DVSA Rev
Theory Test Questions
Guide to passing the driving test and Truckers' Handbook

Combined Edition

MALCOLM GREEN

THE CHOIR PRESS

First published in the United Kingdom in 2018 by The Choir Press

Although the author and publisher have made every effort to ensure that the
information in this book was correct when published, the author and publisher do not
assume and hereby disclaim any liability to any party for any loss, damage, or
disruption caused by errors or omissions, whether such errors or omissions result from
negligence, accident, or any other cause.

The information in this book is meant to supplement, not replace, proper driver training.
Like any activity involving motor vehicles, equipment and environmental factors, there
is inherent risk. The author and publisher advise readers to take full responsibility for
their safety and the safety of others. Before using the skills described in this book ensure
that your vehicle and all associated equipment is well maintained, and that you do not
operate beyond your level of experience, aptitude and training.

ISBN 978-1-911589-55-6

DVSA Theory disclaimer

Crown Copyright material has been reproduced under licence from the Driver and
Vehicle Standards Agency (DVSA) which does not accept any responsibility for the
accuracy of the reproduction.

The author fully acknowledges the Crown Copyrighted Official Highway Code as being
the source of road signs and symbols used in this publication. The recreation of all signs
and symbols has been undertaken to the highest standard.

Contents

Preface

My aim with this handbook is to help new drivers into work. Under licence the first section of this book contains the full DVSA Theory Test, alongside practical tips and advice on passing the driving test.

The second section simplifies trucking rules and regulations in a bid to try and keep a driver and his/her hard won licence safe from harm. It also comprehensively covers all the hands on information needed. I am a LGV1 driver, still currently trucking, with 19 years in the industry and I've used all my experience plus the added input of an instructor and an examiner to create this handbook.

This book is an insight into what to expect and what will be expected of you. "Forewarned is forearmed". I have taken great pains to create a comprehensive, user friendly guide. This book should be accessible, whether you are just starting out in the industry, returning after an absence of leave, or simply wish to brush up on the ever-changing rules and regulations. For matters of ease, I have used articulated vehicle images to illustrate various procedures. Everything translates into all categories of vehicles i.e. LGV1, 2 , & PCV's.

This book is part of a 3 book series which comprises:

- *The Truckers Handbook* published in 2016

- *DVSA Revision Theory Test Questions and guide to passing the Driving Test Combined Edition* published in 2018

- *DVSA Revision Theory Test Questions and guide to passing the Driving Test and Truckers Handbook Combined Edition* published in 2018

Buyers should note that *The Truckers Handbook* is incorporated in full within this 3-in-1 combined edition

Part 1
Questions and Answers

Introduction
Theory and hazard awareness tests

Arriving at the test centre

You must make sure that when you arrive at the test centre you have all the relevant documents with you. If you don't have them, your test will be terminated and you'll lose your fee.

You'll need:

- your signed photocard licence, or your signed old-style paper driving licence and valid

- passport (your passport doesn't have to be British)

All documents must be original. Photocopies will not be accepted!

Multiple choice questions

The theory test is one test made up from two parts. The first is the multiple choice part consisting of a hundred questions. You select your answers for this part of the test by using a mouse on a computer.

Before you start, you'll be given the chance to work through a practice session for up to 15 minutes to get used to the system. Staff at the test centre will be available to help you if you have any difficulties.

The questions will cover a variety of topics relating to road safety, the environment and documents, as well as other factors specific to driving large vehicles, such as passenger care and load safety. Only one question will appear on the screen at a time, and you'll be asked to mark one correct answer.

Take your time and read the questions carefully. You're given 115 minutes for this part of the test, so relax and don't rush. Some questions will take longer to answer than others, but there are no trick questions. The time remaining is displayed on screen.

You may be allowed extra time to complete the test if you have special needs (e.g dyslexia) and you let the test centre know when booking.

You'll be able to move backwards and forwards through the questions and you can also 'flag' questions that you'd like to look at again. It's easy to change your answer if you want to.

Try to answer all the questions. If you're well prepared, you shouldn't find them difficult.

Before you finish this part of the test, if you have time, you can use the 'review' feature to check your answers. If you want to finish your test before the full time, click the 'review' button and then the 'end' button on the review screen.

Hazard perception

The second part of the test the test consists of a series of computer-generated image (CGI) video clips, shown from a driver's point of view. You'll be using a mouse for this part of the theory test which is designed to test your skill at hazard perception.

Before you start this part of the test you'll be shown a short CGI video that explains how the test works and gives you a chance to see a sample clip. This will help you to understand what you need to do. **You can play this video clip again if you wish**.

During the test, you'll be shown 19 CGI video clips. Each clip contains one or more developing hazards. You should press the mouse button **as soon as you see** a hazard developing that may need you, the driver, to take some action, such as changing speed or direction. The earlier you notice a developing hazard and make a response, the higher your score. There are 20 hazards for which you can score points.

Your response won't change what happens in the scene in any way. However, a red flag will appear on the bottom of the screen to show that your response has been noted.

Before each clip starts, there'll be a 10-second pause to allow you to see the new road situation.

The hazard perception part of the test lasts about 25 minutes. For this part of the test no extra time is available, and you can't repeat any of the clips -you don't get a second chance to see a hazard when you're driving on the road.

You have to pass both parts of the theory test before going forward to doing the practical driving test.

As the theory test is one test made up of two parts, you're required to pass both parts to pass. These parts are made up of multiple choice questions and hazard perception clips, and can be taken at different times.

What is the pass mark?

To pass the multiple choice part of the theory test, you must answer at least 85 out of 100 questions correctly.

To pass the hazard perception part of the test, you must reach the required pass mark of 67 out of a possible 100. There are 19 clips with 20 scorable hazards.

If I don't pass, when can I take the test again?

If you fail your test, you've shown that you're not fully prepared. You'll have to wait at least three clear working days before you take the theory test again.

NOTE: Good preparation will save you time and money.

Questions specific to a single category and DVSA publication references.

The DVSA publishes further driving information books. These are:

- Driving Goods Vehicles. DGV's

- Driving Busses and Coaches. DBC's

- Highway Code. HCr/HCp

- Know Your Traffic Signs. KYTSp

I have added this abbreviated reference to each of these publications on to the revision questions for three purposes. These are to give you the possibility for further reading and easy access to the correct part of the DVSA's book. Also to differentiate between LGV and PCV questions.

Most of the questions refer to drivers of all large vehicles. There are a few questions that are dedicated to PCV drivers only. These will be obvious to you when you read them. They are included for information purposes and for drivers training for both licences.

Section 1 Vehicle weights and dimensions

1.1   What does this road sign mean?

❏ No goods vehicles under 7.5 tonnes maximum authorised mass

❏ No goods vehicles over 7.5 tonnes maximum authorised mass

❏ No goods vehicles over 7.5 metres overall height

❏ No goods vehicles under 7.5 metres overall height

HC p106

It's essential that all limits are complied with to avoid breaking the law and facing possible prosecution. Weight restrictions normally apply to the plated weight of a vehicle, often referred to as the maximum authorised mass (MAM).

1.2   What does this temporary sign mean for drivers of vehicles over 7.5 tonnes maximum authorised mass?

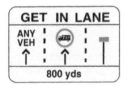

❏ Use either the left-hand or middle lane

❏ Use only the left-hand lane

❏ Use only the middle lane

❏ Use any lane

HC p113, KYTS p131

Lanes at roadworks often have weight restrictions to keep larger vehicles in the left-hand lane. The lanes through the roadworks are often narrow and therefore not wide enough for large vehicles to pass each other safely.

Always look for restriction signs at roadworks. They're usually placed well in advance to give you time to move safely into the correct lane in good time.

1.3   In England and Wales, what's the national speed limit on a single carriageway road for a rigid lorry with a maximum authorised mass of more than 7.5 tonnes?

❏ 30 mph ❏ 40 mph. ❏ 50 mph ❏ 60 mph

HC p40, r124   NI EXEMPT

In England and Wales, vehicles exceeding 7.5 tonnes maximum authorised mass are restricted to a maximum of 50 mph on single carriageway roads. In Scotland, this speed limit is 40 mph.

1.4   You're driving a lorry with a maximum authorised mass of more than 7.5 tonnes along a three-lane motorway. When may you use the right-hand lane?

❏ To overtake slower lorries

❏ When the left-hand lane is closed

❏ If you drive at more than 60 mph

❏ If you're travelling unladen

DGV s4

Use of the right-hand lane on motorways with three or more lanes isn't normally allowed for

• vehicles over 7.5 tonnes maximum authorised mass

• vehicles required to be fitted with a speed limiter

• vehicles towing a trailer.

This rule does not apply in special circumstances, such as when the left-hand lane is closed.

1.5   Where are you most likely to ground a low loader?

❏ On rural roads   ❏ On traffic-calming humps

❏ On yellow rumble strips ❏ On hatched road markings

DGV s2

Traffic-calming measures are becoming more common. Look out for signs warning you of humps in the road ahead. If necessary, change your route rather than take risks.

1.6 You're driving a low loader and you see this sign. What's your main concern at this hazard?

❑ The ground clearance ❑ The weight limit

❑ The height limit ❑ The load's security

DGV s2
You have a responsibility to be aware of the dimensions of your vehicle, including ground clearance. When planning your route, you'll have to consider whether the roads you intend to use have any limits that would apply to your vehicle, such as

• weight • length • height • ground clearance.

1.7 You're driving a vehicle that's over 17 metres (55 feet) long. What should you do at a level crossing?

❑ Cross over using your horn and hazard warning lights

❑ Stop before the crossing and phone the signal operator

❑ Increase your speed to clear the crossing quickly

❑ Stop before the crossing and look both ways before going on

DGV s2
If your vehicle is over 17 metres (55 feet) long and you wish to cross a level crossing, you must stop before the crossing and telephone the signal operator.

1.8 What type of fastening or restraint should you use when carrying a load of steel?

❑ Chains ❑ Straps ❑ Ropes ❑ Sheeting

DGV s2
You're responsible for the safety of the load you're carrying. At no time should the load endanger other road users. It's vital that you make sure your load is secure and safely distributed on your vehicle. How you do this will depend on the

• bulk
• weight
• type of vehicle you're driving (flat bed, curtain side, etc)
• nature of the load.

1.9 You're driving a lorry carrying a load that's 4.5 metres (14 feet 9 inches) wide. What's the maximum speed you're allowed to drive on a motorway?

❑ 10 mph ❑ 20 mph ❑ 30 mph ❑ 40 mph

DGV s2
The speed limits imposed on vehicles carrying abnormal loads can be frustrating for other drivers, but you mustn't be tempted to exceed them. Remember, the more weight you're carrying, the longer it will take you to stop safely.

1.10 What's the speed limit on a dual carriageway when you're carrying a load that's 4.5 metres (14 feet 9 inches) wide?

❑ 15 mph ❑ 25 mph ❑ 35 mph ❑ 45 mph

DGV s2
Vehicles carrying loads between 4.3 metres (14 feet 1 inch) and 5 metres (16 feet 6 inches) wide are subject to lower speed limits. The limit depends on the type of road. On a motorway it's 40 mph (64 km/h), on a dual carriageway it's 35 mph (56 km/h), and on all other roads it's 30 mph (48 km/h).

1.11 What colour are the markings on the rear of lorries over 7.5 tonnes maximum authorised mass?

❑ Red/white ❑ Red/yellow

❑ Black/yellow ❑ Black/white

HC p117
All vehicles over 7.5 tonnes maximum authorised mass must have markings on the rear of the vehicle. These markings are rectangular and are coloured red and yellow. They're there to inform other road users of the characteristics of your vehicle. The markings should be kept clean so that they can be seen clearly at all times, especially at night and in poor visibility.

1.12 When this vehicle transporter turns, how will the overhanging top deck move?

❏ Through a greater arc than the cab

❏ Through a lower arc than the cab

❏ Through a smaller arc than the cab

❏ Through the same arc as the cab

DGV s2
As the top deck is longer than the cab and trailer, it will take up more room as the vehicle turns; you must make sure that you've allowed for the wider swing of the deck. Even if your cab is well clear, the overhanging deck could hit obstructions such as telegraph poles or traffic signs as you go round a corner.

1.13 You're the driver of an articulated car transporter. How will the overhanging top deck move as you turn corners?

❏ Through a smaller arc than the cab

❏ Through a shorter arc than the cab

❏ Through a lower arc than the cab

❏ Through a greater arc than the cab

DGV s2
The longer top deck needs a wider turning circle than the cab below it. To avoid hitting lampposts, telegraph poles, etc, you must allow for this overhang when turning.

1.14 When would the driver of a car transporter need to be most aware of the front overhang of the trailer?

❏ When overtaking ❏ When turning

❏ When loading ❏ When braking

DGV s2
The long overhang at the front of a car transporter can cause problems where street furniture, such as lampposts and traffic signs, is sited close to junctions. Particular problems may be encountered when you're turning right and there are 'Keep left' bollards in the middle of the road you're turning into. Plan your route carefully to avoid such hazards.

1.15 You're scheduled to make a delivery. You arrive at your destination during the morning rush hour. The road is edged with double red lines. What do they mean?

❏ Unload only within a 'white box' area

❏ Unload only within a 'red box' area

❏ Delay your delivery until after the rush hour

❏ Limit your stop to a maximum of 30 minutes

DGV s3, HC p115
White boxes allow you to unload at any time, but during the day the length of stay is restricted. You should check nearby signs for the specific times. At other times, when it's not so busy, there may not be any restrictions on parking.

1.16 You're driving a lorry with a maximum authorised mass of more than 7.5 tonnes. What's the national speed limit for your vehicle on a dual carriageway in England and Wales?

❏ 40 mph ❏ 50 mph ❏ 60 mph ❏ 70 mph

DGV s2, HC p40, r124   **NI EXEMPT**
The speed limit for lorries is lower in Scotland than it is in England and Wales, so be aware – especially if you drive in the border areas.

1.17 Which axle configuration is most effective at preventing petrol tankers from rolling over?

❏ Tandem axles with double wheels

❏ Tandem axles with air suspension

❏ Tri-axles with single wheels

❏ Tri-axles with double wheels

DGV s2
The type of suspension fitted to a vehicle will influence its resistance to 'roll-over'. Modern tri-axle semi-trailers fitted with single wheels on each side extend the tracking width available, making this the most stable configuration.

1.18 What warning does the driver of a petrol tanker have that 'rear wheel lift' is about to become 'roll-over'?

❏ The steering becomes heavy

❏ The driver has very little warning

❏ The air pressure drops

❏ The diff-lock engages

DGV s2
The transition from 'rear wheel lift' to 'roll-over' is more rapid on vehicles equipped with air suspension systems. Make sure you take advantage of any extra training that may be available to drivers of this type of vehicle.

1.19 What effect could a load of hanging meat carcasses cause when you drive around corners or bends?

❏ The wave effect ❏ The camber effect

❏ The gravity effect ❏ The pendulum effect

DGV s2
As you turn a corner, the hanging meat carcasses will all swing to one side of your vehicle, adding extra pulling force towards the outside of the curve. The faster you turn a corner, the greater this force will be. After the corner, the carcasses will continue to swing back and forth, like pendulums, making the vehicle unstable.

1.20 Why do many drivers park at overnight stops with their rear doors close to another lorry?

❏ To keep the load safe

❏ To ensure a clear path

❏ To keep 'same company' lorries together

❏ To stop the theft of their fuel

DGV s3
Load security is extremely important. Make sure you park legally and, preferably, in a well-lit area. Some lorry parks are patrolled regularly by the police or security services.

1.21 What should be fitted to a lorry with a maximum authorised mass of more than 7500 kg?

HC p117
Motor vehicles over 7500 kg maximum authorised mass (MAM) and trailers over 3500 kg MAM should have these markings fitted to the rear of the vehicle/trailer.

1.22 How far can a load overhang at the rear before you must use projection marker boards?

❏ 1 metre (3 feet 3 inches)

❏ 1.5 metres (5 feet 0 inches)

❏ 2 metres (6 feet 6 inches)

❏ 2.9 metres (9 feet 5 inches)

DGV s2
Projection marker boards must be fitted if the load on your vehicle overhangs by more than 2 metres (6 feet 6 inches). This will help other road users who may not notice the projecting load.

1.23 When must you notify telephone companies that you're moving a high load?

❏ When the load's height exceeds 4.00 metres (13 feet)

❏ When the load's height exceeds 4.30 metres 14 feet 2 inches)

❏ When the load's height exceeds 5.00 metres (16 feet 6 inches)

❏ When the load's height exceeds 5.25 metres (17 feet 6 inches)

DGV s2
You should tell telephone companies about your intended route when planning the movement of loads over 5.25 metres (17 feet 6 inches) high. You should tell them in plenty of time before making the journey.

1.24 How wide can a load be before you must use side markers?

❏ 2.0 metres (6 feet 6 inches)

❏ 2.9 metres (9 feet 5 inches)

❏ 3.5 metres (11 feet 5 inches)

❏ 4.3 metres (14 feet 2 inches)

DGV s2
Side markers rnust be displayed if your load is over 2.9 metres (9 feet 5 inches) wide. Make sure that they're clearly visible, at both the front and rear, and that they indicate the actual width of the projection.

1.25 Triangular projection markers are required when your load is wider than 2.9 metres {9 feet 5 inches).What colour are these markers?

❏ Black/yellow ❏ Red/yellow

❏ Black/white ❏ Red/white

DGV s2
The marker boards should be red and white. They must be kept clean and independently lit at night and in poor visibility, so that other road users can see them.

1.26   How should you secure an ISO steel cargo container onto your vehicle or trailer?

❑ Using battens and chocks   ❑ Using straps

❑ Using twist locks   ❑ Using ropes

DGV s2

If you're carrying a steel ISO (International Standards Organization) cargo container, ropes or straps won't be strong enough to take the strain. This type of load requires a special type of restraint using twist locks.

1.27   You're driving an articulated lorry on a narrow road. There's a left-hand bend ahead. Why may you need to move out before driving around the bend?

❑ To leave more room for braking

❑ To prevent anyone from overtaking

❑ To make room for the trailer cutting in

❑ To make sure oncoming drivers see you

DGV s2

You should always be aware of the amount of room your trailer needs when it's going around bends and corners. If you need to go onto the other side of the road, make sure there's no oncoming traffic before you move out.

1.28   What does this sign mean?

❑ Two-axled trailers are prohibited

❑ The bridge is too narrow for vehicles over 7.5 tonnes

❑ The bridge has an axle weight limit of 7.5 tonnes

❑ Vehicles over the weight shown are prohibited

DBC s3, DGV s2

Always look out for road signs, but be especially aware of those that refer to large or heavy vehicles. Get into the habit of checking for signs at junctions. There might be an indication on the junction layout sign. Before you turn, make sure that the road you're using doesn't have any restrictions for the vehicle you're driving.

1.29   What does this sign mean?

❑ Slippery road   ❑ Double bend

❑ Overhead electrified cable ❑ Cable laying ahead

DBC s3, DGV s2

It's essential to know the height of your vehicle before setting off. This should be clearly marked, usually in the cab, and visible from the driving position. Look out for restrictions that you may not have seen on a map - they may be temporary.

1.30   What does this sign mean?

❑ No vehicles over 14 feet 6 inches (4.4 metres) wide

❑ No vehicles over 14 feet 6 inches (4.4 metres) high

❑ Road humps 14 feet 6 inches (4.4 metres) apart

❑ No vehicles over 14 feet 6 inches (4.4 metres) long

KYTS p23

Always be aware of the height of the vehicle you're driving, particularly if you drive different vehicles. If you use a sat-nav, it may show you the height and weight limits on UK roads.

1.31   What does this sign warn of?

❑ Low bridge ahead ❑ Incident ahead

❑ Tunnel ahead   ❑ Accident blackspot ahead

HC p108, KYTS p12

If you're driving a high vehicle, make sure that there's enough headroom available for you to go through the tunnel. There may be additional signs showing height and width restrictions.

1.32   What does this sign mean?

❏ The length of a tunnel

❏ The length of a low bridge

❏ The distance to a tunnel

❏ The distance to a low bridge

HC p108, KYTS p12
As well as a height restriction, the tunnel may have a restriction on the available width of headroom for high vehicles. The advance warning gives you the opportunity to find another route if your vehicle is too high or wide to drive through the tunnel.

1.33   When must you take extra care if you're driving a vehicle more than 3.0 metres (10 feet) high?

❏ When driving over narrow bridges

❏ When driving up steep hills

❏ When driving near airports

❏ When driving under overhead cables

DBC s3, DGV s2, KYTS p24-26
You must take care when approaching any hazard where height is limited. Know the height of your vehicle and what you can drive under safely. If you aren't sure that it's safe, take another route.

1.34   What's the minimum height of an unmarked bridge?

❏ 4.5 metres (15 feet) ❏ 4.7 metres (15 feet 6 inches)

❏ 4.8 metres (16 feet) ❏ 5.0 metres (16 feet 6 inches)

DBC s3,DGV s2
If a height isn't shown on the bridge, the headroom (in the UK) will be at least 5 metres (16 feet 6 inches).

1.35   Who must you tell when your vehicle collides with a bridge?

❏ The police   ❏ The local authority

❏ Your local garage ❏ The fire service

DBC s3,DGV s2
Hitting a bridge with your vehicle can have serious consequences for road and rail traffic. You must tell the police about the incident immediately. If the bridge is a railway bridge, call the railway authority as well as the police to report the incident.

1.36   Your vehicle has collided with a railway bridge. What information must you give the railway authority when you telephone them?

❏ The make and model of your vehicle

❏ The type of bridge

❏ The vehicle's height

❏ The bridge number

DBC s3,DGV s2
The railway authority needs to know immediately if one of their bridges has been hit. You'll need to tell them the number of the bridge so they can identify it. The railway authority will then take action to prevent railway passengers from being put at risk.

1.37   What do bells hanging across the road warn drivers of?

❏ Weight restriction ahead

❏ Trams crossing ahead

❏ Overhead electric cables ahead

❏ Railway level crossing ahead

DBC s3, DGV s2, KYTS p26
If your vehicle touches bells suspended over the road, they'll obviously ring. This will warn you that your vehicle exceeds the safe travelling height beneath electrified overhead cables ahead. You must stop immediately and either find another route or take advice.

1.38   What does this sign mean?

❏ The width of the road is 6 feet 6 inches (2 metres)

❏ No vehicles over 6 feet 6 inches (2 metres) wide

❏ No vehicles over 6 feet 6 inches (2 metres) high

❏ Trailer length must not exceed 6 feet 6 inches (2 metres)

HC p106, KYTS p18

You must always be aware of the size of your vehicle. Look out for road signs that show a width restriction. There should be an indication of this at the entrance to the road.

Don't get into a situation where you have to reverse out of a narrow road because you haven't seen a sign.

1.39   What does this motorway sign mean?

❏ 11 tonnes weight limit

❏ Stop: all lanes ahead closed

❏ Leave the motorway at the next exit

❏ Lane ahead closed

HC p102, KYTS p90-91

Warning lights show when there's danger ahead. This includes

• lane closures • incidents • fog • icy roads.

1.40   You're driving on a motorway and you see this sign. What does it mean?

❏ End of restriction

❏ End of crawler lane

❏ End of weight limit

❏ End of hard shoulder

HC p102, KVTS p90-91

Look out for variable-message warning signs telling you about

• lane closures • speed limits • hazards.

When you're clear of the restriction, you'll see a sign telling you that it has ended.

1.41   In which of these places might there be a restriction on vehicles over a certain length?

❏ On motorway.   ❏ At freight terminals

❏ In road tunnels . ❏ On dual carriageways

DBC s3, DGV s2

Look out for restrictions on long vehicles. Length restrictions are found where there isn't much room to turn (for example, in a tunnel) or where there's a risk of grounding.

1.42   At this roundabout, you want to take the fourth exit. What limit is in force on this road?

❏ Height

❏ Weight

❏ Width

❏ Length

DBC s3, DGV s2, KYTS p25

Look out for signs giving you advance warning of height restrictions. As a professional driver, you should always know the height of your vehicle or load. If you aren't sure of the safe height, stop and check.

1.43   You're driving a large vehicle on a narrow road with passing places. What will you need to be most aware of?

❏ Its length   ❏ Its roof height

❏ Its ground clearance ❏ Its weight

DBC s3, DGV s2

If your vehicle is too long to fit into a passing place, you may need to wait opposite one. This will allow a following or approaching driver to pass. When you use this type of road, you need to plan and look well ahead to avoid meeting another road user at an inappropriate place.

1.44   What type of road surface will increase your stopping distance by up to ten times?

❏ Bumpy   ❏ Icy   ❏ Worn   ❏ Wet

DBC s4, DGV s4, HC r126

To prevent your wheels from locking, you'll need to brake very gently on ice. Give yourself as much room and time as possible to stop. If your front wheels lock, you can't steer, and that will mean you can't avoid any obstacle in your path.

1.45 By how much can your stopping distance increase in icy weather?

❑ 2 times ❑ 4 times ❑ 10 times ❑ 20 times

DBC s4, DGV s4, HC r126
It's vital that you give yourself enough separation distance when driving on icy roads – ten times as much as in normal conditions. You should brake gently to reduce the risk of losing control.

1.46 What's the maximum speed allowed for a vehicle towing a trailer on a motorway?

❑ 40 mph ❑ 50 mph ❑ 60 mph ❑ 70 mph

OBC s2, DGV s3, HC p40
Vehicles towing caravans or trailers on motorways are limited in two ways

• the maximum speed is 60 mph

• on motorways with more than two lanes, towing vehicles aren't allowed in the outside lane, unless other lanes are closed.

1.47 What should you check when you've just overtaken a motorcyclist on a motorway?

❑ Your speedometer ❑ Your left-hand mirror

❑ Your right-hand mirror ❑ The road ahead

OBG s4, DGV s4
When overtaking with a long vehicle, it's very important to be aware of the position of the road user you're passing. Check the nearside mirror to make sure you've passed safely before returning to the left. Be especially careful when overtaking motorcyclists, as they may be affected by the draught from your vehicle.

1.48 You're driving a large vehicle in a straight line. When is it most stable?

❑ During harsh acceleration ❑ During gentle braking

❑ During gentle acceleration ❑ During harsh braking

DBC s2, DGV S2
A vehicle is most stable when travelling in a straight line under gentle acceleration. Sudden acceleration, steering or braking can cause severe loss of control. For maximum control, keep your driving as smooth as possible.

1.49 What does this sign mean?

❑ Warning of lorry crossing a one-way road

❑ No entry for vehicles over 32 feet 6 inches (9.9 metres) long

❑ No entry for vehicles over 32.6 tonnes

❑ Warning of lorry straight ahead

KYTS p17
You need to know the length of your vehicle as well as its weight, height and width. Places where the length of your vehicle may be relevant are

• road tunnels • level crossings • ferries • bridges.

1.50 You're driving a long vehicle. What should you do when you want to turn right at a painted mini-roundabout?

❑ Make sure none of your wheels touch the roundabout

❑ Avoid going over the roundabout if possible

❑ Go ahead, and turn right at the next junction

❑ Carefully mount the left-hand kerb to make more room

DBC s6, DGV s6
When turning at a mini roundabout, It's unlikely that you'll be able to avoid going over the marked area. You should, however, avoid going over the roundabout where possible.

1.51 What should you consider when planning a route for your journey?

❑ Weight restrictions ❑ Speed cameras

❑ Speed-limit changes ❑ One-way streets

DBCs3, DGVs2
You should plan your route to avoid vehicle width, height and weight restrictions that would affect your vehicle and load. Planning to avoid busy times can also reduce journey times and fuel costs.

1.52 Your vehicle is more than 3 metres (9 feet 10 inches) high. Where is this information displayed?

❑ On the windscreen ❑ On the weight plate

❑ In the driver's cab ❑ In the engine bay

DBC s6, DGV s6
It's a legal requirement that information about a vehicle's height can be seen by the driver from their seat.

It's important to know the height of your vehicle so that you can avoid any height restrictions on your route.

1.53 The height of your vehicle is 4.2 metres (14 feet). What should you do as you approach this bridge?

❏ Keep to the centre of the arch and give way to oncoming traffic

❏ Drive through slowly, keeping to the left of the marked limits

❏ Keep to the centre of the arch and take priority over oncoming traffic

❏ Drive through quickly, keeping to the left of the marked limits

DBC s3, DGV s2
The headroom under bridges in the UK is at least 5 metres (16 feet 6 inches) unless marked otherwise. However, this might refer only to the highest point of an arch. If your vehicle hits a bridge, you must report the incident to the police. If a railway bridge is involved, you must also report it to the railway authority.

1.54 Unless otherwise shown, what's the minimum headroom under bridges in the UK?

❏ 4.0 metres (13 feet)

❏ 4.1 metres (13 feet 4 inches)

❏ 5.0 metres (16 feet 6 inches)

❏ 5.5 metres (18 feet)

DBC s3, DGV s2
Every year, there are hundreds of incidents in the UK where vehicles hit railway or motorway bridges. Most involve buses, coaches and lorries. Make sure your route doesn't take you under a bridge that's too low for your vehicle. If you hit a bridge, you'll be putting yourself and any passengers at risk, and you could cause a major disruption to road and rail transport.

1.55 Where can you park large vehicles at night without needing to use parking lights?

❏ In an off-road parking area

❏ On a road with a 20 mph speed limit

❏ At least 10 metres (32 feet) away from any junction

❏ In most lay-bys

DBC s4, DGV s4
Off-road lorry and coach parks are often well lit and patrolled by police or security firms. Never leave your vehicle unlit on a public road or in a lay-by after dark.

1.56 When should you allow for the effects of a speed limiter?

❏ When you're cornering

❏ When you're braking

❏ When you're overtaking

❏ When you're changing gear

DBC s4, DGV s3
Forward planning is important whenever you consider overtaking another road user. You should carefully assess the speed of the vehicle you intend to overtake. Remember that your vehicle's speed is limited and this could considerably increase the distance and time needed to complete the manoeuvre safely.

1.57 When should you consider the effect a speed limiter will have on your vehicle?

❏ When braking   ❏ When changing gear

❏ When overtaking ❏ When reversing

DBC s4, DGV s3
Plan well ahead before overtaking. Be aware that a speed limiter may cause you difficulties when overtaking another vehicle, particularly when climbing a hill.

1.58 What does this sign mean?

❏ Hump bridge

❏ Risk of grounding

❏ Uneven road

❏ Road liable to subsidence

DBC s3, DGV s2, HC p109
If you see this sign, be aware that there's a danger of grounding. This can happen where there's a pronounced bump in the road, such as at a level crossing or a hump bridge.

1.59   What should be your main concern as you approach this sign?

❏ Your vehicle's height
❏ Your vehicle's width
❏ Your vehicle's weight
❏ Your vehicle's length

DBC s3, DGV s2, HC p109
At hump bridges, there's a risk of long vehicles grounding. If you aren't sure whether the floor of your vehicle will clear the bridge, find another route.

1.60   You're driving a long vehicle on a two-lane road. What should you do if you want to turn left into a narrow side road?

❏ Keep well to the left on the approach

❏ Move out to the right immediately before turning

❏ Keep to the left and turn later than normal

❏ Straddle the lanes to make more room for the turn

DBC s2, DGV s2
When you're driving a long vehicle, you'll often need to straddle lanes to turn into narrow side roads. When you do this, watch out for smaller vehicles – especially motorcycles and cycles – trying to squeeze past on your inside.

1.61   Where must the repair of a speed limiter be carried out?

❏ At an authorised speed-limiter centre

❏ At any DVSA site

❏ At any dealer centre

❏ At the depot by a mechanic

DBC s1, DGV s2
Speed limiters may only be repaired by authorised speed-limiter centres. They'll ensure that all the connections are sealed and that the system is tamperproof.

1.62   Where can the axle weight limits be found?

❏ On the vehicle plate ❏ On the operator's licence

❏ On the wheel rims   ❏ On the weighbridge printout

DBC s2, DGV s3
Individual axle weights are shown on the vehicle plate. This can be found in a prominent place on both the vehicle and trailer.

1.63   By approximately how much would 15 passengers increase the weight of your vehicle?

❏ 0.5 tonnes   ❏ 1 tonne   ❏ 2.5 tonnes   ❏ 3 tonnes

DBC s3
You must be aware of the maximum authorised mass (MAM) of your vehicle. This refers to its total weight, including both passengers and luggage. Fifteen passengers would add approximately 1 tonne to the weight of your vehicle. You should also allow for any luggage that they may be carrying.

1.64   As a guide, how many passengers equal 1 tonne?

❏ 15   ❏ 20   ❏ 25   ❏ 30

DBC s3
Your bus will move away more slowly and handle differently when fully laden with passengers and their luggage. You'll have to make allowances for this, especially when moving off uphill.

1.65   How would you know that a weight-limit sign doesn't apply to the bus you're driving?

❏ By a plate fitted beneath the weight-limit sign

❏ By the colour of the weight-limit sign

❏ By a plate attached to the vehicle

❏ By a certificate carried by the driver

DBC s3
Some weight restrictions apply to large goods vehicles only and not to passenger-carrying vehicles. Look for a plate beneath a restriction sign that indicates this.

Road signs show weight restrictions in various ways. You should make yourself familiar with all of them, so that you're in no doubt about their meaning and relevance.

1.66 You're driving a bus on a local service. When can you use this lane?

❏ Between 4.00 pm and 6.30 pm only

❏ Before 4.00 pm and after 6.30 pm only

❏ At any time of the day

❏ Any time except Saturdays

DBC s3
As a local-service bus driver, you may use the bus lane at any time. The restrictions apply to other road users, to keep the lane clear for you at peak times. Don't be tempted to speed when driving up the inside of slow-moving or stationary traffic. Be alert for pedestrians who may be trying to cross the road.

1.67 What's the national speed limit for buses and coaches on a dual carriageway?

❏ 55 mph   ❏ 60 mph   ❏ 65 mph   ❏ 70 mph

HC p40
Don't be tempted to drive on the limiter when using dual carriageway roads. The speed limit for passenger-carrying vehicles is 60 mph. Be considerate to faster-moving traffic by not using the middle or outside lanes unnecessarily.

1.68 What does a D1 category licence allow you to drive?

❏ Buses with a maximum of 16 passenger seats

❏ Buses with a maximum of 24 passenger seats

❏ Buses with a maximum of 32 passenger seats

❏ Buses with a maximum of 48 passenger seats

DBC s7
The D1 category allows you to drive any bus with 9 to 16 passenger seats for hire or reward.

1.69 Where can a driver find their vehicle's unladen weight recorded?

❏ On the dashboard of the vehicle

❏ On the driver's duty roster

❏ On the side of the vehicle

❏ On the depot noticeboard

DBC s3
The driver of a passenger-carrying vehicle needs to know the vehicle's limits. These include its weight, height, width and length, and its seating and standing capacity. The unladen weight should be displayed on the nearside of the vehicle.

1.70 What category of licence is required to drive an articulated bus?

❏ D.   ❏ D+E   ❏ D1   ❏ D1+E

DBC s1, 7
A full category D licence entitles you to drive all buses and coaches, including the articulated type.

A full category D licence on its own doesn't cover you to drive buses or coaches drawing detachable trailers of more than 750 kg; for this you'll need a D+E licence.

1.71 The front of your bus overhangs well past the front wheels. Why should you allow for this when cornering?

❏ The steering will be much heavier

❏ Your speed will be more difficult to control

❏ You might hit something close to the road

❏ You'll need to brake earlier than normal

DBC s3
The front of a bus or coach often extends well beyond the front wheels. Make allowances for this when turning. Try to avoid overhanging the pavement where possible, but if you have to do this, look out for fences, posts, traffic signs, etc. Be especially careful where pedestrians are present; for example, in bus stations.

1.72 Your bus has a speed limiter fitted. What other related item must it have?

❏ An audible warning device for the driver

❏ A plate in the cab showing the limited speed

❏ A warning sign on the back of the bus

❏ A manual override switch for emergencies

DBC s3
A bus equipped with a speed limiter must also be fitted with a plate showing the speed setting. This must be fitted in an obvious position, where it can be clearly seen.

1.73   A speed limiter is fitted to a bus. Where must the speed-limiter setting be displayed?

❏ In the driver's cab

❏ On the nearside of the vehicle

❏ On the rear of the vehicle

❏ On the driver's side at the front of the vehicle

DBC s3
If a speed limiter is fitted to a vehicle, there must be a notice showing the speed at which it's set, clearly displayed in the driver's cab.

1.74   What does the term 'maximum authorised mass' (MAM) mean?

❏ The weight of your vehicle, with passengers but no luggage

❏ The weight of your vehicle, without passengers or luggage

❏ The weight of your vehicle, with luggage but no passengers

❏ The weight of your vehicle, with both luggage and passengers

DBC s3
Maximum authorised mass (MAM) means the total weight of a vehicle or trailer, including the maximum load that can be carried safely when it's being used on the road. It's also known as gross vehicle weight (GVW) or permissible maximum weight. You're responsible for making sure the MAM isn't exceeded when the vehicle is fully loaded.

1.75   How do speed limiters normally work?

❏ By applying the service brake

❏ By applying the secondary brake

❏ By reducing the fuel supplied to the engine

❏ By changing to a lower or higher gear

DBC s1
Most speed limiters work by taking a speed signal from the tachograph and transmitting it to the engine management system. This reduces the fuel supply to the engine, and allows the speed of the vehicle to be controlled to specific limits. The speed at which a limiter is set must be shown on a plate clearly displayed in the cab. You should be aware of the effect a speed limiter will have on your vehicle, especially when overtaking.

1.76   What's a vehicle's turning circle?

❏ The number of turns of the steering wheel between locks

❏ The amount of space needed for the vehicle to turn

❏ The amount by which the vehicle overhangs kerbs

❏ The distance by which a vehicle cuts corners

DBC s3
You should be familiar with the room your vehicle needs to make turns or carry out a manoeuvre. You'll need to consider this as you approach junctions and road layouts. If you're driving a new or temporary vehicle, familiarise yourself with its characteristics before you drive on public roads.

Section 2 Drivers' hours and rest periods

2.1 Why are goods vehicle drivers' hours of work controlled?

❑ To encourage vehicle sympathy

❑ To help road safety

❑ To ensure fair road use

❑ To improve vehicle security

DGV s3

Drivers need to be alert at all times. Fatigue is a recognised danger for professional drivers, so working conditions are governed by EU rules. These set a maximum driving time and minimum requirements for rest and break periods. Setting limits on the length of time a driver can work combats fatigue and so helps road safety.

2.2 What does controlling goods vehicle drivers' hours help to improve?

❑ Fuel economy   ❑ Road safety

❑ Traffic calming   ❑ Journey planning

DGV s3

EU drivers' hours regulations are a series of rules that specify maximum driving time and minimum rest and break periods. These rules are in place to help road safety. Drivers who break them are subject to heavy fines and could lose their licence to drive lorries.

2.3 What must you do when driving under the rules for domestic drivers' hours?

❑ Keep a written record of hours worked

❑ Only record any driving off public roads

❑ Keep a written record of driving time only

❑ Always use a vehicle fitted with a tachograph

DGV s3

Domestic rules apply to certain journeys within Great Britain that aren't subject to EU rules. Under domestic rules you must keep a written record of your hours of duty when driving goods vehicles.

2.4 You must have enough tachograph charts with you for your journey. When do you need to start a new chart?

❑ Every 10 hours   ❑ Every 24 hours

❑ Every 36 hours   ❑ Every 48 hours

DGV s3

If you're using a vehicle equipped with an analogue tachograph, you'll need at least one chart for every 24 hours. Your employer should supply you with enough tachograph charts for your entire journey.

2.5 What period of time does one tachograph chart cover?

❑ 24 hour.   ❑ 48 hours   ❑ 5 days   ❑ 7 days

DGV s3

Your tachograph chart is a legal document; it's a record of your work covering a rolling 24-hour period. Drivers who break the rules are subject to heavy fines and could lose their vocational licence. Altering your tachograph chart with intent to deceive is against the law and could lead to a prison sentence. Similar penalties exist for those who permit such offences.

2.6 What should you do if your tachograph chart becomes dirty or damaged?

❑ Continue with the same chart and enter the details in writing

❑ Use a spare chart and destroy the damaged one

❑ Use a spare chart and attach it to the damaged one

❑ Continue to use the chart

DGV s3

If your current tachograph chart becomes damaged, you should start another and then attach it to the damaged one. Your records must be clear and up to date at all times. It's sensible to carry more tachograph charts than you think you'll need for your journey. Then you'll be able to use a spare if one becomes dirty or damaged.

2.7 During your break, your vehicle will be moved by another person. What should you do with the tachograph chart?

- ☐ Leave the chart in the vehicle and record the changes on the back
- ☐ Put in a new chart on your return to the vehicle
- ☐ Switch to rest mode to record the break
- ☐ Remove the chart and make a manual record of the break period

DGV s3

If your vehicle is likely to be used by another person while you're away from it, you should take your tachograph chart with you. Your break from driving should be entered on the reverse of the chart.

2.8 You've been driving a lorry without a break for four-and-a-half hours. Under EU rules, you must now take a break. How long must this break be?

- ☐ 30 minutes ☐ 35 minutes
- ☐ 40 minutes ☐ 45 minutes

DGV s3

If you're driving under EU rules, you mustn't drive continuously for more than four-and-a-half hours without taking a break. If you've driven continuously for four-and-a half hours, you must take a break of at least 45 minutes. Include your stops in the timetable when planning your journey.

2.9 You're driving a lorry on a motorway and you start to feel drowsy. What should you do when there are no service areas or exits for some distance?

- ☐ Stop on the hard shoulder and rest
- ☐ Open the window and turn down the heating
- ☐ Slow down and use the hazard warning lights
- ☐ Increase your speed to get to the next service area sooner

DGV s3

During very cold weather, it's tempting to have the heating in the cab turned on full. Be aware that this may help to make you feel drowsy, especially after you've eaten a meal. Open the window slightly to let in some fresh air until it's safe for you to stop and rest.

2.10 You're driving a lorry. During the journey you begin to feel ill and are unable to concentrate. What should you do?

- ☐ Stop in a safe place and seek help
- ☐ Continue your journey and keep your windows open
- ☐ Increase your speed to finish your work earlier
- ☐ Keep stopping at regular intervals for rest

DGV s3

If you become unwell, it will affect your ability to concentrate. You must be fully alert and ready for any hazards that might occur while you're driving. Stop in a safe place and call for help. You may have to call out a relief driver to complete the journey for you.

2.11 What should you do to prevent your load from being stolen?

- ☐ Give a lift to a stranger
- ☐ Make sure all doors and windows are locked
- ☐ Discuss your load with members of the public
- ☐ Have wind deflectors fitted

DGV s3

Be careful of giving lifts to strangers; some employers actively discourage it. Allowing strangers in your cab or telling people about your load could put the security of your vehicle and load at risk, and may put you in danger.

2.12 How can you reduce the likelihood of theft of your load when leaving your vehicle overnight?

- ☐ Park with the rear doors close to another vehicle
- ☐ Park with the rear doors well away from another vehicle
- ☐ Park with the front doors well away from another vehicle
- ☐ Park with the front doors close to another vehicle

DGV s3

Theft of loads from commercial vehicles is a serious problem. You should take steps to safeguard your load when leaving the vehicle overnight. Simply parking with the rear doors close to another vehicle or a wall can act as an effective deterrent to thieves.

2.13 What security precautions should you take if you're carrying a high-value load and have to park and sleep overnight in the cab?

- ❏ Lock the doors but leave a window open for ventilation
- ❏ Make sure the doors and windows are secure
- ❏ Stay at the same location regularly
- ❏ Park in a quiet, unlit, non-residential area

DGV s3
Both your load and your vehicle can be a target for thieves. Taking simple precautions, such as securing the windows and doors, can deter thieves and help ensure your own safety.

2.14 You're often involved in the carrying of high-value goods. What security measures can you adopt?

- ❏ Vary your routes and rest stops
- ❏ Always discuss details of your load
- ❏ Give lifts to anyone for added security
- ❏ Keep your journeys to a strict routine

DGV s3
When carrying high-value goods, you can become a target for thieves. Avoid developing a set routine or pattern. Vary your routes whenever possible to make it difficult for thieves to predict when and where your cargo can be intercepted.

2.15 Where should you park your trailer if you have to leave it unattended?

- ❏ In a public car park ❏ On the public highway
- ❏ On secure premises ❏ In a quiet residential area

DGV s3
Theft of vehicles is common. You're responsible for the safety and security of your vehicle and trailer. Try to avoid leaving any trailer unattended unless it's on approved secure premises.

2.16 When should your trailer be fitted with a kingpin or drawbar lock?

- ❏ When it's being driven on a motorway
- ❏ When it's being driven abroad
- ❏ When it's being used partially loaded
- ❏ When it's left unattended

DGV s3
A kingpin or drawbar lock is a visible and effective deterrent to thieves wishing to steal an unattended trailer.

2.17 Before starting driving, which of the following should you complete on the centre field of your tachograph chart?

- ❏ The starting point of your day's journey
- ❏ Details of the goods carried
- ❏ The name and address of your employer
- ❏ The amount of daily rest taken prior to starting the shift

DGV s3
Before starting your journey, you must record a number of items on your tachograph chart. One of these is where the journey begins.

2.18 During your working day, you change to another vehicle with the same type of tachograph. How should you keep your tachograph record up-to-date?

- ❏ Use the chart that's already in the other vehicle
- ❏ Take the chart with you and use it in the other vehicle
- ❏ Record your driving hours in a record book
- ❏ Install a new chart in the other vehicle

DGV s3
If you change vehicles during the working day, you should take your chart with you and use it in the next vehicle. This isn't always possible, however, as charts produced by different manufacturers may not be interchangeable. In this case, you should use another chart, making sure that all the information for the day is recorded.

2.19 Which of the following is good practice in keeping your lorry and its load safe?

- ❏ Parking in a quiet area, out of sight
- ❏ Making sure the back doors are accessible
- ❏ Parking in a well-lit lorry park
- ❏ Showing your papers to anyone who stops you

DGV s3
Load security is one of the many responsibilities of the driver. When choosing a site to park your vehicle overnight, you should always look for a location that's legal and well lit. Many allocated lorry parks are patrolled by the police or security firms.

2.20   You're driving a lorry at night. What can you do to help yourself stay alert?

☐ Eat a heavy meal before setting off

☐ Keep plenty of cool, fresh air moving through the cab

☐ Keep the cab warm and comfortable

☐ Drive faster to get to your destination sooner

DGV s3
Make sure you have enough rest before you start a night shift. Driving at night can be tiring and you must be able to stay alert for the whole of your shift.

Making sure that there's enough fresh air in the cab can help you to stay alert. Stale, warm air can dull your senses and cause drowsiness.

2.21   How can you reduce the risk of your lorry or trailer being stolen?

☐ Fit an alarm and immobiliser

☐ Park alongside another vehicle or a wall

☐ Use the same route and stop in the same places for your rest periods

☐ Park in quiet areas, away from other vehicles

DGV s3
You're responsible for your vehicle, so you should reduce the risk of it being stolen. Plan any lengthy stops for places where your vehicle will be safest, such as a well-lit rest stop at night. Also have an alarm and immobiliser fitted to the vehicle by a security specialist.

2.22   You're planning to carry high-value goods on a regular basis. Whose advice should you seek?

☐ Other drivers in your area

☐ Your local crime-prevention officer

☐ Other operators in your area

☐ Your local road-safety officer

DGV s3
High-value cargoes are often targeted by thieves. Operators are recommended to seek advice from their local crime-prevention officer to help prevent their vehicles and loads from being stolen.

2.23   What period of time makes up a driver's week?

☐ 00.00 hours Monday to 24.00 hours the following Sunday

☐ 00.00 hours Sunday to 24.00 hours the following Saturday

☐ Any 7 consecutive days

☐ Any 56 hours driven

DGV s3
A driver's week is defined as a period from 00.00 hours on Monday to 24.00 hours the following Sunday.

2.24   While you're driving, you notice your tachograph isn't working. What should you do?

☐ Stop immediately and don't drive until it's been repaired

☐ Report it to the nearest police station

☐ Phone the vehicle testing authority and report the fault

☐ Continue your journey but make a manual record

DGV s3
If you can't return to base within a week of the tachograph becoming defective, it must be repaired during the journey. While it's broken, you must keep a manual record.

2.25   What can happen to drivers who break EU tachograph regulations?

☐ They can be given three warnings

☐ They can have their passport withdrawn

☐ They can be heavily fined

☐ They can be let off if they're new to using tachographs

DBC s3, DGV s3
The driver must take responsibility and follow the drivers' hours and tachograph rules. Failure to do so can result in legal action and penalties – such as a fine.

2.26   What must you do when using a vehicle fitted with an analogue tachograph?

❑ Carry enough approved charts

❑ Use damaged charts if they're clean

❑ Use dirty charts if they're undamaged

❑ Reuse charts twice

DBC s3, DGV s3
Make sure you carry enough approved tachograph charts for your journey. Store your spare charts in a plastic wallet to keep them clean and undamaged.

2.27   The analogue tachograph on your vehicle becomes faulty. How long do you have before you must have it repaired?

❑ One day   ❑ Three days

❑ One week   ❑ Two weeks

DBC s3, DGV s3
If the tachograph on your vehicle becomes faulty, you should take it to an approved tachograph repairer as soon as possible. If you can't return to your base within a week of finding the fault, it must be repaired while you're away. While the tachograph is faulty or broken, you must keep a manual record of your activities.

2.28   An enforcement officer keeps one of your tachograph charts. Who should sign the back of the replacement chart?

❑ You, the drive.   ❑ Your transport manager

❑ The vehicle owne.   ❑ The officer

DBC s3, DGV s3
When an enforcement officer keeps a record chart, the driver should ask the officer to sign the back of the replacement chart. They'll need to give their name, telephone number and the number of charts they've kept. The replacement chart must be used to continue the journey. You should always carry more blank charts than you think you'll need.

2.29   An enforcement officer keeps your analogue tachograph records. How should they endorse the replacement charts?

❑ With their name   ❑ With their service number

❑ With their home address ❑ With their date of birth

DBC s3, DGV s3
If your records are kept by an enforcement officer, you should ask the officer to endorse the replacement charts with their name and telephone number. The enforcement officer should also record the number of charts they keep. Alternatively, they can give you a receipt for the charts.

2.30   Why should you carry spare tachograph charts?

❑ As a defence against a speeding prosecution

❑ To record when you've been in a traffic delay

❑ For recording extra loading duties and overtime

❑ To replace the original chart if it gets dirty

DBC s3, DGV s3
Your employer should supply enough approved charts for your journey. They should include spares in case any get damaged or are taken by an authorised inspecting officer.

2.31   Under EU rules, a driver must take regular breaks from driving. What maximum period of continuous driving is allowed?

❑ 3 hours   ❑ 4 hours   ❑ 4.5 hours   ❑ 5.5 hours

DBC s3, DGV s3
It's essential that you don't become drowsy through driving for excessively long periods. EU rules are in place to prevent this. You must take a break after a maximum of 4.5 hours of continuous driving. Your work details must be available for inspection by enforcement staff. Make sure that you know the rules for the journey and the type of vehicle you're driving.

2.32   You've been driving non-stop since 5.00 am. The time is now 9.30 am. Under EU rules, what length of break must you take?

❑ At least 15 minutes   ❑ At least 30 minutes

❑ At least 45 minute.   ❑ At least 60 minutes

DBC s3, DGV s3
You must take an uninterrupted break of 45 minutes after four-and a-half hours of driving. This break may be replaced by two shorter breaks of at least 15 and 30 minutes, taken in that order, during the four-and-a-half hours. During any break, you mustn't drive or do any other work.

2.33   Under EU rules, what's the maximum daily driving time allowed?

☐ 9 hours, extended to 11 hours on three days of the week

☐ 10 hours, extended to 11 hours on two days of the week

☐ 9 hours, extended to 10 hours on two days of the week

☐ 10 hours, extended to 11 hours on three days of the week

DBC s3, DGV s3
You're allowed to extend your daily driving time twice a week, to 10 hours a day. A 'day' is generally any 24-hour period that starts when you begin driving (or other work) again, after the last daily or weekly rest period.

2.34   Under EU rules, your minimum daily rest is 11 hours. On three days of the week this may be reduced to what length of time?

☐ 7 hours   ☐ 8 hours   ☐ 9 hours   ☐ 10 hours

DBC s3, DGV s3
Under EU rules, you must have a minimum daily rest of 11 consecutive hours. A reduced daily rest period is any period of rest of at least 9 hours, but less than 11 hours.

2.35   Under EU rules, your daily rest can be reduced to 9 hours. For how many days per week is this allowed?

☐ One day   ☐ Two days   ☐ Three days   ☐ Four days

DBC s3, DGV s3
Under EU rules, you must have a minimum daily rest of 11 consecutive hours. However you may reduce this to 9 hours for up to three days in any one week.

2.36   Under EU rules, how long should your normal daily rest period be?

☐ 8 hours   ☐ 11 hours   ☐ 13 hours   ☐ 14 hours

DBC s3, DGV s3
Drivers' hours and rest periods are controlled in the interests of road safety. A driver's daily rest period should normally be 11 hours, but this may be reduced to 9 hours for three days in one week. It's a serious offence to break these rules and anyone doing so is liable to a heavy fine and even imprisonment.

2.37   Under EU rules, what's the normal weekly rest period that must be taken?

☐ 40 hours   ☐ 41 hours   ☐ 42 hours   ☐ 45 hours

DBC s3, DGV s3
The working week is defined as from 00.00 hours on Monday to 24.00 hours on the following Sunday. When taking the weekly rest period, a daily rest period must normally be extended to at least 45 consecutive hours.

2.38   A vehicle fitted with an analogue tachograph has two drivers. How should they use the tachograph?

☐ Share the same tachograph chart

☐ Use a separate tachograph chart for every driving period

☐ Use their own tachograph chart

☐ Not use the tachograph for such duties

DBC s3, DGV s3
Your tachograph chart is your personal work record and should only reflect the hours that you drive or do other work. The law says that these charts should be held on file by your employer for at least one year. Enforcement officers can ask for charts to be handed over for inspection.

2.39   You're making a journey with a co-driver. When the other person is driving, how should you show this time?

☐ As a daily rest period   ☐ As a weekly rest period

☐ As a break in daily driving ☐ As driving time

DBC s3, DGV s3
You may only record a break when you're not doing any other type of work. You're allowed to take a break on a double-manned vehicle while the other crew member is driving, but any break must be a minimum of 15 minutes.

2.40   What does a tachograph record?

☐ Load weight   ☐ Driving time

☐ Fuel consumption   ☐ Engine temperature

DBC s3, DGV s3
The tachograph is a tool designed to help you be a safe and responsible driver. The tachograph records details of your journey, including time driven, speed and rest periods.

2.41 Which symbol on your tachograph shows your break/rest period?

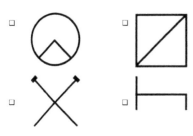

☐ ☐ ☐ ☐

DBC s3, DGV s3

A tachograph allows you to select the mode or task that you're undertaking. Time spent on that task is then recorded automatically. Each task has a different symbol. You need to know the meaning of each, so that your records are correct. The modes are: driving, doing other work, on duty and available for work, and taking a break or rest.

2.42 What does this tachograph chart symbol mean?

☐ Driver at rest

☐ Chart not required

☐ Other work

☐ Driving

DBC s3, DGV s3

Each activity has a different symbol. You should know what they mean, so that you can select the correct one. You're responsible for recording all your activities correctly.

Some tachographs don't have a 'driving' mode switch. These tachographs will automatically record driving time whenever the vehicle is moved, whatever mode the switch is set to.

2.43 What is the 'mode' switch on a tachograph used to record?

☐ Who's driving   ☐ Illness

☐ Weekly rest periods ☐ Other work

DBC s3, DGV s3

As you change activities during the day, you should change the mode switch on the tachograph to record each activity. Failure to operate the mode switch could get you into trouble with your employer or the authorities.

2.44 At the end of your working week, you've driven a total of 56 hours. Under EU rules, what's the maximum number of hours you can drive in the following week?

☐ 34   ☐ 36   ☐ 38   ☐ 40

DBC s3, DGV s3

If you've driven a total of 56 hours in any one week, you can only drive for 34 hours in the following week. Keep your own record to make sure that you don't exceed these hours.

2.45 Your vehicle is fitted with an analogue tachograph. What should you do if you need to exceed the normal drivers' hours due to an emergency?

☐ Continue using the same tachograph chart and write an explanation on the back

☐ Remove the tachograph chart and make a manual record of the rest of the journey

☐ Continue using the same tachograph chart, without any explanation or record

☐ Remove the tachograph chart and tell your employer the reason

DBC s3, DGV s3

In an emergency, you may exceed the drivers' hours rules. As long as road safety isn't put at risk, you can drive for longer to deliver your passengers, your vehicle or its load to safety. In these circumstances, you should note all the reasons on the back of your tachograph chart.

2.46 What's most likely to cause tiredness?

☐ Making frequent and regular stops

☐ Taking driving breaks on board the vehicle

☐ Having insufficient breaks from driving

☐ Using vehicles with automatic gearboxes

DBC s3, DGV s4

Tiredness will affect your concentration. Don't allow yourself to become tired through not taking proper breaks or rest periods. As a professional driver, you have a responsibility either for goods or for passengers, as well as for overall road safety. Make sure your vehicle is well ventilated, so you don't become drowsy between rest periods.

2.47   What should you do if you start to feel tired or unable to concentrate while you're driving?

❑ Stop as soon as it's safe to do so

❑ Wind down a window and carry on

❑ Switch on the radio and complete your journey

❑ Speed up to get to your destination sooner

DBC s3, DGV s4

If you start to feel tired, you should stop as soon as it's safe to do so, even if you aren't due a break.

Make sure that you get enough sleep before you're due to work, especially if you're on an early shift.

2.48   What should you do if you feel tired after driving for two and-a-half hours?

❑ Slow down to a safer speed

❑ Reduce your planned driving time to three hours

❑ Stop as soon as it's safe to do so

❑ Take a less busy route

DBC s3, DGV s4

Most incidents happen as a result of a lapse in concentration. Don't let this happen to you. If you start to feel tired, you won't perform as well as you should. Your reactions will slow down, and your anticipation and judgement of hazards will become flawed. If you feel tired, stop and rest as soon as it's safe to do so.

2.49   What should you do if you suddenly become tired while you're driving on a motorway?

❑ Stop on the hard shoulder and rest

❑ Leave by the next exit and find a place to stop

❑ Stop on the next slip road and rest

❑ Stop on the verge of the motorway and rest

DBC s3, DGV s4

If you're driving for long distances on a motorway, have plenty of rest stops. Many incidents have been caused by drivers falling asleep at the wheel. If you feel yourself becoming tired, you need to leave the motorway and find a safe place to stop; usually this would be the next service area.

2.50   Where can you stop if you feel tired while you're driving on a motorway?

❑ On the hard shoulder   ❑ At a service station

❑ On a slip road   ❑ In a deceleration lane

DBC s3, DGV s4

Travelling long distances on a motorway can be boring. Looking at the same thing for a long period of time can make you feel tired and affect your concentration. If you start to feel tired, leave the motorway by the next exit and stop in a safe place to rest. Ideally you should use a service area, where you can rest and take some refreshment before you restart your journey.

2.51   What should you do if you have to leave your vehicle unattended for a very short time?

❑ Leave a note in the window explaining you'll be back soon

❑ Leave the keys available in case of obstruction

❑ Keep the engine running but lock the doors

❑ Secure the vehicle and lock the doors

DBC s3, DGV s3

Take all the precautions you can to remove opportunities for theft. Lock your vehicle, especially when making deliveries and leaving the vehicle unattended.

2.52   The time is 10.00 am. You've been driving non-stop since 6.00 am. Under EU rules, what's the longest you may now drive without a break?

❑ 15 minutes   ❑ 30 minutes

❑ 40 minutes   ❑ 45 minutes

DBC s3, DGV s3

The maximum driving period under EU rules is 4 hours 30 minutes. After this, you must take a break of at least 45 minutes.

Planning your route will allow you to take your statutory rest periods in a safe place, such as a service area, where you can get food, drink and a rest.

2.53 Under EU rules, you may drive for up to nine hours a day. What maximum may this be increased to on two days of the week?

❑ 9.5 hours ❑ 10 hours ❑ 11 hours ❑ 11.5 hours

DBC s3, DGV s3
You're permitted to extend the daily limit of nine hours to 10 hours twice a week. Don't drive for more than the maximum hours allowed, as you risk a heavy fine and may lose your licence.

2.54 Under EU rules, you can drive for a maximum of nine hours a day. On how many days each week can this be extended to 10 hours?

❑ One day   ❑ Two days

❑ Three days   ❑ Four days

DBC s3, DGV s3
Under EU rules, your normal daily driving time mustn't exceed nine hours. This nine-hour period is defined as the time between

• any two daily rest periods, or
• a daily rest period and a weekly rest period.

You're allowed to extend these hours to 10 hours twice a week.

2.55 How many days does a driver's smart card normally cover?

❑ 7 ❑ 14 ❑ 21 ❑ 28

DBC s3, DGV s3
The smart card will record information covering a period of about 28 days. If you use It beyond this period, some of the recorded information will be overwritten.

2.56 Under EU drivers' hours regulations, a 45-minute break must be taken after 4.5 hours of driving. What shorter breaks can this be split into?

❑ One of 10 minutes, plus one of 35

❑ One of 15 minutes, plus one of 30

❑ One of 20 minutes, plus one of 25

❑ One of 40 minutes, plus one of 5

DBC s3, DGV s3
Under EU regulations, you must take a break of at least 45 minutes after four-and-a-half hours of driving. You may choose to take this break during the driving period. In this case, it can be split into two breaks of at least 15 and 30 minutes, taken in that order.

2.57 You're driving under EU tachograph regulations and lose your smart card. When must you inform the relevant authority?

❑ Within 5 day.   ❑ Within 7 days

❑ Within 14 days ❑ Within 28 days

DBC s3, DGV s3
As a professional driver, you have a responsibility to report any loss or theft of your digital smart card. You must inform the nearest relevant authority within seven days.

2.58 How long is a digital tachograph driver smart card valid?

❑ One year   ❑ Three years

❑ Five years   ❑ Ten years

DBC s3, DGV s3
Digital tachograph driver smart cards are valid for a maximum of five years. You should receive a reminder about three months before the expiry date. However, it's your responsibility to make sure that you apply for a new card at least 15 days before the old one expires.

2.59 Which authority must you contact if your tachograph card is lost or stolen?

❑ The police

❑ The Driver and Vehicle Licensing Agency

❑ A tachograph centre

❑ The Driver and Vehicle Standards Agency

DBC s3, DGV s3   NI Exempt
Driver cards for digital tachographs are issued by the Driver and Vehicle Licensing Agency in Swansea. In Northern Ireland, the cards are issued by the Driver and Vehicle Agency. Tell them if your card is lost or stolen.

2.60 Where can you get a replacement driver tachograph card?

❑ The Driver and Vehicle Licensing Agency

❑ The Driver and Vehicle Standards Agency

❑ Any MOT test centre

❑ A tachograph centre

DBC s3, DGV s3   NI Exempt
Driver cards for digital tachographs are issued by the Driver and Vehicle Licensing Agency. In Northern Ireland, the cards are issued by the Driver and Vehicle Agency. They can send you a replacement card, for a fee.

2.61 A driver is convicted of obstructing an enforcement officer in the course of their duties. Under EU drivers' hours regulations, what's the maximum fine they can receive?

☐ Unlimited ☐ £3000 ☐ £4000 ☐ £5000

DBC s3, DGV s3, HC p126
EU drivers' hours regulations say that any driver who fails to comply with, or obstructs, an enforcement officer in the course of their duties can face an unlimited fine.

2.62 When are you allowed to alter your tachograph record?

☐ If there are two or more drivers

☐ If your journey is over 50 miles

☐ At no time

☐ When you have no spare charts

DBC s3, DGV s3
Altering drivers' hours records or tampering with a tachograph with intent to deceive is a criminal offence. You, and anyone else involved, could go to prison. You could also lose your licence.

2.63 You're driving under EU drivers' hours. How is a week defined under these rules?

☐ Between 00.00 hours on Monday and 24.00 hours the following Sunday

☐ Any seven-day period

☐ Between 00.00 hours and 24.00 hours six days later

☐ A working period of 56 hours

DBC s3, DGV s3
The rules define a week as a period between 00.00 hours on Monday and 24.00 hours the following Sunday. You must make sure that you don't exceed any weekly driving limit.

2.64 Which type of digital tachograph card is used by an approved calibration centre when they're recalibrating the tachograph?

☐ Control card ☐ Company card

☐ Driver card ☐ Workshop card

DBC s3, DGV s3
The workshop card is available only to approved calibration centres. There are three other types of digital tachograph card:
• driver card, used by the driver
• company card, used by an operator
• control card, used by enforcement authorities.

2.65 Which digital tachograph card is only available to enforcement authorities?

☐ Control card ☐ CPC card

☐ Company card ☐ Workshop card

DBC s3, DGV s3
Various types of smart card are used in digital tachograph systems:
• driver card, used by drivers
• company card, used by operators
• workshop card, available only to approved calibration centres
• control card, available only to Driver and Vehicle Standards Agency (DVSA) officials and the police, for carrying out enforcement.

2.66 Drivers must have a driver smart card for use in digital tachographs. Where can you obtain a replacement smart card in Great Britain?

☐ The Driver and Vehicle Licensing Agency

☐ Highways England

☐ A tachograph calibration centre

☐ The Post Office

DBC s3, DGV s3   Ni Exempt
In Great Britain, a replacement smart card can only be obtained from the Driver and Vehicle Licensing Agency (DVLA). In Northern Ireland, they're available from the Driver and Vehicle Agency (DVA).

2.67 Who's responsible for the issue of tachograph charts to a bus or lorry driver?

☐ The driver's employer

☐ The Driver and Vehicle Standards Agency

☐ The authorised calibration centre

☐ The local MOT testing centre

DBC s3, DGV s3
The driver's employer is responsible for the issue of tachograph charts. The driver must ensure that the correct information is recorded on the chart.

2.68 How can you find out when an analogue tachograph was last recalibrated?

□ From a date on the tachograph chart

□ By contacting the vehicle's manufacturer

□ By checking the vehicle's service record

□ From a plaque on or near the tachograph

DBC s3, DGV s3
An analogue tachograph must be checked every two years and recalibrated every six years. A plaque on or near the tachograph will show when it was last checked.

2.69 When must an analogue tachograph be recalibrated?

□ Every two years   □ Every four years

□ Every six years   □ Every eight years

DBC s3, DGV s3
When an analogue tachograph is installed and calibrated, an installation plaque is fixed near the tachograph. This shows the date of the most recent tachograph calibration. Under EU rules, this must take place every six years.

2.70 Your vehicle breaks down during a journey. You continue by driving in another vehicle with the same type of tachograph. What must you do with your tachograph chart?

□ Leave it in the broken-down vehicle

□ Take it with you for security, but use a new chart in the new vehicle

□ Telephone the testing authority for permission to drive without a chart

□ Take it with you, and use it in the new vehicle

DBC s3, DGV s3
When changing vehicles, you should also record certain pieces of information, including the closing odometer reading, the registration number of the new vehicle, the odometer start reading and the time of the vehicle change.

2.71 Under EU rules, what's the maximum driving time allowed in any two consecutive weeks?

□ 85 hours □ 90 hours □ 100 hours □ 105 hours

DBC s3, DGV s3
Under EU rules, the maximum number of hours that you can drive in any two consecutive weeks is 90 hours. These don't have to be split evenly, but the total amount of driving time in any one week mustn't exceed 56 hours. Don't exceed your driving hours; heavy fines can be given to drivers who break the law.

2.72 How often must an analogue tachograph be checked at an approved calibration centre?

□ Every year   □ Every two years

□ Every five years □ Every six years

DBC s3,DGV s3
An analogue tachograph must be checked every two years and recalibrated and sealed every six years. This must be done at an approved calibration centre. Digital tachographs, unlike analogue ones, must be recalibrated every two years.

2.73 You're driving a bus with 18 seats on an excursion from London to Scotland. Which drivers' hours rules should you use?

□ AETR only   □ Domestic

□ EU only   □ EU and AETR

DBC s3
If you're driving a bus on an excursion (that is, not a regular journey) and your vehicle has 18 or more seats, you must use EU rules and record the details.

2.74 After driving continuously for the maximum period under EU rules, a bus driver must take a break. What's the minimum duration of this break?

□ 15 minutes   □ 30 minutes

□ 45 minutes   □ 60 minutes

DBC s3
After driving for a period of no more than 4.5 hours, you must take a break of at least 45 minutes, which mustn't be interrupted. If you're carrying passengers, they'll probably also be grateful for a break. Taking breaks at the correct time will keep you and your passengers safe and comfortable.

2.75   When may a driver take their rest period in a parked vehicle?

❑ If it's fitted with a bunk

❑ If a smoke alarm is fitted

❑ If the vehicle's in an authorised coach park

❑ If there are no passengers on board

DBC s3
Some vehicles are fitted with sleeping accommodation for the driver. If your vehicle has this facility, you're allowed to take your daily rest period there, provided your vehicle is stationary.

2.76   What should you do if you're asked to leave your bus by an official who isn't in uniform?

❑ Comply with the request

❑ Ask to see a warrant card

❑ Refuse to leave the vehicle

❑ Invite the official abroad

DBC s3
If you're asked to leave your vehicle by an official who isn't in uniform, ask to see their warrant card. The official is likely to be an enforcement or police officer, but don't presume this.

2.77   What must the driver do when they leave their bus unattended?

❑ Check that the tachograph chart is removed

❑ Check that the gear lever is in reverse

❑ Check that the gear lever is in first

❑ Check that the· parking brake is applied

DBC s2
Make sure that your vehicle is safe whenever you leave it unattended. Always stop the engine and apply the parking brake.

2.78   When are bus operators required to use tachographs for regular journeys?

❑ When the journey is more than 10 km

❑ When the journey is more than 20 km

❑ When the journey is more than 50 km

❑ When the journey is more than 80 km

DBC s3
Operators of buses used for regular journeys of more than 50 km must use tachographs.

Section 3 Braking Systems

3.1 When is trailer swing most likely to occur on a lorry and drawbar combination?

☐ While you're braking on a bend

☐ While you're using an endurance brake

☐ While you're steering at slow speed and fully loaded

☐ While you're moving off at an angle

DGV s2
The forces that act on your vehicle if you brake while cornering can lead to instability and may cause trailer swing. You should try to plan ahead so that you brake smoothly and in good time as you approach a bend.

3.2 Your vehicle is fitted with a 'diff-lock'. When would you normally use it?

☐ While driving on straight roads

☐ While towing an empty trailer

☐ While driving on muddy construction sites

☐ While uncoupling a trailer

DGV s2
The differential allows the drive wheels to rotate at different speeds; this is necessary for the vehicle to negotiate corners and bends. On a slippery surface, however, it can cause problems: if one wheel has less traction, it can spin, resulting in a complete loss of drive. The 'diff-lock' prevents the wheels from turning independently and so helps to stop this happening.

3.3 What colour is the auxiliary line on a three-line braking system?

☐ Red   ☐ Blue   ☐ Green   ☐ Yellow

DGV s2
If you're driving an articulated vehicle or a trailer combination, it's vital that you understand the rules that apply to coupling and uncoupling the brake lines. If you take a practical driving test with a trailer, you'll be expected to demonstrate this during the test. The lines are colour-coded: red is the emergency line, blue is the auxiliary line and yellow is the service line. They must be connected strictly in accordance with the correct procedure.

3.4 The emergency line is common to both two-line and three-line brake systems. What colour is it?

☐ Red   ☐ Blue   ☐ Black   ☐ Yellow

DGV s2
The red emergency line is common to both two-line and three-line braking systems. Always set the parking brake before disconnecting any brake line.

3.5 Air-brake systems usually have two lines. Which additional line is fitted on a three line system?

☐ Emergency   ☐ Service   ☐ Electrical   ☐ Auxiliary

DGV s2
The blue (auxiliary) line isn't used when connecting to a two-line system. Follow the manufacturer's instructions about what to do with this third line.

3.6 In frosty weather, what precaution could a lorry driver take to prevent moisture from freezing in the air-brake system?

☐ Drain the air tanks daily

☐ Cover the air tanks with a blanket

☐ Keep the engine at high revs when starting

☐ Pump the brakes

DGV s2
You should make sure that you drain the air tanks daily to avoid moisture in the system. Most modern vehicles have an automatic draining system, which should be checked regularly.

3.7 How can a lorry driver avoid brake fade?

☐ Ensure that the air tanks are drained before journeys

☐ Check that the air pressure is correct

☐ Make sure that the parking brake is applied before stopping

☐ Select an appropriate gear before downhill gradients

DGV s2
Using the brakes to control a lorry's speed as it's driven down a hill will cause them to get hot. If they overheat, they can become less effective – a condition known as brake fade. By selecting a low gear, the engine's resistance will slow the lorry. This reduces the demands on the brakes, making them less likely to overheat.

3.8 When are exhaust brakes most efficient?

❏ At high engine speed, while in low gears

❏ At low engine speed, while in high gears

❏ During stop/start town work

❏ While travelling at a constant speed on a motorway

DGV s2

An exhaust brake alters the engine's exhaust flow, using it to help control the vehicle's speed. It's most efficient when the engine is running at a high speed and the vehicle is in a low gear, such as when descending a long hill. Using the exhaust brake can relieve the service brakes, preventing them from overheating and fading.

3.9 What's the principal braking system on a lorry called?

❏ The endurance brake   ❏ The service brake

❏ The parking brake   ❏ The jake brake

DGV s2

The service brake is usually operated by the brake pedal. It's used to control the speed of the vehicle and to bring it to a halt safely. It may also incorporate an anti-lock braking system.

3.10 You're driving an articulated lorry. What could happen if you change to a lower gear while you're going too fast?

❏ The vehicle could jack-knife

❏ The engine could stall

❏ The brakes could fail

❏ The trailer could uncouple

DGV s2

Severe braking or selecting a gear too low for your road speed can cause the tractor unit to slow more quickly than the trailer. The trailer can then pivot around the coupling (fifth wheel), causing the vehicle to jack-knife. Jack-knifing is more likely to occur with an unladen vehicle, particularly on a bend or curve.

3.11 When is an articulated vehicle most at risk of jack-knifing?

❏ When it's fitted with an endurance brake (retarder)

❏ While it's manoeuvring slowly

❏ While it's under heavy braking

❏ When it's fully loaded

DGV s2

Heavy braking can cause an articulated vehicle to become unstable and may even lead to jack-knifing; this is more likely to occur when the trailer is unladen.

3.12 Your lorry is stuck in snow. You use the diff-lock to move off. When should you switch the diff-lock off?

❏ Only after selecting top gear

❏ Once the engine has warmed up

❏ As soon as the vehicle is moving

❏ As soon as the snow has cleared

DGV s2

You must always disengage the diff-lock as soon as the vehicle is moving. The differential allows the rear wheels to revolve at different speeds, and this allows the vehicle to follow a curved path. Attempting to turn with the diff-lock engaged could result in the vehicle continuing straight on.

3.13 Your tractor unit has three air lines. You're connecting to a trailer that has two air line couplings. What colour is the line you shouldn't connect to the trailer?

❏ Red ❏ Yellow   ❏ Black   ❏ Blue

DGV s2

When connecting a three-line tractor unit to a two-line trailer, the blue line is the one that shouldn't be connected to the trailer. This is the auxiliary line. Always follow the manufacturer's advice: it may be necessary to reconnect the extra line to the tractor unit.

3.14 You're driving an articulated lorry that has three air lines connected to the trailer. What's the purpose of the red line?

❏ It's the emergency line   ❏ It's the service line

❏ It's the auxiliary line   ❏ It's the electrical line

DGV s2

The red emergency line is common to both two-line and three-line brake systems. The other colours are

• blue – auxiliary

• yellow – service.

3.15 You're driving a tractor unit fitted with two air lines. You want to couple to a trailer that has three air-line couplings. How should the air lines be connected?

☐ The trailer auxiliary line should be left unconnected

☐ The trailer service line should be left unconnected

☐ Only the service line should be connected

☐ Only the auxiliary line should be connected

DGV s2
A two-line system consists of the emergency line (red) and the service line (yellow). You need to understand the rules that apply to safe connection of brake systems and mixing two-line and three-line systems.

3.16 Your lorry is equipped with anti-lock brakes.What's the correct procedure for stopping in an emergency?

☐ Apply the footbrake firmly in a pumping action until the vehicle has stopped

☐ Apply the footbrake firmly and continuously until the vehicle has stopped

☐ Apply the footbrake and handbrake until the vehicle has stopped

☐ Apply the handbrake only

DGV s2
When your vehicle has anti-lock brakes and you need to stop in an emergency, you should keep your foot firmly on the brake pedal until the vehicle stops; this will allow the system to work. Although anti-lock brakes contribute to safety, they don't reduce your stopping distance or take away the need to drive with good planning and anticipation.

3.17 What does changing to a lower gear on a long downhill gradient help to avoid?

☐ Brake fade   ☐ Clutch slip

☐ Excessive engine revs ☐ Tyre wear

DGV s2
Engaging a lower gear and using engine braking will help you to control your speed as you're going downhill. This reduces the demands on the brakes, and helps to prevent them from overheating. This will reduce the likelihood of brake fade.

3.18 You have to drive onto a muddy building site. Why should you switch on your diff-lock?

☐ To make your steering lighter

☐ To improve your fuel consumption

☐ To increase your engine power

☐ To make the wheels less likely to spin

DGV s2
Engaging the diff-lock means that the driven wheels are locked together. This reduces the likelihood of wheel spin. Remember to switch off the diff-lock as soon as you're on firm ground again, otherwise you could damage the transmission.

3.19 How will anti-lock brakes improve your vehicle's safety?

☐ They allow you to follow other vehicles more closely

☐ They help you keep steering control while braking heavily

☐ They let you drive faster on wet roads

☐ They enable you to brake later than normal

DBC s2, DGV s2
When your steering wheels are locked – as can happen in a skid – you can't steer the vehicle. Anti-lock brakes help you to keep steering control while you're braking heavily, but they aren't a substitute for good forward planning. Anticipation and planning ahead will minimise the risk of skidding more effectively than relying on your braking system.

3.20 What could prevent air pressure from building up in an air-brake system in frosty weather?

☐ Moisture in the air may form bubbles in the brake fluid

☐ The air will contract, reducing the pressure

☐ The dampness may cause valves to rust

☐ Moisture drawn in with the air may freeze and cause a blockage

DBC s2, DGV s2
When air is compressed, moisture condenses and collects in the air tanks. This can find its way along the network of pipes connected to the brakes. In frosty weather, the moisture can freeze in the pipes, blocking them completely. On modern vehicles, the air is dried before it's compressed and the air tanks drain automatically to shed any moisture. On older vehicles, the air tanks need draining manually.

3.21   What should you do if the brake air-pressure warning light comes on while you're driving?

❏ Stop and get help without delay

❏ Report the fault when you return to your depot

❏ Build up the pressure by accelerating

❏ Drain the air tanks and continue normally

DBC s2, DGV s2
When a warning light or device indicating a loss of brake pressure comes on, you rnust stop safely and get the fault put right immediately. The safety of you, your load, your passengers and all other road users is at risk.

3.22   You've just started the engine. What must you do if the brake air-pressure warning light is showing?

❏ Report it as a fault   ❏ Keep the parking brake on

❏ Switch your engine off ❏ Engage the clutch

DBC s2, DGV s2
Even though the warning light is showing, there may be sufficient pressure to release the parking brake. However, you mustn't do this, because there may not be enough air pressure to operate the service brake.

3.23   Your vehicle is fitted with an anti-lock braking system. What's it designed to allow you to do?

❏ Drive at faster speeds

❏ Brake much later than normal

❏ Apply the brakes more quickly

❏ Stop safely in an emergency

DBC s2, DGV s2
Anti-lock braking systems sense when the wheels are about to lock. The sensor control releases the brakes and immediately applies them again. It will do this many times per second. This both prevents skidding and enables the driver to steer – something that's impossible when the steering wheels are skidding.

3.24   Your vehicle is fitted with an anti-lock braking system. When should you check that it's working properly?

❏ Before each servico

❏ At the start of each working day

❏ At the start of each working week

❏ Before every journey

DBC s2, DGV s2
Modern anti-lock braking systems rely on electronics for their operation. A warning light on the dashboard shows that the system is operating. This light will usually go out when the vehicle reaches about 6 mph (10 km/h).

3.25   What will 'pumping' the brake pedal in a vehicle fitted with anti-lock brakes cause?

❏ Increased effectiveness ❏ Reduced effectiveness

❏ Reduced brake wear   ❏ Increased brake wear

DBC s2, DGV s2
Before driving a vehicle fitted with anti-lock brakes, refer to the handbook. This will give you details of the manufacturer's recommended method of use. Remember, anti-lock brakes will enhance your skills, but they can't replace them.

3.26   You're driving a vehicle fitted with anti-lock brakes. What should you do when braking in an emergency?

❏ 'Pump' the brake pedal harshly

❏ Apply minimum force to the brake pedal

❏ Use the exhaust brake (retarder) before the footbrake

❏ Apply firm, continuous pressure to the brake pedal

DBC s2, DGV s2
Applying a firm, continuous brake pressure will enable the anti-lock braking system (ABS) to function properly. However, ABS is becoming increasingly sophisticated, so you should read the vehicle manufacturer's handbook for its advice about using the system.

3.27   What's 'brake fade'?

❏ Reduction of air pressure

❏ Smooth progressive braking

❏ Reduction of braking effectiveness

❏ Low hydraulic brake fluid level

DBC s2, DGV s2
Continually using the brakes could cause them to overheat. When that happens, they become less effective. This is called brake fade, and it occurs most often when the driver has to control the vehicle's speed on a long downhill gradient. To help prevent brake fade, use tho endurance brake (retarder) and a lower gear to keep the vehicle's speed in check, rather than the wheel-mounted brakes.

3.28 'Brake fade' is a loss of effectiveness of the brakes when they overheat. When would 'brake fade' be most likely to happen?

❑ On a long journey

❑ On a long downhill gradient

❑ On the approach to hazards

❑ On a long uphill gradient

DBC s2, DGV s2
Continuous use of the brakes will cause them to overheat, and in extreme cases they'll become ineffective. When you're going downhill, the momentum of your vehicle will cause you to gather speed very quickly. Use the endurance brake (retarder) and stay in a low gear to reduce the need to use the brakes.

3.29 What should you do when driving a large vehicle down a steep hill?

❑ Partly apply the parking brake

❑ Select the vehicle's highest gear

❑ Use the endurance brake

❑ Put the gear lever into neutral

DBC s2, DGV s2
When approaching a long hill, you should take note of any early warning signs. Reduce your speed and select the appropriate gear in good time. Using an endurance brake (retarder), if fitted, will help control your speed.

3.30 What should anti-lock brakes let you do when you have to stop in an emergency?

❑ Brake more gently

❑ Brake much later

❑ Maintain steering control

❑ Stop over a long distance

DBC s2,DGV s2
Anti-lock brakes are a driver aid, and can help you maintain steering control while braking. However, you mustn't rely on them to get you out of trouble or expect to be able to make sudden direction changes if you're going too fast.

3.31 Your vehicle has anti-lock brakes. How does this affect you when you're braking normally?

❑ There's no need to alter the way you brake

❑ You'll be able to brake much later

❑ You'll need to brake more firmly

❑ There's no need to brake so early

DBC s2,DGV s2
Plan well ahead to enable you to brake normally. Don't rely on anti lock brakes to compensate for deficiencies in your driving.

3.32 Where would you see an escape lane?

❑ Outside a fire station

❑ Alongside a bus lane

❑ Before a motorway exit

❑ Down a steep hill

DBC s2,DGV s2
An escape lane is for use in emergencies, usually when brakes have become hot and faded or failed completely while descending a long, steep hill. A sign will show you the direction of the road, and a chequered area, usually straight ahead, defines the escape route.

3.33 When would you use an escape lane?

❑ When motorways merge

❑ When carrying a dangerous cargo

❑ When your brakes have failed

❑ When emergency repairs are needed

DBC s2,DGV s2
Escape lanes are found on steep downhill sections of road. They're designed to give a 'run-off' area, usually straight ahead, to allow vehicles to stop in an emergency. This is usually when brakes have faded or failed on large vehicles.

3.34   When can an endurance brake (retarder) be especially useful?

❏ While driving down long hills

❏ When driving on steep cambers

❏ As a way to reduce gear changes

❏ To improve fuel consumption

DBC s2,DGV s2
Plan ahead and use your endurance brake (retarder) to help keep your speed in check on long downhill gradients. This can help to prevent your brakes from overheating and fading.

3.35   You're driving down a long hill. What should you use to prevent the brakes from overheating?

❏ The anti-lock braking system

❏ The footbrake

❏ The secondary brake

❏ The endurance brake (retarder)

DBC s2, DGV s2
Endurance brakes or 'retarders' help to control a vehicle's speed. They operate by applying resistance to slow the vehicle without using the wheel brakes, so avoiding brake fade. The methods used include: increased engine braking, exhaust braking and transmission-mounted devices.

3.36   What system is used to control a vehicle's speed without using the footbrake?

❏ A secondary brake

❏ An endurance brake (retarder)

❏ A differential lock

❏ An emergency air system

DBC s2, DGV s2
Large vehicles can be fitted with various types of endurance brake (retarder). Make sure you're familiar with how the system operates on the vehicle you're using. Don't risk a crash or collision through ignorance.

3.37   When should an endurance brake (retarder) be used?

❏ On motorways only   ❏ When braking quickly

❏ When you stop or park ❏ On long downhill slopes

DBC s2, DGV s2
An endurance brake can help to control your speed on long downhill slopes without using the service brake. Reducing the use of the service brake helps to prevent the brakes from overheating and reduces the risk of brake fade.

3.38   Your vehicle is fully loaded. Where should you be braking when dealing with bends?

❏ As close to the bend as possible

❏ As you start to turn the wheel

❏ When halfway around the bend

❏ When driving in a straight line

DBC s2, DGV s2
When a vehicle changes direction, forces are applied to the vehicle and its load. Braking at the same time can result in additional forces being introduced, and this can lead to a loss of control. For this reason, braking should be carried out while driving in a straight line, so preventing these forces from acting together.

3.39   A lorry is overtaking you on a two-lane motorway. What should you do if it doesn't have the speed to get past?

❏ Continue at the same speed

❏ Be prepared to reduce your speed

❏ Increase your speed and force the lorry to drop back

❏ Brake hard to allow the other driver to cut in

DBC s4, DGV s4
Always be prepared to give way to overtaking lorries or buses. Maintaining your speed will only block the motorway to other traffic unnecessarily. You may find yourself in a similar situation if the limiter on your vehicle doesn't allow you enough speed to successfully overtake another vehicle.

3.40 What should you do after driving through a flood?

□ Carry out an emergency stop

□ Drive in a low gear with the footbrake lightly applied

□ Avoid braking until the brakes have dried out

□ Pump the footbrake when approaching hazards

HC r121
If you have to drive through a flood, do so with caution. Once out of the flood, you need to test your brakes to make sure they're working properly. To do this, check what's behind you, then drive in a low gear with the brakes gently applied.

3.41 What can coasting downhill seriously affect?

□ The air brakes   □ The cooling system

□ The tachograph   □ The electrical systems

DBC s2, DGV s2
Air-brake systems rely on an engine-driven compressor to keep the reservoir tanks at their operating pressure. Coasting downhill and relying on the brakes to control your speed could result in the loss of sufficient air pressure to operate the brakes effectively.

3.42 When does 'brake fade' occur?

□ When the brakes get too hot

□ When the brakes get too cold

□ When the brakes get too dry

□ When the brakes get too wet

DBC st, 2, DGV s2
Continuous use of the brakes can result in them overheating and losing their effectiveness. This is known as 'brake fade' and it's most likely on long downhill gradients.

3.43 How can you help to prevent 'brake fade'?

□ Use the endurance brake

□ Apply the parking brake

□ Select neutral for a short distance

□ Repeatedly pump the brake pedal

DBC s1, 2, DGV s2
Brake fade occurs when the brakes overheat. Good forward planning and correct use of the gears when descending hills, together with proper use of the endurance brake (retarder), can help to prevent brake fade.

3.44 What causes 'brake fade'?

□ Continuous use of the brakes

□ Repeated pumping of the brakes

□ Loss of air pressure in the system

□ Badly worn brake pads

DBC st, 2, DGV s2
Continuous use of the brakes on a long downhill gradient can cause them to overheat and become ineffective. This is called brake fade. You should use a low gear to enable the engine's braking effect to help control your speed. Also use the vehicle's retarder, if fitted. As well as reducing the likelihood

3.45 Where must extra care be taken when using an endurance brake {retarder)?

□ On uneven roads   □ On slippery roads

□ On downhill gradients □ On uphill gradients

DBC s2, DGV s2
The endurance brake (retarder) slows the vehicle without the use of the wheel-mounted brakes. However, care should be taken in slippery conditions, when the retarder's effect can be powerful enough to cause a skid.

3.46 You're stationary. The brake air-pressure warning light comes on. Why should you keep the parking brake on?

□ Because the vehicle will suddenly roll backwards

□ Because it will cause the air pressure to rise

□ Because the service brake may not stop you

□ Because it will make the warning light go out

DBC s2, DGV s2
Even though a warning device indicates low air-brake pressure, you may still be able to release the parking brake. If you do this and start moving, the service brake may be ineffective and you may not be able to stop.

3.47 You're about to drive a vehicle fitted with air-assisted hydraulic brakes. Why might the brake pedal feel hard when you press it?

☐ The vacuum pump isn't working

☐ The pedal movement needs adjusting

☐ The brakes are locked on fully

☐ The brake-fluid reservoir is empty

DBC s2, DGV s2
If the brake pedal is hard to press, this could mean a loss of vacuum or a fault in the vacuum pump. You shouldn't drive the vehicle until the fault has been repaired.

3.48 Your vehicle is fitted with an air-assisted hydraulic braking system. What would warn you that the vacuum pump isn't working?

☐ The brake pedal feels spongy when pressed

☐ The brake pedal has little resistance

☐ The brake pedal feels hard when pressed

☐ The brake pedal travels a long way

DBC s2, DGV s2
The pump creates a vacuum in the servo unit. This reduces the amount of pressure you need to apply to the brake pedal. Without this vacuum, it's extremely difficult to press the brake pedal down.

3.49 Your vehicle is fitted with hydraulic brakes. Why might the brake pedal go down too far when it's pressed?

☐ There's too much fluid in the braking system

☐ The pedal travel requires adjustment

☐ The vacuum exhauster isn't working

☐ There isn't enough fluid in the braking system

DBC s2, DGV s2
A loose brake pedal would suggest a serious loss of fluid from the hydraulic system. Don't drive your vehicle until the fault has been checked and fixed by a qualified person.

3.50 You're about to drive a vehicle fitted with hydraulic brakes. What should you check before driving the vehicle?

☐ The hydraulic-brake fluid level

☐ The power-steering fluid level

☐ The cooling-system fluid level

☐ The windscreen-washer fluid level

DBC s2, DGV s2
It's important to check all fluid levels during your daily checks, but it's especially important to remember the hydraulic fluid reservoir. A loss of fluid could lead to brake failure.

3.51 Your vehicle is fitted with air-assisted hydraulic brakes. What would warn you that there isn't enough air in the system?

☐ An increase in pressure on the air gauge

☐ A buzzer or light

☐ The exhaust brake won't work

☐ Brake fade

DBC s2, DGV s2
If a warning buzzer or light alerts you to a loss of air pressure, you should stop on the side of the road immediately. You should have enough air in reserve to allow you to do this safely. Don't start or continue your journey until the fault has been repaired.

3.52 Which coloured band on the rev counter makes the best use of engine braking?

☐ Blue   ☐ Red   ☐ Amber   ☐ Green

DBC s2, DGV s2
There are usually four coloured bands on the rev counter: green, amber, blue and red. The blue band will allow you to make the best use of engine braking. Try to keep in this band when going down a steep hill.

3.53 Your vehicle is fitted with air brakes. What does it mean if a brake warning light shows when you've just started the engine?

☐ Low air pressure

☐ Increased air pressure

☐ The parking brake isn't working

☐ The air reservoirs are fully charged

DBC s2, DGV s2
It's dangerous to drive a vehicle with low air pressure. To alert you to this, all vehicles are fitted with a warning light and/or buzzer. Don't move your vehicle if this warning shows or sounds.

3.54 Your vehicle is fitted with air-assisted hydraulic brakes. What fault would you suspect if the brake pedal becomes hard to press?

☐ The brake system has a loss of vacuum

☐ The brake linings are worn

☐ The brake shoes need adjusting

☐ The brake system requires more fluid

DBC s2, DGV s2
A fault in the vacuum pump could be the cause of a stiff brake pedal. There could also be a leaking connection allowing air into the vacuum. Don't continue your journey until the fault has been fixed.

3.55 Which component will last longer when you use a retarder?

☐ The brake linings   ☐ The catalytic converter

☐ The exhaust system   ☐ The transmission

DBC s2, DGV s2
By using a retarder, the life of the brake linings is extended. This is because a retarder works by slowing the vehicle without using the wheel-mounted brakes.

3.56 What should you do when an air-pressure warning device activates?

☐ Continue to drive the vehicle

☐ Drain the air tanks

☐ Stop and have the fault put right

☐ Pump the brake pedal repeatedly

DBC s2, DGV s2
Air-brake systems are fitted with a warning device that operates if the air pressure in the tanks drops below a safe level. There may be a warning buzzer and/or pressure gauges. You must be aware of the function of all gauges on your vehicle, and check them as you drive.

3.57 You're driving down a snow-covered hill. Why should you take care when using an independent endurance brake (retarder)?

☐ Your brakes could overheat

☐ Your speed could increase

☐ Compressed air could escape

☐ The drive wheels could lock

DBC s2, DGV s2
Select an appropriate gear in good time and, if your vehicle has a dashboard-mounted lever, apply the endurance brake (retarder) in stages. Braking too much, too soon may result In locking your drive wheels.

3.58 What should you avoid when using an independent endurance brake (retarder) on slippery roads?

☐ The front wheels spinning

☐ The drive wheels locking

☐ Brake-pad wear

☐ Anti-skid road surfaces

DBC s2, DGV s2
The endurance brake (retarder) usually operates by applying resistance, via the transmission, to the vehicle's driven wheels. If the road is slippery, the tyres may lose grip and the wheels will lock.

3.59 You're about to drive an unfamiliar vehicle. What should you do if you think there may be moisture in the air-brake reservoir?

☐ Assume the system has automatic drain valves

☐ Find out whether you need to drain the system manually

☐ Nothing; it's the vehicle owner's responsibility

☐ Leave the engine running for a while before driving

DBC s2, DGV s2
Moisture in the braking system can cause serious problems, especially in cold weather, when it could freeze and stop the brakes from working. Most modern vehicles have a system that drains automatically, but make sure you know which system is fitted to any vehicle that you drive.

3.60 You're about to start a journey in very frosty weather. What's the likely cause of low air-brake pressure?

☐ Engine temperature too low

☐ Weak engine anti-freeze mixture

☐ Brake pedal needs adjustment

☐ Frozen moisture in the storage tanks

DBC s2
Air-brake systems use air from the atmosphere, which contains moisture. The moisture condenses under pressure, resulting in water in the system. Make sure the air tanks are drained daily to remove any water and to help prevent the system from freezing in cold weather.

3.61 When should an anti-lock braking system (ABS) warning light turn off?

☐ When the brakes are used for the first time

☐ When the ABS comes into operation

☐ When road speed is 6 mph (10 km/h) or more

☐ When the secondary braking system is used

DBC s2

Every vehicle fitted with anti-lock brakes must have a warning light in the cab of the vehicle. The warnings may differ between manufacturers, but on all types the warning light should come on when the ignition is switched on, and turn off when the vehicle reaches a speed of 6 mph (10 km/h). If the light stays on, there may be a fault; you should have the brakes checked before continuing your journey.

3.62 What's the most powerful brake on a bus?

☐ Secondary brake

☐ Anti-lock braking system

☐ Endurance brake (retarder)

☐ Service brake

DBC s2

The most powerful and effective brake on the vehicle is the service brake, and this should be used in normal circumstances. Well-maintained brakes should apply an even pressure to all the wheels, providing an efficient, controlled stop.

3.63 What should you do when making a short stop, facing uphill?

☐ Hold the vehicle on the clutch

☐ Hold the vehicle on the footbrake

☐ Select neutral and apply the parking brake

☐ Apply the parking brake after stopping

DBC s2

As with stopping in any other situation, if you have to make a stop on an uphill gradient, wait until the vehicle has come to a halt before applying the parking brake.

3.64 You're about to move off in a vehicle that has automatic transmission. What must you do before you select 'D' (drive)?

☐ Put your foot on the footbrake

☐ Signal to move off

☐ Alter your seat position

☐ Adjust your mirrors

DBC s2

It's important to apply the footbrake before you engage 'D' (or drive), so your vehicle doesn't creep forward or roll back out of control when you're about to move away. This can be dangerous; for example, if there's another road user close behind.

3.65 What's an advantage of progressive braking?

☐ Improved passenger safety and comfort

☐ Increased air-brake pressure

☐ Avoidance of 'brake fade'

☐ Longer rest periods

DBC s2

The way you drive matters. The safety and comfort of your passengers is your priority; if you have the correct attitude when you're driving, your passengers will be assured of a comfortable and pleasant journey.

Good forward planning and anticipation will help you avoid having to turn or brake suddenly.

Section 4 The driver

4.1 You're approaching a green traffic light and are going straight ahead. What should you do when the traffic ahead, beyond the junction, has stopped and is queuing?

☐ Go forward if your vehicle will clear the junction

☐ Drive slowly across the junction

☐ Maintain your speed and sound your horn

☐ Stop across the junction until the traffic clears

HC r176
Look well ahead and plan your approach to all junctions. Even if the traffic lights are green, don't go forward if queuing traffic will cause you to block the junction. Be aware of the length of your vehicle and how much space it needs to clear the junction.

4.2 What rules apply to the wearing of seat belts fitted to your lorry?

☐ It's not advisable

☐ It's advisable

☐ It's required by law

☐ It's not required by law

DGV s3, HC r99-102
If seat belts are fitted to your lorry, you must wear them. Exemptions are allowed for holders of medical exemption certificates and for delivery drivers when travelling less than 50 metres (162 feet).

4.3 You're driving this box van and are waiting to turn right. What should you do just before turning?

☐ Wave the pedestrian across

☐ Check your left-hand mirror and blind spot

☐ Wave out the blue car (arrowed)

☐ Check your right-hand mirror and blind spot

HC r180
Always make a final check in your mirrors and check your blind spots before you turn. Another driver or a motorcyclist may have committed themselves to overtaking traffic behind you before realising you intend to turn.

4.4 What will you have to deal with when you're driving at night?

☐ Headlight dazzle

☐ Other drivers speeding

☐ Cold weather conditions

☐ Dazzle from shop windows

DGV s4
At night, the headlights of oncoming traffic can dazzle you, reducing how much you can see of the road ahead. Reduce your speed so that you can safely respond to any situation that may arise and make sure you've dipped your headlights.

4.5 You're driving a lorry in a busy town. A driver pulls out in front of you and you have to brake hard. What should you do?

☐ Overtake as quickly as possible

☐ Stay calm and accept the error

☐ Flash your lights to show your annoyance

☐ Sound your horn and speed up

DGV s1
Some drivers might emerge from a junction when it's not safe to do so. In this situation, understand that other drivers might make mistakes. Don't intimidate them by driving aggressively to teach them a lesson.

4.6 Your lorry is fitted with a driver's seat belt. When may you drive without wearing it?

☐ When you're making deliveries that are less than 50 metres apart

☐ When you're towing at less than 50 mph

☐ When you're working less than 50 hours in a week

☐ When you're less than 50 miles away from your depot

HC r99
It's compulsory for drivers and passengers to wear seat belts. However, if you're making deliveries that are less than 50 metres apart, you may leave the seat belt undone. It would be impractical to keep fastening and unfastening your seat belt over such short distances.

4.7 You've been issued with protective clothing. Who's responsible for its use?

❏ You, the driver

❏ The insurance company

❏ The Health and Safety Executive

❏ Your employer

DGV s3
Protective clothing will usually be provided by your company. However, it's your responsibility to make sure that you use it properly.

4.8 You're driving on a motorway. What does it mean when a lorry ahead of you switches on its hazard warning lights?

❏ There are speed cameras ahead

❏ The lorry is about to overtake

❏ The lorry is leaving the motorway

❏ Traffic further ahead may be stopping

HCR r116
When someone ahead of you switches on their hazard warning lights, it means that they've spotted a hazard that you may not be able to see yet. Slow down and be ready to stop if necessary.

4.9 What should you do if you lose your way in heavy traffic?

❏ Stop at traffic lights and ask pedestrians

❏ Shout to other drivers to ask them the way

❏ Drive on until you find a safe place to stop

❏ Check a map as you keep moving with the traffic

HC r150
Driving in heavy traffic needs 100% concentration. If you become lost, find a safe place to stop before checking a map or asking for directions. Don't risk losing concentration by glancing at a map while driving, even if you're in traffic that keeps stopping.

4.10 Where are you most likely to find pedestrians stepping into the road?

❏ Motorways   ❏ One-way streets

❏ Wooded areas ❏ Shopping areas

DBC s1, DGV s1
In shopping areas, pedestrians frequently want to cross the road. They may be hidden by parked vehicles before stepping out into your path. Keep your speed down and be aware of the risk of pedestrians suddenly walking into the road.

4.11 What's most likely to cause danger to a group of horse riders?

❏ Powerful brake lights

❏ Leaving plenty of room

❏ The noise of your vehicle

❏ Reacting too early

DBC s4,DGV s4
The hiss of air-assisted mechanisms, as well as engine noise, can easily startle horses. Keep the noise to a minimum by gentle use of the brakes and, if necessary, stopping and turning your engine off.

4.12 What should you do when passing sheep on a road?

❏ Pass quickly and quietly

❏ Sound your horn gently

❏ Drive very slowly

❏ Keep your vehicle moving

DBC s4, DGV s4
Animals can be very unpredictable. You should give them as much room as you can, keep your speed and noise to a minimum to avoid panicking them, and always be ready to stop if necessary.

4.13 When is your nearside mirror likely to endanger pedestrians?

❏ When driving over a speed hump

❏ When driving near a hospital

❏ When driving close to the kerb

❏ When driving past a car park

DBC s1, DGV s4
When you drive too close to the kerb, there's a risk that your nearside mirror could strike the head of a pedestrian. Be aware of this hazard and, if you see pedestrians close to the road, make sure you leave them enough room.

4.14 What can prevent you from holding a bus or lorry driving licence?

❏ Heart disorders

❏ Dyslexia

❏ Skin problems

❏ Stomach problems

DBC s1, DGV s1
An illness that could affect you while you're driving, such as a heart condition, may make it unsafe for you to drive. You must tell DVLA if you develop any serious illness or disalbility that's likely to last more than three months and that could affect your driving. Partial blindness and mental disorders can also prevent you from getting a driving licence for large vehicles.

4.15 You're about to drive a vehicle you've never driven before. What should you consider when adjusting your seat?

❏ Your distance from the controls

❏ Being able to reach your sat-nav

❏ The tension in the seat belt

❏ The wear on the seat fabric

DBC s3, DGV s3
Being seated properly is very important when driving long distances. A poor driving position can quickly cause fatigue. You should make sure that you can reach all the controls comfortably.

4.16 Why is it important to adjust your head restraint properly?

❏ To make you more comfortable

❏ To protect your neck in a collision

❏ To help you relax while you're driving

❏ To maintain a good driving position

DBC s3, DGV s3
Your head restraint should be adjusted so that, in the event of a collision, it protects your neck from whiplash injury.

4.17 When may you drive without wearing your seat belt?

❏ When reversing

❏ When carrying out a hill start

❏ When making an emergency stop

❏ When driving slowly

DBC s2, DGV s3
You can legally remove your seat belt when carrying out a manoeuvre that involves reversing. Don't forget to put it back on again when you've finished.

4.18 You're driving along this road. What should you do if the red van cuts in close in front of you?

❏ Accelerate to get closer to the red van

❏ Give a long blast on the horn

❏ Drop back to leave the correct separation distance

❏ Flash your headlights several times

DBC s4, DGV s4
There are times when other road users make incorrect or ill-judged decisions. Try to stay calm and don't retaliate or react aggressively, especially as your vehicle is likely to be larger and more intimidating than the other person's. Always put safety first.

4.19 You're approaching a large puddle near the left-hand kerb. What should you do if pedestrians are close to the water?

❏ Ignore the puddle

❏ Brake suddenly and sound your horn

❏ Try to avoid splashing the pedestrians

❏ Wave at the pedestrians to keep back

DBC s1, DGV s4
The effect of your vehicle driving through a puddle will be to throw water onto the pavement. If there are pedestrians close by, they could be splashed with the water. Be considerate and, if it's safe to do so, avoid driving through the puddle.

4.20 What should you do if a long, heavily laden lorry is taking a long time to overtake you?

❏ Speed up   ❏ Slow down

❏ Hold your speed   ❏ Change direction

DBC s4, DGV s4
A long lorry with a heavy load will need more time to pass you than a car. It won't be able to accelerate enough to pass you quickly, especially on an uphill stretch of road. Be considerate to the lorry driver – ease off the accelerator and allow the lorry to pass.

4.21 You're driving a slow-moving vehicle on a narrow, winding road. What should you do to let other vehicles overtake you?

☐ Wave them past   ☐ Stop in a safe place

☐ Show a left-turn signal   ☐ Drive more slowly

HC r169
Don't frustrate other road users by driving for long distances with a queue of traffic behind you. This could cause them to lose concentration and overtake in an unsafe way. Stop where it's safe and let them pass.

4.22 When should you use your vehicle's horn?

☐ To warn others of your presence

☐ To allow you right of way

☐ To greet other road users

☐ To signal your annoyance

DBC s1, 4, DGV s1, 4, HC r112
Only use your horn to warn people of your presence when they may not have seen you. Don't use it to greet others, to show impatience, or to give or claim priority.

Your horn mustn't be used between 11.30 prn and 7.00 am in a built-up area, or when your vehicle is stationary, unless another vehicle poses a danger.

4.23 You're following a car being driven slowly by a learner driver. What should you do if it isn't safe to overtake it?

☐ Flash your lights so the driver sees you

☐ Be patient and stay well behind

☐ Switch your hazard lights on

☐ Drive along the centre line of the road

DBC s4, DGV s4
Learner drivers are often nervous. If you stay well back, this will reduce the risk of incidents occurring if they make a mistake, and you won't intimidate them. Remember, you were once in that situation yourself.

4.24 What should you do if you're signalled to stop by a police officer in a patrol car?

☐ Brake harshly to a stop

☐ Drive on until you reach a side road

☐ Stop on the left as soon as it's safe

☐ Stop immediately wherever you are

HC r106
If a police officer signals for you to stop, stop as soon as possible in a safe place on the left.

4.25 You're being followed by a marked police car. As well as flashing the headlights, what will the police officer do to signal you to stop?

☐ Signal with the right indicator

☐ Signal with the left indicator

☐ Switch on the hazard warning lights

☐ Switch on the rear fog lights

HC r106
When a police officer is following you and wants you to stop, they'll flash the vehicle's headlights and signal with the left indicator. You should stop in a safe place as soon as possible.

4.26 Your vehicle is fitted with a hand-held telephone. What should you do before taking or making a call?

☐ Find a safe place to stop

☐ Reduce your speed to less than 30 mph

☐ Steer your vehicle with one hand

☐ Be very careful when dealing with junctions

HC r149
Telephone calls can distract you, meaning that you're not in proper control of your vehicle. If you need to use a telephone when driving, find a safe place to stop first. Better still, use a phone answering service and listen to your messages at the end of your journey.

4.27 A mobile telephone is fitted to your vehicle. When should it be used?

☐ When you're stopped in a safe place

☐ When travelling slowly

☐ When on a motorway

☐ When in light traffic

HC r149
It's illegal to use a hand held phone while driving. When you've stopped in a safe place, you can concentrate on your call or message. Using a phone while driving means you won't have full control of your vehicle. This could result in a collision, with serious or even fatal consequences.

4.28 You approach a pelican crossing that goes straight across the road. How must you treat it if it has a central island?

❑ As one crossing in daylight only

❑ As one continuous crossing

❑ As two separate crossings

❑ As two crossings during darkness

HC r197
A pelican crossing that goes straight across the road must be treated as one continuous crossing even if it has a central island. The lights controlling the crossing show to both directions of traffic. You must give way to pedestrians who are still crossing when the amber light is flashing.

4.29 What does the flashing amber light mean at a pelican crossing?

❑ Stop if you can do so safely

❑ Give way to pedestrians already on the crossing

❑ Stop and wait for the green light

❑ Give way to pedestrians waiting to cross

HC r196
Pedestrians use push-button controls to activate the signals. Pelican crossings have no red-and amber stage before green. Instead, they have a flashing amber light. This means you must give way to pedestrians on the crossing, but you may proceed if the crossing is clear.

4.30 What should you do at a zebra crossing?

❑ Rev your engine to encourage pedestrians to cross quickly

❑ Park only on the zigzag lines on the left

❑ Always leave the crossing clear in traffic queues

❑ Wave pedestrians to cross if you intend to wait for them

HC r195
When traffic is heavy, plan well ahead so that you don't block crossings. Leave them clear so that pedestrians can cross safely.

4.31 A coach is overtaking you. What should you do when it's safe for the coach to move back to the left?

❑ Do nothing and let the driver decide

❑ Switch your sidelights on and off

❑ Flash your headlights once

❑ Flash your headlights twice

DBC s4, DGV s4
When you're being overtaken, the other driver has to decide when it's safe to complete the manoeuvre. Don't give an unofficial signal, however well intended. There may be a hazard you're unable to see from your position.

4.32 What should you do when you're being followed by an ambulance showing a flashing blue light?

❑ Stop to let it pass as soon as it's safe to do so

❑ Accelerate quickly to get away from it

❑ Ignore it if possible, unless you're forced to let it pass

❑ Brake harshly and immediately to a stop in the road

HC r219
When an ambulance is displaying a flashing blue light, try to stop in a safe place to allow it to pass. Make sure you don't endanger any other road users or commit an offence; for example, by driving past a red traffic light.

4.33 Should you give way to a car showing a flashing green beacon?

❑ Yes, because it's a doctor going to an emergency

❑ Yes, because it's a fire-crew support vehicle

❑ No, because it's a slow-moving vehicle

❑ No, because it's a breakdown vehicle

DBC, s4, DGV s4, HC r219
If you see a vehicle with a green flashing light, it will be a doctor on an emergency call, so give way by pulling over and letting the vehicle pass. But don't just stop suddenly – choose a safe place as soon as you can to let the doctor's car pass safely.

4.34   What type of emergency vehicle has a green flashing beacon?

❑ Fire engine   ❑ Road gritter

❑ Ambulance   ❑ Doctor's car

DBC, s4, DGV s4, HC r219
A green flashing light on a vehicle means the driver or passenger is a doctor on an emergency call. Give way to them if it's safe to do so. Be aware that the vehicle may be travelling quickly or may stop suddenly.

4.35   You stop for pedestrians at a zebra crossing. What should you do if they don't start to cross immediately?

❑ Be patient and wait   ❑ Sound your horn

❑ Drive on   ❑ Wave them to cross

HC r195
If you stop for pedestrians and they don't start to cross, be patient. Don't wave them across or sound your horn. This could be dangerous if the driver of an approaching vehicle isn't aware of them. The driver may not have seen or heard your signal, making it very dangerous for the pedestrians to start to cross.

4.36   Why could it be dangerous to wave people across at pedestrian crossings?

❑ There may be another vehicle coming

❑ They may be distracted

❑ They may not see your signal

❑ They may not be ready to cross

HC r195
You should always try to stop, if it's safe, for people waiting at pedestrian crossings. However, avoid waving them to cross. Another driver may not have seen them, may not have seen your signal or may not be able to stop safely.

4.37   What danger should you be most aware of if you're driving close to the kerb in a busy shopping area?

❑ The nearside mirror striking the heads of pedestrians

❑ The amount of fuel being used when driving slowly

❑ Solid white line markings in the centre of the road

❑ Traffic lights that may suddenly change to green

DBC s4, DGV s1
When you need to drive close to the kerb, be aware of the dangers.

- Pedestrians may step off the kerb.
- The nearside mirror may be at a pedestrian's head height.
- Cyclists may be tempted to pass you on your left if you're driving slowly in congested conditions.

4.38   Which of these is an unsafe place to park your vehicle or trailer?

❑ At an overnight service area

❑ Near the brow of a hill

❑ In the yard at a factory

❑ In a lay-by in a built-up area

HC r234
Don't park where you would endanger or inconvenience others. If your choice of parking place obstructs drivers, riders or pedestrians, move to a more suitable area.

4.39   What must you check before setting out on a journey?

❑ Your mirrors are tinted   ❑ Your mirrors are convex

❑ Your mirrors are concave ❑ Your mirrors are clean

DBC s3, 4, DGV s3, 4
It's important to know what's happening behind as well as ahead. Your mirrors must always be clean and properly adjusted.

4.40   A group of schoolchildren are standing close to the left-hand kerb. What should you do as you drive past?

❑ Check your offside mirror

❑ Check your nearside mirror

❑ Switch on your headlights

❑ Switch on your hazard warning lights

DBC s4, DGV s4
As you approach the children, consider whether you need to sound the horn as a warning. Always check your nearside mirror as you pass any hazards on the left, so that you know when your vehicle is clear of the hazard.

4.41 You're driving at the legal speed limit. What should you do if a vehicle comes up quickly behind, flashing its headlights?

❑ Accelerate to maintain a gap behind you

❑ Touch the brake pedal sharply to show your brake lights

❑ Maintain your speed and prevent the vehicle from overtaking

❑ Allow the vehicle to overtake

HC r168
Don't try to enforce the speed limit by blocking another vehicle's progress. This is likely to cause the other driver to become more frustrated. Slow down or move over when it's safe and allow the other vehicle to pass.

4.42 What should you do when a vehicle pulls out in front of you at a junction?

❑ Swerve past it and sound your horn

❑ Flash your headlights and drive up close behind

❑ Slow down and be ready to stop

❑ Accelerate past it immediately

DBC s4, DGV s4
Plan ahead and learn to anticipate hazards. Give yourself more time to react to any problems that might occur – such as a vehicle pulling out unexpectedly. Be tolerant of other road users who don't behave correctly. Don't react by flashing your lights, sounding your horn or making gestures, as any show of aggression on the road can quickly lead to a serious incident.

4.43 How is drinking alcohol likely to affect your driving?

❑ You'll have faster reactions

❑ You'll become colour-blind

❑ You'll feel more confident

❑ You'll be able to concentrate better

DBC s3, DGV s3, HC r95
Alcohol can increase confidence to a point where a driver's behaviour might become 'out of character': someone who normally behaves sensibly suddenly takes risks and enjoys it. Never let yourself or your friends get into this situation.

4.44 What can seriously affect your concentration while driving?

❑ Contact lenses ❑ Fresh air

❑ Tinted windows ❑ Tiredness

DBC s3, DGV s3
Tiredness can seriously affect your concentration – even to the point of falling asleep. You always need to be alert so that you can safely deal with the constantly changing environment around your vehicle.

4.45 How does alcohol affect your driving?

❑ It speeds up your reactions

❑ It increases your awareness

❑ It improves your coordination

❑ It reduces your concentration

DBC s3, DGV s3, HC r95
Concentration and good judgement are needed to be a good, safe driver. You're strongly advised not to drink any alcohol before driving. Alcohol can stay in your system for 24–48 hours, so you should also consider your intake the day and night before driving.

4.46 You've been convicted of driving while unfit through drink or drugs. What will increase in cost when you start driving again?

❑ Vehicle tax ❑ Insurance premiums

❑ Vehicle test certificate ❑ Driving licence

DBC s3, DGV s3
If you've been convicted of drink or drug-driving, statistically you're a risk to yourself and others on the road. For this reason, when you're able to drive again, insurance companies may charge you a high premium to insure your vehicle.

4.47 What should you do if you've had a few alcoholic drinks at a party?

❑ Have a strong cup of coffee and then drive home

❑ Drive home carefully and slowly

❑ Go home by public transport

❑ Wait a short while and then drive home

DBC s3, DGV s3
Drinking black coffee or waiting a few hours won't make any difference. Alcohol takes time to leave the body, so you should find a way to get home without using your vehicle; for example, by public transport. Depending on how much you've had to drink, you may even be unfit to drive the following morning.

4.48   As a driver, what should you do when you attend a social event?

❑ Drink plenty of coffee after drinking alcohol

❑ Avoid busy roads after drinking alcohol

❑ Avoid drinking alcohol completely

❑ Avoid drinking alcohol on an empty stomach

DBC s3, DGV s3
Avoiding alcohol will always be the safest option. There are many factors that influence how alcohol will affect you, such as height, weight and gender. It's better not to risk a single alcoholic drink before you drive.

4.49   It's been eight hours since you last had an alcoholic drink. What effect could the alcohol have on your driving?

❑ You may still be over the legal drink-drive limit

❑ You'll have no alcohol in your system

❑ Your driving won't be impaired

❑ You can't be breathalysed

DBC s3, DGV s3
Alcohol can take a long time to leave the body. You may feel all right to drive, but its effect will last for many hours.

4.50   Your doctor has given you a course of medicine. Why should you ask whether it's safe to drive?

❑ Drugs make you a better driver by quickening your reactions

❑ You'll have to let your insurance company know about the medicine

❑ Some types of medicine can cause your reactions to slow down

❑ The medicine you take may affect your hearing

DBC s3, DGV s3
Some medicines can have side effects that affect your driving. Ask your doctor whether you'll be safe to drive while taking the medicine that's been prescribed.

4.51   You've been taking medicine for a few days, and it has made you feel drowsy. Today you feel better, but you still need to take the medicine. When should you drive?

❑ Only if your journey is necessary

❑ Only at night on quiet roads

❑ Only if someone goes with you

❑ Only after checking with your doctor

DBC s3, DGV s3
Take care; it's not worth taking risks. Always check with your doctor to be absolutely sure. The medicine may have an effect on you later in the day and for longer than you think.

4.52   What should you do if you aren't sure whether your cough medicine will affect your driving?

❑ Ask your doctor for advice

❑ Drive a little more slowly

❑ Drive if you feel all right

❑ Ask a friend for advice

DBC s3, DGV s3
If you're taking medicine or drugs prescribed by your doctor, check that they won't affect your driving. If you forget to ask when you visit the surgery, check with your pharmacist.

4.53   You take some cough medicine given to you by a friend. What must you do before driving?

❑ Drink some strong coffee

❑ Ask your friend whether taking the medicine affected their driving

❑ Check the label to see whether the medicine will affect your driving

❑ Make a short journey to see whether the medicine is affecting your driving

DBC s3, DGV s3
Never drive after taking drugs you don't know about. They might affect your judgement and perception – and, therefore, endanger lives.

4.54   What should you do if you're driving along a motorway and become tired?

❑ Stop on the hard shoulder at a safe place to rest

❑ Leave the motorway at the next exit and take a rest

❑ Close your windows and turn up the radio volume

❑ Close your windows and set the heating to warm

DBC s3, DGV s3
If you feel the onset of tiredness, you need to take a break. This might be at a motorway service station, but if there isn't one nearby you'll need to leave at the next exit and find a safe place to stop and rest.

4.55   You're about to drive home. What should you do if you feel very tired and have a severe headache?

☐ Wait until you're fit and well before driving

☐ Drive home, but take painkiller tablets

☐ Drive home if you can stay awake for the journey

☐ Wait for a short time, then drive home slowly

DBC s3, DGV s3
All your concentration should be on your driving; any pain you feel will distract you. Be safe and wait until you're fit before starting your journey.

4.56   What should you do if you're feeling tired but there's nowhere to stop safely?

☐ Increase your speed to find a stopping place more quickly

☐ Ensure a supply of fresh air

☐ Gently tap the steering wheel

☐ Keep changing speed to improve your concentration

DBC s3, DGV s3
If you're travelling on a long journey, plan your route before you leave. This will help you to

• be decisive at intersections and junctions

• plan your rest stops

• know approximately how long the journey will take.

Make sure that the vehicle you're travelling in is well ventilated. A warm, stuffy atmosphere can make you drowsy, which will impair your judgement and perception.

4.57   When will your reactions be slower?

☐ When driving while you're tired

☐ When driving in fog

☐ When driving too quickly

☐ When driving in rain

DBC s3, DGV s3
Try to avoid becoming tired by taking plenty of rest stops and allowing fresh air into your vehicle.

4.58   What should you do if you're taking medication that could affect your driving?

☐ Seek medical advice ☐ Make short journeys only

☐ Drive only at night   ☐ Drink plenty of water

DBC s3, DGV s3
Check all medicines for their side effects, such as drowsiness. If you're unsure, ask your doctor or pharmacist to explain how you might be affected by the medication.

4.59   What should you do if you feel tired while driving on a motorway?

☐ Stop on the hard shoulder for a rest

☐ Carry on, but drive slowly

☐ Leave the motorway at the next exit

☐ Try to complete your journey more quickly

DBC s3, DGV s3
Don't continue to drive if you feel the onset of tiredness. Find a safe place to stop for a rest. Walking around in the fresh air during your break will help but it's no substitute for adequate rest.

4.60   You've driven a long distance and feel tired. Your tachograph shows that you haven't exceeded your driving hours. What should you do in these circumstances?

☐ Park in a suitable place and rest

☐ Reduce your speed and drive more slowly

☐ Carry on driving to use up your hours

☐ Increase your speed and reduce your journey time

DBC s3, DGV s3
The smallest lapse in concentration can result in loss of control. Even when your tachograph would allow you to drive for longer, stop somewhere safe and rest if you feel your driving may be affected by your tiredness.

4.61   What might misuse of drugs or alcohol lead to?

☐ Better concentration   ☐ Better eyesight

☐ Withdrawal of a driving licence ☐ Faster reactions

DBC s3, DGV s3
Misuse of drugs and/or alcohol may lead to the withdrawal of your driving licence. Future insurance premiums will probably increase as well.

4.62   What should you do if a front tyre bursts while you're driving on a motorway?

❑ Loosen your grip on the steering wheel

❑ Brake firmly to a stop

❑ Hold the steering wheel firmly

❑ Drive to the next service area

DBC s3, DGV s3

A front tyre bursting will seriously reduce your control of the vehicle. Keep calm and resist the temptation to brake hard or swerve. Hold the steering wheel firmly and try to get the vehicle onto the hard shoulder while allowing it to slow down gradually. Stop as far to the left as possible and switch on your hazard warning lights.

4.63   Your vehicle breaks down on a motorway and you need to call for help. Why may it be better to use an emergency roadside telephone rather than a mobile phone?

❑ It connects you to a local garage

❑ Using a mobile phone will distract other drivers

❑ It allows easy location by the emergency services

❑ Mobile phones don't work on motorways

DBC s4, DGV s4

On a motorway, it's best to use a roadside emergency telephone so that the emergency services are able to locate you easily.

4.64   When are you most likely to lose concentration while you're driving?

❑ When you use a mobile phone

❑ When you switch on the windscreen wipers

❑ When you switch on the heated rear window

❑ When you look at the door mirrors

HC r149

Using a hand-held mobile phone while driving is illegal. It will distract you from your driving, because your attention is split between the phone call and your driving.

4.65   What should you do if you want to make a business call on your mobile phone while you're driving?

❑ Make. the call but take extra care

❑ Use the cruise control while you're making the call

❑ Stop in a safe place before making the call

❑ Reduce speed while you make the call

HC r149

It's illegal to use a hand-held mobile phone while you're driving, other than to call 999 or 112 in a genuine emergency. Switch it off before you start driving and use the messaging facility. You can pick up messages when you stop for a rest break. If you must make a call, stop in a safe place before using the phone.

4.66   You're driving on a single carriageway. When may you use your mobile phone?

❑ Only when you're receiving a call

❑ Only when you're suitably parked

❑ Only when you're driving at less than 30 mph

❑ Only when you're driving an automatic vehicle

HC r149

It's illegal to use a hand-held mobile phone while you're driving. Park in a suitable place before receiving or making a call or text.

4.67   What effect will using a mobile phone have on your driving?

❑ Your vehicle will be harder to steer

❑ Your field of vision will be reduced

❑ Your attention will be diverted from the road

❑ Your vehicle's electronic systems will be disrupted

HC r149

Driving today requires all of your attention, all of the time. Any distraction, however brief, is dangerous. This is why it's illegal to use a hand-held mobile phone while you're driving.

4.68   Your vehicle breaks down on the hard shoulder of a motorway. What should you do if you decide to use your mobile phone to call for help?

❑ Stand at the rear of the vehicle while making the call

❑ Use the speed-dial function to save time

❑ Set the tachograph to 'Other work' before making the call

❑ Check your location from the marker posts on the left

DBC s4, DGV s4
In an emergency, time can be of the essence. The emergency services need to know your exact location. Before you phone, get the post number from the nearest marker post on the edge of the hard shoulder. Give this to the emergency services, as it will help them to locate you.

4.69   How should you answer a mobile phone call while you're driving?

❑ Reduce your speed wherever you are

❑ Stop safely before answering

❑ Keep one hand on the steering wheel

❑ Slow down and allow others to overtake

HC r149
No phone call is important enough to endanger someone's life. If you must be contactable when driving, plan your route to include breaks where you can catch up on telephone messages in safety. Always choose a safe place to take a break.

4.70   You're overtaking a lorry. What should you do if you see the driver flash their headlights?

❑ Move back to the left when you judge it's safe to do so

❑ Take their signal to mean it's safe to move back to the left

❑ Stop; there must be something wrong with your vehicle

❑ Flash your hazard warning lights and move back to the left

DBC s4, DGV s4
Never presume what someone means when they flash their headlights, as they might be signalling to someone else. Use your own judgement and wait until it's safe to complete your manoeuvre.

4.71   A bus has stopped at a bus stop ahead of you. What should you do if its right-hand indicator is flashing?

❑ Flash your headlights and slow down

❑ Slow down and give way if it's safe to do so

❑ Sound your horn and keep going

❑ Slow down and then sound your horn

HC r223
Give way to buses whenever you can do so safely, especially when they signal to pull away from bus stops. Look out for people who have left the bus and wish to cross the road. Also look out for people rushing to catch a bus: they may be more concerned about catching the bus than watching for traffic.

4.72   You've stopped for an elderly pedestrian who's slowly crossing the road. What should you do if traffic behind you is being held up?

❑ Edge forward slowly and make them hurry

❑ Stay where you are and allow them to cross in their own time

❑ Steer slowly around them to ease the build-up of traffic

❑ Get out of your vehicle and wave them across

HC r207
Elderly pedestrians can be hesitant and may move slowly when crossing the road. Also, their awareness of traffic may be limited because of hearing or visual impairment. Be patient and show courtesy and understanding.

4.73   How should you let other vehicles overtake when you're driving a slow-moving vehicle along a narrow road?

❑ Maintain a steady speed ❑ Wave them past

❑ Give a left-turn signal   ❑ Pull in when you can

HC r169
Drivers queuing behind you may make hasty or ill-judged decisions in an effort to overtake. If you see a queue of traffic building up behind, give way as soon as you can do so safely by pulling in to the left.

4.74   How is using a hands-free phone likely to affect your driving?

❏ It will improve your safety

❏ It will increase your concentration

❏ It will reduce your view

❏ It will divert your attention

DBC s1, DGV s1, HC r149
While you're using a phone, your attention will be divided between the call and the road. This means you're unable to take in all that's happening around your vehicle. You need to be concentrating on your driving all of the time, and especially when dealing with a hazard.

4.75   You're driving on the motorway and want to use your mobile phone. What should you do before using it?

❏ Reduce your speed to 40 mph

❏ Stop on the hard shoulder

❏ Move into the left-hand lane

❏ Stop in a safe place when you can

DBC s1, DGV s1, HC r149
Plan your journey and take breaks to keep in touch if necessary. When driving on motorways, you can't just stop to use your mobile phone. You'll need to turn off the motorway or wait until you reach the next service area. Avoid being distracted by switching your phone off while you're driving; use the message facility to listen to any calls when you've parked safely.

4.76   What effect will drinking alcohol have on your driving?

❏ Better forward planning

❏ A false sense of confidence

❏ Faster reactions

❏ Greater awareness of danger

DBC s3, DGV s3
Drinking alcohol will reduce your ability to drive safely. One drink is too many if you're going to drive.

4.77   You're driving on a motorway. There's been a collision on the opposite carriageway. What should you do if drivers ahead are slowing to look?

❏ Concentrate on the road ahead

❏ Slow down to take a look

❏ Stop on the hard shoulder

❏ Overtake using the hard shoulder

HC r282
Drivers passing incidents often end up having collisions themselves when they're distracted by the scene. You need to keep your concentration in a situation like this and ignore what's happening on the other carriageway.

4.78   What do you need to be aware of when driving a vehicle fitted with power-assisted steering?

❏ It causes less tyre wear

❏ It prevents you from oversteering

❏ It makes it easier for you to steer

❏ It only works at high speeds

DBC s1, DGV s6
Power-assisted steering operates when the engine is running. If a fault develops, much greater effort is required to turn the steering wheel. Don't attempt to drive a vehicle if you're aware of a fault in the power-steering system.

4.79   What should you do if a car driver makes a mistake that causes you to brake?

❏ Keep calm and don't retaliate

❏ Overtake and sound your horn

❏ Drive close behind and sound your horn

❏ Flag the driver down and explain the mistake

DBC s1, DGV s1
Sometimes other road users disobey the rules or make errors of judgement. Try to accept this calmly and learn from their mistakes.

4.80   What should you do if you're upset by another driver's behaviour?

❏ Stop and take a break

❏ Shout abusive language

❏ Gesture to them with your hand

❏ Follow them, flashing your headlights

DBC s1, DGV s1
Tiredness may make you more irritable than you would be normally. You might react differently to situations because of it. If you feel yourself becoming tense, take a break.

4.81   What should you do if another driver does something that upsets you?

❑ Stay calm and don't retaliate

❑ Let them know how you feel

❑ Flash your headlights several times

❑ Sound your horn

DBC s1, DGV s1

Sometimes other drivers or riders make a mistake. If this happens, try not to let it worry you. Don't react by sounding the horn, flashing your headlights or shouting at the other driver; it won't help the situation. A professional driver will remain calm and stay focused on their driving.

4.82   You're driving in fast-moving traffic along a motorway. What should you do if there's a stationary queue of traffic ahead?

❑ Move to the hard shoulder

❑ Change lanes

❑ Switch on your rear fog lights

❑ Switch on your hazard warning lights

DBC s4, DGV s4

Traffic queues on the motorway are fairly common, often due to the volume of traffic at peak times or to incidents. If you see a queue of stationary traffic ahead, switch on your hazard warning lights for a short while to warn those behind you of a hazard ahead.

4.83   You're turning right onto a dual carriageway from a side road. What should you do if your vehicle is too long for the gap in the central reservation?

❑ Move forward and wait in the middle

❑ Wait until it's clear in both directions

❑ Move out, blocking traffic from the right

❑ Edge out slowly so other traffic will see you

DBC s6, DGV s6, HC r173

When turning right onto a dual carriageway, don't stop in the gap in the central reservation unless your vehicle will fit in the gap without any overhang. When it's busy, consider turning left and using a roundabout further up the road so you don't have to cross the central reservation.

4.84   You want to turn left at a junction. What affects the position you take up as you approach the junction?

❑ The length of your vehicle

❑ The axle weight of your vehicle

❑ The camber of the road

❑ The type of road surface

DBC s6, DGV s6

Plan well ahead and take care if you need to move out or straddle lanes due to the length of your vehicle. Other road users may not understand your reasons for doing this and may try to pass on your left. Check your mirrors before and as you turn. It's better to use extra space on the road you're leaving than to find there's not enough room when you turn in.

4.85   What should you do when you have to travel a long distance?

❑ Allow plenty of time for your journey

❑ Plan to go at busy times

❑ Avoid all national-speed-limit roads

❑ Prevent other drivers from overtaking

DBC s4, DGV s4

Always allow plenty of time for your journey, in case of unforeseen problems such as punctures, breakdowns, road closures or diversions. You'll feel less stressed and less inclined to take risks if you're not under time pressure.

4.86   What can you do to help maintain concentration while you're driving?

❑ Eat sugary snacks when on duty

❑ Have regular meals and rest breaks

❑ Don't eat at all when on duty

❑ Avoid meals containing bread

DBC s1, 3, DGV s1, 3

Being as healthy and alert as possible will make you safer on the road. Take regular meal and rest breaks, and keep to foods that contain complex carbohydrates, such as bread and vegetables. These release energy slowly and will keep you satisfied for longer than foods with a high sugar content.

4.87 What's the best type of fluid to drink during work time?

□ Bottled water ☐ Sugary canned drinks

□ High-caffeine drinks ☐ Hot chocolate

DBC s1, DGV s1
Water is the ideal drink, because it quenches your thirst for longer than tea or coffee. It's a good idea to carry water when you're driving, especially in very hot weather. The medical profession recommends that you drink 1.5 to 2 litres of water per day.

4.88 What should you do to help your concentration when you have to drive through the night?

□ Eat lots of snacks while you're driving

□ Eat a big meal in the middle of your shift

□ Eat a meal at the beginning of your shift

□ Eat nothing during your period of work

DBC s1, DGV s1
Concentration will be improved by eating regular, light meals timed to fit in with your scheduled rest periods. If you don't eat at all, your blood sugar levels will drop and you'll feel tired. If you just eat snack foods, most of which are sugary or high in fat, your energy levels will peak and then drop – and eating while you're driving is a dangerous distraction.

4.89 When is there a particular risk of sleep-related incidents?

□ Between 2 am and 7 am

□ Between 11 pm and 2 am

□ Between 6 pm and 11 pm

□ Between 7 am and 2 pm

DBC s3, DGV s3
There's a particular risk when driving between 2 am and 7 am. This is when the 'body clock' is programmed. for sleep in most people. There's another, smaller, dip between 2 pm and 4 pm. If you feel that tiredness is affecting your ability to drive, stop in a safe place and rest.

4.90 Approximately what percentage of sleep-related vehicle incidents (SRVIs) involve commercial vehicles?

□ 40% ☐ 55% ☐ 70% ☐ 95%

DBC s3, DGV s3
Research shows that approximately 40% of SRVIs involve commercial vehicles. The consequences are usually very serious because of the size of the vehicle and the fact that there is no braking before the impact.

4.91 Poor eating habits can increase your risk of long-term health problems. What may result from a poor diet?

□ Deafness ☐ Epilepsy

□ Lung disease ☐ Heart disease

DBC s1, DGV s1
A poor diet can increase your risk of ill health. It may cause obesity, diabetes or heart disease, which can increase your risk of sudden incapacity at the wheel. There's a greater risk of developing a serious illness – and ultimately an early death. Smoking and a lack of exercise will increase the risks.

4.92 What should you do when you've been driving for a long time and are fighting sleep?

□ Stop and rest ☐ Open a window

□ Play loud music ☐ Stretch your arms

DBC s3, DGV s3
The only effective solution to driver sleepiness is to stop in a safe place and take a break.

4.93 Where do most sleep-related vehicle incidents occur?

□ On motorways ☐ In one-way streets

□ On rural roads ☐ On tourist routes

DBC s3, DGV s3
Driving at a constant speed for long periods, such as on a motorway, can cause drowsiness. Falling asleep while driving accounts for a significant proportion of vehicle incidents. You should plan and take regular rest stops, but if you feel the onset of tiredness between these breaks, stop and rest in a safe place.

4.94 At what age are men most at risk from sleep-related vehicle incidents (SRVIs)?

□ 30 years and under ☐ 31-45 years

□ 46-59 years ☐ 60 years and over

DBC s3, DGV s3
SRVIs are more evident in young male drivers, who tend to ignore or deny how they're feeling. The greatest risk is between the hours of 2.00 am and 7.00 am, when the body clock is in a trough. Make sure you take sufficient rest breaks and don't ignore feeling sleepy.

4.95   What should you try to do when your vehicle has a front-tyre blow-out?

❑ Hold the steering wheel firmly and slow down gradually

❑ Steer to the right-hand side and brake firmly

❑ Don't use your brakes under any circumstances

❑ Brake hard and steer towards the affected side

DBC s4, DGV s4

With a front-tyre blow-out, you won't be able to steer properly. Keep a firm hold of the steering wheel and slow gradually to a stop. Don't brake hard or steer sharply.

4.96   When can you drive without wearing a seat belt?

❑ When you hold a medical exemption certificate

❑ When the seat belt is too large for your use

❑ When you're driving on a motorway

❑ When the speed limit is 30 mph or less

DBC s2, DGV s3, HC r99

When seat belts are fitted to your vehicle, they must be worn unless you hold a valid medical exemption certificate. People making deliveries or collections in goods vehicles are also exempt, when they're travelling less than 50 metres (162 feet).

4.97   How will your body clock affect your driving between 2.00 am and 7.00 am?

❑ You're more likely to fall asleep at the wheel

❑ You're more likely to feel road rage

❑ You're more likely to break the speed limit

❑ You're more likely to drive too close to the vehicle in front

DBC s3, DGV s3

A significant number of sleep related vehicle incidents involve commercial vehicles. There's a particular risk when driving between 2.00 am and 7.00 am, because this is when the body clock craves sleep. It's important to take proper rest before, during and between driving duties.

4.98   What's provided specifically to protect you against neck and whiplash injuries?

❑ An air-sprung seat   ❑ Anti-lock brakes

❑ A collapsible steering wheel ❑ A head restraint

DBC s3, DGV s3, HC r97

If you're in a collision, a properly adjusted head restraint can help to reduce the risk of neck injury. However, an incorrectly adjusted head restraint could worsen any damage to your neck.

4.99   When are you allowed to drive a bus without wearing the seat belt?

❑ When the seat belt is uncomfortable

❑ When it's a lap-only type of seat belt

❑ When you're reversing the vehicle

❑ When your passengers are children

DBC s2

If your vehicle is fitted with a seat belt, you must wear it unless you're exempt for medical reasons. You may also remove it before a reverse manoeuvre. If the fitting of the belt is uncomfortable and it prevents you from obtaining a safe driving position, report this to your employer.

4.100   What must be clearly displayed on your bus?

❑ The route timetable

❑ The location of all bus stops

❑ The emergency-exit location

❑ Your employee number

DBC s1

Make sure that your vehicle displays all the information required by law (the 'legal lettering'): the seating/standing capacity and the locations of the emergency exit, fuel cut-off switch and electrical isolator.

4.101   You're driving on a dual carriageway. When would you use the nearside mirror?

- ☐ To check that the driver's door is closed properly

- ☐ After overtaking, to see whether it's safe to return to the left

- ☐ To see whether any passengers want the next bus stop

- ☐ To look for following traffic moving out to overtake

DBC s4

Use your nearside mirror when you've overtaken another vehicle. This is particularly important on dual carriageways or motorways, where it can take some distance to overtake safely. Look carefully to make sure you're far enough ahead and can safely return to the left lane.

4.102   What should you do while you're driving a bus in a built-up area?

- ☐ Keep junctions clear

- ☐ Reduce your stopping distance

- ☐ Stay ahead of cyclists and motorcyclists

- ☐ Allow less time for passengers to board

DBC s4

Blocking other vehicles' access to side roads is inconsiderate and can cause congestion. You should look at the flow of traffic and be aware of junctions when you're slowing down or stopping.

Section 5 Carrying passengers

5.1 What's your main responsibility as a bus driver?

☐ The safety and comfort of your passengers

☐ Keeping to a strict timetable

☐ The collecting of fares

☐ The issuing of tickets

DBC s1
Your passengers should be your first consideration. It's your responsibility to deliver them to their destination safely and on time. You should also treat passengers courteously at all times.

5.2 How can a bus driver show care for their passengers?

☐ By taking fares while moving, to save time

☐ By reaching destinations early

☐ By not speaking when taking fares

☐ By stopping close to the kerb

DBC s1
At bus stops, stop close to the kerb, where it's safe and convenient for your passengers to get on and off. Accelerating as you move off can easily unsteady a passenger. Try to wait until all passengers are seated or settled before moving off.

5.3 What's the main reason for using smooth acceleration when you're driving a bus?

☐ To reduce wear on the tyres

☐ To reduce wear on the engine

☐ To improve fuel consumption

☐ To improve passenger comfort

DBC s1
Operators often publicise journeys as being comfortable, convenient and fast. You play an important part in delivering this standard of service.

5.4 How can you avoid harsh braking?

☐ Pump the brakes when approaching a bus stop

☐ Use only the gears to slow down

☐ Use the parking brake just before stopping

☐ Plan ahead and take early action on all stops

DBC s2
Your first duty is to your paying customers, who want to reach their destination comfortably and safely. Harsh braking can cause your passengers to be thrown forward on the bus, so avoid this by looking and planning well ahead. Give yourself plenty of time to react to traffic situations.

5.5 Where are passengers likely to be thrown when a bus driver brakes harshly?

☐ To the front of the bus ☐ To the rear of the bus

☐ To the nearside   ☐ To the offside

DBC s2
When approaching hazards or bus stops, you should always be aware of how your passengers will be affected by the change in speed. Late, harsh braking as passengers leave their seats can take them by surprise and cause them to fall towards the front of the bus, possibly injuring themselves or others. Wherever possible, avoid harsh braking by planning ahead, giving yourself time to reduce speed smoothly.

5.6 How can you avoid harsh braking?

☐ Gently apply the parking brake

☐ Plan ahead and take early action

☐ Slow down by using your gears only

☐ Pump the brake pedal several times

DBC s2
Always look well ahead. Early planning and anticipation will help you avoid the need to brake harshly. It's important that you give your passengers a smooth journey, especially if any of them are having to stand.

5.7 When would passengers be most likely to notice weight transfer?

☐ When the vehicle is parking

☐ When the vehicle is cornering

☐ When the vehicle is reversing

☐ When the vehicle is overtaking

DBC s2
A smooth ride at all times isn't always easy to achieve. However, scanning ahead for hazards will help you avoid late braking and cornering too fast.

5.8 Well ahead of you are traffic lights on green. What should you do in case the lights change to red?

☐ Accelerate to make sure you can cross before they change

☐ Slow down to avoid the need to stop suddenly

☐ Accelerate, but warn your passengers you may have to stop

☐ Carry on at a constant speed, but be ready to sound your horn

DBC s4
If you're approaching a set of traffic lights and you can see they've been on green for a while, be prepared for them to change. Ease off the accelerator and be ready to come to a gradual stop if you need to. Don't try to beat the red light; it may change as you come closer, causing you to brake late and harshly. Think of your passengers.

5.9 Why should a bus driver avoid stopping harshly?

☐ To preserve the tyres

☐ To avoid wear on the brakes

☐ To keep the passengers safe

☐ To stop the suspension bouncing

DBC s2
Passengers are very vulnerable when they're standing in a moving vehicle. Inconsiderate use of the footbrake can easily cause them injury – especially if they're young or infirm. Some passengers may not wait until you've stopped before leaving their seat. If you seem to be in a hurry, they may even leave their seat early because they don't want to feel responsible for holding you up.

5.10 Where may passengers be thrown when a bus takes a bend too fast?

☐ Towards the outside of the bend

☐ Towards the inside of the bend

☐ Towards the front of the bus

☐ Towards the rear of the bus

DBC s2
Turning corners or travelling around bends too quickly will push passengers towards the outside of the bend. In addition, the weight of the passengers being transferred to one side of the vehicle will make the bus even more unstable. This will make steering out of the bend more difficult.

5.11 What would contribute to the safety and comfort of your passengers?

☐ Giving change on the move

☐ Driving with the door open

☐ Thinking and planning well ahead

☐ Braking hard before reaching a bend

DBC s1
Thinking and planning well ahead will help you to deal competently and safely with hazards and other road users. A safe, comfortable ride, even when you're under pressure, will be appreciated by your passengers.

5.12 What should you be most aware of before moving off from a standstill?

☐ Passengers making phone calls

☐ Passengers smoking on the bus

☐ Passengers asking you directions

☐ Passengers getting off the bus

DBC s1
Check your nearside external and internal mirrors before you move away, in case anyone is attempting to board or leave your vehicle. Always give passengers time to be seated safely before you move away.

5.13   Your bus is fitted with seat belts. When should passengers wear them?

❏ During journeys of more than 20 minutes

❏ Only when travelling in EU countries

❏ Only when travelling on motorways

❏ At all times

DBC s2

As a driver of a bus, you may be responsible for several passengers at any given time. If a situation occurs where you have to brake or steer harshly, your passengers could be thrown about the vehicle. In these circumstances, there's a significant risk of injury from fittings on board, such as luggage racks, handrails and poles. If seat belts are provided for passengers, they should wear them.

5.14   Which of these is a legal requirement for every bus?

❏ A fire extinguisher   ❏ A current timetable

❏ A mobile phone or radio ❏ A working tachograph

DBC s4

Every bus must carry a fire extinguisher. Make sure that you know where it's located and how to use it, so that you're fully prepared in the event of a fire.

5.15   What must be clearly labelled on a bus?

❏ The location of the air vents

❏ The location of the first-aid equipment

❏ The location of the security cameras

❏ The location of the bus station

DBC s4

It's essential to know the location of first-aid equipment, the fuel cut off device and the fire extinguisher on every bus that you drive. Take time to familiarise yourself with their location whenever you drive a different vehicle. When you take your PCV test, you'll be asked questions on safety.

5.16   A passenger is boarding your bus. What does it mean if they're carrying a white stick with a red ring painted on it?

❏ They have a learning difficulty

❏ They have poor vision and hearing

❏ They have a physical disability

❏ They have a speech problem

DBC s1

A person carrying a white stick or a long white cane may be visually impaired. If the stick has a red ring or red-and-white checks painted on it, they also have impaired hearing. Be prepared to help if they appear to need it, or if they ask for assistance.

5.17   What should a bus driver do to help passengers have a good journey?

❏ Keep to the timetable regardless of comfort

❏ Drive on before people are seated

❏ Look ahead when issuing tickets

❏ Be courteous and polite

DBC s1

Nobody likes to be late, but you shouldn't let the pressure of your timetable make you feel you have to rush people. Being pleasant to your passengers and showing them some common courtesies will encourage them to use your service again.

5.18   Why should you look at passengers when you're collecting fares from them?

❏ To see if they're carrying bags

❏ To remove the threat of violence

❏ To be courteous and polite

❏ To show them you're in charge

DBC s1

You're a representative of your company, so showing passengers that their custom is appreciated will encourage them to travel with you again.

5.19   What should you do when dealing with passengers who have hearing difficulties?

❏ Shout as loudly as you can

❏ Ask another passenger to help them

❏ Hurry to get them to their seats

❏ Look at them when speaking to them

DBC s1

Passengers who are hard of hearing may want to lip read. Make sure that they're able to see your face clearly when you speak to them.

5.20　What's the purpose of a kneeling bus?

❏ To improve passenger comfort on bumpy roads

❏ To help with access under low bridges

❏ To allow the step height to be raised and lowered

❏ To give more clearance over speed ramps

DBC s1
A kneeling bus uses air suspension to lower the front entrance, giving easier access for passengers. This is especially helpful for people who have difficulty climbing steps, are disabled or use wheelchairs. Make sure you're properly trained to use this equipment.

5.21　Why would this sign be fitted to the front and rear of a bus?

❏ The bus may be carrying children

❏ Children must be accompanied by an adult

❏ The bus is carrying blind people

❏ The driver will help disabled people

DBC s1
If you're carrying children on your vehicle and it isn't on a scheduled route used by the general public, the bus must display this sign to the front and rear. When carrying children to and from school, it's likely that you'll have to make several stops in places other than recognised bus stops. Think carefully before you stop. Don't cause unnecessary inconvenience to other road users.

5.22　You're driving a bus displaying this sign. When can you use its hazard warning lights?

❏ When stopped at a pedestrian crossing

❏ When children are getting on or off the vehicle

❏ When approaching a school crossing patrol

❏ When there's a sign warning of a school ahead

DBC s1
You may be driving in the rush hour, when traffic is heavy, so when you stop you're permitted to show your hazard warning lights. This will tell other road users that children are getting on and off the bus. Look out for passing traffic and make sure that all your passengers get on and off safely.

5.23　Your bus has broken down at night. Why should you move your passengers to the front of the bus?

❏ To keep the bus stable

❏ To help you see clearly out of the back window

❏ To limit injuries in the event of a rear-end collision

❏ To keep them informed about the breakdown

DBC s4
Passenger safety should be your priority. You should take every precaution to ensure they're out of danger.

5.24　What should you do when you're driving a coach at night and you have passengers on board?

❏ Stop more often　　❏ Switch off the radio

❏ Keep the interior lit　❏ Close the curtains

DBC s4
Passengers should be able to move about the vehicle in safety. You should make sure that all interior lights are in working order before you start your journey.

5.25　What should you do if there's a fire on the upper deck of your bus?

❏ Move all the passengers to the lower deck

❏ Get all the passengers off the bus

❏ Make sure passengers have the belongings

❏ Open all the windows on the upper deck

DBC s4
Fire can spread extremely quickly. Your priority is the safety of your passengers: you must get them off the bus straight away. If at all possible, disconnect electrical lines and cut off the fuel supply. Fire can destroy a vehicle very quickly.

5.26 What are kneeling buses designed to improve?

❑ Access for the driver   ❑ Access to the luggage bay

❑ Access for passengers ❑ Access for maintenance

DBC s1
Some buses are equipped with air or hydraulic systems that allow the step level to be lowered. These are known as kneeling buses and have been designed to allow people to board more easily. Don't forget to raise the step again before moving off.

5.27 You're driving a bus carrying passengers at night. Why should you always switch on the interior lights?

❑ It will help you see the road ahead

❑ So that passengers can see to move around

❑ It will help passengers to see outside

❑ So that you can see your controls

DBC s4
Passengers need a properly lit area so they can move around safely.

5.28 Which passengers should you especially watch for as you move off?

❑ Those smoking in the lower saloon

❑ Those standing in the upper saloon

❑ Those avoiding paying the correct fare

❑ Those attempting to board the bus

DBC s1
Always check your nearside mirror before moving away. A passenger may be attempting to open the door to board the bus, or running to jump aboard an open platform. Also check for passengers trying to get off the bus as you move away.

5.29 What could you do to help a passenger who has difficulty walking?

❑ Drive quickly, so that the passenger has a shorter journey

❑ Wait until the passenger has sat down before moving away

❑ Make sure the passenger has a window seat

❑ Suggest that the passenger stands near the door

DBC s1
Try to wait until your passengers have sat down before you move off. This is even more important if they're elderly or have difficulty walking. Offer help when you think it might be needed – and remember, a smile goes a long way.

5.30 You're the driver of a bus displaying reflective yellow school-bus signs. When are you allowed to use hazard warning lights?

❑ When parked to take a rest period

❑ When children are boarding the bus

❑ When slowing down to approach a bus stop

❑ When slowing down to find a parking space

DBC s1
Buses carrying schoolchildren must display a distinctive yellow reflective sign on the front and rear, unless they're running a scheduled service for the general public. Buses displaying the sign are permitted to use hazard warning lights when they've stopped for schoolchildren to get on or off.

5.31 You're parking your coach at a coastal resort. What should you do if your passengers will still have access to the vehicle?

❑ Ask the passengers to take all of their belongings

❑ Park with the gear lever in neutral

❑ Ensure the storage lockers are left open

❑ Leave a responsible person on the coach

DBC s3
If passengers have access to your coach, it must never be left unattended. In particular, they mustn't be able to get into the cab area of the vehicle. You or another responsible person must always be there to supervise the coach.

5.32 What should you be especially aware of while you're driving a double-deck bus on a road with a steep camber?

❑ Lampposts   ❑ Parking meters

❑ Parked cars   ❑ Litter bins

DBC s2
When driving high-sided vehicles, such as double-deck buses, changes in the road camber can affect your vehicle. As the bus leans towards the kerb, there's a risk that shop awnings, trees and street furniture, such as lampposts, could strike the top deck.

5.33 What's the likely weight difference between an empty bus and a bus with 75 passengers on board?

❑ 5 tonnes ❑ 10 tonnes ❑ 15 tonnes ❑ 20 tonnes

DBC s3
Your vehicle will handle very differently when it's full, compared with when it's empty. Having 75 passengers on board would increase the weight of the bus by about 5 tonnes – and the passengers may also have luggage. It will take longer to build up speed and the vehicle will be more difficult to stop. Forward planning and controlled braking will be required to allow for this extra weight.

5.34 It's important to be able to work out the weight difference between a full bus and an empty one. How many passengers will add about 1 tonne to the vehicle's overall weight?

❑ 8   ❑ 15   ❑ 25   ❑ 30

DBC s3
You should also make allowances for any luggage your passengers may bring on board. An average of two cases per passenger on a 50-seat coach will add about 1.5 tonnes to the overall weight of your bus or coach.

5.35 What must buses and coaches display when they're used for school contract work?

❑ School-bus signs

❑ Flashing amber beacons

❑ Triangular warning signs

❑ No overtaking' signs

DBC s1
Vehicles carrying schoolchildren display the 'school bus' sign to alert other drivers to the danger of children crossing the road. As the bus driver, you must make every effort to ensure the children's safety when boarding or getting off your bus, as well as during their journey with you.

5.36 What should you do if a passenger comments on exhaust smoke in the bus?

❑ Report it as soon as you return to the depot

❑ Stop and have the fault put right

❑ Avoid heavy revving of the engine when stationary

❑ Have the emissions checked at the next vehicle inspection

DBC s2
If exhaust fumes are getting into the vehicle, this could be a danger to your passengers. Stop as soon as it's safe to do so and have the fault put right before continuing.

5.37 What do you have to be aware of when driving a double-deck bus on a road that has a steep camber?

❑ 'Keep left' islands   ❑ A smooth road surface

❑ Pedestrian crossings   ❑ Overhanging trees

DBC s2
A road that has a steep camber will slope sharply towards the kerb, causing your bus to lean towards the pavement or verge. This brings a risk of collision with objects such as overhanging trees, lampposts and bus-stop roofs.

5.38 What does good passenger care include?

❑ Making criticisms of other road users

❑ Providing a commentary on the route

❑ Talking to passengers while driving

❑ Helping passengers who need directions

DBC s1
Always show consideration to passengers, whether they have special needs or not. Try to imagine what assistance you would like if you were in their position.

5.39 Your bus is fitted with lifts or ramps for less mobile passengers. Who should operate this equipment?

☐ Wheelchair attendants   ☐ Fully trained people

☐ Bus-company employees   ☐ Accompanying nurses

DBC s1

Make sure that you're fully trained in the safe use of lifts, ramps and securing devices. If you drive a vehicle fitted with this equipment, never let untrained people operate it.

5.40 What does a kneeling bus improve?

☐ Access for disabled people

☐ Stability when cornering

☐ Passenger comfort at higher speeds

☐ Access for the driver

DBC s1

Kneeling buses are equipped with air or hydraulic systems that allow the vehicle body to be lowered. This improves access for disabled and elderly passengers. Remember to return the mechanism to its travelling position before moving off.

5.41 Your double-deck bus breaks down on a busy road. Where should you ask your passengers to move to?

☐ The rear of the bus   ☐ The top deck

☐ The lower deck   ☐ The front of the bus

DBC s2

The greatest risk to a stationary bus is being hit from behind. Moving your passengers forward could reduce the risk of injury if such a collision occurred.

5.42 What should you watch for when you drive away from a bus stop?

☐ Passengers who avoid paying the correct fare

☐ Passengers smoking in the lower saloon

☐ Passengers leaving the bus

☐ Passengers using expired travel passes

DBC s1

Even though you've started to drive away, passengers may still try to get off the bus. You should also check your nearside mirror for any passengers trying to get on as you're moving away.

5.43 What must you do before moving off when you're driving a service bus?

☐ Finish issuing tickets to passengers

☐ Ensure your fuel tank is above a quarter full

☐ Take off your sunglasses

☐ Make sure all passengers have a seat

DBC s1

On regular services, traffic congestion can soon put you behind schedule. Nevertheless, you have a responsibility to your passengers at all times not to take shortcuts or jeopardise their safety; for example, by driving off while you're still issuing tickets.

5.44 Your bus breaks down on the motorway. What should you do if it isn't feasible to remove your passengers from the vehicle?

☐ Move passengers to the rear of the bus

☐ Move passengers to the front of the bus

☐ Move passengers to the middle of the bus

☐ Tell passengers to stay in the same seats

DBC s4

Stop as far to the left as possible on the hard shoulder. Make sure all your passengers have moved as far as possible to the front of the vehicle; this will reduce the risk of injury if a passing vehicle runs into the back of the bus. Use an emergency telephone to call for assistance.

5.45 What's a bus driver's first priority?

☐ The safety and comfort of passengers

☐ Keeping to the timetable

☐ Completing tachograph records correctly

☐ Making sure the destination is clearly marked

DBC s1

Bus drivers have responsibilities beyond those of other drivers. Your passengers have paid for a service, and they should arrive at their chosen destination safely.

Customers are more likely to travel with you again if they receive a safe, courteous and comfortable service.

5.46 You're driving a one-person-operated bus. What should you do while issuing tickets at a bus stop?

- ❑ Signal right, so you're ready to move off
- ❑ Turn on your hazard warning lights
- ❑ Make sure you've cancelled any signal
- ❑ Signal left, to let others know you're not ready to move off

DBC s1

Giving wrong signals causes uncertainty and confusion to other road users. Only give signals that are relevant and timed to match your actions.

5.47 You're the driver of a one-person-operated double-deck bus. How do you stay aware of passengers on the top deck?

- ❑ By counting passengers up and down the staircase
- ❑ By frequent checks upstairs while stopped at bus stops
- ❑ By listening to passengers in the upstairs gangway when approaching bus stops
- ❑ By making full use of the internal mirror system

DBC s1

If you're driving a one-person-operated double-deck bus, you must make sure that you use your internal mirrors. You need to be able to see passengers who are about to descend the stairs. Consider their safety and avoid harsh braking and steering.

5.48 You're driving a double-deck bus. Why do you need to know if anyone is using the stairs?

- ❑ The upper deck is only to be used when the lower deck is full
- ❑ Tickets for the upper deck are more expensive
- ❑ Passengers using the stairs could fall if the bus brakes or swerves
- ❑ No-one under 18 years old may use the stairs

DBC s1

You must always be aware of anyone using the stairs. Be particularly careful to avoid any sudden movement, such as when braking or cornering, as this could cause passengers to stumble.

5.49 Where should you stop when you're stopping to collect passengers at a bus stop?

- ❑ Close to the kerb   ❑ Away from the kerb
- ❑ After the bus stop   ❑ Before the bus stop

DBC s1

If passengers aren't waiting at the bus stop, it can be tempting to stop near where they're standing. This may not be a safe place for your vehicle or for other road users. Be professional and be safe; stop in the correct position.

5.50 Where should you stop to make it easy for passengers leaving or joining your bus?

- ❑ Next to soft grass   ❑ Alongside guard rails
- ❑ Near parked cars   ❑ Close to the kerb

DBC s1

You should stop as close to the kerb as you can, so that passengers can reach the safety of the pavement without any difficulty.

5.51 A bus stop is blocked and you can't get into it. What's the most important thing you should do before opening the exit door?

- ❑ Try to get the bus stop cleared
- ❑ Carry on to the next bus stop
- ❑ Check for traffic on the left
- ❑ Check for traffic on the right

DBC s3

Make sure that you allow your passengers to get on or off the vehicle safely. If you're unable to stop close to the kerb, don't open the doors until you're sure it's safe. You must take care of your passengers at all times.

5.52 Several parked cars are blocking your bus stop. What should you do before allowing passengers to leave the bus?

- ❑ Move on to the next bus stop
- ❑ Check it's clear of traffic on the left
- ❑ Try to find the car owners
- ❑ Check it's clear of traffic on the right

DBC s3

Always check your nearside mirror before opening the door to allow passengers to alight. When you've stopped away from the kerb, it's important to warn the passengers to look out for cyclists and to expect a long step down onto the road. Be ready to offer help if they need it.

5.53   What should you do before allowing passengers off your bus?

❑ Collect their used tickets

❑ Activate an audible warning system

❑ Check mirrors before opening doors

❑ Ask if they have luggage to collect

DBC s3

Passenger safety is your main responsibility. Before you allow them to step down from the bus, you should always check your mirrors to make sure there's nothing approaching that could endanger them.

5.54   Passengers may be in a hurry to get off the bus as you approach a bus stop. What should you do to reduce any dangers?

❑ Insist that passengers stay seated until the bus stops

❑ Stop just before the bus stop and let passengers get off

❑ Let passengers on to the bus before letting passengers off

❑ Keep the passenger doors closed until the bus has stopped

DBC s3

Passengers may have left their seats early and may be standing up, waiting to get off. Don't brake harshly or open the doors until the vehicle has stopped.

5.55   When can you drive a bus at night without having the interior lights switched on?

❑ When the passengers want to sleep

❑ When most passengers want the lights off

❑ When there are no standing passenger

❑ When there are no passengers

DBC s4

Whenever passengers are on board, the interior lighting must be left on. It may be turned off when the bus is empty.

5.56   You're driving a bus in hot weather. Can the passenger door be left open to let in fresh air?

❑ Yes, this is normal practice

❑ No, unless all passengers are seated

❑ Yes, unless carrying schoolchildren

❑ No, this isn't allowed

DBC s4

Under no circumstances should you drive with your passenger door open. An open door invites people to make rash decisions to enter or leave the vehicle as you're about to move away; this can be extremely dangerous.

5.57   How would your bus benefit from an air suspension system?

❑ Fuel consumption will be reduced

❑ Passenger comfort will be increased

❑ It will allow you to drive faster

❑ Your brakes will be more effective

DBC s2

Air suspension will increase passenger comfort and can also help to reduce wear on road surfaces – which is why it's also known as 'road-friendly suspension'.

5.58   A disabled person is getting on your bus. What should you do if they're having problems, but say they can manage?

❑ Be prepared to move off

❑ Smile and offer to help them

❑ Ask them politely to hurry up

❑ Do nothing; you can't leave your seat

DBC s1

Disabled people like to keep their independence. However, if they're having problems, be prepared to offer help.

5.59   When may the built-in TV and video equipment be used on a coach?

❑ When the coach is moving slowly

❑ When it can't be seen by the driver

❑ During long motorway journeys

❑ During a coach tour

DBC s2

To prevent drivers from becoming distracted, TV or video equipment must be out of their sight. While passengers are being entertained, they can be sure the driver is concentrating on delivering them safely to their destination.

5.60 What must be fitted to new buses, to benefit people with disabilities?

❑ Internal mirror   ❑ Radio telephone

❑ Automatic transmission   ❑ Priority seating

DBC s2
All new buses and coaches must be easily accessible for disabled passengers. They must have ramps, priority seating and colour contrasted fittings.

5.61 Who should benefit from priority seating?

❑ Those with heavy luggage

❑ Those with a weekly pass

❑ Those who get on first

❑ Those with disabilities

DBC s1
Since 2000, all new buses and coaches must be accessible to people with disabilities. These vehicles must have ramps, priority seating and colour-contrasted handrails and steps.

5.62 A passenger using a wheelchair wants to get on your bus. When may you need to deny them access?

❑ When the wheelchair won't fit in the luggage rack

❑ When the boarding device has failed to work

❑ When the passenger must remain in a wheelchair

❑ When the heater on the vehicle isn't working

DBC s1
It's unfortunate, but machinery will sometimes break down despite the best efforts to service it. Don't risk the health and safety of a person with a disability, or other passengers, by struggling to get them on without the proper equipment.

5.63 Your bus is accessible to wheelchair users. In what situation can you refuse to allow them access?

❑ When the designated space is occupied

❑ When you're running behind schedule

❑ When traffic behind you will be held up

❑ When you're shortly due to take a break

DBC s1
It's illegal for bus and coach operators to discriminate against people with disabilities. You must always make reasonable adjustments to the way that any service is provided. This means that you must allow wheelchair users access to the designated space – unless it's already been taken by another wheelchair user.

5.64 You're driving a school bus carrying children. When can you make physical contact with a passenger?

❑ In a medical emergency

❑ To prevent fare dodging

❑ When carrying luggage

❑ When fastening seat belts

DBC s1
All physical contact with children should be avoided except in specific circumstances such as genuine self-defence, a medical emergency, or to prevent a serious offence or threat to anyone's safety.

5.65 What should you wear when making a walk-round check of your coach?

❑ Ear protectors   ❑ Protective goggles

❑ High-visibility vest   ❑ Face mask

DBC s3
You should make yourself clearly visible when you're working outside your vehicle and close to moving traffic.

5.66 You're about to drive on a route where you'll be picking up wheelchair users. What must be checked before leaving the depot?

❑ The boarding device ❑ The radio

❑ The door seals   ❑ The heater

DBC s1
It's a legal requirement that you should make reasonable adjustments to provide for people with disabilities. You should make sure that any ramp or lift is in place and in good working order before leaving the depot.

5.67   When can you refuse access to a wheelchair user?

❑ When the lift has stopped working

❑ When the wheelchair won't fold up

❑ When the heater has stopped working

❑ When the wheelchair is too heavy to lift manually

DBC s1
You won't have failed in your statutory duties if the boarding device breaks down and there's no other means of assisting the passenger.

5.68   Why may you be unable to allow a person in a wheelchair to enter your bus?

❑   Passengers are standing in a wheelchair space and can't move elsewhere

❑   You'll take time to load the wheelchair and fall behind schedule

❑   The wheelchair passenger will have to stand up

❑   You can't collapse the wheelchair

DBC s1
If a wheelchair space is occupied by standing passengers and luggage, you might not be able to allow a wheelchair user on the bus. This may occur on a bus that's almost full to capacity. You won't have failed in your statutory duties towards the wheelchair user.

5.69   You're at a bus stop. What should you do if passengers are standing on the open platform?

❑ Put the chain across the platform

❑ Ask them to hold on tight

❑ Move off but drive more slowly

❑ Wait until they're inside the bus

DBC s1
A bus driver must never allow their passengers to ride on an open platform. Anyone standing on an open platform is at risk should the driver have to brake harshly, swerve or suddenly change direction.

Section 6 The road

6.1 What should you do when you overtake a cyclist on a two-way road?

- ❑ Pass closely, staying about 1 metre (3 feet 3 inches) from the kerb

- ❑ Go past quickly and move back to the left sharply

- ❑ Leave plenty of room and check your nearside mirror before returning to the left

- ❑ Give a right-turn signal after you've moved out to overtake

DGV s4
Only overtake when it's safe to do so, and don't use the size of your vehicle to intimidate approaching traffic. When overtaking a cyclist, leave plenty of room and, before returning to the left, check in your nearside mirror to make sure you've passed them safely.

6.2 Your lorry has a curtain-sided body. Your route will take you over several high level bridges. Why should you check the weather forecast before starting your journey?

- ❑ Rain can make crossing bridges very difficult for large vehicles

- ❑ In hot weather, the bridges might be closed to heavy traffic

- ❑ You won't be able to cross the bridges if it's frosty

- ❑ High-level bridges may be closed to certain vehicles in windy weather

DGV s4
In exposed places, such as high level bridges, viaducts or some motorways, high winds can cause the road to be closed to certain vehicles. If you're driving a high sided vehicle and high winds are forecast, plan an alternative route in case your intended·route is closed.

6.3 What should you do when you want to join a motorway where traffic is flowing freely?

- ❑ Keep to a low speed until you see a gap on the motorway

- ❑ Build up your speed on the slip road before joining the motorway

- ❑ Stop at the start of the slip road and move off when you see a gap

- ❑ Use the hard shoulder, if necessary, to build up speed

DGV s4
Normally, you should avoid having to stop before joining a motorway. Use the slip road to build up your speed so that you can emerge safely. If it's extremely busy, there may be rare occasions when you have to stop and then filter into the traffic. This is most likely to happen where traffic is queuing; for example, at roadworks.

6.4 What should you do before driving your high-sided lorry in windy weather?

- ❑ Check your wind deflector

- ❑ Check your spray-suppression equipment

- ❑ Plan your route in advance

- ❑ Only half-load your lorry

DGV s4
In high winds, some exposed roads, bridges and viaducts are closed to high-sided vehicles. Plan your route with care and try to avoid these areas. Also plan an alternative route in case of road closure.

6.5 You're overtaking another lorry. What should you do if you start to lose speed due to an uphill gradient?

- ❑ Continue at the same speed and in the same position

- ❑ Try to force the vehicle you were overtaking to drop back

- ❑ Try to force the vehicle you were overtaking to speed up

- ❑ Ease off and drop behind the vehicle you were trying to overtake

DGV s4
If you try to overtake another vehicle and realise that you're unable to complete the manoeuvre, ease off the accelerator and drop back behind the vehicle. If the vehicle you're trying to overtake is large, then it will take a long time to pass. You should assess whether you have the time and power to complete the manoeuvre before you try to overtake.

6.6   How could you reduce the problems caused by a strong side wind when driving an empty curtain-sided vehicle on an exposed bridge?

☐ Tie one curtain open and lock open the rear doors

☐ Leave both curtains closed

☐ Tie both curtains open

☐ Tie open the curtain on the side the wind's blowing from

DGV s2

If you're driving an empty curtain-sided vehicle, you can help to lower the resistance to side wind if you tie the curtains open. The air will then be able to flow across the flat bed of the vehicle. This will reduce any loss of control, particularly when crossing exposed viaducts or bridges.

6.7   When is a high-sided vehicle most affected by side wind?

☐ When it's stationary

☐ When it's travelling loaded

☐ When it's being reversed

☐ When it's travelling empty

DGV s2

Take care if you're driving an empty high-sided vehicle when it's windy. Watch for places where the conditions could suddenly change, such as a gap between buildings or when passing under a bridge. Reduce your speed and stay alert for other road users who are also affected by these weather conditions.

6.8   You're driving an empty curtain-sided vehicle. Why might you consider tying the curtains open?

☐ To use less fuel

☐ It's a legal requirement

☐ To prevent the curtains from tearing

☐ To reduce the effect of side wind

DGV s2

Closed curtains on large empty vehicles can hold the wind. Strong side wind can blow a semi-trailer off course and, in severe cases, can blow the whole vehicle over onto its side. To reduce the risk of this happening, you should tie the curtains open.

6.9   When will a box van be most affected by side wind?

☐ When travelling empty   ☐ When stationary

☐ When travelling fully laden ☐ When reversing

DGV s2

High-sided vehicles such as box vans are affected by side wind, particularly when they're empty. Drivers should slow down and stay alert for other road users affected by the windy conditions.

6.10   You're driving a lorry towards a high bridge on a windy day. What should you expect?

☐ Changed weight limits   ☐ No restrictions for lorries

☐ Minimum speed limits   ☐ Lane closures

DGV s2

In windy weather, exposed stretches of road may have lane closures or there may be diversions for some types of vehicle. Consider this when you're planning your journey; delays will add to your driving time.

6.11   Which of these vehicles is most at risk from strong side wind?

☐ A laden lorry with box body

☐ An unladen lorry with box body

☐ An unladen lorry with platform body

☐ A laden lorry with platform body

DGV s2

An unladen vehicle that also has high sides will be vulnerable to the effects of strong side wind. An evenly distributed load will help to keep the vehicle more stable, but the higher the vehicle is, the more it will be affected. Be aware that such a vehicle may become unstable or difficult to control in windy conditions.

6.12   In strong winds, an overtaking lorry can cause additional air turbulence that can affect other road users. Which vehicle is most at risk from this turbulence?

☐ A car ☐ A delivery van ☐ A motorcycle ☐ A coach

DGV s4

Vehicles such as motorcycles, bicycles and caravans could be blown off course by strong winds. You should be aware that your vehicle could cause additional buffeting when you overtake, so allow them plenty of room.

6.13   Which vehicle is most at risk in windy conditions?

❏ High-sided lorry ❏ Saloon car

❏ Tractor unit ❏ Single-deck bus

DGV s2
High-sided vehicles are severely affected by side wind because of the large surface area of the bodywork. The risk of loss of control is increased if the vehicle is unladen.

6.14   When are air deflectors most effective?

❏ When there's a side wind

❏ When there's a headwind

❏ When reversing

❏ When there's a strong tailwind

DGV s2
Air deflectors reduce wind resistance by streamlining the vehicle. They're most effective when there's a headwind. The streamlining also reduces the vehicle's fuel consumption.

6.15   You're driving your lorry on the motorway. What should you do when visibility Is reduced by heavy rain and spray?

❏ Maintain a constant speed

❏ Use main-beam headlights

❏ Double your dry-weather separation distance

❏ Stay in the left-hand lane

DGV s4
Rain makes the road surface slippery and reduces tyre grip. Doubling your separation distance should allow you the extra time and space you'll need to slow down and stop safely.

6.16   What should you do before driving your lorry away from a wet construction site at the side of a motorway?

❏ Turn on your amber beacon

❏ Drain the air tanks

❏ Hose down the wheels

❏ Set your tachograph to 'other work'

DGV s4
Before leaving a construction site, check your vehicle for mud and for debris wedged between double rear wheels. It's important that you prevent any mud or debris from being deposited on the road, where it could be a danger to other road users.

6.17   You're driving a lorry from a wet construction site onto a motorway. Why must you take extra precautions before leaving the site?

❏ Your view from the cab will be obscured by plant machinery

❏ It's an offence to emerge from a works site onto a motorway

❏ Your lorry's spray-suppression equipment will be inoperative

❏ It's an offence to deposit mud on a road

DGV s4
You should take precautions against dropping mud on the road, because it's a hazard to other road users. It's also an offence for which you could be prosecuted.

6.18   What ground conditions are suitable for a tipper lorry to tip its load?

❏ Soft and level ❏ Soft and downhill

❏ Solid and uphill ❏ Solid and level

DGV s2
When discharging a load from a tipper vehicle, the centre of gravity is raised as the tipper body rises. To avoid the vehicle rolling over, it's vital that it's positioned on a level, solid surface before the tipper mechanism is engaged.

6.19   You're driving a lorry of more than 7.5 tonnes maximum authorised mass along a motorway. When can you use the right-hand lane to overtake?

❏ When the motorway has two lanes

❏ When the motorway has three lanes

❏ When there's a 50 mph speed limit

❏ When there's a 40 mph speed limit

DGV s4
You may use the right-hand lane to overtake on a two-lane motorway. Lorries weighing more than 7.5 tonnes, vehicles that are required to be fitted with speed limiters, and vehicles towing trailers aren't allowed to use the right-hand lane of a motorway with three or more lanes, except in special circumstances.

6.20 You're driving on a motorway. You look in your mirrors and see smoke coming from your rear tyres. What should you do?

❑ Reduce speed for the rest of your journey

❑ Drive on the hard shoulder until the smoke stops

❑ Stop as soon as it's safe to do so

❑ Ignore it; this is normal when driving at speed

DGV s4
A tyre may burst or shred if it overheats. This could result In serious loss of control. Stop on the hard shoulder as soon as it's safe to do so and call for help.

6.21 You're on a wet, level road, driving at 50 mph. What's the minimum time gap you should leave between your vehicle and the one in front?

❑ One second   ❑ Two seconds

❑ Three seconds   ❑ Four seconds

DGV s4
The usual advice is to leave a minimum time gap of two seconds, but on wet roads you should leave at least double that time. Always take the road and weather conditions into account when you're driving.

6.22 You're driving an articulated lorry on a three-lane motorway. When can you drive in the right-hand lane?

❑ When overtaking a slow-moving car in the middle lane

❑ When the escort vehicle of an oversized load signals you to pass

❑ If no speed limiter is fitted to your lorry

❑ If your lorry is unladen

DGV s4
Articulated lorries aren't allowed to drive in the right-hand lane of motorways with three or more lanes. The only exceptions are when an escort vehicle gives you a signal, when road signs indicate, or when directed by a police officer.

6.23 You're driving on a motorway and it's raining heavily. What should you do when spray is causing poor visibility?

❑ Use dipped headlights

❑ Use sidelights only

❑ Remove spray-suppression equipment

❑ Use the two-second rule

DGV s4
Whenever visibility is reduced, use dipped headlights to make your vehicle easier to see. During and after heavy rain, you should also reduce speed and increase your distance from the vehicle in front.

6.24 What might happen if using the brakes continuously causes them to overheat?

❑ The brakes will work better

❑ The brakes will be less effective

❑ The brake pedal will become stiff

❑ The air pressure will increase

DBC s2, DGV s2
Whenever you brake, the brakes convert the moving energy of your vehicle into heat. Continuous use of the brakes, particularly from high speed or on long steep descents, can cause the shoes and drums to overheat. This will make them less effective and, in some cases, they may not work at all.

6.25 What do you need to be careful of when you're driving in high winds?

❑ Fallen trees   ❑ Poor visibility

❑ A risk of grounding ❑ Steep gradients

DBC s4, DGV s4
In severe weather conditions, you should be aware of the dangers of fallen trees or damaged branches that may fall on your vehicle. Be prepared in case a fallen tree is lying across the road just around a bend.

6.26 What do you need to be aware of when you drive over an exposed suspension bridge?

❑ The swaying of the bridge

❑ The width of the lanes

❑ The effect of strong side wind

❑ The overhanging bridge cables

DBC s4, DGV s4
On exposed bridges, the wind can be particularly strong. If the bridge has two lanes, one may be closed in windy conditions to act as a buffer lane. In severe conditions, these bridges are often closed to high-sided vehicles, caravans and motorcycles.

6.27 You're driving through the night. What could it mean if your steering feels lighter than normal?

❑ Your tyres are losing pressure

❑ There's a leak in the power-steering pump

❑ There's ice or frost on the road

❑ There isn't enough tread on your tyres

DBC s4, DGV s4
When you're in a warm cab, you may not notice the drop In outside temperature. One of the first signs of an icy road is a lack of 'feel' in the steering. If this happens, slow down and increase the distance between your vehicle and the one in front.

6.28 You're in the centre lane of a motorway, overtaking another vehicle. What should you do before returning to the left-hand lane?

❑ Signal left, then check your mirror

❑ Wait for the other driver to flash their headlights

❑ Check ahead and then your nearside mirror

❑ Check behind for fast traffic in the right-hand lane

DBC s4, DGV s4
Never return to the left-hand lane until you're sure that you're well clear of the vehicle you've just overtaken. Don't cut in too soon and don't rely on the other driver flashing you in. Make your own judgement about when it's safe to move into the left-hand lane.

6.29 What should you do as you approach a zebra crossing?

❑ Stop before the zigzag lines

❑ Wave pedestrians across the road

❑ Sound the horn and flash headlights

❑ Be prepared to stop in good time

DBC s6, DGV s6
Always keep your speed down as you approach a zebra crossing. This will allow you to stop safely if necessary. Look well ahead for anyone about to reach the crossing or waiting to cross.

6.30 You're driving a high-sided vehicle on a motorway. You should anticipate the effects of side wind.When is this most likely to happen?

❑ When passing signs ❑ On exposed sections

❑ In contraflow systems ❑ In service areas

DBC s4, DGV s4
Motorways often have exposed sections of road, placing high sided vehicles at risk in side wind. When there are extremes of weather, listen to and watch out for weather forecasts. That way, you can plan your journey for the safest time, or make a decision on whether you should travel at all.

6.31 You're driving a high-sided vehicle in very windy conditions. Where should you avoid travelling?

❑ Across suspension bridges

❑ Up steep hills

❑ Along country lanes

❑ Through road tunnels

DBC s4, DGV s4
In windy weather, try to avoid routes where you would have to drive across suspension bridges and other exposed stretches of road. Plan a route that takes you across lower ground and where you'll be less exposed.

6.32 You're driving in heavy rain. What should you do if your steering suddenly feels very light?

❑ Brake very sharply

❑ Steer towards the centre line

❑ Ease off the accelerator

❑ Increase your speed

DBC s4, DGV s4
In wet conditions. water can build up between your tyres and the road surface. This is known as aquaplaning and it will cause your vehicle to slide. Try to regain control by easing off the accelerator to gradually lose speed. Don't brake or steer until your tyres are gripping the road again.

6.33 Why should you be especially aware of parked cars when you're driving at night?

❑ There are more of them

❑ They're more likely to move off

❑ The drivers may be drunk

❑ They can park without lights

DBC s4, DGV s4
Vehicles below 2500 kg laden weight may park without lights on roads with a speed limit no greater than 30 mph. In dark streets. you may not be able to see them clearly.

6.34 You're waiting at a T-junction. What should you do if you see a vehicle is coming from the right, with its left indicator flashing?

☐ Move out and accelerate hard

☐ Wait until the vehicle starts to turn in

☐ Pull out before the vehicle reaches the junction

☐ Move out slowly

DBC s4, DGV s4
Try to anticipate the actions of other road users. When you're waiting at a junction, don't emerge until you're sure of their intentions; their signals might be misleading.

6.35 You're driving along a motorway and see this sign. What does it mean?

☐ There's a steep downhill section ahead

☐ Only lorries and buses are allowed to use that lane

☐ Vehicles fitted with speed limiters must use that lane

☐ There's a long uphill gradient ahead

DBC s4, DGV s4
Where a motorway has a long or steep gradient, slow-moving large vehicles might get In the way of other traffic. To help the traffic flow, an extra lane – called a crawler lane – is sometimes found on these gradients. This helps the traffic to flow by providing the slower heavy vehicles with a dedicated lane on the left.

6.36 You're about to pass this car. What's the main hazard you should be aware of?

☐ Sunlight reflecting off the car windscreen

☐ The driver's door may suddenly open

☐ Its alarm may be activated

☐ The narrow pavement on the right

HC r152
You don't know what the driver of this car will do. Be prepared for any hazard. The driver may not have seen you. Planning ahead will allow you to be in the correct gear and at the correct speed to cope if this hazard develops.

6.37 What should you do when you park your vehicle on a two-way road at night?

☐ Use the parking lights

☐ Switch off all lights

☐ Put a traffic cone behind your vehicle

☐ Park underneath a street lamp

DBC s4, DGV s4
Large vehicles are required by law to use parking lights when parked at night, unless in a designated off-road parking area. Also, unless you're in a one-way street, you must only park on the left-hand side. It's generally much better to park off-road if you can, particularly if you're going to be stationary for a long period of time.

6.38 When would weight transference be most likely to occur?

☐ When you're reversing

☐ When you're loading

☐ When you're overtaking

☐ When you're cornering

DBC s2, DGV s2
You must take extra care when your vehicle is carrying a load. When cornering, weight will be transferred away from the direction in which you're turning. Also, when you're braking, weight can be transferred in several different directions.

6.39 How will gravity affect a laden vehicle going downhill?

☐ The vehicle will use more fuel

☐ Stopping distances will be decreased

☐ More braking effort will be required

☐ The load will be more stable

DBC s2, DGV s2
Always plan ahead and take note of gradient warning signs. On downhill gradients, you can help control your vehicle's speed and avoid brake fade by selecting a lower gear in good time.

6.40 When do long vehicles sometimes need to straddle lanes?

☐ When turning at tight junctions

☐ When travelling empty

☐ When driving on motorways

☐ When coming to contraflow systems

DBC s2, DGV s2
When driving a long vehicle around corners, it's sometimes necessary to adopt a different road position to avoid mounting the kerb or colliding with street furniture such as lampposts or traffic signs. Other road users may not understand what you intend to do next. Watch them carefully and always signal in good time.

6.41 What should you do when you drive in windy weather?

☐ Maintain a constant speed in exposed areas

☐ Anticipate how the weather may affect other road users

☐ Always keep to your intended route

☐ Stay close to smaller or vulnerable vehicles as you overtake them

DBC s4, DGV s4
Cyclists, motorcyclists, caravans and high-sided vehicles can be very vulnerable in high winds. Plan well ahead and consider the difficulties they may be having. Remember, some routes may be closed to certain vehicles and you may need to use an alternative route.

6.42 High-sided vehicles can be affected by side wind. On which type of road is this most likely?

☐ Narrow country lanes

☐ Open roads

☐ Slip roads

☐ Motorway underpasses

DBC s4, DGV s4
You should take account of the weather forecast when you plan your route. You're most likely to be subjected to side wind on exposed routes; for example, on long bridges, open roads and exposed stretches of motorway.

6.43 Where would you anticipate problems when you're driving a high-sided vehicle on a windy day?

☐ In road tunnels   ☐ On high-level roads

☐ In dead ground   ☐ On ring roads

DBC s4, DGV s4
Listen to the weather forecast and plan your route to avoid exposed or high-level roads if windy weather is expected.

6.44 Which vehicle is least likely to be affected by high wind?

☐   ☐

☐   ☐

DBC s4, DGV s4
The car is the most stable of the vehicles shown. However, all vehicles are affected by side wind and buffeting from larger vehicles. Be aware that your speed and road position could cause unnecessary turbulence when passing smaller vehicles.

6.45 What's a buffer lane?

☐ A safety lane for vehicles blown off course

☐ A lane for overtaking safely

☐ A lane to park in until the wind drops

☐ The only lane to be used in high winds

DBC s4, DGV s4
During high winds, one of the lanes on a high bridge might be closed to traffic to create a buffer lane. The buffer lane is kept free to prevent vehicles from being blown into the path of other road users in the next lane. The closure of this lane may cause traffic congestion and delay.

6.46 Where would you expect to find buffer lanes?

☐ In built-up areas   ☐ On high-level bridges

☐ On country roads   ☐ In roadworks

DBC s4, DGV s4

Buffer lanes are often found in places that are frequently subjected to high winds. Examples include high-level bridges, high-level roads, exposed viaducts and exposed stretches of motorway. Listen to the weather forecast, which should tell you of any need to re-plan your route.

6.47 When is a buffer lane most likely to be in use?

☐ When it's windy   ☐ When it's raining

☐ When it's foggy   ☐ When it's icy

DBC s4, DGV s4

A buffer lane is used when the wind begins to cause a risk to high-sided vehicles. At other times, it will be a normal lane. Don't use the buffer lane unless your vehicle has been blown off course into the lane, or you need to use it to avoid an incident or collision.

6.48 What's the best way to control your vehicle when driving on snow?

☐ Keep the engine revs high and spin the wheels

☐ Drive in your vehicle's lowest gear

☐ Keep the engine revs high and slip the clutch

☐ Drive slowly, in a higher gear than normal

DBC s4, DGV s4

Driving slowly will give you better control of your vehicle. By using a high gear, you reduce the chance of your wheels spinning and skidding on the snow.

6.49 You're driving a large vehicle in gusty conditions. Which vehicle is most likely to be affected by buffeting when you overtake it?

☐ A motorcycle   ☐ A flat-bed lorry

☐ A car   ☐ A loaded tanker

DBC s4, DGV s4

The lighter the vehicle, the more likely it is to be affected by the buffeting from your vehicle in windy weather. Give motorcyclists and cyclists extra room when you overtake them, as your vehicle's draught can easily upset their control and balance.

6.50 It's very windy and you're overtaking a motorcyclist on a motorway. What should you be aware of that may cause them problems?

☐ Your exhaust smoke   ☐ Your engine noise

☐ The buffeting effect ☐ The tyre noise

DBC s4, DGV s4

Give them plenty of room. Watch carefully in your nearside mirror, as the high winds and the buffeting effect from your vehicle may blow them off course.

6.51 Why should you be aware of motorcyclists on a motorway when there are gusty winds?

☐ They may be blown into your path

☐ They may leave at the next exit

☐ They may suddenly stop on the hard shoulder

☐ They may position to turn right

DBC s4, DGV s4

On motorways, there are often exposed stretches of road where vulnerable vehicles can be affected by side wind. A gust of wind can even blow a motorcyclist out of their lane. Try to anticipate how the wind may affect others and give them plenty of room.

6.52 Which road users are most at danger from the turbulence from your vehicle?

☐ Lorry drivers   ☐ Coach drivers

☐ Tractor drivers   ☐ Car drivers towing caravans

DBC s4, DGV s4

Remember that the buffeting caused by large vehicles can affect other road users, including

• cars towing caravans

• motorcyclists.

6.53 Which road users are most likely to be affected by the turbulence created by large vehicles travelling at speed?

☐ Drivers of low-loaders

☐ Drivers towing caravans

☐ Drivers of tankers

☐ Drivers of emergency vehicles

DBC s4, DGV s4

Caravans are relatively light but have a large surface area. This makes them vulnerable to the turbulence created by large vehicles travelling at speed. The blast of air can destabilise the caravan, causing it to snake, and in extreme cases they can be blown over.

6.54 You're overtaking a motorcycle in windy conditions. Why should you check your nearside mirror?

❑ To check your road position

❑ To see if the rider is in control of their motorcycle

❑ To see if other vehicles have been affected

❑ To check that it's properly adjusted

DBC s4, DGV s4

You must check the nearside mirror during and after overtaking a motorcyclist. Make sure that the rider is still in control and that your vehicle's draught hasn't caused them to lose their balance.

6.55 Which vehicles are most likely to be affected by high winds?

❑ Slow-moving vehicles   ❑ Track-laying vehicles

❑ Front-wheel-drive vehicles ❑ Curtain-sided vehicles

DBC s4, DGV s4

In very windy conditions, certain types of vehicle can be blown off course. These include box vans, curtain-siders, caravans and motorcycles. Make allowances for how the wind might affect these vehicles, especially if you're overtaking.

6.56 You're driving a high-sided vehicle on a motorway. Where should you be especially aware of the effects of side wind?

❑ In cuttings   ❑ Through tunnels

❑ Across viaducts   ❑ Passing large signs

DBC s4, DGV s4

On motorways, be especially careful when driving over bridges and viaducts. The road here is exposed and in windy weather there's a risk of strong side wind, which may blow you off course or even blow your vehicle over. In severe windy weather, these routes are often closed to drivers of high-sided vehicles.

6.57 You're on a motorway and the surface is still wet after rain. Why should you take care when you're overtaking?

❑ Wet roads may cause more buffeting

❑ Other vehicles will have their lights on

❑ Vehicles may be parked on the hard shoulder

❑ The road may still be slippery

DBC s4, DGV s4

Rain, combined with oil, rubber particles, dirt and debris on the road surface, reduces the tyres' grip on the road. It can be especially slippery when it rains after a long dry spell.

6.58 It's raining. Why would a motorcyclist steer around drain covers on a bend?

❑ To reduce the risk of skidding

❑ To avoid puncturing the tyres

❑ To improve their view around the bend

❑ To avoid splashing pedestrians

DBC s4, DGV s4

Drain covers usually have a metal surface. When wet, these covers are slippery and can cause a motorcycle to skid; be prepared for riders to avoid them.

6.59 What's the minimum distance you should allow for braking when it's raining heavily?

❑ The normal distance

❑ Twice the normal distance

❑ Three times the normal distance

❑ Five times the normal distance

DBC s4, DGV s4

If you're travelling in heavy rain, you should be aware that it could take twice as long for you to stop as it would in dry weather. Increase your distance from the vehicle in front to allow for the longer stopping distance.

6.60 You're driving on a motorway. What should you do if your view ahead is restricted by heavy spray?

❑ Move into the lane on the right

❑ Use the two-second rule

❑ Switch on your dipped headlights

❑ Leave the motorway at the next exit

DBC s4, DGV s4

If you're travelling on a motorway and your view ahead is poor, then you should reduce your speed. Leave at least four seconds between your vehicle and the one in front, and make sure that others can see you by using your dipped headlights.

6.61 What's the greatest risk to your safety when you're overtaking on a motorway in very wet weather?

☐ Your engine may get flooded

☐ Your braking distance may be reduced

☐ Your steering may become heavy

☐ Your tyres may lose grip

DBC s4, DGV s4
In very wet conditions, tyres may be unable to clear all the water from their path. This can result in a layer of water building up between the road and the tyre – a situation known as aquaplaning. To regain control, ease off the accelerator and, as the vehicle slows, the tyres should regain their grip. It's safer to reduce the risk of aquaplaning occurring by driving more slowly in very wet weather.

6.62 What should you be aware of when you're overtaking on a motorway while it's raining heavily?

☐ Manhole covers will be slippery

☐ Visibility will be reduced by spray from traffic

☐ Your braking distances will be reduced

☐ There'll be distracting bright reflections

DBC s4, DGV s4
Other road users can be affected by the spray from large vehicles, severely reducing their vision. Always take care when you need to change lanes: signal in good time and watch your mirrors carefully before pulling out in these conditions.

6.63 Why can visibility be worse when driving at high speed in wet weather?

☐ Drivers bunch together when it's raining

☐ Headlights will dazzle you more easily

☐ Windscreen wipers obstruct your view

☐ More spray will be thrown up

DBC s4, DGV s4
Higher speeds will cause more spray to be thrown up by vehicles' tyres – particularly the tyres of larger vehicles and trailers. Always use dipped headlights in poor visibility caused by rain and spray.

6.64 What should you do if you intend to overtake a lorry that's throwing up spray?

☐ Get much closer before moving out

☐ Wait until the other driver gives a left signal

☐ Move out earlier than normal

☐ Wait for the lorry to slow down on a hill

DBC s4, DGV s4
If you wish to overtake a vehicle that's throwing up spray, move out earlier than normal. This will help to limit the reduction in vision that the rear spray will cause before you pass.

6.65 You're driving in wet weather. What effect will faulty spray-suppression equipment have on other drivers?

☐ Their vision will be increased

☐ Their vision will be reduced

☐ They'll be able to overtake more easily

☐ They'll need to use intermittent wipers

DBC s4, DGV s4
Spray-suppression equipment reduces the amount of spray thrown up to other road users. Check the equipment regularly to make sure it's secure and undamaged.

6.66 Why are brushes fitted to this vehicle's wheel arch?

☐ To clear mud from the tyres on building sites

☐ To remove objects from the tyre tread

☐ To stop snow building up behind the wheel

☐ To reduce spray on wet roads

DBC s4, DGV s4
The brushes are part of a spray-suppression system. They reduce the amount of water thrown up at the sides and rear of the vehicle. Check them regularly for security. If they become worn, make sure they're replaced.

6.67 When should you check your vehicle's spray-suppression equipment?

❑ Only when you'll be using a motorway

❑ Before setting out on every journey

❑ Only as part of a pre-winter check

❑ Once per year before the MOT test

DBC s4, DGV s4
You should always check all your spray-suppression equipment before a journey. Don't ignore it just because it's dry when you set out. The weather can change on the way.

6.68 What component fitted to your vehicle will help following drivers in wet weather?

❑ Spray reducers   ❑ Side-panel skirts

❑ Wind deflectors   ❑ Catalytic converter

DBC s4, DGV s4
Spray reducers or spray-suppression equipment are attachments fitted around the wheel arches of large vehicles. They effectively trap spray thrown up from the wheels, which would otherwise reduce visibility for other road users.

6.69 This vehicle is fitted with spray-suppression equipment. In what weather conditions will it be most useful?

❑ Rain

❑ Snow

❑ Wind

❑ Fog

DBC s4, DGV s4
The spray-suppression equipment helps to prevent water from being thrown up and causing reduced visibility, for you and other drivers. Driving at a reduced speed in wet conditions will also help to reduce the amount of water thrown up by your vehicle's tyres.

6.70 How should you drive through flood water?

❑ Slowly, in a low gear, with engine speed high

❑ Slowly, in a high gear, with engine speed low

❑ As quickly as possible to cause the least delay

❑ At normal speed when you have spray reducers fitted

DBC s4, DGV s4
It's important to use a low gear and keep the engine speed high to prevent water from entering the engine through the exhaust system. In these circumstances, it may be necessary to slip the clutch to keep the road speed as low as possible.

6.71 You're on a motorway, approaching a working snow plough. Why should you stay behind it?

❑ It's illegal to overtake snow ploughs

❑ Snow ploughs are left-hand-drive only

❑ Your speed could cause snow to drift behind

❑ There may be deep snow ahead

DBC s4, DGV s4
There's no way of knowing how deep the snow could be ahead. If you overtake and then become stuck in the snow, you may cause problems for the snow plough, particularly if you block the road.

6.72 You're driving in heavy rain. Why do you need to increase your distance from the vehicle in front?

❑ To prevent rain from entering the vehicle's braking system

❑ To let other motorists move into the gap

❑ To allow for an increased stopping distance

❑ To reduce the risk of water spraying into the filters

DBC s4, DGV s4
Extra care is needed when driving in heavy rain. Reduce your speed and switch on dipped headlights. Tyres will have less grip on a wet road and it will take up to twice the distance to stop when compared with good dry conditions.

6.73 You're driving a large vehicle In heavy rain on a motorway. You slow down to reduce the risk of aquaplaning. For what other reason should you slow down?

❑ To force other drivers to act properly and slow down

❑ To reduce the amount of spray thrown up

❑ To prevent water from entering the braking system

❑ To stop the electrics getting wet

DBC s4, DGV s4
Driving at high speed on a wet motorway can throw up dense spray, making it very difficult for other drivers to see ahead. Driving more slowly reduces the amount of spray and this makes it safer for other drivers.

6.74 You're driving on a motorway in heavy rain. When are you allowed to use high-intensity rear fog lights?

❏ When visibility is more than 100 metres (328 feet)

❏ Only when the national speed limit applies

❏ Only when you're being followed closely by other traffic

❏ When visibility is reduced to 100 metres (328 feet) or less

HC r114, 226
Heavy rain and the resulting spray from large vehicles travelling at speed can seriously affect visibility on the motorway. Reduce your speed and use your headlights. Don't use high-intensity rear lights unless visibility is reduced to 100 metres (328 feet) or less.

6.75 You're driving on a motorway in heavy rain. What could cause your steering to become unresponsive?

❏ Water reducing the tyres' grip on the road

❏ Tyres becoming hotter in the bad weather

❏ Braking gently and in good time

❏ Water entering the braking system

DBC s4, DGV s4
If a build-up of water prevents the tyres from gripping the road, the steering can become unresponsive. If this happens, ease off the accelerator and slow down gradually.

6.76 You're driving downhill. How will this affect your vehicle?

❏ It will need more engine power

❏ It will take longer to stop

❏ It will increase fuel consumption

❏ It will be easier to change direction

DBC s2, DGV s2
When driving downhill, gravity will cause the vehicle to increase speed. More braking effort will be required, and stopping distances will increase.

6.77 The road is wet. Why should you slow down as you approach this pedestrian?

❏ Because there are no road markings

❏ To avoid splashing them

❏ Because they have priority

❏ To encourage them to cross

DBC s4, DGV s1
When the roads are wet, have consideration for pedestrians walking or standing near the kerb.

6.78 Why is tailgating dangerous?

❏ You're likely to be distracted

❏ Your engine will overheat

❏ Your view to the rear is reduced

❏ Your view ahead is reduced

DBC s1, 4, DGV s1
Tailgating is very dangerous because there isn't enough room to stop if an emergency arises. It's also intimidating for the driver that you're following.

6.79 When may you use your vehicle's hazard warning lights while it's moving?

❏ When you've just overtaken another vehicle

❏ When you need to reverse for some distance

❏ When you're on a motorway and traffic ahead slows suddenly

❏ When one of your lights has failed

DBC s4, DGV s4
While moving, hazard warning lights may only be used on a motorway or unrestricted dual carriageway to warn drivers behind of a need to slow down, due to a hazard ahead.

6.80 You're driving in town and see these lights flashing. What would you expect to see ahead?

□ Contraflow system

□ Uneven road surface

□ Children crossing the road

□ Roadworks ahead

DBC s4, DGV s4

These lights warn that children are likely to be crossing the road on their way to and from school. Slow down and watch out for them.

6.81 Where are these lights found?

□ On approach to a level crossing □ Near a fire station

□ On approach to a motorway □ Near a school

DBC s4, DGV s4

Flashing amber lights are found near schools. They warn you that children are likely to be crossing the road on their way to and from school. Drive slowly until you're clear of the area.

6.82 What problem may you have when driving at night?

□ It's more difficult to keep to speed limits

□ There'll be an increase in traffic

□ You'll have reduced visibility

□ It takes longer to stop

DBC s4, DGV s4

You must be able to stop safely in the distance that you can see to be clear ahead. This will be the distance illuminated by your headlights or by street lights and will generally be less than you can see in daylight.

6.83 Why should you take extra care when overtaking at night?

□ Every driver will normally be tired

□ Large vehicles are subject to a 10% speed reduction

□ Speed and distance are harder to judge

□ Most towns aren't adequately lit

DBC s4, DGV s4

In the darkness, it will be difficult to assess the road ahead – especially if there are bends or hills, which may prevent you from seeing oncoming vehicles.

6.84 You're driving along a motorway in thick fog at night. The reflective studs are red on your left and white on your right. Which lane are you in?

□ The right-hand lane □ The hard shoulder

□ The left-hand lane □ The middle lane

DBC s4, DGV s4, HC r132

The red studs on your left indicate the edge of the hard shoulder, while the white studs are used between the lanes. Using more than one reference point will help you to be certain of your position.

6.85 You're driving in the left-hand lane on a three-lane motorway. What should you check for before moving into the middle lane to overtake a slower vehicle?

□ Traffic behind in the right-hand lane, returning to the middle lane

□ Traffic that's intending to leave at the next exit

□ Traffic ahead moving into the right-hand lane

□ Traffic behind that's trying to pass on your left

DBC s4, DGV s4

Traffic behind that's returning from the right-hand lane is a hazard to be aware of before you move into the middle lane to overtake. Checking your blind spot can help you see these vehicles before you commit to changing lanes.

6.86 What should you do before changing lanes to overtake on a motorway?

□ Check your mirrors carefully

□ Change to a lower gear

□ Look over your left shoulder

□ Increase your speed gently

DC s4, DGV s4

Check your mirrors to make sure that it's safe to overtake. Remember that traffic coming up behind will be travelling at a faster speed.

6.87   Which lane should you use when you're driving on a clear motorway, at the speed limit for your vehicle?

❑ Any lane   ❑ The middle lane

❑ The right-hand lane   ❑ The left-hand lane

DC s4, DGV s4

You should remain in the left-hand lane unless you're overtaking other vehicles. Don't be inconsiderate and stay in the centre lane or other overtaking lanes when you've finished overtaking.

6.88   You're driving in the left-hand lane of a motorway. What should you do when you see a large vehicle merging from a slip road ahead?

❑ Try to race and get ahead of it

❑ Leave the other vehicle to adjust its speed

❑ Stay at the maximum speed allowed for your vehicle

❑ Be ready to adjust your speed

DBC s4, DGV s4

It's not always possible for drivers in the left-hand lane to change lanes to let joining traffic merge. However, you should be ready to adjust your speed to help the joining driver merge safely.

6.89   You're driving at the speed limit in the left hand lane of a motorway. What should you do if you see lorries merging from a slip road ahead?

❑ Try to accelerate past them

❑ Move to the next lane if it's safe

❑ Brake heavily and let them merge

❑ Expect them to stop and let you pass

DBC s4, DGV s4

Only change lanes if doing so won't inconvenience another road user. Merging drivers have a responsibility to give way, if necessary, and not force their way onto the main carriageway. Planning ahead will ensure you're prepared to deal with these situations.

6.90   Why should you take care before moving into the centre lane of a three-lane motorway?

❑ The centre lane is narrower than the left-hand lane

❑ The bridge height clearance will be less in the centre lane

❑ Traffic in the centre lane may be travelling much faster than you

❑ The reflective studs may be missing in the centre lane

DBC s4, DGV s4

Always indicate your intentions in good time; this will allow others time to alter their speed and course if necessary. Always check your blind spots before changing lanes.

6.91   When may vehicles over 7.5 tonnes maximum authorised mass (MAM) use the right-hand lane of a motorway to overtake?

❑ When the motorway has three lanes

❑ When vehicles are stopped on the hard shoulder

❑ When the motorway has two lanes

❑ When other vehicles are turning right

DBC s4, DGV s4

Goods and passenger vehicles with a MAM of more than 7.5 tonnes, those required to be fitted with a speed limiter, and vehicles towing trailers must not use the right-hand lane on a motorway with more than two lanes, unless there are exceptional circumstances.

6.92   You've just overtaken another vehicle on a motorway. What should you avoid when moving back to the left?

❑ Cutting in   ❑ Increasing your speed

❑ Changing gear   ❑ Signalling

DBC s4, DGV s4

After overtaking, check your nearside mirror carefully before moving back to the left. Don't rely on the other driver flashing their headlights, because only you can make the decision that it's safe.

6.93 What's a crawler lane for?

❑ To enable other traffic to overtake on the nearside

❑ To enable large vehicles to park out of the way

❑ To enable slow-moving traffic to move further over to the left on uphill gradients

❑ To enable emergency vehicles to get quickly to the scene of an incident

DBC s4, DGV s4
On a motorway where there's a long uphill gradient, there may be a crawler lane. This helps the traffic to flow by making an extra lane available on the left for slower, heavy vehicles.

6.94 What does this motorway sign mean?

❑ You're approaching a long downhill slope

❑ You're approaching a long uphill slope

❑ You're approaching a 'lorries only' lane

❑ You're approaching a service area

DBC s4, DGV s4
The term 'crawler lane' doesn't mean the lane is only for extremely slow vehicles. It's advising you of an extra lane on the left. Crawler lanes are usually built on sections of road where the length of the gradient is such that some large vehicles will be slowed to the point where they become a hazard for other road users.

6.95 When should you use a crawler lane?

❑ When letting faster traffic overtake you

❑ When turning right from a major road

❑ When parking to have a rest

❑ When slowing down for a motorway exit

DBC s4, DGV s4
Many vehicles are very powerful and can maintain speed even when climbing a gradient Even if your vehicle is capable of maintaining speed, you can still use the crawler lane to make it easier for other road users to overtake safely.

6.96 What should you do before overtaking on a single carriageway road?

❑ Flash your headlights at oncoming traffic

❑ Look ahead for road junctions

❑ Drive very close to the vehicle in front

❑ Make a final check in your left-hand mirror

HC r167
Before overtaking, you need to make sure it's safe to carry out the manoeuvre. As part of your check, look well ahead for road junctions. You shouldn't overtake as you approach a road junction, because if a vehicle emerges, or has to wait to turn, you could risk a collision.

6.97 When shouldn't you overtake?

❑ When the speed limit has been reduced

❑ When you're approaching motorway slip roads

❑ When you would have to break the speed limit

❑ When your view of the road ahead is clear

HC r166-167
Never commit yourself to overtaking unless you're absolutely certain that you have the time and space to complete the manoeuvre safely. Don't take any risks that will endanger other road users.

6.98 You've just overtaken another large vehicle. How do you know when it's safe to move back to the nearside lane?

❑ By waiting for the driver you've overtaken to flash their headlights

❑ By checking your nearside mirror

❑ By using your hazard warning lights as a signal

❑ By moving to the nearside, hoping the other vehicle will slow down

DBC s4, DGV s4
While overtaking, you'll need to judge carefully when to return to the nearside lane. Check your left-hand (nearside) mirror to make sure the rear of your vehicle is well clear. You should allow for the length of both vehicles and take into account the speed difference. Don't cut in too soon on the vehicle you've overtaken, and don't rely on signals from other drivers; they may be signalling to someone else.

6.99 You're driving on a dual carriageway and Intend to overtake the vehicle ahead. What should you do if there's a car approaching quickly behind you in the right-hand lane?

☐ Stay behind the slower vehicle

☐ Signal right and move out

☐ Move up closer to the slower vehicle

☐ Signal left while waiting for the car to pass

DBC s4, DGV s4
You should allow the faster moving vehicle to overtake safely. If you pull out to overtake at this time, you'll cause the car behind to brake sharply. Don't use the size of your vehicle to intimidate. Be professional and show consideration to other road users.

6.100 What should you do after overtaking on a dual carriageway?

☐ Move back to the left when it's safe to do so

☐ Indicate left, then right

☐ Wait for the other driver to flash their headlights

☐ Switch your rear lights on and off

DBC s4, DGV s4
Signal if necessary and move back to the left as soon as It's safe to do so. Don't drive for long distances in the centre or right-hand lane unnecessarily.

6.101 You're driving a long vehicle and want to tum right at a roundabout ahead. How should you signalif you need to occupy the left-hand lane?

☐ Signal left on approach

☐ Signal right on approach

☐ Give no signal on approach

☐ Give a right signal after entering the roundabout

DBC s6, DGV s6
There are times when, due to the size of your vehicle, you'll have to take up part of another lane. If you need to do this, make sure that you use effective observation all around. Be aware that other road users might not understand the reasons for your position on the road. You should signal your intentions and take up your position in good time.

6.102 When do drivers of long vehicles need to straddle lanes?

☐ When they need to avoid braking sharply

☐ When driving on motorways

☐ When they need to avoid mounting the kerb

☐ When coming to contraflow systems

DBC s6, DGV s6
When you have to straddle the lanes at small roundabouts or junctions, always signal in good time. Be alert for inexperienced road users who may, without realising, put themselves Into a dangerous position.

6.103 What should you do as you approach these roadworks?

☐ Check your mirrors   ☐ Select a higher gear

☐ Flash your headlights ☐ Use your endurance brake

DBC s4, DGV s4, HC r288
Before changing direction, you should check your mirrors for any vehicles that may be overtaking. An overtaking driver or rider might not have seen the narrowing road ahead. You should let them get past before you move across to the right.

6.104 What should you do when you're overtaking a motorcyclist in very windy conditions?

☐ Allow extra room

☐ Overtake slowly

☐ Sound your horn as you pass

☐ Keep close as you pass

DBC s4, DGV s4
Cyclists and motorcyclists may become unbalanced by your vehicle passing too close. Plan ahead and give them plenty of room. Remember that your large vehicle can cause a vacuum, which will suck the rider towards it. The noise and close proximity of your vehicle can also startle them, and could cause them to swerve suddenly.

6.105 You're driving behind two cyclists. They're approaching a roundabout in the left-hand lane. What should you expect them to do?

☐ Go in any direction   ☐ Turn left

☐ Turn right   ☐ Go straight ahead

DBC s4, DGV s4

When following cyclists onto a roundabout, be aware that they might not take the exit you expect them to. Cyclists approaching in the left-hand lane may be turning right. They may not have been able to get into the correct lane due to heavy traffic, so give them room.

6.106 What should you do before you start to overtake a lorry?

☐ Look well ahead for uphill gradients

☐ Check your position in the left-hand mirror

☐ Change quickly to a higher gear

☐ Close right up before pulling out

DBC s6, DGV s6

Plan your overtaking carefully. The weight of your vehicle, combined with the restrictions imposed by a speed limiter, is likely to make your vehicle lose speed on uphill gradients. You should take this into consideration before attempting to overtake another moving vehicle.

6.107 You're in the left-hand lane on a three-lane motorway. Why should you check for any vehicles in the right-hand lane before you overtake?

☐ They may be moving faster than you

☐ They may move back to the middle lane as you move out

☐ They may cut in sharply behind you

☐ They may accelerate briskly in front of you

DBC s4, DGV s4

Vehicles overtaking in the right-hand lane may return to the centre lane when they've finished their manoeuvre. You should look for this before starting to pull out. Don't rely on the size of your vehicle to claim right of way.

6.108 What does it indicate if you see white lights on a vehicle at night?

☐ It's moving away from you

☐ It's stationary and facing away from you

☐ It's ahead of you and braking

☐ It's facing towards you

DBC s4, DGV s4

At night, you can tell whether a vehicle is facing towards or away from you by the colour of its lights. Additionally, its brake lights or indicators can give you information about its direction and intentions. This information helps you to make safe driving decisions.

6.109 You're driving at night. Why should you ensure that all your lights are clean and working correctly?

☐ To allow following drivers to use dipped headlights

☐ To prevent the battery from overcharging

☐ So that other road users can see the size of your vehicle

☐ So that the intensity of street lighting can be reduced

DBC s4, DGV s4

As well as headlights and tail lights, large vehicles have additional lighting to help other road users see the size of the vehicle. All lights should be clean and working properly. Driving at night when your vehicle is poorly lit is dangerous for you and other road users.

6.110 You're driving in fog. When should high-intensity rear fog lights be used?

☐ When visibility falls below 100 metres (328 feet)

☐ When visibility falls below 200 metres (656 feet)

☐ When visibility falls below 300 metres (984 feet)

☐ When visibility falls below 400 metres (1312 feet)

DBC s4, DGV s4, HC r114, 226

In dense fog, large vehicles are no more visible than any other. If visibility falls below 100 metres (328 feet), use your fog lights to help other drivers see you.

6.111 You're driving in fog that's starting to clear. When should you switch off your high Intensity rear fog lights?

❏ When visibility is more than 10 metres (32 feet)

❏ When visibility is more than 50 metres (164 feet)

❏ When visibility is more than 75 metres (246 feet)

❏ When visibility is more than 100 metres (328 feet)

HC r114, 226
Switch off your fog lights when fog starts to clear and visibility improves to more than 100 metres (328 feet). Don't leave your fog lights on when the fog has cleared, because they can cause unnecessary glare or distraction for other drivers.

6.112 In fast traffic, when should you leave a two-second gap between your vehicle and the one in front?

❏ When the roads are dry

❏ When it's raining and the roads are wet

❏ When the roads are icy

❏ When you're driving in fog

DBC s4, DGV s4, HC r126
In good dry conditions, you should leave a two-second gap between your vehicle and the one ahead. When the weather is bad, you'll have to keep a greater distance, because it will take you longer to stop. In wet weather it will take up to twice the distance; in icy weather this could increase to ten times as far.

6.113 What should you do if you see a vehicle too close behind when you're driving in traffic on the motorway?

❏ Increase your distance from the vehicle in front

❏ Touch the brake pedal sharply to show your brake lights

❏ Briskly accelerate away from the vehicle behind

❏ Switch your rear fog lamps on and off

DBC s4; DGV s4
The faster the traffic is moving, the greater the distance that needs to be kept between vehicles to maintain safety margins. If you find another vehicle driving too close behind you, gradually reduce your speed to increase your distance from the vehicle in front. You'll then be able to brake more gently when you need to, reducing the likelihood of the vehicle behind running into the back of your vehicle.

6.114 What should you do If an overtaking vehicle pulls in too close in front of you?

❏ Slow down   ❏ Stay close behind

❏ Overtake when you can ❏ Flash your headlights

DBC s4; DGV s4
Always maintain a safe following distance from the vehicle in front. If another vehicle pulls into the gap, slow down to re-establish a safe following distance.

Following too close is dangerous and places you and other road users in unnecessary danger; your view of the road ahead will be seriously reduced, and you won't be able to see or plan effectively.

6.115 You're driving at 50 mph (80 km/h) on a dry, level road. What gap should you leave between your vehicle and the one in front?

❏ One vehicle length

❏ Two vehicle lengths

❏ At least a one-second gap

❏ At least a two-second gap

DBC s4, DGV s4, HC r126
'Tailgating' – travelling too close to the vehicle in front – is very dangerous, because it doesn't give you enough distance to stop safely.

Leave at least a two-second gap in good conditions, and increase this to four seconds in wet weather.

6.116 You're following a large vehicle. How can you improve your view ahead?

❏ Drop further back   ❏ Move over to the right

❏ Move over to the left ❏ Overtake as soon as you can

DBC s4; DGV s4
Staying well behind the vehicle in front will improve your view of the road ahead. This will give you more time and room to react to hazards. Use the two-second rule to make sure you're not too close. Don't move out to the right, as this could put you into the path of an oncoming vehicle or obstruct smaller vehicles that wish to overtake.

6.117   What must you be certain of before you overtake at night?

❑ You can see well ahead

❑ The road's well lit

❑ There's an overtaking lane

❑ You're outside a built-up area

DBC s4; DGV s4

It's more difficult to judge speed and distance accurately in the dark. Darkness can also hide bends and dips in the road. Plan ahead, and be sure that you have time and space to complete your overtaking safely.

6.118   How much longer will your stopping distance be in snow than in dry weather?

❑ Twice as long   ❑ Four times as long

❑ Five times as long ❑ Ten times as long

DBC s4; DGV s4, HC r126

In icy or snowy weather, your stopping distance can increase by up to ten times. Because snowy weather increases the distance needed to stop, you must look further ahead and leave an increased safety margin.

6.119   How should you slow down or stop when you're driving on an icy road?

❑ Brake gently and in good time

❑ Always use the retarder

❑ Change down through the gears

❑ Use the parking brake in a rapid on-and-off movement

DBC s4; DGV s4

When you have to slow down or stop, you should always avoid harsh, late braking. This is particularly important on icy or slippery roads, where you need to brake gently and in good time to make sure you keep control of your vehicle.

6.120   How should you use the brakes in icy weather?

❑ Suddenly   ❑ By pumping the brake pedal

❑ Gently   ❑ After using the gears first

DBC s4; DGV s4

In poor conditions, all braking should be controlled, in good time and when travelling in a straight line. Try to avoid braking and turning at the same time. Look well ahead to assess and plan your actions.

6.121   When should you use the two-second rule?

❑ To keep a safe distance from the vehicle in front when it's raining

❑ To keep a safe distance from the vehicle in front when conditions are good

❑ To keep a safe distance from the vehicle in front when it's icy

❑ To keep a safe distance from the vehicle in front in queuing traffic

DBC s4; DGV s4, HC r126

Use the two-second rule when conditions are good and you're driving on roads carrying faster-moving traffic. Choose a fixed reference point, and when the vehicle ahead passes that point say to yourself 'Only a fool breaks the two-second rule.' If you reach the object before you finish saying this, you're too close and you need to drop back and check again.

6.122   Why is it dangerous to follow a large goods vehicle too closely?

❑ Your field of vision will be seriously reduced

❑ Your cab will fill with fumes

❑ Your engine will overheat

❑ Your brakes will overheat

DBC s4, DGV s4

Staying back will increase your view of the road ahead. This will help you to see any hazards that might occur and will allow you more time to react. It will also allow the driver in front to see you in their mirrors.

6.123   What time gap should you leave when you're following a vehicle on a wet road?

❑ At least one second   ❑ At least two seconds

❑ At least three seconds ❑ At least four seconds

DBC s4; DGV s4, HC r126

Wet roads will increase the time it takes you to stop. Four seconds is the minimum gap you should leave on wet roads. This is double the gap you should normally keep from the vehicle in front on good, dry roads.

6.124 The entrances to roundabouts are often slippery when they're wet. How should you deal with this hazard?

☐ Stay in the left-hand lane

☐ Brake in good time

☐ Use the handbrake

☐ Stop before emerging

DBC s4, DGV s4

The entrances to roundabouts are often worn. This can make the surface slippery, especially when it's wet. You should plan your approach and brake in good time.

6.125 You're driving in wet conditions. What should you try to do before braking?

☐ Make sure that the gear lever is in neutral

☐ Make sure that all spray-suppression equipment is working

☐ Make sure that there's no mist on your rear-view mirrors

☐ Make sure that your vehicle is travelling in a straight line

DBC s2, 4, DGV s4

If you need to brake when the road surface is wet, do so while your vehicle is travelling in a straight line. This will reduce the risk of skidding. As a professional driver, you should routinely brake in good time, so that you don't brake and change direction at the same time.

6.126 You're driving a fully laden vehicle approaching an uphill gradient. What will happen if you start to overtake?

☐ You'll be able to get past more quickly

☐ The weight of the load will help you go faster

☐ You'll take longer to get past

☐ You'll need to use a high gear

DBC s4, DGV s4

Always plan well ahead before overtaking. Take into consideration the size of your vehicle and whether there's a gradient ahead. The load on your vehicle will slow you down on an uphill gradient. It may be better to wait until you're on the level before trying to overtake.

6.127 You're on a motorway and there's a strong side wind. Which vehicle is particularly at risk?

☐ A motorcycle   ☐ A taxi

☐ A sports car   ☐ A road tanker

DBC s4, DGV s4

Motorcycles can be very vulnerable to strong side wind. Allow extra room when overtaking them in windy weather. Check your nearside mirror while alongside and before moving back to the left.

6.128 You're driving at a speed of 50 mph (80 km/h) in good, dry conditions. What distance should you stay behind the vehicle in front?

☐ At least 23 metres (75 feet)

☐ At least 36 metres (118 feet)

☐ At least 53 metres (175 feet)

☐ At least 73 metres (240 feet)

DBC s4, DGV s4

You should always leave a safety margin between your vehicle and the one In front. This gap will give you a better view of the road ahead. It will also allow you time to react if the traffic in front changes speed or direction.

6.129 You're driving on a motorway after it's been raining heavily. What should you do if spray is being thrown up, causing poor visibility?

☐ Keep a two-second gap

☐ Reduce your separation distance

☐ Remove spray-suppression equipment

☐ Use dipped headlights

DBC s4, DGV s4

When visibility is poor or the road is wet, leave a greater separation distance – at least a four-second time gap from the vehicle in front. You should also reduce speed and use dipped headlights.

6.130 You'll be driving a high-floor coach. You'll be going over several high bridges. Why should you check the weather forecast before starting your journey?

- ❑ Rain can make crossing bridges very difficult for buses and coaches
- ❑ In hot weather, the bridges might be closed to heavy traffic
- ❑ You won't be able to climb the bridges if it's frosty
- ❑ Some roads may be closed to certain vehicles in high winds

DBC s4
Some exposed places are frequently subject to high winds. These include high-level bridges and roads, viaducts and some motorways. Check the weather forecast and plan an alternative route. Remember, you're responsible for your passengers' safety. Don't ignore warnings of severe winds.

6.131 It's raining heavily. What effect could this have when you overtake a cyclist?

- ❑ Spray could affect their control
- ❑ Exhaust fumes are more toxic when it's raining
- ❑ Noise from your engine will be louder
- ❑ Buffeting will be reduced

DBC s4
When passing other road users – especially motorcyclists and cyclists – in wet weather, the spray from your vehicle could affect their control. Leave plenty of room as you pass, and look in your left hand mirror to check that they're still in control.

6.132 How is a strong wind likely to affect your bus?

- ❑ Steering will be easier
- ❑ Your stopping distances will be reduced
- ❑ Your stopping distances will be greater
- ❑ Steering will be more difficult

DBC s4
Be alert for places where the road is shielded from the wind. When you leave this shelter, the wind may suddenly blow you off course, making steering more difficult.

6.133 What will affect a double-deck bus more than a single-deck bus?

- ❑ Strong wind   ❑ Heavy rain
- ❑ Thick fog   ❑ Dense spray

DBC s4
If you're driving a double-deck bus, you'll feel the effect of the wind more than you would on a single deck vehicle. This is because the vehicle's height increases the surface area that can be affected by the wind.

6.134 You're driving a bus on a windy day. What should you do when you're overtaking a motorcyclist?

- ❑ Pass close to shield them from the wind
- ❑ Move back early to protect them from buffeting
- ❑ Pass wide in case they're blown off course
- ❑ Signal left so they know you're pulling in

DBC s4
In strong wind, motorcyclists can be blown off course. Allow them plenty of room when you're overtaking, in case they're blown into your path.

6.135 In which type of weather is spray-suppression equipment particularly useful?

- ❑ Rain   ❑ Ice   ❑ Fog   ❑ Wind

DBC s4
If there's heavy rain, the spray-suppression equipment fitted to your vehicle will protect other road users from loss of vision when following or passing your vehicle. Check the wheel arches to make sure the fitments haven't worked loose and no parts have broken off. Well-maintained equipment will force the spray back down onto the road, instead of out to the rear and the sides of the vehicle.

6.136 You're driving a long bus. When would you need to straddle lanes?

- ❑ Only when joining a bus lane
- ❑ On all bends and corners
- ❑ On the approach to all roundabouts
- ❑ To avoid mounting the kerb

DBC s2
There may be times when you have to take up part of another lane in order to make a turn or manoeuvre. Use your mirrors and check for other traffic that might try to move into the gap you've left to make your turn. Signal and take up your position in good time.

6.137 What must bus and coach drivers do when they park their vehicle on the road at night?

❑ They must park under street lights

❑ They must park within 25 metres (82 feet) of a street light

❑ They must leave all the interior lights switched on

❑ They must leave their parking lights switched on

DBC s4
All buses and coaches and most minibuses – depending on their weight – must have their parking lights switched on when they're parked on the road at night. Make sure that all your lights are clean and working properly.

6.138 You're driving a bus at night on a road without street lighting. Why could it be dangerous to overtake?

❑ There may be unseen dips or bends in the road

❑ You may dazzle other drivers

❑ It's harder to concentrate

❑ It's harder to keep control in the dark

DBC s4
On unlit roads, it's more difficult to see bends, junctions or dips ahead. This could prevent you from seeing oncoming traffic, pedestrians or cyclists. Unless the road is well lit or you're on a dual carriageway, ask yourself whether overtaking is absolutely necessary.

6.139 Why do some buses have marker lights along their sides?

❑ To make them easier to overtake

❑ To help the driver when reversing

❑ To help any passengers getting on or off

❑ To make them easier to see at junctions

DBC s4
Newer buses and coaches have marker lights along the side; these ensure that they're visible as they emerge at junctions, roundabouts and in other situations. If your vehicle has marker lights fitted, they must all be clean and working.

6.140 You're driving a bus. Where should you be aware of the risk of grounding?

❑ On a hump bridge   ❑ In a crawler lane

❑ On a left-hand bend   ❑ In a narrow street

DBC s3
You must be aware of the risk of grounding; for example, on a hump bridge. Look ahead for advance warning signs. If you decide to divert to avoid the hazard, make sure your new route doesn't also have a restriction that would be impassable for your vehicle.

Section 7 Incidents, accidents and emergencies

7.1 What should you do when there's a fire in your vehicle's engine compartment?

❏ Open all windows

❏ Try to remove the load

❏ Flag down a passing motorist

❏ Cut off the fuel supply

DGV s4
If you suspect a fire, try to isolate the source. If possible, disconnect electrical leads and cut off the fuel supply.

7.2 What training must you take before driving a lorry loaded with toxic substances?

❏ How to use fire-fighting equipment

❏ How to operate a forklift truck

❏ How to operate a lorry-mounted crane

❏ How to use breathing apparatus

DGV s2, 3
Vehicles carrying dangerous goods and other materials that may pose a hazard are subject to detailed emergency procedures. These procedures must be followed. Appropriate fire-fighting equipment must be available and the driver must be trained in its use.

7.3 You're approaching a bridge that has no height restriction on it. What's the minimum height under the bridge?

❏ 3.6 metres (11 feet 10 inches)

❏ 4.4 metres (14 feet 5 inches)

❏ 4.8 metres (16 feet

❏ 5 metres (16 feet 6 inches)

DBC s3, DGV s2
The headroom under bridges in the UK is at least 5 metres (16 feet 6 inches), unless otherwise stated. Where the overhead clearance is arched, this headroom is normally only between the limits marked.

7.4 What should you do first to help someone who's unconscious at the scene of an incident?

❏ Try to get them to drink water

❏ Look for any witnesses

❏ Take the numbers of any vehicles involved

❏ Check that they're breathing

DBC s4, DGV s4
Gently tilt the unconscious person's head to clear their airway. Check for at least 10 seconds that the casualty is breathing by looking for movement in the chest, listening for sounds and feeling for breath on your cheek. Get someone to call the emergency services.

7.5 What must you do if you're involved in a traffic incident?

❏ Drive on for help

❏ Inform the police within seven days

❏ Stop at the scene

❏ Drive to the nearest police station

DBC s4, DGV s4
If your vehicle is involved in a traffic incident, you must stop. Follow the guidance set out In The Highway Code if there's injury or damage to any other person, vehicle or property.

7.6 Your vehicle is Involved in an incident where someone is injured. You don't produce your insurance certificate at the time. How soon must you report the incident to the police?

❏ 24 hours   ❏ 48 hours   ❏ 72 hours   ❏ Seven days

DBC s4, DGV s4   Ni Exempt
If you don't give your name and address at the time of an incident, report it to the police as soon as you can, or in any case within 24 hours. If any other person is injured and you don't produce your insurance certificate to the police at the time of the incident, or to any other person who has reasonable grounds to request it, you must also

• report the incident to the police as soon as possible, or in any case within 24 hours

• produce your insurance certificate to the police either when reporting the incident or within seven days (five days in Northern Ireland) at any police station.

7.7 You're at the scene of an incident. What does it mean if there's a plain orange rectangle displayed on one of the vehicles?

❑ It's carrying dangerous good

❑ It's carrying a first-aid kit

❑ It's carrying medical supplies

❑ It's unladen

DBC s4, DGV s4
Vehicles that carry dangerous goods have badges displayed on the side and rear. The badges are orange and show the type of material that's being carried. Make a note of this and report it to the emergency services when you contact them.

7.8 You arrive at an incident where someone is suffering from severe burns. What should you do to help?

❑ Douse the burns with cool wate

❑ Remove anything stuck to the burns

❑ Burst blisters that form on the burns

❑ Apply ointment to the burns

DBC s4, DGV s4
Clean, cool water will cool the burning tissue and help prevent further damage. It will also reduce swelling, minimise shock and alleviate pain.

7.9 You're waiting for the emergency services to arrive at the scene of an incident. A pedestrian's leg is bleeding heavily, but there's nothing embedded in the wound. What could you do to help?

❑ Apply firm pressure to the wound

❑ Dab the wound to stop the bleeding

❑ Put the casualty into the recovery position

❑ Wrap an ice pack near the wound

DBC s4, DGV s4
Before helping the pedestrian, you should protect yourself from contact with blood. If there's nothing embedded in the wound, you can stem the flow of blood by applying pressure to the wound area. As soon as practical, fasten a pad to the wound with a bandage or cloth.

7.10 At the scene of an incident, an injured person is lying in a busy road. What's the first thing you should do to help?

❑ Treat the person for shock

❑ Warn other traffic

❑ Place them in the recovery position

❑ Make sure the injured person is kept warm

DBC s4, DGV s4
You should warn other road users that there has been a incident. You can do this by displaying an advance warning triangle or by switching on hazard warning lights or other lights. However you choose to warn people of the incident, make sure it doesn't put you or others at risk.

7.11 You're the first person to arrive at an incident where people are badly injured. What's the first thing you should do?

❑ Switch on your own hazard warning lights

❑ Contact the local radio station to tell them about the incident

❑ Try and get people who are injured to drink something

❑ Move the people who are injured clear of their vehicles

DBC s4, DGV s4
If you're the first to arrive at an incident, further collisions and fire are the immediate concerns. Switch on your hazard warning lights to warn other traffic. Stop any running vehicle engines to reduce the risk of fire. Don't assume that someone else has called the emergency services – do it yourself. Don't move casualties trapped in vehicles unless they're in danger.

7.12 You arrive at an incident where a motorcyclist is lying in the road, unconscious and bleeding. The area is safe and the emergency services have been called. What's the first priority when checking the rider?

❑ Remove their helmet

❑ Stop the bleeding

❑ Check their airway is open

❑ Move them off the road

DBC s4, DGV s4
At a traffic incident, the danger of further collisions and fire needs to be dealt with and the emergency services must be called. When helping a casualty, follow the DR ABC procedure, as this has been designed by medical experts to give the best outcome while waiting for the emergency services to arrive. Don't remove a motorcyclist's helmet unless it's essential to do so.

7.13 You're the first person to arrive at an incident where a motorcyclist is lying unconscious and unresponsive. You've warned other traffic and called the emergency services. What's the first check you should make on the casualty?

☐ Whether their airway is open

☐ Whether they're bleeding

☐ Whether they have broken bones

☐ Whether they have any bruising

DBC s4, DGV s4
At the scene of an incident, first make sure there's no danger of further collisions or fire before calling the emergency services. If the casualty is unresponsive, check that their airway is open and that they're breathing normally. Don't remove their helmet unless it's essential, as this could make an injury worse.

7.14 You arrive at the scene of an incident and someone is unconscious. What's the first thing you should do to help them?

☐ Take the numbers of the vehicles involved

☐ Try to get them to drink water

☐ Check that they're breathing

☐ Look for any witnesses

DBC s4, DGV s4
The priority when dealing with an unconscious person is to make sure their airway is open and they can breathe. Stay with the casualty and make sure someone rings for an ambulance.

7.15 You've stopped at the scene of an incident where there are casualties. What should you do to help while waiting for the emergency services to arrive?

☐ Keep injured people warm and comfortable

☐ Clear debris from the road

☐ Keep injured people on the move by walking them around

☐ Give injured people a warm drink

DBC s4, DGV s4
If you stop to give help at an incident and there are casualties, don't move injured people unless there's further danger. Keep them warm, comfortable and calm. Don't give them anything to drink.

7.16 You arrive at the scene of an incident where someone is injured. What should be given urgent priority?

☐ Deal with the danger from further collisions or fire

☐ Get the casualty a warm drink

☐ Take details of any witnesses

☐ Take the numbers of the vehicles involved

DBC s4, DGV s4
Make the area safe and call the emergency services first. If you're able to give first aid, follow the DR ABC procedure. If you feel you aren't capable of carrying out first aid, consider taking some training. It could save a life.

7.17 You're at the scene of an incident. How can you help someone suffering from shock?

☐ Reassure them confidently

☐ Offer them a cigarette

☐ Keep them moving

☐ Give them a warm drink

DBC s4, DGV s4
Immediate treatment can help to reduce the effects of shock. Reassure the casualty and try to keep them warm and comfortable. Only move a casualty if it's necessary for their safety.

7.18 What should you do if you're the first person to arrive at the scene of an incident?

☐ Warn other traffic to prevent further collisions

☐ Take photographs of the scene

☐ Offer a calming cigarette to those involved

☐ Ask everyone who isn't injured to leave

DBC s4, DGV s4
Warn other traffic of the incident, without putting yourself or others at risk. Once the danger of further collisions is dealt with, call the emergency services. While you're waiting for them to arrive, keeping casualties or witnesses calm is important, but never offer a cigarette because of the risk of fire.

7.19 There's been an incident. What can you do to help a driver who's suffering from shock?

❏ Give them a drink

❏ Offer them a cigarette

❏ Ask who caused the collision

❏ Reassure them confidently

DBC s4, DGV s4

You can help someone suffering from shock by talking to them and reassuring them confidently. Don't leave them alone or give them anything to eat or drink.

7.20 You arrive at the scene of an incident where a motorcyclist is lying in the middle of the road and unconscious. What's the first thing you should do?

❏ Move the rider out of the road

❏ Warn other traffic

❏ Clear the road of debris

❏ Give the rider reassurance

DBC s4, DGV s4

At the scene of an incident, the first priority is to prevent any further collisions by warning traffic. You can warn other traffic by switching on hazard warning lights or displaying an advance warning triangle, or by any other appropriate means.

7.21 You're trying to resuscitate a casualty who isn't breathing. For how long should you continue compressions if they haven't started breathing again?

❏ Give up if you think they're dead

❏ Keep trying for up to two minutes

❏ Until medical help arrives and takes over

❏ Keep trying for up to four minutes

DBC s4, DGV s4

If you're trying to resuscitate someone, it's important that you don't give up on them. Make sure that someone has called the emergency services and continue trying to resuscitate the casualty until a medical professional takes over.

7.22 When should you stop trying to resuscitate a casualty?

❏ When you think they're dead

❏ When they can breathe without help

❏ When they've turned blue

❏ When you think the ambulance is coming

DBC s4, DGV s4

If you're trying to resuscitate a casualty, don't give up until a medical professional takes over. Never assume that someone's dead. People who aren't breathing can survive longer than you may imagine when given CPR.

7.23 You arrive at the scene of an incident. A casualty has an injured arm that's bleeding heavily. What could you do to help while waiting for the emergency services to arrive?

❏ Remove clothing around the wound

❏ Dab the wound

❏ Get them a drink

❏ Try to stem the flow of blood

DBC s4, DGV s4

You should first protect yourself from exposure to blood – many first-aid kits contain surgical gloves. To stem the flow of blood, you should apply firm pressure over the wound. If there's an object in the wound, you'll need to build up padding on either side and make sure you don't press on the object.

7.24 You arrive at the scene of an incident. The emergency services have already been called. A pedestrian is bleeding heavily from a leg wound, but their leg isn't broken. What could you do to help them?

❏ Dab the wound to stop the bleeding

❏ Give them some painkiller tablets

❏ Apply firm pressure to the wound

❏ Fetch them a warm drink

DBC s4, DGV s4

You should first protect yourself from exposure to blood – many first-aid kits contain surgical gloves. To stem the flow of blood, you should apply firm pressure over the wound. If there's an object stuck in the wound, you should leave it in place and build up padding on either side, making sure you don't press on the object.

7.25   At an incident, a casualty is unconscious but still breathing. Why would you move them?

❏ Because an ambulance is on the way

❏ Because bystanders advise you to

❏ Because there's further danger

❏ Because they look uncomfortable

DBC s4, DGV s4
Moving a casualty could cause further injury, so it's important that this is only done If there's danger to them where they are.

7.26   At an incident, you suspect a casualty has back injuries. What's the best way to help them?

❏ Offer them a drink   ❏ Leave them where they are

❏ Raise their legs   ❏ Offer them a cigarette

DBC s4, DGV s4
If you attempt to move a casualty who has a spinal injury, it could cause further damage. Make sure an ambulance has been called for and talk to the casualty to keep them calm.

7.27   The area around an incident is safe. What's the best way to help an injured person?

❏ Get them out of their vehicle

❏ Give them a drink

❏ Give them something to eat

❏ Keep them in the vehicle

DBC s4, DGV s4
Don't move a casualty who's in a safe place, as this could worsen any injury they may have. Only move a casualty if they're in danger – for example, from passing traffic. You may also need to move them if you need to give lifesaving first aid, such as opening their airway.

7.28   You're stopped by a police officer for a suspected motoring offence. Which document will you always be asked to produce?

❏ Your driving licence

❏ Your vehicle registration document

❏ Your vehicle's MOT certificate

❏ Your theory test certificate

DBC s4, DGV s4
If you can't produce your driving licence when asked to do so by a police officer, you may be asked to produce it at a police station within a certain time.

7.29   At the scene of an incident, a person has become hysterical. How should you calm them down?

❏ By leaving them to quietly recover

❏ By engaging them in banter

❏ By giving them a hot drink

❏ By talking to them quietly and firmly

DBC s4, DGV s4
Someone who has been involved in or witnessed a crash will be in no mood for humour. The best way to calm them is by remaining calm yourself, and talking quietly and firmly to them.

7.30   You're at an incident. Why may It be harmfull to move a casualty?

❏ You could damage your back

❏ You could get blood on your hands

❏ You could be accused of assault

❏ You could cause more injury

DBC s4, DGV s4
Be especially careful about moving casualties at the scene of an incident. Inexperienced handling of a casualty could cause more injury, or even prove to be fatal. Only move casualties if they're in danger; for example, from fire.

7.31   At the scene of a crash, a casualty is in contact with live electrical cables. What should you use to break the electrical connection?

❏ A metal pole

❏ Woollen gloves

❏ A damp piece of cloth

❏ A length of wood

DBC s4, DGV s4
At the scene of an incident, if there are any casualties who are in contact with live electricity, don't touch them with your hands – even if you're wearing gloves. You should use a dry, non-conducting item, such as a wooden sweeping brush or plastic spade. You mustn't give first aid until you're sure the electrical contact has been broken, otherwise you'll be putting yourself in danger.

7.32   Where should you stand when using a motorway emergency telephone?

❏ In front of the barrier

❏ Facing the oncoming traffic

❏ With your back to the traffic

❏ Looking towards the grass verge

DBC s4, DGV s4

Motorway phones are free and easily located. You should face the oncoming traffic while using them, so that you can see approaching vehicles.

7.33   Which type of fire extinguisher shouldn't be used on flammable liquids?

❏ Water (red)   ❏ Foam (cream)

❏ Dry powder (blue) ❏ Carbon dioxide (black)

DBC s4, DGV s4

It's very important to know the correct fire extinguisher to use. They'll carry a coloured label or badge telling you their contents. Make sure you learn which extinguisher is which, as using the wrong one could be dangerous and may spread the fire further. For example, you should never use a water extinguisher on burning oil.

7.34   Your vehicle breaks down on a motorway. What should you do if you can't get it fully onto the hard shoulder?

❏ Stand at the edge of the carriageway to warn others

❏ Place a warning triangle in the lane behind your vehicle

❏ Wear a bright jacket and stand In the lane behind your vehicle

❏ Call for help using the nearest emergency telephone

DBC s4, DGV s4

Standing on or near the edge of the carriageway is very dangerous. Your priority is to alert the emergency services by using an emergency roadside telephone. This connects to an operator, who'll get help out to you as soon as possible. In most cases, this is preferable to using a mobile phone, as it will show the operator your precise location.

7.35   Your engine catches fire. What should you do before attempting to put the fire out?

❏ Shut off the fuel supply

❏ Open the engine housing wide

❏ Drive to the nearest fire station

❏ Empty the air tanks

DBC s4, DGV s4

An engine fire is serious. If the fire breaches the fuel lines, it can easily spread to the fuel tank. If that happens, both the vehicle and its cargo will probably be lost. Therefore, your priority is to shut off the fuel supply.

7.36   What should you do before driving Into a tunnel?

❏ Switch off your radio

❏ Remove your sunglasses

❏ Close your sunroof

❏ Switch on your windscreen wipers

DBC s4, DGV s4

Before driving into a tunnel, you should take off your sunglasses. If you don't, you'll find that your vision is restricted – even in a tunnel that appears to be well lit.

7.37   What should you do when you drive into a tunnel?

❏ Use parking lights   ❏ Use front spotlights

❏ Use dipped headlights ❏ Use rear fog lights

DBC s4, DGV s4

Before entering a tunnel, you should switch on your dipped headlights; these help you to see and be seen. In many tunnels, using headlights is a legal requirement. You should also remove your sunglasses before you drive into a tunnel.

7.38   What should you do before entering a tunnel?

❏ Put on your sunglasses

❏ Check your tyre pressures

❏ Change to a lower gear

❏ Tune your radio to a local channel

DBC s4, DGV s4

On the approach to many tunnels, a board will indicate a local channel or radio frequency that you should tune into. This should give a warning of any incident or congestion in the tunnel ahead. Severe loss of life has occurred in tunnel fires. Getting advance warning of any problems ahead will help you to take appropriate action in good time.

7.39   You're driving through a congested tunnel. What should you do it you have to stop?

❏ Stop very close to the vehicle in front to save space

❏ Ignore any message signs as they're never up to date

❏ Keep a safe distance from the vehicle in front

❏ Put your headlights on full beam

DBC s4, DGV s4

It's important to keep a safe distance from the vehicle in front at all times. This still applies in congested tunnels, even if you're moving very slowly or have stopped. If the vehicle in front breaks down, you may need room to manoeuvre past it.

7.40   You're driving through a tunnel. What should you do if your vehicle breaks down?

❏ Switch on hazard warning lights

❏ Remain in your vehicle

❏ Wait for the police to find you

❏ Rely on CCIV cameras seeing you

DBC s4, DGV s4

If your vehicle breaks down in a tunnel, it could present a danger to other traffic. First, switch on your hazard warning lights. If there are passengers in your vehicle, take them to the nearest exit point. You should then call for help from an emergency telephone. Don't rely on being found by the police or being seen by a CCTV camera. The longer a vehicle stays in an exposed position; the more danger it poses to other traffic.

7.41   Your vehicle catches fire while you're driving through a tunnel. What should you do if the vehicle can still be driven?

❏ Leave it where it is, with the engine running

❏ Stop, then walk to an emergency telephone point

❏ Park it away from the carriageway

❏ Drive it out of the tunnel if you can do so

DBC s4, DGV s4

If it's possible, and you can do so without causing further danger, it's safer to drive a vehicle that's on fire out of a tunnel. The greatest danger in a tunnel fire is smoke and suffocation.

7.42   What should you do when you're driving through a tunnel in heavy traffic?

❏ Stay close to the vehicle in front to reduce congestion

❏ Switch off your dipped headlights to reduce dazzle

❏ Closely follow the tail lights of other vehicles

❏ Follow the instructions given by variable message signs

DBC s4, DGV s4

In congested tunnels, you should always obey the instructions given by variable message signs and tunnel officials. Listen out for radio announcements and observe the road signs and signals. Keep your distance from the vehicle in front.

7.43   A vehicle has rolled over and caught fire. The driver's hands and arms have been burned. How could you help the driver?

❏ Douse the burns with cool water

❏ Try to put out the fire

❏ Remove smouldering clothing

❏ Remove anything sticking to the burns

DBC s4, DGV s4

Don't remove anything sticking to a burn. You may cause further damage and introduce infection into the wound. If you can, douse the burn with clean, cool water for at least 10 minutes.

7.44   At an incident, a casualty has stopped breathing. How could you help them?

❏ By opening their airway

❏ By tilting their head as far forward as possible

❏ By raising their legs

❏ By giving them something to drink

DBC s4, DGV s4

To help a casualty who isn't breathing, you should open their airway by placing your fingers under their chin and lifting it forward. This will open their airway but if there are no signs of breathing you should then start CPR.

7.45 You've been involved in an incident and damaged some property. What should you do if nobody else is present and your vehicle is still roadworthy?

☐ Stop, then report the incident to the police within 24 hours

☐ Leave the scene. Don't report the incident if there are no witnesses

☐ Stop, then report the incident to the police after 48 hours

☐ Leave the scene. Don't report the incident if there were no injuries

DBC s4, DGV s4   NI EXEMPT

If you're involved in an incident that causes damage or injury to a person or property, you must stop. You must also give your details to anyone who has reasonable grounds to ask for them. If you don't do this, you must inform the police as soon as possible and in any case within 24 hours.

7.46 You've had an incident while driving through a tunnel. You aren't injured but your vehicle can't be driven. What's the first thing you should do in this situation?

☐ Rely on other drivers to phone the police

☐ Switch off the engine and switch on hazard warning lights

☐ Take the names of witnesses and other drivers

☐ Sweep up any debris that's in the road

DBC s4, DGV s4

If you're involved in an incident in a tunnel, be aware of the danger this can cause to other traffic. You should immediately switch on your hazard warning lights and switch off your engine.

7.47 While driving through a tunnel, your vehicle catches fire. What's the first thing you should do if the vehicle can't be driven out of the tunnel?

☐ Wait for the police; tunnels are regularly patrolled

☐ Stay with your vehicle; you'll be seen by the CCTV cameras

☐ Stop at the side of the road and switch off the engine

☐ Don't put out the fire; wait for the emergency services

DBC s4, DGV s4

If your vehicle catches fire in a tunnel and it can't be driven, stop on the side of the road, as far away from passing traffic as possible. Turn off the engine and warn other traffic by switching on your hazard warning lights.

7.48 You're at the scene of an incident. What would suggest someone is suffering from shock?

☐ A flushed complexion   ☐ Being alert

☐ Rapid shallow breathing ☐ Being very hungry

DBC s4, DGV s4

The effects of shock may not be immediately obvious. Try to recognise the warning signs early; prompt treatment can help to deal with it. Symptoms include a rapid pulse, pale grey skin, sweating and rapid shallow breathing.

7.49 What's the first thing you should try to do if your vehicle catches fire while you're driving through a tunnel?

☐ Drive out of the tunnel

☐ Stop at the side of the tunnel

☐ Stop and put out the fire

☐ Stop and leave the vehicle immediately

DBC s4, DGV s4

If your vehicle catches fire in a tunnel, you should first try to drive it out – but only if you can do so safely.

7.50 You arrive at the scene of an incident. How should you deal with someone who is hysterical?

☐ Talk to them quietly and firmly

☐ Let them wander off to calm down

☐ Restrain them physically

☐ Shout loudly to get their attention

DBC s4, DGV s4

A person who's hysterical may do things that you wouldn't expect. Try to keep the distressed person calm and safe until the emergency services arrive.

7.51 You're at the scene of a traffic incident. What are the symptoms of someone suffering from shock?

☐ Rapid pulse and sweating

☐ Flushed complexion and deep breathing

☐ Slow pulse and dry skin

☐ Muscle spasms and an itchy rash

DBC s4, DGV s4
Prompt treatment can help to deal with shock. Warning signs to look for include rapid pulse, sweating, pale grey skin, and rapid shallow breathing. While waiting for help to arrive, keep the casualty warm and comfortable, and speak reassuringly to them.

7.52 You're at the scene of a collision. People are injured. What should be done when the risk of further collisions has been dealt with?

☐ Pull people who are hurt out of their vehicles

☐ Clear a parking area for the emergency services

☐ Make sure the emergency services have been called

☐ Get the casualties to drink something sweet

DBC s4, DGV s4
Make sure you or someone else has called the emergency services. Check the casualties and, if you feel able to give first aid, do so. Alternatively, ask any bystanders if they can help.

7.53 You're driving a coach carrying elderly people. You arrive at the scene of an incident. What should you do If the emergency services have already arrived?

☐ Ask your passengers to find out what's happening

☐ Don't tell your passengers anything in case you upset them

☐ Leave your passengers on the bus and see what's happening

☐ Tell your passengers what's happening without upsetting them

DBC s4
At the scene of an incident, you should tell your passengers what has happened, while reassuring them that they're not in danger. Explain to them that the emergency services are dealing with it and they should remain on the coach.

7.54 What should you do if your bus has been involved in an incident with other vehicles?

☐ Switch off your headlights

☐ Switch off the fuel supply

☐ Switch off the air conditioning

☐ Switch off the destination signs

DBC s4
The risk of fire will be reduced if all fuel supplies are switched off. However, don't put yourself or your passengers at any risk. If there's a fire, call the fire service.

7.55 What must you do if your bus has hit a parked vehicle and the owner can't be found?

☐ Report the incident to the police within seven days

☐ Report the incident to the owner as soon as possible

☐ Report the incident to the owner within seven days

☐ Report the incident to the police within 24 hours

DBC s4   Ni Exempt
If you damage a parked vehicle and the owner isn't around, you must report it to the police within 24 hours. This applies to any property you might have damaged. In Northern Ireland, all incidents must be reported to the police immediately.

7.56 How should you care for a passenger who's in shock?

☐ Give them liquids

☐ Keep them moving

☐ Encourage them to sleep

☐ Keep them warm

DBC s4
After an incident, passengers who aren't obviously injured may be suffering from shock. Reassure them and keep them warm. Don't give them anything to eat or drink. Call the emergency services and keep yourself and any injured passengers calm until professional help arrives.

7.57 A passenger on your bus has stopped breathing. You help them by giving CPR. When should you stop doing this?

❏ When they can breathe on their own

❏ When you think the passenger has died

❏ When their skin has turned blue

❏ When you think the ambulance is coming

DBC s4

You should only stop resuscitation when the passenger can breathe on their own or a professional medical person can take over.

7.58 Your bus is involved in an incident. What should you do if you have a passenger who's unconscious but still breathing?

❏ Get medical help ❏ Check their pulse

❏ Give them liquid ❏ Lie them on their back

DBC s4

If one of your passengers is unconscious but breathing, get medical help immediately. Only move them if there's a danger of further injury and you're moving them to a place of safety while you wait for help to arrive.

7.59 Your bus has stopped at the scene of an incident. Why should you consider moving your passengers to the front of the bus?

❏ To improve weight distribution

❏ To reduce the risk of injury from a rear-end collision

❏ To be closer to emergency exits

❏ To be witnesses to the incident

DBC s4

If there's a risk that another vehicle could run into the back of your bus, you should move your passengers forward to a safer position.

7.60 Your bus hits a low railway bridge. Nobody is injured. When and to whom should you report the incident?

❏ Immediately, to your employer

❏ Within 24 hours, to the railway authority

❏ Within seven days, to the police

❏ Immediately, to the railway authority

DBC s3

If your bus hits a railway bridge, you must inform the railway authority immediately, as the impact may have damaged the bridge and made it unsafe. You should find the telephone number on or near the bridge. It's very important to do this as soon as possible, so that all rail traffic is stopped. You must also inform the police immediately, or in any case within 24 hours.

7.61 While driving through a tunnel, your coach catches fire. What should you do if the vehicle can't be driven any further?

❏ Move the passengers to the rear of the coach

❏ Get the passengers off and keep them together

❏ Make sure the passengers stay in their seats

❏ Move the passengers to the front of the coach

DBC s4

If your coach catches fire and it can't go any further, stop at the side of the road, switch the engine off and switch on your hazard warning lights. Your immediate responsibility is to your passengers. Get them off the coach, keep them together and take them to the nearest emergency exit.

7.62 You're carrying a bus full of passengers. What must you do if you see smoke coming from the engine compartment?

❏ Move the passengers to the front of the bus

❏ Open the engine cover to investigate

❏ Drive to the bus station for a replacement bus

❏ Get everyone off the bus quickly and safely

DBC s4

Smoke from the engine compartment is very serious, as fire within a vehicle can spread very quickly. Your priority is to make sure that all passengers get off the bus as quickly and safely as possible.

7.63 Your bus catches fire in a tunnel and can't be driven any further. What should you do when you've stopped safely at the side of the road?

❏ Move your passengers to the nearest tunnel exit

❏ Use the extinguisher to put out the fire

❏ Keep your passengers together in front of the vehicle

❏ Stand behind your vehicle and warn other drivers

DBC s4

If your vehicle catches fire and you can drive it out of the tunnel, you should do so. If you can't do this, stop at the side of the road and switch off the engine. Move your passengers calmly but quickly to the nearest exit.

Section 8 Vehicle condition

8.1 What's the main reason for cleaning your wheels and tyres when you leave a building site?

❑ To keep the tyres in good condition

❑ To prevent the tyres from damaging the road surface

❑ To reduce air leakage from the tyre valves

❑ To stop mud dropping onto the road

DGV s4
If your wheels leave mud on the road, you must arrange for it to be cleared. A slippery, muddy surface could cause danger to other road users.

8.2 Your vehicle has double rear wheels. Why should you check them before leaving a building site?

❑ To make sure the diff-lock is engaged

❑ To make sure the diff-lock is disengaged

❑ To check that the load-sensing valve is operating correctly

❑ To make sure bricks or debris aren't wedged between the wheels

DGV s2
While driving on a building site, bricks, mud or other debris can become lodged between a lorry's double rear wheels. When you leave the site and increase your road speed, anything lodged between the tyres could be thrown out. This flying debris can be a hazard for drivers of following vehicles and can create dangerous road conditions, especially for motorcyclists.

8.3 What should you check before you drive off a muddy building site onto the road?

❑ The diff-lock is disengaged

❑ The diff-lock is engaged

❑ The steering lock is engaged

❑ The twist lock is disengaged

DGV s4
Attempting to drive at normal speeds with the diff-lock engaged is dangerous; it will severely affect your steering control. The diff-lock is designed to be used in slippery conditions, at low speed, when maximum traction is required.

8.4 You're driving a lorry along a motorway. You notice that you're losing tread from one of your tyres. What should you do?

❑ Stop on the hard shoulder and phone for assistance

❑ Stop on the hard shoulder and change the wheel

❑ Continue driving to the next service station

❑ Continue driving and leave by the next exit

DGV s2
Continuous high speeds on the motorway can cause the tyres to become hot and to shred. If you notice this happening, you must stop on the hard shoulder as soon as it's safe to do so. It's dangerous to drive a defective vehicle.

8.5 What's the minimum depth of tread required over three-quarters of the breadth of a lorry tyre?

❑ 1 mm ❑ 1.5 mm ❑ 2.5mm ❑ 5 mm

DGV s2, 4
Tyres are your lorry's only contact with the road. It's essential that this contact gives you the grip you need to control your vehicle at all times. For that reason, goods vehicles must have a tread depth of at least 1 mm across three quarters of the breadth of the tread and in a continuous band around the entire circumference.

8.6 What's the final thing you should do after recoupling a trailer?

❑ Connect the brake lines

❑ Release the trailer parking brake

❑ Connect the electrical lines

❑ Raise the trailer legs

DGV s6
It's important to work methodically when uncoupling or recoupling a tractor unit and trailer. After recoupling, check that all connections, systems and lights are working correctly.

8.7 When should your lorry coupling system (fifth wheel) be checked and lubricated?

□ Only prior to an MOT test

□ Every 6 months

□ Yearly

□ Regularly

DGV s2
Maintenance of the fifth wheel should be carried out regularly, ideally monthly or every 10 000 km.

8.8 You're driving a new articulated lorry that's fully laden. You notice that the steering feels heavy. What's the most likely reason?

□ The road is icy   □ The power steering is faulty

□ The lorry is new □ The load on the trailer has shifted

DGV s2
Heavy steering could mean there's a fault with the power steering. It should be investigated as soon as possible. Many large vehicles can become undriveable if the power steering fails completely.

8.9 When should wheel nuts be checked?

□ After driving down a steep hill

□ Soon after initial tightening

□ Just after driving on a motorway

□ After unloading

DGV s2
Always have wheel nuts checked soon after their initial tightening. They should be tightened to the torque specified by the vehicle manufacturer.

8.10 What would you secure with a dog clip?

□ The kingpin release handle □ The air lines

□ The parking brake   □ The diff-lock

DGV s6
When recoupling, you must connect the dog clip to secure the kingpin release handle.

8.11 How frequently should the components of a fifth-wheel coupling be inspected?

□ Daily   □ Weekly   □ Monthly   □ Yearly

DGV s2
A fifth wheel must be maintained properly. It requires regular lubrication and inspection. This should be carried out monthly or every 10 000 km – whichever comes first.

8.12 What should you check for wear or damage on a drawbar unit?

□ Dog clip   □ Fifth wheel

□ Kingpin release handle □ Eyelet coupling

DGV s2
The eyelet coupling on drawbar units should be checked regularly for damage or wear. It should be kept lubricated with heavy-duty grease.

8.13 What's the fifth-wheel coupling used for?

□ To connect the tractor unit to the trailer

□ To support the trailer when it's detached

□ To prevent the trailer from jack-knifing

□ To attach air lines to the trailer

DGV s2
The fifth-wheel coupling is a device to connect the tractor unit to the trailer. It allows articulation between the tractor and trailer, and it should be regularly maintained.

8.14 How often should the components of the fifth-wheel coupling be inspected?

□ Every 3000 miles (5000 km)

□ Every 6000 miles (10 000 km)

□ Every 9000 miles (15 000 km)

□ Every 12 000 miles (20 000 km)

DGV s2
Fifth-wheel couplings need regular inspection and lubrication. This should be carried out either every 6000 miles (10 000 km) or monthly – whichever is the sooner.

8.15 What happens to diesel fuel when it gets hot?

☐ It expands ☐ It liquefies ☐ It shrinks ☐ It waxes

DGV s2
When a full diesel fuel tank heats up, the fuel expands and can be forced out of the breather vent and onto the road. This wastes fuel and makes the road surface very dangerous for other road users.

8.16 You're checking your vehicle's tyres before starting a long motorway journey. What check should be made on each tyre?

☐ Air pressure ☐ Tracking

☐ Valve clearance ☐ Tyre profile

DBC s2, DGV s2
All tyres must be properly inflated and in good condition. Tyre failure on a motorway can have serious consequences. This can be avoided by checking your tyres at the start of each journey.

8.17 What should you do if you notice that two wheelnuts are missing from one of the wheels on your vehicle?

☐ Continue your journey

☐ Drive to the nearest tyre depot

☐ Use a nut from another wheel.

☐ Park and phone for assistance

DBC s2, 3, DGV s2, 3
If you notice any missing wheel nuts, park and phone for assistance. It's essential that all wheel fixings are in place and tightened to the torque specified by the manufacturer. Checks should be made before you start any journey, but make a visual check every time you start up again after a rest stop.

8.18 What would be illegal?

☐ Using different makes of tyre on the same axle

☐ Using a tyre with a recut tread

☐ Using a tyre with a tread depth of 1.3 mm

☐ Using a tyre with exposed ply or cord

DBC s2, DGV s2, 4
You should check your tyres as part of your routine check of the vehicle. A damaged tyre – such as one with exposed ply – can have a major effect on your vehicle's handling and will make it a danger to you and other road users.

8.19 In very cold weather, moisture can freeze In your vehicle's air storage tanks. What can you do to help prevent this from happening?

☐ Cover the air tanks with a blanket

☐ Drain the tanks daily

☐ Use the brakes frequently

☐ Pump the brakes

DBC s2, DGV s2
In very cold weather, moisture in the storage tanks can freeze. Ice can form in the pipes and this will result in loss of pressure, which could cause brake failure. Make sure that you drain the tanks daily as part of a routine. Most modern vehicles are fitted with automatic bleed valves. Check that they're working properly and that air-drying systems are effective.

8.20 What does this warning light on the instrument panel mean?

☐ Low oil pressure ☐ Battery discharge

☐ Braking-system fault ☐ Door open

DBC s2, DGV s2
You should be familiar with all warning lights and buzzers fitted to your vehicle. If you're driving the vehicle for the first time, make sure that you know the function of each. If the brake warning light shows a fault in the system, stop as soon as it's safe to do so. Report the fault, and don't continue until it's been corrected.

8.21 You're driving along a motorway. What should you do if the air-pressure warning device starts to operate?

☐ Stop immediately in the lane you're in

☐ Continue slowly to the next service area

☐ Stop on the hard shoulder as soon as possible

☐ Leave the motorway at the next exit

DBC s2, DGV s2
If the air-pressure warning activates, you should have enough air to allow you to stop safely on the hard shoulder. Don't delay stopping, as further loss of air may cause the brakes to lock on. Switch on the hazard warning lights. Use the nearest emergency telephone to call for assistance.

8.22 Your vehicle has broken down at night on a two-way road. How should you try to leave the vehicle?

❑ On the left of the road ❑ Partly on the pavement

❑ On a grass verge   ❑ On the right of the road

DBC s4, DGV s4
If your vehicle breaks down, try to stop on the left, facing in the same direction as the flow of traffic. This will help other drivers to see you, as your red reflectors will show to the rear. Don't stop on the pavement, as the weight of the vehicle may damage paving stones and underground services.

8.23 What should you do if your power-assisted steering fails suddenly?

❑ Continue driving to the nearest repair centre

❑ Return to the depot

❑ Continue your journey at a slower speed

❑ Park and get help

DBC s4, DGV s6
Faulty power steering will make your steering wheel very difficult or almost impossible to turn. Continuing to drive could cause danger to you and other road users. You should park safely and get help.

8.24 Your steering suddenly becomes heavy to turn. What could make this happen?

❑ An uneven road surface

❑ A loss of air-brake pressure

❑ A faulty parking brake

❑ A fault with the power-assisted steering

DBC s2, DGV s6
If the steering becomes heavy, the power-assisted steering may have failed. It's also possible that your vehicle has a puncture or the load might have shifted. You should stop safely, investigate the cause and call for help if necessary.

8.25 What should you do if the brake pedal becomes hard to press?

❑ Continue to drive and report it at the end of the day

❑ Pump the brake pedal continuously

❑ Drain the air tanks and then continue

❑ Park and phone for help

DBC s2, DGV s2
As soon as you detect a fault on your vehicle, you must take action. Where faulty brakes are concerned, you need to seek help immediately. Always report minor faults as soon as you detect them. Minor faults can become major ones if they aren't repaired quickly.

8.26 Why do air tanks on brake systems need to be drained?

❑ To remove excess coolant

❑ To remove rain water that's seeped into the system

❑ To remove any oil leaks that collect here

❑ To remove moisture drawn in from the atmosphere

DBC s2, DGV s2
Moisture in the air condenses as the air pressure increases. This moisture can be transmitted around the braking system and is especially dangerous in cold weather. It can lead to ice forming and blocking the valves and pipes.

8.27 You're checking your vehicle. What should you do if you discover an air leak in the braking system?

❑ Drive slowly to the nearest garage

❑ Check the leak from time to time on your journey

❑ Leave the vehicle parked and report the fault immediately

❑ Start your journey and report the fault on your return

DBC s2, DGV s2
Under no circumstances should you attempt to move or drive a vehicle with an air leak in the braking system. Report the fault immediately, or arrange to have it repaired. Place a warning sign in the cab, telling other drivers not to drive the vehicle and why.

8.28 A loud buzzer sounds in your vehicle. What's this most likely to indicate?

❑ Low oil pressure   ❑ Low air pressure

❑ Low tyre pressure ❑ Low fuel level

DBC s2, DGV s2
Warning buzzers are linked to many systems on modern vehicles, including the air brakes. A warning light on the dashboard may help you identify the system that's caused the problem. Stop in a safe place until the fault has been identified and put right. Get professional help if necessary.

8.29 What proportion of the width of a tyre must have at least the legal minimum depth of tread?

❑ One-quarter ❑ One-half

❑ Five-eighths ❑ Three-quarters

DBC s2, DGV s2
Keeping your vehicle's tyres in good condition will give them a good grip on the road and will improve the vehicle's overall stability. Each tyre must have at least the minimum legal depth of tread across three-quarters of its width. Renew tyres well before they wear to less than that.

8.30 You discover that one of your rear brakelight bulbs has failed. How soon should it be replaced?

❑ Immediately ❑ On return to your base

❑ Within five days ❑ At the next service

DBC s4, DGV s4
Bulbs should be replaced as soon as you're aware that they've failed. Carry a stock of all the various bulbs used on your vehicle, so you can repair a fault without delay.

8.31 What can you add to diesel fuel to prevent it from becoming less effective at low temperatures?

❑ Anti-freeze ❑ Anti-waxing additives

❑ Petrol ❑ Paraffin

DBC s2, DGV s2
In extremely cold weather, you'll have to use diesel fuel with anti-waxing additives to stop the fuel lines from freezing up. During the winter months, these additives are usually put in by the fuel companies.

8.32 You're about to start a long journey midway through the day. What should you do if you notice that the sidelights work but the headlights are faulty?

❑ Don't drive until they're repaired

❑ Drive only until the light begins to fade

❑ Avoid driving on motorways after dark

❑ Drive only if the weather is good

DBC s2, DGV s3
To comply with the law, all lights must be in good working order, even in daylight when they're not being used. Before you set out, make sure that everything is working and get any faulty lights fixed. You may need to use your headlights or other lights if you're delayed or find yourself driving in conditions of reduced visibility.

8.33 Before starting a journey, you want to check your brake-system warning lights. What can you do when these aren't operated by the ignition switch?

❑ Look for a check switch on the dashboard

❑ Get someone behind to check your brake lights

❑ Check them at the end of your journey

❑ Pump the brake pedal a number of times

DBC s2, DGV s2
A warning-lights check is sometimes performed automatically when the ignition is switched on. However, you may need to do this manually by operating a separate check switch. Never start a journey without carrying out this check. If there's a problem, have it repaired before you set off.

8.34 On motorways, you're usually driving at higher speeds for long distances. What effect can this have on your tyres?

❑ They'll be more likely to overheat and disintegrate

❑ They'll have lower rolling resistance

❑ They'll need less air pressure

❑ They'll become very slippery

DBC s2, 4, DGV s2
Driving at higher speeds and for longer periods, such as on motorways, can cause your tyres to overheat and disintegrate. You should make a point of checking them when you stop for a break.

8.35 You notice that one of your tyres has a bulge in the side wall. What will happen if you drive the vehicle?

❑ Your tachograph reading won't be accurate

❑ Your speedometer will give an incorrect reading

❑ The vehicle will become unstable on corners

❑ You'll break the law and risk prosecution

DBC s2, DGV s2
It's a legal requirement that your tyres have at least the minimum permitted depth of tread and are in good condition before you start any journey. Make sure that you inspect them before setting off, and at regular intervals.

8.36   What's the purpose of a preheating device?

☐ To heat the cab

☐ To heat the gearbox

☐ To heat the combustion chambers

☐ To heat the seat

DBC s2, DGV s4

Most diesel engines have glow plugs to preheat the combustion chambers, so helping the engine to start when it's cold. When the ignition is switched on, the preheat warning lamp will show and the glow-plugs will rapidly heat up.

In cold weather, the starter should only be operated when the glow plugs reach operating temperature and the warning light goes out.

8.37   Where does a high-pressure fuel injector deliver fuel?

☐ Into the carburettors

☐ Into the combustion chamber

☐ Into the manifold

☐ Into the crankcase

DBC s2, DGV s2

Most diesel engines use a high-pressure fuel-injector system that will deliver pressurised fuel directly into the combustion chamber of the engine. This system is known as a direct-injection engine.

8.38   Why is it important to avoid overfilling the engine with oil?

☐ It could leave an oil stain on the road

☐ It will increase the amount of exhaust gases

☐ It could increase pressure in the engine and cause damage

☐ It will damage the exhaust system

DBC s4, DGV s2

Too much oil in an engine can be just as bad as too little. Overfilling an engine can create excess pressure, cause oil leakage through seals and result in expensive damage.

8.39   Why should you use an approved coolant solution in your engine's cooling system?

☐ To protect the coolant from freezing

☐ For easier starting from cold

☐ To prevent the air tank from freezing

☐ For effective cab heating

DBC s2, DGV s2

Coolant solution is also known as anti-freeze. It provides protection from freezing and also contains a corrosion inhibitor that prolongs the life of the cooling system. Remember to check the coolant level regularly.

8.40   What's it advisable to do when you replace a tubeless tyre?

☐ Fit the same valve   ☐ Replace the valve

☐ Have the valve checked   ☐ Clean the valve

DBC s2, DGV s2

Always get expert advice when dealing with tyres. It's good practice to have a new valve fitted when replacing a tubeless tyre. Good garages and specialist tyre services know the regulations.

8.41   When should you check the oil level in your engine?

☐ When the engine is running

☐ When the engine is cold

☐ When the engine is warm

☐ When the engine is hot

DBC s2, DGV s2

Oil is vital for lubrication of the engine. It should be checked regularly and topped up as necessary. You should always check your engine's oil level when the engine is cold and your vehicle is parked on the level.

8.42   When should anti-freeze be used in the cooling system?

☐ In winter only   ☐ All year round

☐ In summer only   ☐ When starting from cold

DBC s2, DGV s2

Today, all water-cooled engines use a mixture of water and anti-freeze to make up the coolant. As well as helping to keep the engine at its correct operating temperature, the anti-freeze acts as a corrosion inhibitor to prolong the life of the cooling system.

8.43   What does this warning light on the instrument panel mean?

❑ Low fuel pressure   ❑ Low oil pressure

❑ Low water pressure   ❑ Low air pressure

DBC s2, DGV s2

You should be familiar with all the warning lights fitted to your vehicle. The oil warning light indicates low oil pressure or lack of oil. If it lights up, report the fault and don't continue until it's been corrected.

8.44   What does it mean if the ignition warning light comes on while you're driving?

❑ The oil pressure is low ❑ There's an electrical fault

❑ The air pressure is low ❑ There's a hydraulic fault

DBC s2, DGV s2

The ignition light should go out when the engine has started. If it fails to go out or comes on while you're driving, it means that there's an electrical fault of some kind.

8.45   What do the codes shown on the side walls of bus and lorry tyres refer to?

❑ Tread pattern   ❑ Minimum temperature

❑ Maximum load   ❑ Running pressure

DBC s2, DGV s2

Tyres have codes shown on the wall of the tyre. These refer to the maximum load and speed capability of the tyre.

8.46   What will happen if you follow a regular vehicle maintenance schedule?

❑ It will reduce breakdowns

❑ It will increase fuel bills

❑ It will allow heavier loads to be carried

❑ It will reduce insurance premiums

DBC s2, DGV s3

You can reduce the chance of a breakdown with routine maintenance and regular checks on your vehicle.

8.47   What should you do before changing a wheel on your vehicle?

❑ Leave the parking brake off

❑ Use wheel chocks if available

❑ Dismantle the wheel and tyre

❑ Get someone to check the other tyres

DBC s2, DGV s2

Always make sure your vehicle is secure and level before a wheel is changed. Apply the parking brake and use chocks if they're available. When the replacement wheel is fitted, all wheel nuts/studs should be retightened to the correct torque.

On a motorway, never attempt to change a wheel yourself. Use the emergency telephones to call for assistance.

8.48   You've had to change a wheel on your vehicle. When should the wheel nuts be checked again?

❑ At the next service interval ❑ When they're cold

❑ When they're hot   ❑ Shortly afterwards

DBC s3, DGV s2

When refitting a wheel, the nuts should be tightened to the correct torque. They should be rechecked after about 30 minutes if the vehicle hasn't moved, or after 40 to 80 km (25 to 50 miles) of driving.

8.49   How can vehicle breakdowns be reduced?

❑ By driving slowly   ❑ By regular servicing

❑ By regular cleaning   ❑ By avoiding bad weather

DBC s2, DGV s2

Following the vehicle manufacturer's guidelines for service intervals will enable worn components to be replaced before they fail. This will help prevent costly breakdowns.

8.50   Why should your engine oil be changed at the recommended intervals?

❏ To reduce friction and wear

❏ For better steering control

❏ To prevent oil leaks

❏ To improve clutch wear

DBC s2, DGV s2
The oil and filter will get dirty in normal use. If you follow the service-interval guidance, your engine will remain protected and properly lubricated, making it less likely to break down.

8.51   Where should you park your vehicle before checking the engine oil level?

❏ On sloping ground   ❏ On a steep gradient

❏ On flat ground   ❏ On a downhill slope

DBC s2, DGV s2
If you check the engine oil level when your vehicle is standing on a slope, the reading on the dipstick won't be accurate. Park it on flat ground, so the dipstick shows the true level.

8.52   What could happen if you overfill your engine with oil?

❏ The handling may improve

❏ Exhaust emissions could be reduced

❏ Some gaskets might be damaged

❏ You could wait longer before the next service

DBC s2, DGV s2
If you overfill the engine with oil, you could cause the engine to build up too much pressure when it's running. This could cause damage to oil seals and gaskets.

8.53   You've stopped on a firm, level surface. What's the first thing you must do before you uncouple the trailer?

❏ Lower the trailer legs to the ground

❏ Apply the parking brake

❏ Release the brake air lines

❏ Uncouple the electrical lines

DBC s2, DGV s6
Before leaving the cab, it's very important to secure the vehicle by applying the parking brake. After leaving the cab, apply the trailer parking brake.

8.54   You're uncoupling a trailer. What must you do before disconnecting any of the air lines?

❏ Drain the air tanks

❏ Apply the trailer parking brake

❏ Lower the landing gear

❏ Disconnect the electrical line

DGV s6
Whenever you uncouple a trailer, you must work through the uncoupling process methodically. Start by making sure that the brakes are applied on both the vehicle and the trailer.

8.55   When should you check the wheel nuts on your vehicle?

❏ Before any journey

❏ Only before long trips

❏ Every 1000 miles (1600 km)

❏ Annually

DBC s2, 3, DGV s2
Always have a walk round your vehicle and visually check the wheel nuts whenever you take a break. When a wheel is replaced, it's important to have the wheel nuts rechecked shortly after their initial tightening. Wheel nuts must always be tightened to the torque specified by the manufacturer.

8.56   What should you do if thick black smoke is coming from the exhaust of your vehicle?

❏ Continue on to the nearest garage

❏ Return to your depot and report the problem

❏ Stop in a safe place and get help

❏ Drive slowly with your hazard warning lights on

DBC s2, DGV s2
Causing excessive smoke is an offence and could contribute to causing an incident or collision. You could also end up creating serious traffic problems if your vehicle breaks down in a difficult location.

8.57   You hit the kerb at speed. What part of your vehicle should you check for damage?

❏ Exhaust   ❏ Brakes   ❏ Lights   ❏ Tyres

DBC s2, DGV s2
Hitting the kerb at speed can split the tyre or put the steering and suspension geometry out of alignment. Have it checked as soon as possible. A sudden puncture in a front tyre could result in a loss of steering control and a serious crash.

8.58   What's most likely to cause a burst tyre?

□ Frequent gear changing in varying conditions

□ Running tyres under-inflated

□ Always operating in cool weather

□ Mixing tyres with different tread depth

DBC s2, DGV s2
Tyres can become very hot during sustained high-speed driving. If they're under-inflated or damaged, there's a risk they'll burst or disintegrate. Check for excessive heat when you stop for a break.

8.59   When can 'selective' or 'block' gear changing be used?

□ To change down in gear only

□ To change up in gear only

□ To change gear to a low speed only

□ To change either up or down in gear

DBC s2, DGV s2
'Block' gear changing means changing up or down to the most appropriate gear without going through each gear in turn. It reduces the number of gear changes, and this can improve fuel consumption.

8.60   When would you use 'kickdown' on a vehicle that has automatic transmission?

□ To give quicker acceleration

□ To apply the emergency brakes

□ To stop more smoothly

□ To go down a steep hill

DBC s2, DGV s2
Depending on road speed, pressing the accelerator pedal firmly to the floor will activate a switch that allows the gearbox to select a lower gear for improved acceleration.

8.61   What's the most likely cause if your steering starts to feel heavy?

□ Faulty power steering   □ An icy road

□ A burst rear tyre   □ A wet road

DBC s2, DGV s6
Modern large vehicles are fitted with power-assisted steering. If the steering feels heavy, then there's likely to be a fault, which should be investigated and repaired as soon as possible.

8.62   Your vehicle suffers a tyre blow-out. How could this create a hazard for other road users?

□ Scattered debris   □ Skid marks

□ Suspension failure   □ Axle damage

DBC s2, DGV s2
When a tyre explodes, fragments are thrown over a wide area. This can create a serious hazard for other drivers. You should regularly check your tyres for cuts, damage and pressure. Frequent checks and proper maintenance can help prevent a blow-out.

8.63   The Driver and Vehicle Standards Agency (DVSA) and the police carry out spot checks for faulty vehicles. What will happen to the vehicle if serious defects are found?

□ It will be impounded until a new driver is found

□ It will be restricted to 30 mph for the remainder of the journey

□ It will be prohibited from further use until the defects are rectified

□ It will be ordered back to the depot to unload goods or passengers

DBC s3, DGV s3   NI Exempt
DVSA or the police can order an immediate prohibition. The vehicle may be immobilised and you won't be able to drive it until the faults have been rectified. Details are notified to the traffic commissioner. Never use a vehicle that you know is faulty.

8.64   At a Driver and Vehicle Standards Agency (DVSA) roadside check, your vehicle is found to have serious defects and you may no longer use it. Who will DVSA share this information with?

□ The Driver and Vehicle Licensing Agency

□ The Traffic Commissioner

□ The Road Transport Industry Training Body

□ The Bus, Coach and Commercial Vehicle Council

DBC s3, DGV s3   NI Exempt
DVSA and the police carry out frequent roadside checks of commercial vehicles. Where serious defects are found, the vehicle is taken out of use until they're put right. Details of the prohibition are shared with the traffic commissioner.

8.65 What could happen if there isn't enough oil in your engine?

❑ It may run faster   ❑ It may break down

❑ It may use less fuel   ❑ IIt may produce more power

DBC s2, DGV s2
You should check your oil level regularly and pay attention to any oil warning devices. A damaged engine can be very expensive to mend. It could also cause sudden and unexpected loss of control, putting you and others in danger.

If your engine seizes, you should make every effort to stop in a safe place.

8.66 While driving, your engine-oil warning light comes on. Why could it be dangerous to continue driving?

❑ The brakes will fai

❑ The engine may be damaged

❑ You'll need to have the vehicle serviced

❑ You'll need to replace the carburettor

DBC s2, DGV s2
Lack of oil could cause the engine to seize, and this could cause sudden and unexpected loss of control. You could break down in a dangerous position and put yourself and other road users at risk.

8.67 Bus and lorry tyres have codes on their side walls. What do these codes refer to?

❑ Running pressure   ❑ Speed capability

❑ Minimum temperature   ❑ Tread depth

DBC s2, DGV s2
Codes are shown on the wall of the tyre. These refer to the maximum load and speed capability of the tyre.

8.68 What's the advantage of energy-saving tyres?

❑ Greater tread depth   ❑ Reduced rolling resistance

❑ Less tread depth   ❑ Increased rolling resistance

DBC s2, DGV s2
When changing or fitting new tyres, consider buying energy-saving tyres. These have a reduced rolling resistance and improved efficiency, which helps to keep fuel costs down.

8.69 A tyre has been replaced on your vehicle. What precautions should be taken when tightening the wheel nuts?

❑ Tighten the nuts in a clockwise direction

❑ Fully tighten each nut before moving to the next

❑ Tighten the nuts evenly with a torque wrench

❑ Tighten the nuts with an air-operated power tool

DBC s2, DGV s2
When a wheel is refitted, the wheel nuts/studs should be tightened gradually and diagonally across the wheel. You should tighten the nuts to the specified torque setting, using a calibrated torque wrench.

8.70 Why are energy-saving tyres effective?

❑ They have a reduced rolling resistance

❑ They cost less to produce

❑ They have no tread pattern

❑ They don't puncture at high speed

DBC s2, DGV s2
Energy-saving tyres keep fuel costs down because they have a lower rolling resistance and better grip than ordinary tyres. You should consider this when replacing your tyres.

8.71 Where can you get advice to help carry out minor repairs?

❑ DVLA guidance notes

❑ EU and UK directives

❑ The Health and Safety Executive

❑ The vehicle handbook

DBC s2, DGV s2
The vehicle handbook will clearly explain what maintenance may be carried out by the driver. Always refer to it and comply with the safety guidance that it contains. However, you need to be aware of your employer's policy on making any minor repairs.

8.72 Where can you get advice about carrying out repairs to your vehicle?

❑ Workshop manuals

❑ DVLA guidance notes

❑ EU and UK directives

❑ The Health and Safety Executive

DBC s2, DGV s2
Workshop manuals give detailed technical advice about the servicing, maintenance and repair of your vehicle. They're essential for anyone who wants to service or repair their own vehicle.

8.73   What could happen if you overfill your engine with oil?

☐ Loss of power   ☐ Lower emissions

☐ Better handling   ☐ Longer service intervals

DBC s2, DGV s2

If the engine contains too much oil, the moving parts can hit the oil surface, causing a loss of power or even damage to the engine. Excess pressure may damage oil seals, causing oil to leak onto the road, creating a slippery and dangerous road surface.

8.74   What's the purpose of the oil filter?

☐ To prevent the engine from overheating

☐ To give better fuel consumption

☐ To prevent the engine from over-revving

☐ To collect metal particles from the oil

DBC s2, DGV s2

As the lubricating oil is pumped around the engine, It collects tiny fragments of metal from the moving parts. The oil filter is designed to remove these fragments. Most filters are designed to be replaced at service intervals.

8.75   Which tool is essential for fitting a road wheel?

☐ Torque wrench   ☐ Ring spanner

☐ Open-end spanner   ☐ Adjustable wrench

DBC s2, DGV s2

It's essential that all wheel nuts are tightened to the specified torque with a calibrated torque wrench. The wheel nuts, fixings and markers should be checked every day before you start your journey.

8.76   What's the most likely reason for a diesel-engined vehicle running erratically in very cold weather?

☐ The endurance brake engaging

☐ The air conditioning not working

☐ The speed limiter operating

☐ The fuel partly solidifying

DBC s2, DGV s2

If diesel fuel becomes very cold, it can partially solidify. Additives are used by the fuel companies to try to prevent this. Any solidifying (waxing) of the fuel can prevent it from flowing properly and cause the engine to run erratically or even stop.

8.77   What do heated fuel lines prevent?

☐ The cab temperature from dropping

☐ The radiator from freezing

☐ The windows from misting

☐ The diesel from solidifying

DBC s2, DGV s2

In cold weather, diesel fuel can solidify as it starts to freeze. This is known as waxing. Waxing prevents the fuel from flowing properly and this can stop the engine from running.

8.78   Why should you carry out a daily walk-round check before setting off?

☐ To check your route

☐ To check for any parking violations

☐ To check your schedule

☐ To check for any defects

DBC s3, DGV s3

You have a legal responsibility to make sure that your vehicle is fully roadworthy. Daily walk-round checks give you the chance to look for any defects with your vehicle.

8.79   What happens to diesel fuel when It gets hot?

☐ It expands   ☐ It liquefies   ☐ It shrinks   ☐ It waxes

DBC s2, DGV s2

On a hot day, the fuel in your tank will expand. If this happens when the tank has been filled to the brim, fuel will spill onto the road. This can be very dangerous or even fatal for other road users – especially motorcyclists. Allow for this expansion when filling your tank.

8.80   What must vehicle operators provide for their drivers?

☐ A system for reporting vehicle defects

☐ A daily update on all motorway hold-ups

☐ A hands-free mobile communications system

☐ A fuel-saving incentive scheme

DBC s3, DGV s3

The operator must have a system in place so that drivers can report defects and have them repaired property.

8.81 You're driving a three-axle double-deck bus. Why should you take extra care when using full steering lock?

❑ Passengers might alter the angle of tilt

❑ The power steering might fail

❑ You may damage the air suspension

❑ You may scrub the rear tyres

DBC s2
Very low speed is advisable to reduce damage to the rearmost tyres when the vehicle is on full lock. When you're driving around tight corners, the rear wheels will follow a different path from the front wheels. You should be alert to anything the rear wheels or bodywork might strike.

8.82 You're driving a three-axle double-deck bus and have the steering turned onto full lock. What should you do to avoid rear tyre scrub?

❑ Use the highest gear possible

❑ Drive at a very low speed

❑ Apply the exhaust brake (retarder)

❑ Reduce the pressure in the rear tyres

DBC s2
When turning tight corners, allow for the course the wheels will take. A very low speed is advisable when the steering is on full lock. This is to minimise any scrubbing effect on the rear tyres.

8.83 You're driving a double-deck bus. What's the minimum depth of tread required over three-quarters of each tyre's width?

❑ 0.8 mm   ❑ 1 mm   ❑ 1.6 mm   ❑ 2mm

DBC s2
It's essential that the tyres on your vehicle are in good condition. You must never forget that you have passengers on board. Their safety must be your priority. At no time should the depth of the tread be less than 1 mm over three-quarters of the width of the tyre.

8.84 What should you do if you notice that your coach's right rear indicator isn't working?

❑ Continue your journey using arm signals

❑ Get it repaired before continuing

❑ Get it repaired on your return to the depot

❑ Get your passengers to their destination and then repair it

DBC s3
All lights must be in working order, even in daylight. A faulty right rear indicator could cause a serious incident if another motorist attempts to overtake as you change lanes or turn right.

8.85 Before each journey, you should check all warning lights. What should you do if a warning light remains lit?

❑ Report the fault when you return

❑ Have the fault checked before setting off

❑ Have the fault checked at the next service

❑ Ignore it until the fault shows up

DBC s3
Many buses and coaches have a large panel of warning lights on the dashboard. A system check built into the ignition system will allow you to check that all the warning-light bulbs are working before you start your journey. If a warning light stays on, there's a fault. Have it checked before continuing. Remember, your passengers' lives are in your hands.

8.86 Why should you check your tyres more frequently on a coach with three axles?

❑ Punctures can be more difficult to detect

❑ Air pressure is more easily lost

❑ The wheels will need balancing more often

❑ You've no room for a spare wheel

DBC s2
Tyre checks should be made as a matter of routine. Inspect both the inside and outside walls, as well as the treads, for signs of wear, damage, bulges, separation and exposed cords.

8.87 Some buses have different-sized wheels on the front and rear. What do you need to be aware of when driving at high speeds on long journeys?

❑ The tyres on the larger wheels are more likely to overheat

❑ The tyres on the smaller wheels are more likely to overheat

❑ The tyres on the larger wheels are more likely to lose pressure

❑ The tyres on the smaller wheels are more likely to lose pressure

DBC s2
Because small wheels need to rotate faster, their tyres are more likely to overheat on long journeys at speed. Make sure you check them when you take rest stops.

8.88   How frequently should a driver carry out a walk-round check?

☐ Daily   ☐ Weekly

☐ Every 100 miles ☐ Every 1000 miles

DBC s3
Drivers should carry out a walk-round check daily, as part of a routine. They have a legal responsibility to take all reasonable precautions to ensure that legal requirements are met before they drive any vehicle.

8.89   What should you do before stopping a turbocharged engine?

☐ Release the air-suspension valve

☐ Allow the engine to idle

☐ Select reverse gear

☐ Rev the engine sharply

DBC s4
You should always allow engines fitted with turbochargers to idle for about a minute before stopping the engine. This prevents the turbine bearings from being starved of oil.

8.90   A passenger tells you they've noticed that a wheel nut is missing from your bus. How often should you check your vehicle's wheel nuts?

☐ At the end of every week

☐ At the start of every week

☐ Every day before starting out

☐ Only at every service interval

DBC s3
It's essential to make sure that all wheel nuts are tightened with a correctly calibrated torque wrench. The wheel nuts should be checked every day before you start your journey. If a passenger tells you they've noticed that a wheel nut is missing, check It Immediately. If there's a problem, don't move off until it's been rectified.

8.91   What should you do when you park a vehicle that's fitted with a turbocharger?

☐ Rev the engine up, then switch it off

☐ Switch the engine off immediately

☐ Allow the engine to idle, then switch it off

☐ Switch the engine off and on repeatedly

DBC s3
An engine fitted with a turbocharger should be allowed to idle for about a minute before it's switched off. This prevents the turbocharger bearings from being starved of oil.

8.92   You're driving at night on a very busy road when your headlights fail. What should you do if the fuse box is on the outside of the bus, on the right-hand side?

☐ Ask a passenger to watch for traffic

☐ Drive on without lights

☐ Fix the problem yourself

☐ Wait for the breakdown services

DBC s4, HC r274–275
Fast-moving traffic is passing close by, so wait for the breakdown services to arrive. Their vehicle will provide protection while your vehicle is repaired or recovered.

8.93   Your coach often tows a trailer. How often should you check the trailer tyres for pressure?

☐ At least once a week when they're cold

☐ At least once a month when they're hot

☐ At least once a week when they're hot

☐ At least once a month when the trailer is fully laden

DBC s2, 4
Just like your bus tyres, your trailer tyres must be in good condition. You might not tow a trailer on every journey you make, but when you do, check the trailer tyres while they're cold and make sure they're suitable for the load they'll carry.

8.94   The bus you're driving is fitted with automatic transmission. When would you use kickdown?

☐ When stopping in an emergency

☐ When changing to a higher gear

☐ When driving at slow speed

☐ When needing brisk acceleration

DBC s2
The kickdown facility on automatic transmission allows a lower gear to be engaged to allow faster acceleration (for example, when overtaking). This is achieved by firmly pressing the accelerator to the floor.

8.95 Your coach is fully laden. What's the most likely reason for the steering feeling heavy?

❏ An icy road ❏ A burst rear tyre

❏ Faulty power steering ❏ Too many passengers

DBC s2
All modern vehicles have some form of power-assisted steering, which will be able to cope with everything the vehicle requires. If the steering feels heavy, the power-steering system could be faulty and needs to be checked before you continue your journey.

8.96 Why are frequent tyre checks advisable on a tri-axle double-deck vehicle?

❏ These tyres are more likely to deflate

❏ Punctures can be difficult to detect

❏ Blow-outs are more common on these vehicles

❏ Tyre pressures are difficult to maintain

DBC s2
On multi-axled vehicles, the inside wheels on the rear twin-axle are the most difficult to check for punctures and damage. A deflated tyre will transfer the weight to the second tyre of the twin-axle pair. This will overload it and could cause it to burst.

8.97 When should the driver of a coach wear gloves?

❏ To load and stow passengers' luggage

❏ To operate a lift for disabled passengers

❏ To handle the fares

❏ To top up the oil or water levels

DBC s2
Even the best-maintained vehicles accumulate a certain amount of grime around the engine. If this comes into contact with skin, it can cause irritation and may lead to conditions such as dermatitis. By wearing gloves, you can also keep your hands and cuffs clean to present a smart appearance to your customers.

8.98 You're driving a six-wheeled double-deck bus. What do you need to know about punctures on the rear tyres?

❏ They're much easier to detect

❏ They're more likely to happen

❏ They're more difficult to detect

❏ They're less likely to happen

DBC s2
The handling of a six-wheeled bus or coach is not much different from that of a two-axle vehicle, except that punctures can be more difficult to detect.

8.99 What should you regularly check on the tyres of your bus?

❏ The tyre manufacturer's details are displayed

❏ The tyre pressures are all correct

❏ The dust caps are all in place

❏ The tread depths are equal on all tyres

DBC s2
Tyre care is especially important. You should routinely check tyre pressures and general tyre condition. An unroadworthy vehicle will endanger the lives of your passengers.

8.100 What will result from having over-inflated tyres?

❏ You'll have improved acceleration

❏ The tyres will wear more quickly

❏ The tyres will give better grip

❏ The fuel consumption will be reduced

DBC s2
Your tyres must be in good condition and properly inflated to the manufacturer's recommended pressure. Research has shown that the tyres most likely to fail are those that have been over-inflated.

8.101 What should you do before uncoupling your trailer?

❏ Disconnect the battery

❏ Park on a firm, level surface

❏ Park in a well-lit location

❏ Unload some of the cargo

DBC s2
Before uncoupling a trailer, always make sure that you've parked on firm, level ground and applied the trailer parking brake.

Section 9 Leaving the vehicle

9.1 What should you be careful of when stopping on the left in a busy place?

☐ There's good access to unload

☐ You've disconnected all the air lines

☐ Your nearside mirror doesn't strike the head of a pedestrian

☐ You change your tachograph mode

DGV s4
When stopping on the left, you should always be aware of pedestrians, particularly if they're close to the edge of the road. The height of your nearside mirror can vary depending on the size and type of vehicle you're driving. If in doubt, approach these situations with caution and stop if necessary.

9.2 You've just parked a lorry on the side of the road. What should you do just before dismounting from the cab?

☐ Make sure the radio is turned down

☐ Check the rear-view mirrors

☐ Make sure the hazard warning lights are on

☐ Check that all the windows are closed

DGV s3
Getting out of the cab on the offside, directly into the road, can be hazardous – especially if traffic is travelling at speed. Use your mirrors to check that it's safe to leave the vehicle. Be sure to use all proper footholds and hand grips when you leave the cab.

9.3 Where are you allowed to park a long, rigid vehicle?

☐ At a pedestrian crossing ☐ At a bus stop

☐ At a school entrance   ☐ At a service area

DGV s3
It's important that you always select a place to park that's both safe and legal. Don't park on or too close to a pedestrian crossing or a school entrance; this would restrict the view for drivers and pedestrians. Don't park at a bus stop either, because buses would then have to stop in the road, creating a hazard for other traffic and for passengers getting on or off the bus.

9.4 Where should you park a semi-trailer if you plan to leave it unattended?

☐ On a residential street

☐ On a steep hill

☐ In a lorry park

☐ In a lay-by

DGV s3
If you need to park and leave a semi-trailer, find a safe place. Don't park it in a lay-by or anywhere it could be an obstruction or a danger. Leave lay-bys for drivers who wish to stop and rest. Find a place off the road – preferably a lorry park or somewhere safe that will also reduce the risk of theft.

9.5 Which of the following is important when you're getting out of a lorry cab?

☐ Checking your load is secure

☐ Using the mirrors

☐ Turning off the radio

☐ Disconnecting the air lines

DGV s3
When getting out of your lorry cab, it's essential that you check it's safe to dismount by checking your mirrors and looking out for traffic. When you're safely down, it's then a good idea to walk round and check your tyres, load, lights, brake lines, electrical connections, etc.

9.6 You're the driver of a fuel tanker. What danger should you be aware of when opening the tank hatches?

☐ Low air pressure   ☐ Speed limiters

☐ Slippery walkways ☐ Emergency air lines

DGV s2
Take your time when you're using walkways at high levels. Spilt fuel can make the surface slippery and increase the risk of falling.

9.7 You're working on the platform of a flat bed lorry. What's the safest way to get down to the ground?

❑ Use a suitable set of steps

❑ Jump down wearing non-slip shoes

❑ Use ropes to lower yourself down

❑ Climb down facing away from the vehicle

DGV s3
Every year, many people are seriously injured by falling from vehicles. Using suitable steps will lessen the chance of falling. Be aware of the dangers when loading or unloading vehicles.

9.8 What do you need to consider when transporting a high-value cargo of cigarettes?

❑ There'll be a risk of theft or hijack

❑ There'll be more Revenue and Customs checks

❑ You'll be allowed to take fewer rest breaks

❑ You'll need to maintain your regular route

DGV s3
If you're carrying a high-value load, you should consider your personal safety. There's always the possibility of an attempted theft. Watch out for and report anything unusual, such as people taking a special interest in you or your vehicle.

9.9 What should you consider having on your vehicle to combat theft?

❑ Roof markings   ❑ Diff-lock

❑ Air horns   ❑ Tinted windows

DGV s3
Roof markings on lorries can help police air-support units to identify stolen vehicles. Fleet operators, particularly those that regularly carry vulnerable or dangerous loads, are encouraged to use these markings.

9.10 When should you use your mirrors?

❑ As you signal   ❑ To check the blind spot

❑ Occasionally   ❑ Before opening your door

DGV s3, 4
You must be aware of the position of other road users, so that you know how they may be affected by your actions. Before opening your door, it's important to check the mirrors, as well as looking around for passing or approaching vehicles and pedestrians.

9.11 What must you do before you leave your vehicle?

❑ Empty the air tanks

❑ Adjust your mirrors

❑ Apply the parking brake

❑ Check that the warning lights are working

HC r239
The parking brake must always be set whenever you leave the vehicle. It's an offence not to leave your vehicle properly secured.

9.12 What should you do before leaving your vehicle parked on a public road?

❑ Remove your tachograph chart

❑ Switch off the engine

❑ Adjust the mirrors

❑ Put the gear lever into reverse

HC r239
It's an offence to leave a vehicle unattended on a public road with the engine running. Take care if you have to open the cab door directly into the road. Look for passing traffic – especially cyclists or motorcyclists – that may not be visible in your mirrors.

9.13 What should you be aware of before opening your cab door?

❑ Vehicles passing near the door

❑ The height of your cab from the ground

❑ Loose grab rails near the door

❑ People crossing the road behind you

HC r239
It can be dangerous for vehicles passing close by if you open the door carelessly. Always look properly to make sure that it's safe – checking the blind spots as well as using the mirrors – before you get out of the cab.

9.14 When should you use hazard warning lights?

❑ To warn other drivers that you're towing

❑ When approaching queuing traffic on a motorway

❑ When parked illegally on a busy road

❑ To thank a driver for giving way to you

HC r116
The only time you may use hazard warning lights while driving is when you're on an unrestricted dual carriageway or motorway and you want to warn other drivers of a hazard or obstruction ahead. Only use them for long enough to make sure your warning is seen.

9.15 You need to stop and get out of your vehicle. When should you use the parking brake?

❑ After the service brake has been released

❑ Only if you park on a gradient

❑ Whenever you leave the vehicle

❑ After the air pressure has dropped

HC r239
It's an offence to leave your vehicle unattended at any time without applying the parking brake.

9.16 You've parked on the roadside. What must you do before leaving the vehicle?

❑ Reset the retarder

❑ Stop the engine

❑ Switch off the tachograph

❑ Remove your personal items

HC r239
Before leaving your vehicle parked, you must stop the engine. The parking brake must be set and the vehicle should be safe and secure when you leave the cab.

9.17 When may hazard warning lights be used while driving?

❑ To thank a driver who has let you move back to the left after overtaking

❑ As a warning to drivers that you're towing another vehicle

❑ To show you want to go ahead when your position suggests otherwise

❑ When on motorways or dual carriageways, to warn drivers behind of a hazard ahead

HC r116
Use your hazard warning lights on a motorway or unrestricted dual carriageway to warn following drivers of an obstruction or hazard ahead. This will alert drivers who may not be able to see the hazard due to the size of your vehicle.

9.18 What should you try to do when you lift a heavy box or suitcase?

❑ Lift and twist together

❑ Look down all the time

❑ Lean sideways and lift

❑ Look ahead when the load is secure

DBC s1, DGV s1
Once you have a secure hold on the object, keep your head up and bend your knees.

9.19 What's the best way to lift a heavy object?

❑ Twist your back while lifting

❑ Have a stable position

❑ Hold the load at arm's length

❑ Lift the load as quickly as possible

DBC s1, DGV s1
To lift a load manually, your feet should be apart, with one leg slightly forward to help you keep your balance. Place one foot alongside the load if it's on the ground. Be prepared to move your feet to keep a stable position.

9.20 How should you stand when you're lifting a heavy object?

❑ Leaning sideways

❑ In a stable position

❑ With one leg straight

❑ Keeping your feet together

DBC s1, DGV s1
Always think of your own and others' physical safety before lifting any heavy object. Plan the lift and move any other items out of the way. Decide whether you need assistance.

9.21   When can a bus driver use hazard warning lights?

❑ When children are getting off a school bus

❑ To thank a driver who has given way

❑ When stopping at a pedestrian crossing

❑ When parking a bus on yellow lines

DBC s1
All drivers may use hazard warning lights to warn other road users of danger on specific occasions. When you're driving a school bus, you may also use these lights when you've stopped and children are getting on or off the bus.

9.22   When do you need to take account of your vehicle having air suspension?

❑ When you're passing animals or horse riders

❑ When you're travelling up a steep gradient

❑ When you're parked close to another vehicle

❑ When you're driving in falling snow

DBC s4
Vehicles fitted with air suspension can sometimes move a considerable amount when the airbags are inflated. If you're parked too close to another vehicle or obstruction, this could result in collision damage.

9.23   What should your passengers do with their belongings when you arrive at your destination?

❑ Place them on luggage racks

❑ Take everything with them

❑ Place them on the seats

❑ Leave them with you

DBC s3
Passengers shouldn't leave any personal property on the vehicle, unless it can be locked in secure luggage compartments.

9.24   What should you do before getting out of your bus?

❑ Apply the parking brake

❑ Change the destination board

❑ Put the hazard warning lights on

❑ Check the air-pressure gauges read full

DBC s3
Don't park where you'll cause obstruction or inconvenience to other road users. It's an offence to leave your bus with the engine running and/or without applying the parking brake.

9.25   What must you do before leaving your bus?

❑ Apply the parking brake

❑ Count the fares

❑ Reset the odometer

❑ Operate the fuel cut-off switch

DBC s4
Before you leave your bus, you must always apply the parking brake.

9.26   What should you wear while unloading luggage from your coach?

❑ High-visibility vest

❑ Heatproof gloves

❑ Safety goggles

❑ Ear protectors

DBC s3, 4
Very often, you'll load or unload luggage by the roadside. For your own safety, make yourself visible to other traffic.

Section 10 Vehicle loading

10.1 How should you load a vehicle?

❏ Spread the load evenly

❏ Load it towards the rear

❏ Load it towards the front

❏ Arrange the load to make it easy for unloading

DGV s2
It's your responsibility to make sure that the vehicle's load is spread evenly, to avoid overloading individual axles. Overloading carries severe penalties for the driver and operator.

10.2 You're going to drive an articulated lorry with an ISO container on the trailer. How should the container be secured to the trailer?

❏ The container must be secured by ropes

❏ The container must be secured using the locking levers

❏ The container must be held up against the headboard

❏ The container must be sealed

DGV s2
ISO (International Standards Organization) cargo containers should only be carried on lorries or trailers with the appropriate securing points. These are designed to lock into the container body.

10.3 You're using three sheets to cover your load. Which is the correct overlap?

DGV s2
Keep a check in your mirrors as you're driving to make sure that the sheets are secure. Air can force itself under the sheets and work them loose.

10.4 You're covering a load using more than one sheet. Why should you start with the rearmost sheet, then work forwards?

❏ To stop you tripping when walking on the load

❏ To stop wind and rain from getting under the sheets

❏ To make it much easier to fold up the sheets

❏ To make it easier to carry longer loads

DGV s2
If the load is sheeted incorrectly, the wind may get underneath a sheet, making it flap about. This is dangerous, as it can catch unsuspecting pedestrians or cyclists, and it can also seriously reduce the driver's view of what's happening behind.

10.5 What's the best knot to use when securing a load with ropes?

❏ A dolly knot

❏ A reef knot

❏ A slip knot

❏ A bowline knot

DGV s2, 7
If a load is being secured with ropes, you must make sure it's tied securely to the body of the unit. The most effective method of tying is with 'dolly knots'. These are non-slip knots that hold firmly.

10.6 Why are ropes unsuitable to tie down a load of scrap metal?

❏ Ropes are hard to tie

❏ Ropes will loosen in rain

❏ Ropes are hard to untie

❏ Ropes can wear and snap

DGV s2
When securing a load, the driver must use the most suitable type of restraint. Scrap metal is likely to have sharp edges that could wear through straps or ropes. Security of the load is the driver's responsibility; a load that has been correctly secured shouldn't move if an emergency arises.

10.7 You're driving an open tipper lorry carrying loose dry sand. Why should you sheet this load?

❑ To stop the handling from being affected

❑ To stop the load from shifting

❑ To stop the load from blowing away

❑ To stop the tipper mechanism from accidentally operating

DGV s2

If you're carrying a load that consists of loose materials, it must be covered by suitable sheeting. You mustn't risk losing any part of your load. This could cause damage or injury to other road users, and you would be responsible.

10.8 What should you do if the load on your lorry becomes insecure?

❑ Continue at a slower speed to ensure the load doesn't fall off

❑ Attach 'hazard' boards to the load to warn other road users

❑ Park and resecure the load before continuing

❑ Inform base at the earliest opportunity

DGV S2

If you become aware that any part of your load is insecure, you must stop as soon as it's safe to do so. Resecure the load before continuing your journey. If this isn't possible, then you must seek assistance. Don't take risks.

10.9 Tankers carrying liquids can experience the 'wave effect'. What helps to reduce this problem?

❑ Spray guards

❑ Harsh braking

❑ Baffle plates

❑ Wind deflectors

DGV S2

Modern tankers are fitted with baffle plates inside the tank compartment. These help to minimise the movement of liquids and, therefore, reduce the 'wave effect'.

10.10 You're driving an articulated tanker on a straight road. How will the liquid load affect the vehicle as you brake to a stop?

❑ It will try to push the vehicle forward

❑ It will try to push the vehicle to the side

❑ It will make the trailer wheels bounce

❑ It will make the trailer wheels skid

DGV s2

When braking a vehicle carrying a liquid load, it's important to apply even pressure on the brake pedal. Don't relax the pedal pressure until the vehicle has stopped. Secure the vehicle with the parking brake before releasing the footbrake; this will minimise the risk of unintentional movement of the vehicle caused by 'surge' from the liquid load.

10.11 You're driving a tanker that's half full. The inside of the tank isn't divided into compartments. How should you use the footbrake when you're stopping?

❑ Keep pressure on the brake pedal until you've stopped

❑ Relax pressure on the brake pedal before you've stopped

❑ Pump the brake pedal rapidly

❑ Use the footbrake and parking brake together

DGV s2

When braking, always maintain steady pressure on the brake pedal until the vehicle has stopped. This helps to reduce the 'wave effect' that can build up as the liquid load moves when the vehicle changes speed.

10.12 Which type of load would benefit most from being carried on a lorry fitted with road-friendly suspension?

❑ Steel

❑ Timber

❑ Glass

❑ Cables

DGV s2

Fragile loads need extra care in loading and handling. The load must be secured using the most appropriate form of restraint. Air suspension reduces the vibration caused by the impact of the lorry wheels on road surfaces. This also reduces damage to the road, bridges and adjacent structures.

10.13 How wide does a load need to be before an attendant is required?

❏ 2.6 metres (8 feet 5 inches)

❏ 3.0 metres (9 feet 9 inches)

❏ 3.3 metres (10 feet 9 inches)

❏ 3.5 metres (11 feet 5 inches)

DGV s2
Wide loads are a hazard to other road users. In addition to having an attendant with you, you must notify the police if your load is wider than 3.5 metres (11 feet 5 inches). Side markers must also be used to show other road users the limits of your vehicle.

10.14 When is an articulated lorry most likely to jack-knife?

❏ When it's carrying a high load

❏ When its load is carried at the rear of the trailer

❏ When it's unloaded

❏ When it's fully loaded

DGVs2
When the trailer is loaded, the weight of the load presses the trailer tyres firmly onto the road surface, so improving the tyres' grip. Unladen, there is no load bearing down on the tyres, and under heavy braking the trailer wheels can lock or slide across the road surface, making the trailer more difficult to stop. Severe braking can result in jack-knifing: the trailer doesn't slow as quickly as the tractor unit and this causes it to pivot around the coupling.

10.15 You've finished recoupling. How should you make sure that the tractor and trailer are secure?

❏ Try to move forward with the trailer parking brake on

❏ Reverse with the trailer parking brake on

❏ Try to move forward with the trailer parking brake off

❏ Reverse with the trailer parking brake off

DGV s6
Make sure the locking mechanism is secure by selecting a low gear and attempting to move forward. Apply the parking brake again before leaving the cab. Connect the 'dog clip' to secure the kingpin release handle.

10.16 What must you check first when uncoupling or recoupling your trailer?

❏ The lights are working

❏ The tilt-cab mechanism is secure

❏ The trailer brake is applied

❏ The air lines are safely stowed

DGV s6
If the trailer begins moving while you're working on it, you could put yourself and others in great danger. You must make sure that it's properly secured by the brake before you start work.

10.17 You're uncoupling a lorry and trailer. What should you do after disconnecting the electrical line?

❏ Stow it away safely   ❏ Drive forward slowly

❏ Lower the landing gear ❏ Apply the trailer brake

DGV s2
It's important to stow away all your electrical cables and air lines safely to avoid causing injury to others. Connectors left lying around can be a trip hazard and can be damaged if they're run over by another vehicle.

10.18 Your lorry has a demountable body. What should you check before demounting the body?

❏ The rear doors are open

❏ The legs are up

❏ The body is unloaded and empty

❏ The surface is firm and level

DGV s2
If you demount the body on a poor or soft surface, there's a danger of it sinking and becoming difficult to handle. Always think carefully before you demount the body and be sure that the site is suitable.

10.19 How should you adjust your mirrors after recoupling your trailer?

❏ To give a full view of your load

❏ To give a clear view of both pairs of rear wheels

❏ To give a view down each side of the trailer

❏ To give a view of the road on the other side

DGV s2
The view you get in your mirrors may vary, depending on the size of the trailer and the load it carries. Always adjust your mirrors to ensure that you have the best possible view down each side of the trailer before you drive away.

10.20   Which vehicle is most likely to be affected by 'vehicle bounce'?

❑ A long-wheelbase empty vehicle

❑ A short-wheelbase laden vehicle

❑ A short-wheelbase empty vehicle

❑ A long-wheelbase laden vehicle

DGV s2

A short-wheelbase empty vehicle will bounce more noticeably than some long-wheelbase vehicles. This can affect braking efficiency and all-round control. Don't be tempted to push this type of vehicle into bends or corners simply because the vehicle appears to be easier to drive.

10.21   Which type of load should be secured using chains?

❑ Timber planks   ❑ Hay bales

❑ Steel plates   ❑ Canvas sacks

DGV s2

The choice of restraint will depend on the load. For example, ropes are unsuitable for loads such as steel plates, as there's a danger of sharp edges shearing the ropes. For steel plates, chains must be used with a suitable tensioning device.

10.22   Which load is most likely to move forward with some force when you brake sharply?

❑ Heavy material in canvas sacks ❑ Loose sand

❑ Timber secured with dolly knots ❑ Tubular metal

DGV s2

When deciding which type of restraint to use, consider what may, happen if you have to brake sharply. Tubular loads may move forward with some force if you have to brake sharply in an emergency. This could cause serious damage to the vehicle's headboard.

10.23   You're part-loading a lorry with an empty ISO container. Where should you position it on the trailer?

❑ Close to the fifth wheel   ❑ Over the front axle

❑ Close to the trailer edge ❑ Over the rear axles

DGV s2

To increase stability and reduce the risk of the trailer wheels lifting when turning, it's preferable to locate part-loads over the rear axle(s).

10.24   How must spare sheets and ropes be carried on your trailer?

❑ Laid out flat   ❑ Visible from the cab

❑ Tied down securely ❑ Stacked loosely

DGV s2

All spare sheets and ropes carried on the vehicle must be tied down securely to prevent them falling onto the road, where they may be a hazard for other vehicles.

10.25   Which articulated trailer is most at risk of jack-knifing?

❑ A loaded flat-bed trailer

❑ A laden fuel tanker

❑ A loaded high-sided trailer

❑ An unladen trailer

DGV s2

Jack-knifing occurs when the tractor unit is pushed by the semi-trailer pivoting around the coupling (fifth wheel). This is more likely to occur with an unladen vehicle.

10.26   In what circumstances will short-wheelbase vehicles bounce more noticeably than long-wheelbase vehicles?

❑ When laden

❑ When turning

❑ When empty

❑ When travelling slowly

DGV s2

Short-wheelbase vehicles will bounce more noticeably than some long-wheelbase vehicles when empty. This can affect braking efficiency and all-round control.

10.27   What's the main cause of a lorry shedding its load?

❑ Driving on motorways

❑ Driving too fast

❑ Driving over a level crossing

❑ Driving in wet weather

DGV s2

The main causes of lorries shedding their loads are driver errors, such as sudden changes of speed or direction, driving too fast for the conditions, and harsh braking.

10.28 What could happen if you drive a double-deck lorry with the top deck loaded and the lower deck empty?

☐ The lorry will become unstable under normal braking

☐ The brakes will be less effective

☐ The lorry may overturn when cornering

☐ You'll need to change gear more often

DGV s2
It you're only carrying halt a load on a double-deck lorry, this should be carried on the lower deck whenever possible. With only the top deck loaded, your lorry is top-heavy and at risk of overturning as you drive around bends or corners.

10.29 Your lorry has a double-deck body. The top tier is loaded and the lower deck is empty. When will the vehicle be most at risk of overturning?

☐ In thick fog   ☐ In high winds

☐ In hot weather   ☐ In heavy rain

DGV s2
A lorry loaded like this will be top-heavy and more likely to overturn in high winds or when cornering. If you're only carrying half a load, you should try to carry it on the lower deck.

10.30 You're carrying another vehicle piggyback on your lorry. Chocks should be used to secure the wheels. What else should you use to secure the load?

☐ Baffle plates   ☐ Axle stands

☐ Restraining straps   ☐ A scaffolding bar

DGV s2
You should use a suitable restraint and chock the wheels when another vehicle is being carried piggyback. Don't just rely on the other vehicle's parking brake.

10.31 The lorry you're driving is heavily laden. How will the load affect the vehicle if you approach a left-hand bend too fast?

☐ The load will push the lorry to the left

☐ The load will pull the lorry to the right

☐ The load will push the lorry straight on

☐ The load will hold the lorry back

DGV s2
The forces acting on a lorry will try to move it in a straight line as it enters a bend. The greater the weight, the greater the force. If you're going too fast, there's a danger that you could lose your load or tip over.

10.32 You're driving a vehicle with an unladen trailer. What could happen if you change down to a low gear while travelling at speed?

☐ Your vehicle may suddenly accelerate

☐ The endurance brake will come on

☐ You won't be able to brake

☐ Your could lose control of your vehicle

DGV s2
Changing down to an inappropriate gear at too high a speed will cause your vehicle to slow down suddenly. With no separate braking for the trailer, the tractor could be pushed to the point where it turns over.

10.33 Your lorry has a crane fitted. You're loading very heavy items. What should you do when you feel that the ropes or straps may break?

☐ Reposition the load

☐ Use chains and tensioners

☐ Tie two straps together

☐ Continue loading carefully

DGV s2
If there's any danger that the load you're lifting with a crane is too heavy for ropes or straps, or that sharp edges on the load may damage them, you should use chains with compatible tensioners.

10.34 When you're carrying other vehicles piggyback, you should use restraints and the parking brake on each vehicle. What else should you do?

☐ Make sure the vehicles are sheeted

☐ Place chocks under the wheels

☐ Put the heavy vehicles at the top

☐ Rope the vehicles together

DGV s2
Vehicles being carried piggyback must always have chocks applied to their wheels, in addition to a restraint. Never rely on just their parking brake.

10.35   When will an articulated car transporter be least stable?

❏ When only the lower deck is loaded

❏ When only the top deck is loaded

❏ When it's fully laden

❏ When it's unladen

DGV s2
Keeping the centre of gravity as low as possible will improve the handling of a car transporter. Top-heavy loads are more unstable and require more care when turning and cornering.

10.36   What do the legs on a demountable body enable you to do?

❏ Load and unload the body without stopping

❏ Stack one body on top of another

❏ Alter the overall height of the vehicle

❏ Demount the body without a crane or lift

DGV s2
Demountable bodies have legs that can be lowered so that the carrier vehicle can be driven out from underneath the body. This has an advantage over ISO containers, which require some form of crane or lift to remove the container from the trailer.

10.37   What shape are the labels that indicate a vehicle is carrying hazardous cargo?

❏ Diamond   ❏ Triangle   ❏ Circle   ❏ Oval

DGV s2
Hazardous substances in transit are readily identified by a diamond-shaped warning label. This label carries other information to identify the type of hazard more specifically, such as

• flammable gas
• toxic gas
• corrosive agents.

These are just some of the types of hazard encountered. Strict regulations apply to the storage and carriage of these goods. All drivers of this type of load must receive specific certificated training.

10.38   Why are baffle plates fitted to tankers carrying liquids?

❏ To reduce wind resistance

❏ To reduce the wave effect

❏ To stop the brakes from locking

❏ To make the steering lighter

DGV s2
Fluids carried in tankers can move in waves as the vehicle's speed or direction changes. This happens particularly when you brake and then ease off the pedal; the moving wave of liquid causes the vehicle to surge forward. Baffle plates are designed to reduce this surging effect.

10.39   Which of these vehicles will be most at risk of 'roll-over' when laden?

❏   ❏

❏   ❏

DGV s2
'Roll-over' usually happens as a result of the inside rear wheels of an articulated vehicle starting to lift when the driver changes direction sharply. This tends to happen when a driver is changing direction to leave a roundabout. If the load moves during the change of direction, the vehicle is increasingly at risk of rolling over. The problem often involves vehicles carrying fluids in bulk.

10.40   You're unloading an end-tipper lorry. What should you do before tipping the body?

❏ Make sure the vehicle is on a firm, level surface

❏ Park facing uphill to make unloading easy

❏ Make sure the vehicle is on a soft, sloping surface

❏ Park downhill for easier unloading

DGV s2
Unless you're on firm, level ground, there's a risk of your lorry overturning when the body is tipped. Before raising the body, check that you're well clear of overhead obstructions such as power lines.

10.41   Who must you inform if the load on your trailer hits a railway bridge?

❏ The local authority   ❏ DVLA

❏ Highways England   ❏ The railway authority

DGV s2
If your vehicle hits a bridge, you must report it to the police. If a railway bridge is involved, you must also report it to the railway authority. The phone number is usually shown on or near the bridge.

10.42 Which of these best describes a vehicle's payload?

❏ The maximum load the vehicle can carry

❏ The maximum load over each axle

❏ The maximum load plus the weight of the vehicle

❏ The maximum load each tyre can take

DGV s2

The formula used to calculate the payload of a vehicle is the maximum authorised mass (MAM) minus the tare weight. The tare weight is the total weight of the vehicle, including the crew and extra equipment.

10.43 What additional training do you need before transporting frozen foods?

❏ Packaging procedures

❏ Weight-distribution procedures

❏ Waste-handling procedures

❏ Hygiene procedures

DGV s1, 2

When transporting frozen food, you need to know how to operate your refrigeration unit correctly. It's also essential that you're aware of correct hygiene procedures when handling food.

10.44 You've parked your vehicle on level ground to deliver a load of building materials. What should you do before using the vehicle-mounted crane?

❏ Switch the engine off

❏ Turn the steering wheels to the left

❏ Lower the stabilising legs

❏ Set out warning cones

DGV s2

Before using the crane, it's vital to make sure the vehicle is parked on level ground and the stabilising legs are lowered. This will reduce the risk of the load becoming unstable during lifting. Also check for any overhead cables that may obstruct the crane.

10.45 You're loading goods of varying weights. How should they be distributed over the width of the vehicle?

❏ Heavy items at the front, light items at the rear

❏ Light items near the centre line, heavy items towards the sides

❏ Heavy items near the centre line, light items towards the sides

❏ Light items at the front, heavy items at the rear

DGV s2

To achieve maximum stability, the load should be placed to keep the centre of gravity as low as possible. To do this, heavy items should be placed close to the centre line and spread over the full length of the vehicle. Lighter items should be placed along the sides.

10.46 What should you do when you're working on a vehicle platform?

❏ Make sure you can jump down

❏ Walk forward near the edges

❏ Work in stockinged feet

❏ Walk backwards near the edges

DGV s2

When working on a flat-bed or open curtain-sided vehicle, you should always be aware of your proximity to the edge of the platform. It's too easy to concentrate on moving and positioning the load, and lose sight of your own position. Stepping backwards could be fatal, so always make sure you're facing the edge as you approach it.

10.47 Which of these loads needs to be transported at a controlled temperature?

❏ Frozen foods

❏ Timber

❏ Bulk grain

❏ Cement

DGV s1, 2

Some loads need to be transported in special conditions. For example, chilled or frozen foods need to be transported in a refrigeration unit. To drive one of these units, you'll need to be trained in how to use it. You'll also need relevant training in hygiene procedures.

10.48   What will you need to transport livestock on journeys of less than 65 km (40 miles)?

❑ Practical experience In the care of animals

❑ Membership of the RSPCA

❑ No driving convictions

❑ The ability to drive abroad

DGV s1, 2
The type of training required by drivers carrying livestock varies according to the distance, journey duration and species involved. For journeys of less than 65 km (40 miles), no formal qualification is required but you must have practical experience in the care of animals being transported.

10.49   What should you do when transporting a small quantity of livestock that doesn't fill the vehicle?

❑ Allow no direct access to the animals

❑ Check them for disease before you load

❑ Give the animals plenty of space

❑ Create compartments using moveable panels

DGV s1, 2
When transporting livestock, it's important to limit the amount of space they have to move around. If you allow them to move around freely, it could increase the risk of injury to the animals. It will also affect the stability of the vehicle when braking and cornering, and could even cause the vehicle to tip over.

10.50   Your vehicle has a maximum authorised mass of 40 tonnes. The kerbside weight is 15 tonnes. What's your maximum payload?

❑ 15 tonnes

❑ 25 tonnes

❑ 35 tonnes

❑ 45 tonnes

DGV s2
Overloading a vehicle is dangerous. Your stopping distance will increase, and your vehicle could become unstable and difficult to control. You'll need to work out the payload. Do this by taking away the kerbside weight from the maximum authorised mass (MAM). This will give you the maximum weight you can carry.

10.51   You're making several deliveries. What problems may the decreasing payload cause?

❑ You might overload an axle

❑ You'll always have heavy items remaining

❑ You might exceed your kerbside weight

❑ You'll damage the rest of the load

DGV s2
As items are unloaded from the rear of the vehicle, weight will be transferred to the front axle. Take care that this axle doesn't become overloaded. You may need to redistribute the load.

10.52   What can result from overloading an axle?

❑ Reduced braking efficiency

❑ Reduced braking distance

❑ Increased kerbside weight

❑ Increased fuel efficiency

DGV s2
Too much weight on an axle can reduce braking efficiency and cause brake fade. As well as being dangerous, exceeding the axle weight limit is an offence that can result in prosecution.

10.53   What could be the result of overloading an axle while loading a lorry?

❑ Reduced tyre temperature

❑ Damage to the road surface

❑ Damage to the tachograph

❑ Increased tyre life

DGV s2
Overloading an axle has an impact on the environment, causing damage to road surfaces. You also risk a fine and driving penalties.

10.54   You're transporting a skip carrying loose waste. How should the material be carried?

❑ Covered

❑ Shrink-wrapped

❑ While displaying a warning beacon

❑ Under a waterproof membrane

DGV s2
The skip should be covered to prevent any part of the load from blowing away. Loose material blown onto the road could be a danger to other road users and can cause environmental damage.

10.55 You're securing a very heavy load with a ratchet strap. Which anchorage point is unsafe to use with ratchet straps?

❑ Rope hook ❑ Eye bolt ❑ Shackle ❑ 'D' link

DGV s2

Rope hooks aren't designed to withstand high forces. They're usually just welded or bolted to the underside of the platform. Many are so weak that they can easily be distorted by a ratchet buckle when a webbing strap is tightened. Secure anchorage points should be built into the main frame or chassis of the vehicle.

10.56 You're securing a load using chains. Which type of chain is unsafe for securing a load?

❑ Short-link ❑ Round-link ❑ Oval-link ❑ Split-link

DGV s2

Split-link and iron chains shouldn't be used to secure loads, as they're less reliable than solid-link and steel chains. For more information on the suitability of various-sized steel chains, consult the relevant British Standard (BS) leaflets.

10.57 You're securing a load using ropes. What's the minimum diameter of rope that should be used?

❑ 5mm ❑ 10 mm ❑ 15 mm ❑ 20 mm

DGV s2

When using ropes, the ends should be spliced or otherwise treated to prevent fraying. The rope should be of at least three-strand construction, with a normal diameter of at least 10 mm.

10.58 You're loading timber onto a flat-bed lorry. You want to cover it with sheets. Which sheet should be positioned first?

❑ Front ❑ Middle ❑ Rear ❑ Side

DGV s2

When more than one sheet is used to cover and protect a load, the rear sheet should be positioned first. This is so that the overlaps face backwards, rather than forwards, preventing wind and rain from getting between the sheets.

10.59 What's the main reason for covering a skip that you're transporting?

❑ To prevent any spillage

❑ To stop children climbing in

❑ To keep the contents dry

❑ To prevent theft

DGV s2

Debris falling from vehicles can be very dangerous to other road users, so skips need to be covered when they're transported. Falling debris may also cause environmental damage.

10.60 Which cargo needs to be transported at a controlled temperature?

❑ Perishable foods ❑ Barrels of beer

❑ Cement ❑ Silage

DGV s1, 2

Some foods need to be transported at controlled temperatures. Drivers will need to be trained in the use of refrigeration units and correct hygiene procedures.

10.61 Which load may need to be transported at a controlled temperature?

❑ Chemicals

❑ Bulk grain

❑ Sugar

❑ Beer barrels

DGV s2

Some highly dangerous chemicals have to be transported at prescribed temperatures. Drivers must be fully trained in the use of these specially designed, temperature-controlled vehicles.

10.62 Which symbol on a lorry means it's likely to be carrying compressed gases?

DGV s7

Vehicles carrying dangerous or hazardous goods need to have markings on them that clearly identify the load. This could, for example, help the emergency services to deal with any incident quickly and safely.

10.63 What's being carried on a lorry displaying this symbol?

☐ Corrosive materials

☐ Compressed gases

☐ Oxidising agents

☐ Radioactive materials

DGV s7
The symbols on the back or side of a lorry should show the type of material that the vehicle will normally be carrying.

10.64 Which symbol on the back of a lorry means it's carrying a corrosive substance?

☐
☐
☐
☐

DGV s7
If you drive a vehicle carrying dangerous or hazardous material, you must make sure the correct symbol or mark is clearly visible.

10.65 Which symbol on a lorry shows its load is dangerous when wet?

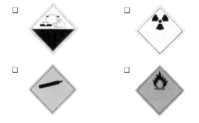

☐
☐
☐
☐

DGV s7
If any vehicle displaying a warning symbol is involved in an incident, the consequences could be serious. The emergency services need to be aware of how a dangerous or hazardous material will behave in different situations; for example, when it's wet.

10.66 You're driving a loaded lorry with curtain sides. What should you do when you see the curtain bulging on one side?

☐ Check the load by carefully entering through the rear door or opposite curtain

☐ Check the load by carefully opening the curtain in the affected area

☐ Continue driving, as this is normal for these types of vehicles

☐ Continue driving at a much reduced speed

DGV s2
You must stop in a safe place as soon as possible. The curtain might be the only support for a slipped load, so don't open it before checking. Check the load by carefully opening the rear door or opposite curtain, if it shows no sign of bulging.

10.67 You're loading a curtain-sided vehicle. What are the curtains for?

☐ Restraint

☐ Protection from the weather

☐ Improved visibility

☐ To reduce noise

DGV s2
Unless the curtains are specifically designed, they must not be used to restrain the load. They should be used to protect it from the weather and provide a level of security. Most companies also use them as a mobile advertisement.

10.68 You're using a lorry-mounted crane to unload building materials. What safety features should you use?

☐ Wheel clamps

☐ Kingpin locks

☐ Jockey wheels

☐ Vehicle stabilisers

DGV s2
When using a lorry-mounted crane, stabilisers should always be used. All drivers should be fully trained and regularly tested on their competence in using stabilisers.

10.69 You intend to move a heavy object using a barrow or trolley. What's the best height for the handles?

❑ Between the shoulder and the waist

❑ As high as you can reach

❑ Between the knee and the waist

❑ As low as possible for comfort

DGV s1
When moving a load, make sure you don't have to bend down or stretch up to reach the handles. Also, try to push rather than pull, so you can see where you're going.

10.70 Your vehicle has a maximum authorised mass of 40 tonnes. The tare weight is 10 tonnes. What's your maximum payload?

❑ 20 tonnes

❑ 30tonnes

❑ 40 tonnes

❑ 50 tonnes

DGV s2
To work out your vehicle's payload, use the following formula: maximum authorised mass (MAM), minus tare weight, equals payload. This is the maximum weight your vehicle can carry.

Section 11 Restricted view

11.1 Some lorries have an extra mirror angled down towards the nearside front wheel. What's this mirror especially useful for?

❏ Overtaking

❏ Parking

❏ Checking your trailer

❏ Turning right

DGV s4
Sitting in a high cab doesn't always give you all-round visibility. Other road users might assume that you can see them and position themselves out of sight close to your vehicle. Making good use of any extra mirrors can help prevent dangerous incidents, especially when parking.

11.2 What should you look for when choosing a site to park your trailer?

❏ The site should be level

❏ The site should be made of concrete

❏ The site should be sheltered

❏ The site should have marked parking bays

DGV s2
Check that the ground is firm and level before you uncouple the trailer. If you need to, place a heavy plank under the legs to distribute the weight and stop the legs sinking into the ground. Don't park illegally. Make sure that your unattended trailer isn't blocking access for others.

11.3 You're behind a parked car. What should you do when you're about to move off?

❏ Start to signal when you've started moving

❏ Move off when there's no oncoming traffic

❏ Check the blind spots before you start moving

❏ Only use your mirrors after you've started moving

DGV s6
Because the body of your vehicle is designed to take loads, your view around it will be restricted. Take extra care to look well out of the window to check the blind spots. Don't forget to check all the mirrors. Check ahead and signal, if necessary, before moving off.

11.4 You're driving a lorry. Why do you need to take extra care when emerging at this junction?

❏ There are bollards in the middle of the road

❏ It's a closed junction

❏ There's a motorcycle on the left

❏ There's a grass verge on the left

DGV s4
Make sure that you signal in good time, so that the motorcyclist behind you knows your intention. You may have to position yourself wide in order to negotiate the junction. Be aware that the motorcyclist may see this as an opportunity to filter through on your nearside. Check your left-hand mirror carefully before you start to turn.

11.5 You're driving this lorry (arrowed). What should you do about the emergency vehicle that's trying to emerge from the side road?

❏ Brake hard to a stop and wave it out

❏ Brake smoothly and allow it to emerge

❏ Drive on; you're on the major road

❏ Turn left to give it a clear view

DGV s4
Good forward planning will allow you to deal safely with this situation. You need to assess how your actions will affect other road users. Acting on impulse can have disastrous consequences.

11.6   What should you do when you're unable to see clearly while you're reversing into a loading bay?

❑ Get someone to guide you into the bay

❑ Use an audible warning signal while reversing

❑ Reverse into the bay until your bumper touches the end wall

❑ Open your door and lean well out while reversing

DGV s4
Don't take chances when reversing in a confined space. It's too easy to crush or kill someone without knowing they're in danger. If in doubt, get help from a reliable person.

11.7   This lorry is turning right from the side road. What should the driver be especially aware of?

❑ The motorcyclist from the right passing the parked van

❑ The vehicles coming from the left along the main road

❑ The pedestrians on the footpath by the main road

❑ The vehicles behind on the minor road

DGV s4
Parked vehicles near junctions can hide smaller road users such as cyclists and motorcyclists.
Double-check before emerging with a large vehicle. If in doubt, move forward slowly into a position where you can safely have another look.

11.8   You're parking your lorry at night. Where must you use parking lights?

❑ On the road   ❑ In a motorway service area

❑ In a factory entrance   ❑ In dock-authority areas

DGV s4
Goods vehicles exceeding 2500 kg laden weight must always have their parking lights switched on when they're parked on the road at night. This includes parking in lay-bys: other drivers entering the lay-by must be able to see the vehicle.

11.9   You're driving a lorry with a sleeper cab. When would a quick sideways glance be helpful?

❑ After driving over a pedestrian crossing

❑ When traffic is merging from the right or left

❑ Before climbing a steep hill

❑ When driving round sharp bends

DGV s4
The size and design of some cabs can create blind spots. This is especially true of a sleeper cab. A quick sideways glance might show something you can't see in your mirrors, especially when traffic is merging.

11.10   Your lorry has a sleeper cab. Why could this make your driving more difficult?

❑ It increases your blind spots

❑ It increases your view of the road ahead

❑ It increases your view in the right-hand mirror

❑ It increases your view in the left-hand mirror

DGV s4
A sleeper cab can create extra blind spots. Look out for vehicles just to the rear offside and nearside of your cab – they could soon become hidden in your blind spots.

11.11   You're waiting to turn right in this lorry (arrowed). What danger should you be most aware of?

❑ The road surface

❑ The 'give way' lines

❑ The hazard line

❑ The motorcyclist

DGV s4
Indicate your intentions in good time, so that both the motorcyclist and pedestrians know you plan to turn right. You should note all potential hazards and keep checking as you turn.

11.12   What's the first thing you should check before moving to the left?

☐ The nearside mirror

☐ The offside mirror

☐ Behind, over your right shoulder

☐ Behind, over your left shoulder

DBC s4, DGV s4

Before you make a turn or a change of direction, however slight, you should always check the mirrors. If you intend to turn left, check your left-hand (nearside) mirror first.

11.13   What's the first thing you should check before moving to the right?

☐ The nearside mirror

☐ Behind, over your left shoulder

☐ Behind, over your right shoulder

☐ The offside mirror

DBC s4, DGV s4

If you intend to turn right, check your right-hand (offside) mirror first. All of your mirrors should be properly adjusted to give a clear view around and behind your vehicle. They should be kept clean at all times and shouldn't be cracked or broken.

11.14   What should you do before moving off?

☐ Extend your right arm out of the window

☐ Just use the offside mirror and move away quickly

☐ Signal right with indicator and arm together

☐ Use your mirrors and look behind

DBC s4, DGV s4

To make sure it's safe, you must use the mirrors well before you make any manoeuvre. For example, you need to use them before moving off, turning, overtaking, slowing or stopping, opening a door, or changing direction, lanes or speed.

11.15   When would you need to check your nearside mirror?

☐ As a final check before turning right

☐ After passing cars parked on the left

☐ Before moving into the lane on your right

☐ When getting out of your cab on the driver's side

DBC s4, DGV s4

As you pass pedestrians or vehicles on your left, you should use your nearside mirror and check that you've passed them safely. You need to allow a good safety margin before you move back to the left.

11.16   The MSM routine should be used when you negotiate a hazard. What do the initials MSM stand for?

☐ Mirrors, signal, manoeuvre

☐ Manoeuvre, speed, mirrors

☐ Mirrors, speed, manoeuvre

☐ Manoeuvre, signal, mirrors

HC r180

Always use the MSM routine when you're approaching a hazard.

M – Mirrors: check the position of the traffic behind you.

S – Signal: signal your intention to slow down or change course in good time.

M – Manoeuvre: a manoeuvre is any change in position, from slowing or stopping the vehicle to turning off a busy road.

11.17   What does this sign mean?

☐ Contraflow bus and cycle lane

☐ With-flow bus and cycle lane

☐ No buses or cycles

☐ Priority to buses or cycles

KYTS p32

Some lanes are set aside for certain types of vehicle. Signs and road markings show the authorised vehicles in words or pictures. There's usually also a sign showing the times that the lane is in operation. Some lanes might only be in operation for a short time. Check the sign and only use the lane if you're allowed to do so.

11.18   What must you do to ensure good all-round vision when driving?

❏ Keep your windows open   ❏ Have a sun visor fitted

❏ Adjust your seat properly   ❏ Keep your lights clean

DBC s3, DGV s3
You must make sure that you adjust the seat so that you're able to reach all the controls and see in all the mirrors before you start to drive any vehicle. You should also be able to lean out of the window and check your offside blind spots.

11.19   When may an audible warning device for reversing be used in areas with a 30 mph speed limit?

❏ Between 7.00 am and 11.30 pm

❏ Between 11.30 pm and 7.00 am

❏ During daylight hours only

❏ At any time of the day or night

DBC s3, DGV s3
Some vehicles are fitted with an audible warning device that sounds when the vehicle is being reversed. As these devices make a loud noise, they shouldn't be used between 11.30 pm and 7.00 am in a built-up area. Audible warning devices are an effective safety feature, but they don't take away the need to use effective observation around the vehicle before and while reversing.

11.20   What will happen if you drive too close to the vehicle in front?

❏ Your view ahead will be reduced

❏ Your view ahead will be increased

❏ Your view of following drivers will be increased

❏ Your view of following drivers will be reduced

DBC s1, DGV s1
The closer you are to the vehicle in front, the less you'll be able to see of the road ahead. You must be aware at all times that you won't be able to see all around your vehicle. This is why you must have an excellent mirror routine and constantly update yourself on what's going on around you.

11.21   Why might it be difficult to see motorcyclists at junctions?

❏ They can be hidden in blind spots

❏ They always ride in the gutter

❏ They wear bright clothing

❏ They ride with their headlights on

DBC s4, DGV s4
When driving large vehicles, windscreen pillars and large mirrors can easily create blind spots as you look left and right at junctions. Altering your body position slightly while looking into the new road can give you an improved view of the traffic. If in doubt, look again and reassess the situation. Don't take chances.

11.22   Why should you check your right-hand mirror just before turning right from a main road into a side road?

❏ There may be pedestrians stepping off the kerb

❏ You need to check your position

❏ Someone may be overtaking you

❏ Your rear view to the left is blocked

DBC s4, DGV s4
Driving a large vehicle will sometimes require you to position your vehicle well to the left before making a tight right turn. Inexperienced drivers or riders may not realise your intentions and may try to overtake you. Make sure you signal in good time and make a final mirror check before committing yourself to the turn.

11.23   What should you check just before you tum left?

❏ The left-hand mirror   ❏ The interior mirror

❏ The right-hand mirror   ❏ The overtaking mirror

DBC s4, DGV s4
When making a left turn with a long vehicle, you may have to adopt an unusual position, well over to the centre of the road. Always signal your intentions in good time, and make good use of the mirrors, especially the left-hand one. Be alert for less experienced road users putting themselves in danger by coming up on your nearside.

11.24   You're driving a long vehicle. What should you be especially careful of before turning left onto a main road?

❏ Pedestrians on the opposite kerb

❏ Cyclists on your left

❏ Solid white lines in the centre of the road

❏ Vehicles directly behind you

DBC s4, DGV s4
You should always check your nearside mirror before any change of direction. Be alert for cyclists and motorcyclists who don't realise the potential danger involved in trying to squeeze through on your nearside when you're waiting at a junction.

11.25 You want to turn right at a roundabout marked with two right-turn lanes. What should you do if there's ample room for your vehicle in either lane?

❑ Use the right-hand of the two lanes

❑ Use the left-hand of the two lanes

❑ Use the left-hand lane, then move to the right as you enter the roundabout

❑ Use the right-hand lane, then move to the left as you enter the roundabout

DBC s4, DGV s4

Using the left-hand lane will make it easier for you to leave the roundabout. If you use the right hand lane, there could be traffic on your left and in your blind spot when you reach your exit and try to move back to the left.

11.26 Your vehicle is fitted with a reverse warning bleeper. How will this affect you when you're reversing?

❑ You'll be able to reverse more accurately

❑ You'll only need to use the offside mirror

❑ You'll need to take all-round observation

❑ You'll only need to use the nearside mirror

DBC s3, DGV s3

The reverse warning bleeper is fitted to your vehicle to warn others near the vehicle that it's reversing. However, it's no substitute for good all-round observation. Get someone to guide you if you can't see clearly where you're reversing.

11.27 What does 'blind spot' mean?

❑ An area of road covered by your right-hand mirror

❑ An area of road covered by your left-hand mirror

❑ An area of road that can't be seen, even with mirrors

❑ An area of road that isn't lit by your headlights

DBC s4, DGV s4

Blind spots can occur when bodywork – such as a door or window pillar – restricts your view. Different types of vehicle have different blind spots.

11.28 You're driving a large vehicle. How does its size and design affect the blind spots?

❑ It will have fewer blind spots than smaller vehicles

❑ It will have more blind spots than smaller vehicles

❑ It will have the same blind spots as other vehicles

❑ It will have no blind spots whatsoever

DBC s4, DGV s4

Take the time to check where the blind spots are when driving a vehicle that's unfamiliar to you. Being aware of the limitations of your mirrors will help you take steps to prevent collisions. Always check the blind spots before changing direction. Frequent and proper use of the mirrors will help you to be aware of a vehicle moving into your blind spot.

11.29 You're turning right at a T-junction. What should you do when your view to the right and left is blocked by parked vehicles?

❑ Lean forward to get a better view without crossing the 'give way' lines

❑ Edge out until you're about 1 metre (3 feet 3 inches) over the 'give way' lines

❑ Ease forward until you can see clearly in all directions

❑ Ask a passenger to assist by waving you out when it's clear

DBC s4, DGV s4

When emerging, if you can't see, don't go. Be aware that there could be an approaching cyclist or motorcyclist hidden by parked vehicles. Edge out very slowly, checking in all directions, and be ready to stop.

11.30 What must you do before you start reversing?

❑ Remove your seat belt

❑ Look all around

❑ Use an audible warning device

❑ Change the tachograph mode

DBC s4, DGV s4

Large or long vehicles have many blind spots. It's vital to check all these areas before starting to reverse and then make sure you keep checking all around while completing the manoeuvre.

11.31 You're reversing your vehicle. What should you do while the audible warning device is operating?

☐ Rely on a clear path behind

☐ Expect others to be aware of your course

☐ Be cautious and keep looking all around

☐ Concentrate solely on your blind areas

DBC s4, DGV s4
Don't rely on an audible warning device to claim right of way. It's your responsibility to be cautious and take all-round observation while you're reversing.

11.32 Some coaches have a mirror on their nearside, angled down to show the front nearside wheel. When should this extra mirror be used?

☐ When you're pulling in after overtaking

☐ When you're pulling in to park at the kerb

☐ Before you pass parked cars

☐ Before you change lanes on a motorway

DBC s4
This mirror offers the most benefit when you're manoeuvring in confined spaces. It shows you where your nearside front wheel is in relation to the kerb or a bay marking line.

11.33 What must you be aware of when you're driving a bus with a high driving position?

☐ The blind area close in front

☐ Passengers will have to look up to you

☐ Your judgement of speed will be impaired

☐ The lack of headroom in the cab

DBC s4
It's essential that you're constantly aware of other road users and pedestrians around you. A routine of effective mirror checking should be established. You must also know when it's essential to make checks in the blind spots; for example, just below the nearside front of the vehicle, where a pedestrian or a cyclist could be out of sight when you move off.

11.34 On a coach with high side windows, it can be difficult to see either side. What should you do before you move off in one of these vehicles?

☐ Get out of your vehicle and stop the traffic

☐ Ask a passenger to make sure it's safe to move off

☐ Indicate before checking all of your mirrors

☐ Open the window and look down and round to the right

DBC s4
High-sided coaches can create extra blind spots; you should be aware of these. You'll need to make additional checks on this type of vehicle, but don't forget your usual observations and mirror checks to make sure it's safe before moving off.

11.35 Your bus has a high seating position. What may be out of sight below the windscreen line?

☐ Following vehicles

☐ Overtaking vehicles

☐ Cyclists and pedestrians

☐ Other buses

DBC s4
If you've been stopped for some time at a bus stop or in a bus station, be aware that cyclists and pedestrians, especially children, can enter your blind spots. They may be out of sight below the windscreen line. Always take all-round observation before manoeuvring, whether you're moving away, parking or reversing.

11.36 Many modern vehicles are fitted with an additional nearside mirror. What does this help the driver to see?

☐ The front wheel in relation to the kerb

☐ The exhaust to check for emissions

☐ The rear of the vehicle when reversing

☐ The distance of the following vehicle

DBC s4
This mirror is specifically positioned so that the driver can see the position of the front nearside wheel in relation to the kerb. Use it when pulling in to park alongside the kerb or when you have to move close to the left in normal driving.

Section 12 Essential documents

12.1 You've been asked to drive a fully loaded petrol tanker back to the depot. It has a maximum authorised mass of 10 tonnes. What must you have before you can drive this vehicle?

❑ A request from the police to move a dangerous load

❑ A fully qualified tanker driver with you for the journey

❑ A valid ADR driver training certificate

❑ A copy of the vehicle's insurance certificate

DGV s2, 3
Drivers of vehicles carrying dangerous goods are required to hold an ADR driver training certificate. This certificate is valid for five years and is issued by DVLA when you've attended an approved course and successfully completed the examination.

12.2 Who's responsible for making sure that cargo arrives undamaged?

❑ The packer ❑ The driver

❑ The sender ❑ The loader

DGV s2, 3
The driver mustn't allow any cargo to be damaged during transit, loading or unloading. This requires a responsible attitude to safeguard the load at all times.

12.3 How many copies of the CMR consignment note are required?

❑ Two ❑ Three ❑ Four ❑ Five

DGV 3
The full name of the CMR is the 'Convention on the Contract for the International Carriage of Goods by Road'. You'll need this document to transport goods internationally by road. Of the four copies required, the consignor, consignee and originator all have one copy, and the fourth travels with the vehicle.

12.4 You hold a full category C licence. What does this entitle you to tow?

❑ A trailer of any weight

❑ A trailer with more than one axle

❑ A trailer up to 750 kg

❑ A curtain-sided trailer

DGV s1, 7
When you pass a test to obtain a C or C1 licence, you can tow trailers up to 750 kg. You can do this without taking a further test.

12.5 You're delivering boxes of chilled food to a supermarket. What specific training would you need?

❑ Hygiene procedures

❑ ADR procedures

❑ Waste-handling procedures

❑ Ecosafe driving procedures

DGV s1
Chilled foods are transported at temperatures above freezing point. Drivers need to be trained in hygiene procedures and how to operate refrigeration units.

12.6 You'll be driving your vehicle in Europe. Which of these documents must you carry?

❑ The vehicle service record

❑ Your medical examination form

❑ Your national driving licence

❑ The vehicle workshop manual

DBC s3, DGV s3
As well as your driving licence, you'll need to carry the insurance certificate and vehicle registration document. Other documentation may also be needed for some countries. Check this before starting your journey.

12.7 What condition could prevent you from holding a lorry or bus licence?

❑ Dyslexia

❑ Partial blindness

❑ Dermatitis

❑ Stomach upset

DBC s1, DGV s1
Any medical condition that could affect your ability to drive a lorry or a bus safely may prevent you from holding a licence. These conditions include serious visual impairment, heart disease and some mental disorders. For more information about medical standards, you should contact the Drivers Medical Branch, DVLA, Swansea.

12.8   You've been convicted of a drink-drive offence and banned from driving. Which entitlement will this ban affect?

❏ Your entitlement to drive all motor vehicles

❏ Your car entitlement

❏ Your lorry entitlement

❏ Your bus entitlement

DBC s3, DGV s3

The dangers of drink-driving are well publicised. Anyone convicted of this offence will lose their entitlement to drive any motor vehicle on the road.

12.9   You're found to be two-and-a-half times over the legal drink-drive limit and are disqualified from driving. Before regaining your licence, who will you have to satisfy that you don't have an alcohol problem?

❏ The local hospital

❏ The Driver and Vehicle Licensing Agency

❏ Alcoholics Anonymous

❏ The Driver and Vehicle Standards Agency

DBC s3, DGV s3   NI EXEMPT

If you're disqualified from driving because you were two-and-a-half times over the legal limit, you'll be classified as a high-risk offender. Before you can regain your licence, you'll have to satisfy the Driver and Vehicle Licensing Agency (DVLA) that you don't have an alcohol problem.

12.10   For how long is a Statutory Off-Road Notification (SORN) valid?

❏ Until the vehicle is taxed, sold or scrapped

❏ Until the vehicle is insured and MOT'd

❏ Until the vehicle is repaired or modified

❏ Until the vehicle is used on the road

HC p122

A SORN allows you to keep a vehicle off the road and untaxed. The SORN remains valid until the vehicle is taxed, sold or scrapped. If you buy a vehicle that has a SORN, the SORN will finish as soon as you buy it. You'll need to make a new SORN if you want to keep the vehicle off the road and untaxed.

12.11   What's a Statutory Off-Road Notification (SORN)?

❏ A notification to tell DVSA that a vehicle doesn't have a current MOT

❏ Information kept by the police about the owner of the vehicle

❏ A notification to tell DVLA that a vehicle isn't being used on the road

❏ Information held by insurance companies to check the vehicle is insured

HC p122

If you want to keep a vehicle untaxed and off the public road, you must make a SORN. It's an offence not to do so. When you've made a SORN, you won't have to pay vehicle tax, but you also won't be able to use the vehicle on the road. The SORN remains valid until your vehicle is taxed, sold, scrapped or exported.

12.12   What's the maximum fine for driving without insurance?

❏ Unlimited   ❏ £500   ❏ £1000   ❏ £5000

HC p126   NI Exempt

It's a serious offence to drive without insurance. As well as an unlimited fine, you may be disqualified or given penalty points.

12.13   What's the current fine for each person Illegally carried into the UK?

❏ Up to £1000   ❏ Up to £2000

❏ Up to £3000   ❏ Up to £4000

DBC s3, DGV s3

The importation of illegal Immigrants into the UK carries heavy penalties. A fine of up to £2000 can be imposed for each illegal immigrant. This fine can be Imposed on each 'responsible person', which includes the vehicle owner, hirer and driver.

12.14   Drivers can be fined for bringing illegal immigrants into the UK. Who else can be fined?

❏ The vehicle repairer   ❏ The vehicle insurer

❏ The vehicle manufacturer ❏ The vehicle hirer

DBC s3, DGV s3

There are heavy fines for those convicted of bringing illegal immigrants into the UK. This can mean a fine for each illegal person carried. The fine can be imposed on each 'responsible person', including the vehicle driver, owner and hirer.

12.15   How can vehicle operators help to prevent the carriage of Illegal immigrants?

❑ By using an effective vehicle security system

❑ By using vehicle tracking devices

❑ By taking out liability insurance

❑ By having effective mobile communications

DBC s3, DGV s3
Current legislation requires all operators to set up an 'effective system' to help prevent the carriage of illegal immigrants. This should Include vehicle security and checking using a checklist. Failure to do this will incur penalties.

12.16   You're returning to the UK and are about to board a ferry. An immigration officer asks to see your documentation. What must you show them Immediately?

❑ Your vehicle registration document

❑ Your driver's hours record

❑ Your operator documentation

❑ Your driving licence

DBC s3, DGV s3
Operators must set up an 'effective system' to prevent the carriage of illegal immigrants. This should include documentation with advice on vehicle security and a list of checks to be made. These papers should be produced immediately if an immigration officer asks to see them.

12.17   A driver is convicted of bringing illegal immigrants into the UK. How is the fine calculated?

❑ For each family group they bring in

❑ For each court attendance they make

❑ For each person they bring in

❑ For each journey they made in the last year

DBC s3, DGV s3
If convicted, the current fine for each illegal immigrant brought into the UK is £2000. This fine can be imposed on each responsible person; this includes the vehicle driver, owner and hirer.

12.18   The Driver Certificate of Professional Competence (Driver CPC) requires you to take training every five years. How many hours of training must you take?

❑ 30 hours   ❑ 35 hours   ❑ 40 hours   ❑ 45 hours

DBC s1, DGV s1
To keep your Driver CPC, you need to take 35 hours of training every five years. This can be split into sessions of at least seven hours each, so you can take one training day a year over the five years if that suits you. The penalties for non-compliance are the same as those for driving without a licence.

12.19   You'll need to take 35 hours of training to maintain your Driver Certificate of Professional Competence (Driver CPC). Over what period must this be carried out?

❑ One year   ❑ Three years
❑ Five years   ❑ Ten years

DBC s1, DGV s1
You must take 35 hours of training every five years to maintain your Driver CPC. This can be done at any time during the five years: all at once or split into sessions of at least seven hours each. The penalties for non-compliance are the same as those for driving without a licence.

12.20   Every five years, you must complete further training to keep your Driver Certificate of Professional Competence (Driver CPC). How many hours of training must you complete over those five years?

❑ 25 hours   ❑ 30 hours   ❑ 35 hours   ❑ 40 hours

DBC s1, DGV s1
Drivers are required to take 35 hours of training every five years to maintain their Driver CPC. This can be split into shorter sessions of at least seven hours each. These can be spread over the five years, so effectively one day's training is taken each year. The penalties for non-compliance are the same as those for driving without a licence.

12.21   You're applying for an LGV or PCV licence for the first time. What will your medical examination include?

❑ An eyesight test   ❑ A numeracy test
❑ A hygiene test   ❑ A literacy test

DBC s1, DGV s1
If you apply for a PCV or LGV licence, you must demonstrate that your eyesight is good enough to drive safely. DVLA (or DVA in Northern Ireland) can give you specific information about this. It's your responsibility to tell DVLA or DVA if your eyesight changes or you can't meet the requirements.

12.22   Which category of licence do you need to drive a tri-axle double-deck coach?

❑ D1   ❑ D   ❑ D1+E   ❑ C

DBC s1
A category D licence allows you to drive a coach or bus of any size. It also allows you to tow a trailer up to 750 kg. If you want to tow a trailer over 750 kg with a bus or coach, you'll need a category D+E licence.

12.23   Why may coaches be subject to a search by immigration authorities at international ports?

❑ For national security

❑ To check for red diesel

❑ For tachograph regulations

❑ To check vehicle condition

DBC s3
Because of the threat to national security, coaches may be searched at ports and the Channel Tunnel. If the authorities aren't satisfied, they may refuse to let you continue.

12.24   You're driving a coach, returning from a European trip. Why should you search the vehicle at the port?

❑ To look for missing property

❑ To ensure duty-free limits aren't exceeded

❑ To prevent the carriage of illegal immigrants

❑ To ensure the vehicle has the correct documentation

DBC s3
A coach driver can be fined up to £2000 for each illegal immigrant carried. The owner and hirer may also be fined the same amount.

12.25   You're making a journey that crosses international borders. Which document should you produce at immigration control?

❑ A list of passengers

❑ A breakdown insurance certificate

❑ A route plan

❑ A list of alcohol on board

DBC s3
When passing through immigration control, you should have a list of all your passengers. They must all be accounted for.

12.26   Which licence category do you need to drive an articulated bus ('bendy bus')?

❑ D1+E   ❑ D   ❑ D+E   ❑ D1

DBC s1
An articulated bus, commonly known as a 'bendy bus', isn't considered to be a bus towing a trailer. Therefore, it can be driven on a category D licence.

12.27   What size of trailer can be towed by the holder of a full category D licence?

❑ 750 kg ❑ 1000 kg ❑ 1250 kg ❑ 1500 kg

DBC s7
A full category D licence entitles you to tow a trailer of up to 750 kg.

12.28   You hold a full category D licence. What entitlement does this give you for towing?

❑ You can't tow a trailer at all

❑ You can tow a trailer not exceeding 750 kg

❑ You can tow a trailer of any weight

❑ You can't tow a trailer with more than one axle

DBC s7
A full category D licence entitles you to tow a trailer of up to 750 kg. If you wish to tow a trailer over 750 kg, you must pass an additional test.

12.29   You intend to drive a minibus for hire or reward. It has more than 16 passenger seats. What's the minimum licence entitlement you need?

❑ C   ❑ C1   ❑ D   ❑ 01

DBC s1, 7
Drivers of buses and coaches with more than 16 passenger seats require a category D licence. Make sure your licence has the correct entitlement for the vehicle you plan to drive.

12.30   Which licence category do you need to drive a bus with 25 passenger seats?

❑ D   ❑ D1   ❑ D+E   ❑ D1+E

DBC s1
Drivers of coaches or buses with more than 16 passenger seats require a category D licence.

12.31   Which authority has the power to impose conditions on a passenger-carrying vehicle (PCV) operator's licence?

❑ The Traffic Commissioner ❑ DVLA

❑ DVSA   ❑ Highways England

DBC s1   NI EXEMPT
Traffic commissioners are responsible for administering the regulations governing a PCV operator's licence. They can take disciplinary action against an operator who falls foul of the legal requirements.

Section 13 Environmental issues

13.1 Your lorry has been fitted with wind deflectors. How will they affect your vehicle?

❑ They'll increase the fuel consumption

❑ They'll reduce the stability

❑ They'll require increased tyre pressures

❑ They'll reduce the wind resistance

DGV s4

Wind deflectors direct the wind either around or over your vehicle, so reducing the wind resistance. The vehicle then requires less power to make progress against the wind, and so will use less fuel.

13.2 What can can-mounted wind deflectors reduce?

❑ Journey times   ❑ Load capacity

❑ Tyre wear   ❑ Fuel consumption

DGV s4

A wind deflector redirects the air flow around the vehicle. This reduces the amount of energy required to drive the vehicle forward and so saves fuel.

13.3 How could you reduce your lorry's fuel consumption?

❑ Fit new brake linings ❑ Fit a high-level exhaust pipe

❑ Fit a larger fuel tank ❑ Fit wind deflectors

DGV s4

Wind deflectors reduce a vehicle's wind resistance and so help reduce fuel consumption.

13.4 You're a driver who's certified to carry dangerous goods. How long is your certificate valid?

❑ One year ❑ Two years ❑ Five years ❑ Ten years

DGV s2

The operator of a UK-registered vehicle engaged in the carriage of dangerous goods should make sure that the driver has a valid vocational training certificate. These certificates are valid for five years.

13.5 What would help to reduce the impact that your lorry has on the environment?

❑ Driving through town centres

❑ Braking in good time

❑ Planning routes to avoid motorways

❑ Racing to make up time

DGV s4

Noise, vibration, exhaust emissions and fuel consumption all contribute to the environmental impact made by a lorry.

Good anticipation and forward planning will help to reduce these effects. Braking in good time saves fuel and so helps reduce exhaust emissions. It also helps reduce wear on the vehicle. its tyres and the road surface.

13.6 What's reduced by fitting a fly sheet tightly over a tipper body?

❑ Drag effect   ❑ Steering effort

❑ Legal load weight   ❑ Load capacity

DGV s2

Drag is caused by wind entering the cavity of an uncovered tipper. If the cavity is covered, then the drag is reduced.

13.7 How could you reduce the fuel consumption of your lorry?

❑ Brake late as often as you can

❑ Fit a cab-mounted wind deflector

❑ Avoid sheeting any bulky loads

❑ Try to increase your overall speed

DGV s4

Wind deflectors lower a vehicle's wind resistance. The vehicle therefore requires less energy to drive it forward, and this reduces its fuel consumption. Ecosafe driving techniques, correct tyre pressures and proper maintenance also help to maximise fuel efficiency.

13.8 When may red diesel be used?

☐ For operators to reduce running costs

☐ For authorised purposes only

☐ For garages to test-drive repaired vehicles

☐ For environmental purposes

DGV s3
Red diesel is subject to less excise duty than standard diesel, so it's considerably cheaper. It may only be used for authorised purposes. Any driver whose vehicle is found to be using this fuel illegally faces penalties.

13.9 You're driving a lorry with a loaded skip. Why should the skip be covered with a net?

☐ To prevent rubbish from falling out of it

☐ To protect the contents from the weather

☐ To make it more visible to other traffic

☐ To stop others from adding to the load

DGV s2
If the load isn't covered, rubbish can be blown onto the carriageway. This can cause danger for other road users, as well as environmental damage. It may also lead to legal action against both the driver and the operator.

13.10 What must you do when you park a lorry weighing more than 7.5 tonnes on a verge for essential loading?

☐ Sign the collection note

☐ Display an orange badge

☐ Obtain the owner's permission

☐ Make sure the lorry is always attended

DGV s4, HC r246
Goods vehicles with a maximum authorised mass of more than 7.5 tonnes (including any trailer) mustn't be parked on a verge without police permission. The only exception is when this is essential for loading and unloading. In these cases, the vehicle mustn't be left unattended.

13.11 What must you have before you can leave a lorry weighing more than 7.5 tonnes unattended on a verge?

☐ Police permission   ☐ A warning triangle

☐ The owner's permission ☐ A loading permit

DGV s4, HC r246
If your vehicle is to be left unattended on a verge, you must first get permission from the police.

13.12 What can help to reduce fuel consumption?

☐ Changing filters regularly

☐ Keeping tyres under-inflated

☐ Always using gears in sequence

☐ Keeping the rev counter in the amber band

DGV s4
Poorly maintained engines use more fuel and emit more exhaust fumes than those that are well maintained. Filters need to be changed on a regular basis. Remember that members of the public are encouraged to report vehicles emitting excessive exhaust fumes.

13.13 What will a correctly adjusted air deflector do?

☐ Save fuel

☐ Reduce tyre wear

☐ Reduce road-surface wear

☐ Cut loading time

DGV s4
Correctly adjusted air deflectors will save fuel. They should be adjusted to guide the airflow over the highest point at the front of the trailer or load and body.

13.14 What would staff from HM Revenue and Customs (HMRC) be looking for at a roadside check?

☐ Red diesel

☐ Vehicle defects

☐ Drivers' hours records

☐ Exhaust emissions

DGV s3
HMRC can check the type of fuel you're using, and the type and legality of your load. Red diesel is dyed gas oil with a lower tax than regular diesel. It can only be used in agricultural and construction vehicles (such as tractors). Red diesel mustn't be used in freight transport.

13.15 Why should the height of a load be kept to a minimum?

❏ To reduce aerodynamic drag

❏ To increase rolling resistance

❏ To increase momentum

❏ To reduce unloading time

DGV s2

Keeping the height of the load as low as possible will reduce the wind resistance of the vehicle. This will help to save fuel. It's particularly relevant when using a flat-bodied lorry or trailer.

13.16 What would be affected by a vehicle with faulty suspension?

❏ Overhead gantries   ❏ Road surfaces

❏ Tyre pressures   ❏ Engine performance

DBC s3, DGV s3

If your suspension is damaged, all the weight of the vehicle compresses the road and anything located below it. The vibrations travel through the ground and can also damage surrounding buildings.

13.17 What makes the pictured vehicle environmentally friendly?

❏ It uses solar power   ❏ It uses diesel fuel

❏ It uses electricity   ❏ It uses unleaded fuel

DBC s2, DGV s2

This is the sign for a tram. These vehicles are powered by electricity and reduce the emissions released into the environment. As they can carry many people, they can help to reduce the number of other vehicles on the road.

13.18 Which vehicles are most likely to cause severe damage to road surfaces?

❏ Lorries ❏ Cars ❏ Motorcycles ❏ Bicycles

DBC s3, DGV s3

Lorries and buses are much heavier than cars and will have a greater impact on the road surface.

13.19 What does air suspension help to protect?

❏ The fuel system   ❏ Tachograph accuracy

❏ Engine emissions ❏ Underground services

DBC s3, DGV s3

Air suspension reduces the pounding of the vehicle on an uneven road surface. This, in turn, reduces the vibrations transmitted to buildings and underground services along the route.

13.20 How can you help to reduce the impact of road transport on the environment?

❏ By avoiding high gears

❏ By reducing rest periods

❏ By braking in good time

❏ By increasing your overall speed

DBC s4, DGV s4

Good forward planning will reduce fuel consumption and engine emissions. This will cause less wear on the vehicle and its tyres, as well as reducing environmental pollution.

13.21 How can you help to protect the environment?

❏ By driving faster to reduce travelling time

❏ By using bypasses and avoiding town centres

❏ By filling your fuel tank with red diesel fuel

❏ By leaving your engine running in traffic jams

DBC s4, DGV s4

By using a bypass, rather than joining the stop/start traffic in a town centre, you're less likely to be held up and can travel at a constant speed. Keeping to a constant speed will reduce the amount of pollution produced by your vehicle.

13.22 How could a professional driver improve their efficiency?

❏ Keep to maximum speeds for shorter journeys

❏ Plan routes to avoid busy times and congestion

❏ Avoid route-planning because of the time it takes

❏ Drive at a faster speed through hazardous areas

DBC s4, DGV s4

If you plan your journey to avoid busy times, you can avoid congestion. That way, your overall journey time may be reduced, so cutting costs and making you a more efficient driver.

13.23 You've just refilled your fuel tank. What must you check before driving away from the fuel pump?

❑ That the tank is completely full up to the filler neck

❑ That the filler cap is vented correctly by keeping it loose

❑ That the filler cap is properly closed and secure

❑ That the tank is nearly full and the filler cap is slightly loose

DBC s2, DGV s2
Leaving the filler cap off, or not properly securing it, could result in a spillage of diesel onto the road. Because diesel is slippery, this would be a major hazard, so make sure to correctly secure the filler cap after use.

13.24 What should you do to prevent fuel spillage?

❑ Stop refuelling when the tank is half full

❑ Use a filtered fuel system

❑ Close and secure the filler cap

❑ Place the drip tray correctly

DBC s2, DGV s2
Fuel spilled on the road is a serious danger to other road users, especially motorcyclists. To prevent this from happening, make sure the filler cap is secure after refuelling.

13.25 You're following a lorry that's leaking fuel. What should you be especially aware of?

❑ The road may be very slippery

❑ The fuel may splash your vehicle

❑ Your brake linings will become slippery

❑ Your spray reducers won't be effective

HC p130
Leaking fuel can make the road extremely slippery. Look out for this, particularly on roundabouts.

13.26 Which large vehicles are more likely to damage the road surface?

❑ Vehicles with a mixture of tyre makes

❑ Vehicles with a mixture of re-cut and new tyres

❑ Vehicles with faulty spray-suppression equipment

❑ Vehicles with faulty suspension

DBC s3, DGV s3
Suspension faults may result in road damage. Road-friendly suspension reduces the impact on the environment, the road surface and under-road services.

13.27 How could you save fuel?

❑ By extending the vehicle's service times

❑ By braking as late as you can

❑ By planning routes to avoid congestion

❑ By selecting lower gears

DBC s4, DGV s4
You should always plan your route. This will ensure you always drive on roads that are suitable for the size and weight of your vehicle. By planning to avoid peak travel times, you can also avoid congestion.

This can save you fuel, as well as reducing your journey times.

13.28 Which fuel provides a reduction in exhaust emissions harmful to human health?

❑ High-sulphur diesel   ❑ Red diesel

❑ Low-sulphur diesel   ❑ Blue diesel

DBC s4, DGV s4
Low-sulphur diesel reduces the levels of sulphur-dioxide particles in exhaust emissions. It's widely available and makes a contribution to reducing emissions that are harmful to human health.

13.29 Which fuel is better for the environment?

❑ Anti-waxing diesel

❑ Low-sulphur diesel

❑ Red diesel

❑ Anti-foaming diesel

DBC s4, DGV s4
Sulphur produces acidic gases. Diesel fuels with lower sulphur content have been produced to reduce exhaust emissions that harm both people and the environment.

13.30 What must you do after filling your fuel tanks?

❏ Check your fuel gauge

❏ Check your tachograph

❏ Securely close the filler caps

❏ Complete the fuel log sheets

DBC s3, DGV s3
Make certain that your filler caps are properly closed, so that you don't spill fuel as you drive along the road.

13.31 You're driving between the hours of 11.30 pm and 7.00 am. When must you switch off your vehicle's reverse warning bleeper?

❏ Before reversing on a road that has a 30 mph speed limit

❏ Before reversing on a road that has a temporary speed limit

❏ Before reversing on a road that has the national speed limit

❏ Before reversing on a road that has a 40 mph speed limit

DBC s3, DGV s3
Your vehicle will make more noise than a car, so you should try to avoid making unnecessary noise at any time of the day or night. This is especially important when you're in a residential area at a time when people are likely to be sleeping.

13.32 What will cause your fuel consumption to increase?

❏ Continuous use of the air suspension

❏ Continuous use of the mirrors

❏ Continuous use of the air conditioning

❏ Continuous use of the electrical retarder

DBC s4, DGV s4
Use your air conditioning only when it's absolutely necessary. Running it continuously increases overall fuel consumption by up to 15%.

13.33 Why are vehicles fitted with air suspension?

❏ To reduce wear to roads

❏ To reduce tyre wear

❏ To improve fuel consumption

❏ To help the driver stay awake

DBC s3, DGV s3
Air suspension provides a smoother journey than traditional suspension and transmits less vibration to the road surface, under-road services and nearby structures, such as bridges. It's considered to be environmentally friendly because it reduces damage to the road network.

13.34 You're driving in a built-up area. Your vehicle is fitted with an audible warning device that sounds when It's reversing. When must you turn off this alarm?

❏ Between midnight and 6.30 am

❏ Between 11.30 pm and 6.30 am

❏ Between 11.30 pm and 7.00 am

❏ Between 12.30 am and 7.00 am

DBC s3, DGV s3
Some vehicles are fitted with an audible warning that sounds when the vehicle is reversing. This is an effective way to warn pedestrians and other road users of a reversing vehicle, but it doesn't take away the need to use effective observation all around your vehicle before and while you're reversing. Don't use the device in built-up areas between 11.30 pm and 7.00 am. Have consideration for the residents and don't disturb them with excessive noise.

13.35 What are the consequences of driving your vehicle when it's emitting excessive exhaust smoke?

❏ Its fuel consumption will improve

❏ Your vision ahead will be reduced

❏ The brakes will fade more easily

❏ You'll be breaking the law

DBC s3, DGV s3
It's illegal to drive a vehicle that's emitting excessive exhaust smoke, so you should get the problem fixed as soon as you're aware of it. Excessive exhaust smoke increases pollution and creates a hazard for other road users.

13.36 What does 'road-friendly' suspension help to reduce?

❏ Damage to level crossings

❏ Damage to river banks

❏ Damage to the road surface

❏ Damage to overhead cables

DBC s3, DGV s3
Road-friendly suspension reduces the vibration caused by the impact of the wheels on the road surface.

13.37 How can you help to ease traffic congestion?

❏ Plan journeys to avoid busy times

❏ Plan journeys to avoid quiet times

❏ Use motorways for all journeys

❏ Avoid motorways altogether

DBC s3, 4, DGV s3, 4
By planning your journey to avoid busy times, you'll avoid the build up of traffic that often occurs.

13.38 You've parked for a short time in a town while you plan your route. What should you do while your vehicle is parked?

❏ Keep the engine running on tick-over

❏ Rev the engine occasionally to maintain air pressure

❏ Hold the engine at a fast tick-over to maintain air pressure

❏ Switch off the engine

DBC s3, DGV s3
Turning off the engine is safer and emits less fumes into the environment. Leaving the engine idling unnecessarily will also waste fuel.

13.39 What can cause unnecessary pollution to the environment?

❏ High-level exhaust systems

❏ Regular servicing

❏ Weak radiator coolant

❏ Poorly maintained vehicles

DBC s3, 4, DGV s3, 4
All drivers should play their part to protect the environment against traffic pollution. Make sure the vehicle you drive is properly maintained. Report any defects, such as excessive exhaust smoke, as soon as you can.

13.40 Diesel fuel has been spilled on the road. Which road users will this be a particular danger for?

❏ Lorry drivers   ❏ Motorcyclists

❏ Horse riders   ❏ Car drivers

DBC s3, DGV s3
Spllt diesel creates a serious risk to other road users, especially motorcyclists. Take care when refuelling and make sure that all filler caps and tank hatches are properly closed and secure.

13.41 You're driving in a built-up area between 11.30 pm and 7.00 am. For what reason can you sound the vehicle's horn?

❏ To greet a friend

❏ To get another driver to move out of your way

❏ To let another road user know you're giving way

❏ To warn another road user who poses a danger

DBC s4, DGV s4
The horn shouldn't be used between 11.30 pm and 7.00 am in a built-up area. The only exception is when another road user is unaware of you and poses a danger.

13.42 Spilled diesel makes the road very slippery. Which vehicles will be most at risk from this hazard?

❏ Motorcycles

❏ Tractors

❏ Buses

❏ Lorries

DBC s3, DGV s3
Take care to secure caps and tank hatches. Diesel is very slippery and, if spilled on the road, it's particularly dangerous to motorcyclists.

13.43 What should you do if you've lost the filler cap for your diesel tank?

❏ Get a replacement before driving

❏ Push a rag into the filler pipe

❏ Drive slowly back to your depot

❏ Only fill the tank half-full

DBC s2, DGV s3
Don't drive without a fuel filler cap in place, as fuel could spill onto the road, especially when you're cornering or turning at a roundabout. Diesel fuel will make the road surface extremely slippery. Any spillage should be reported, so that the emergency services can make the road safe.

13.44 Before starting a journey, it's wise to plan ahead. What would you do to help plan your route?

☐ Look at a map

☐ Contact your local garage

☐ Look in your vehicle service record

☐ Check your vehicle registration document

DBC s4, DGV s4
Planning your journey before you set out can make the drive much easier and reduce traffic congestion. Look at a map to help you do this. You may need maps of different scales, depending on where and how far you're going. Printing or writing down the route can also help. Don't look at the map while you're driving; stop somewhere safe before checking your route again.

13.45 Where can you get help to plan your route before starting a journey?

☐ Your local filling station

☐ A motoring organisation

☐ The Driver and Vehicle Licensing Agency

☐ Your vehicle manufacturer

DBC s4, DGV s4
Most motoring organisation websites allow you to create a detailed plan of your trip, showing directions and distances. Some also include advice on rest and fuel stops. The Traffic England website will give you information on roadworks and incidents, along with expected delay times.

13.46 How can you plan your route before starting a long journey?

☐ Check your vehicle's workshop manual

☐ Ask your local garage

☐ Use a route planner on the internet

☐ Consult your travel agents

DBC s4, DGV s4
Various route planners are available on the internet. Most of them give you options, allowing you to choose the most direct route, the quickest route or a scenic route. The plans may also include rest and fuel stops. Print them off and take them with you, but don't look at them while you're actually driving.

13.47 How can you plan your route before setting out?

☐ Look in a motoring magazine

☐ Only visit places you know

☐ Try to travel at busy times

☐ Print or write down the route

DBC s4, DGV s4
Print or write down your route before setting out. Some places aren't well signed, so using both place names and road numbers may help you avoid getting lost. Find out how far you'll be travelling and plan your rest stops into the route.

13.48 Why is it a good ideas to plan your journey to avoid travelling at busy times?

☐ Your vehicle will use more fuel

☐ There'll be fewer roadworks

☐ It will help to ease congestion

☐ You'll travel a much shorter distance

DBC s4, DGV s4
Avoiding busy times means that you're not adding needlessly to traffic congestion. Other advantages are that you'll use less fuel and you may have an easier journey, making you feel less stressed.

13.49 What's likely to happen if you avoid travelling during peak times?

☐ You're more likely to be held up

☐ Your journey time is likely to be longer

☐ You'll travel a much shorter distance

☐ You're less likely to be delayed

DBC s4, DGV s4
If possible, avoid the early morning, late afternoon and early evening peak times. Doing this should allow you to miss the worst daily traffic jams and to travel in a more relaxed frame of mind, arriving at your destination feeling less stressed.

13.50 Planning your route before starting a journey is a good idea. Why should you also plan an alternative route?

□ Your original route may be blocked

□ Your maps may have different scales

□ It may be more scenic

□ You may get held up by a tractor

DBC s4, DGV s4
It can be frustrating and worrying to find your planned route is blocked by roadworks or diversions. If you've planned an alternative, you'll feel less stressed and able to concentrate fully on your driving. If your original route is mostly on motorways, it's a good idea to plan an alternative using non-motorway roads. Always carry a map with you just in case you need to refer to it – but stop driving before you do so.

13.51 What will happen if you drive smoothly?

□ You'll reduce journey times by about 15%

□ You'll increase fuel consumption by about 15%

□ You'll reduce fuel consumption by about 15%

□ You'll increase journey times by about 15%

DBC s3, 4, DGV s4
By driving smoothly, you'll reduce fuel consumption by about 15%, and you'll reduce the amount of wear and tear on your vehicle. You'll also feel more relaxed and have a more pleasant journey.

13.52 Which driving technique can save you fuel?

□ Using lower gears as often as possible

□ Accelerating sharply in each gear

□ Using each gear in turn

□ Missing out some gears

DBC s4, DGV s4
Missing out intermediate gears, when appropriate, reduces the amount of time you spend accelerating. Your vehicle uses the most fuel when you're accelerating, so reducing this will reduce your vehicle's fuel consumption.

13.53 Usually, a rev counter is divided into coloured bands. Which band should you stay in for maximum fuel economy?

□ Blue □ Green □ Amber □ Red

DBC s2, 3, DGV s2
Most large vehicles have a rev counter (tachometer) that's divided into coloured bands. This helps you to drive in the most fuel efficient way and avoid damage to the engine. The green band is the one that gives adequate torque and power with optimum fuel economy.

13.54 What would be the most likely effect of driving with the rev counter in the red band?

□ You would have optimum fuel economy

□ You would improve engine efficiency

□ You would damage the engine

□ You would create a false tachograph reading

DBC s2, DGV s2
Driving with the rev counter in the red band will cause the engine to wear prematurely and can lead to expensive repairs. This could result in the vehicle being off the road for some time.

13.55 What can be expected after drivers complete a Driver Certificate of Professional Competence (Driver CPC)?

□ Increased vehicle breakdowns

□ Increased fuel consumption

□ Reduced traffic volume

□ Reduced engine emissions

DBC s1, DGV s1
Better knowledge and use of eco safe driving techniques can result in lower fuel consumption and emissions. Other benefits include improved road safety and greater professionalism.

13.56 Why do energy-saving tyres contribute to better fuel economy?

□ They have a reduced rolling resistance

□ They're much easier to manufacture

□ They allow you to travel at higher speeds

□ They allow heat to disperse more quickly

DBC s2, DGV s2
Less fuel will be used to move your vehicle at the same speed if you use a tyre with reduced rolling resistance, rather than one of normal construction. Low rolling-resistance tyres aren't all the same; they have ratings for rolling resistance, wet-weather grip and noise. Specialists can advise on the best tyres for specific requirements.

13.57 Your vehicle is fitted with an engine management system. What will happen if you press the accelerator when you're starting the engine?

☐ An excessive amount of fuel will be used

☐ There'll be an excessive build-up of air pressure

☐ Exhaust emissions will be reduced

☐ Oil consumption will be reduced

DBC s2, DGV s2

When starting an engine fitted with an engine management system, you don't need to press the accelerator, because the engine management system automatically regulates the fuel/air supply. Using the accelerator at start-up wastes fuel, causes increased engine noise and is harmful to the environment.

13.58 What benefit is expected to come from having a Driver Certificate of Professional Competence (Driver CPC) qualification?

☐ A reduction in fuel consumption

☐ An exemption from tachograph regulations

☐ A reduction in vehicle tax

☐ An exemption from all congestion charges

DBC s1, DGV s1

The Driver CPC qualification and training syllabus is designed to lead to enhanced professionalism and improvements in road safety. Other expected benefits are a general reduction in fuel consumption and emissions, resulting from a better knowledge of ecosafe driving techniques.

13.59 You've been stopped at a roadside check. What would staff from the environmental health department be checking?

☐ Licence entitlement   ☐ Exhaust emissions

☐ Tachograph changes   ☐ Illegal immigrants

DBC s3, DGV s3

Local-authority environmental health departments check vehicles' exhaust emissions. They have the power to prosecute the driver and the operator, as do enforcement bodies such as DVSA.

13.60 What helps you to become an ecosafe driver?

☐ Being aware of hazards ☐ Avoiding block changing

☐ Accelerating rapidly   ☐ Using air conditioning

DBC s4, DGV s4

Driving in an ecosafe manner means that you plan well ahead for hazards and react in good time. This can save fuel and is therefore good for the environment.

13.61 What can help to maximise fuel economy?

☐ Cruise control   ☐ Air suspension

☐ Re-grooved tyres ☐ Diff-lock

DBC s4, DGV s4

Using cruise control can help save fuel. The sensitive electronics make continuous micro-adjustments that improve efficiency. It should only be used when you can see well ahead in good road conditions. Be prepared to switch it off immediately if the traffic situation changes.

13.62 How would you benefit from forward planning and early recognition of potential hazards?

☐ You'll use less fuel

☐ You'll use more fuel

☐ You'll be able to stop more quickly

☐ You'll reduce journey times

DBC s4, DGV s4

Poor planning leads to late braking and harsh acceleration. This causes higher fuel consumption and increased emissions, which is harmful to the environment.

13.63 What will cause a noticeable increase in your vehicle's fuel consumption?

☐ Using electric windows ☐ Using a manual sunroof

☐ Using air conditioning   ☐ Using the endurance brake

DBC s4, DGV s4

Using air conditioning continuously can increase fuel consumption by about 15%. Think of the environment and only use it when it's necessary.

13.64 Which ancillary equipment will cause the greatest increase in fuel consumption?

☐ Air suspension   ☐ Air brakes

☐ Air bags   ☐ Air conditioning

DBC s4, DGV s4

A number of ancillary systems use power from the engine to operate. The downside to this is that fuel consumption can increase. Air conditioning can increase fuel consumption by up to 15%.

13.65 You'll be waiting at a terminus for some time. How can you reduce pollution?

❏ By rewing your engine

❏ By switching off your engine

❏ By leaving your engine on tick-over

❏ By keeping your engine at high revs

DBC s4
If you have to wait for long periods of time, you should turn your engine off. Noise and exhaust fumes can cause annoyance as well as pollution.

13.66 You're waiting for some time in a stationary traffic queue. Why should you switch off your engine?

❏ To keep your passengers cool

❏ To save on vehicle air pressure

❏ To reduce exhaust emissions

❏ To reduce radio interference

DBC s3
When you're stationary for any length of time (for example, in a traffic jam), switch off your engine. This will cut exhaust emissions and so help to protect the environment.

13.67 You've been waiting in a traffic queue for several minutes. What should you do if it's clear that you won't be moving soon?

❏ Keep your engine at tick-over speed

❏ Rev your engine occasionally

❏ Switch off your engine

❏ Run the engine at a constant higher speed

DBC s3
Switch your engine off when you're stationary for some time, especially where noise and exhaust fumes may cause annoyance. This can help to protect the environment and save fuel.

13.68 What effect will continuous use of the air-conditioning system have on fuel consumption?

❏ Increase it by about 15%

❏ Increase it by about 30%

❏ Increase it by about 50%

❏ Increase it by about 75%

DBC s3
Avoid using air-conditioning systems for long periods, as they can increase fuel consumption by about 15%. Try to drive with fuel economy and the environment in mind.

13.69 When starting your bus, how should air pressure be built up?

❏ With the doors open

❏ With the service brake on

❏ With the engine ticking over

❏ With the engine revving up

DBC s3
Vehicle designers and bus drivers have a duty to help reduce the effects of pollution on the environment. The most environmentally friendly way to allow air pressure to build up is with the engine running at tick-over.

13.70 What must you check after refuelling your bus?

❏ Your filler caps are securely closed

❏ Your tank is full to the top

❏ The position of the emergency fuel cut-off switch

❏ The low-fuel warning light is working

DBC s2
It's a legal requirement that you check all filler caps are properly closed and secure after refuelling your vehicle.

Section 14 Other road users

14.1   Your vehicle leaks diesel fuel on a roundabout. Who will this affect most?

❏ Drivers of three-wheeled vehicles   ❏ Motorcyclists

❏ Towed vehicles   ❏ Car drivers

HC p130

When diesel fuel spills onto the road, it makes the road surface extremely slippery. This can cause danger for all types of vehicle, but particularly for those with two wheels, which rely on their tyres' grip to remain upright.

14.2   Which vehicles are most likely to be affected by side wind?

❏ Flat-bed lorries   ❏ Tractors

❏ Motorcycles   ❏ Estate cars

DBC s4, DGV s4

You should be aware that motorcyclists are likely to be affected by side wind and can be blown into your path. Adjust your speed so that you can stop or take avoiding action safely if necessary.

14.3   What should you do if the vehicle ahead Is being driven by a learner?

❏ Keep calm and be patient

❏ Drive up close behind

❏ Put your headlights on full beam

❏ Sound your horn and overtake

DBC s4, DGV s4

Learners might take longer to react to traffic situations. Don't unnerve and intimidate them by driving up close behind.

14.4   You're about to overtake horse riders. What could scare the horses?

❏ Sounding your horn

❏ Giving arm signals

❏ Driving slowly

❏ Keeping well back

DBC s4, DGV s4, HC r215

When passing horses, allow plenty of space, slow down and stop if you need to. Animals are easily frightened by sudden or loud noises and can quickly become uncontrollable, so don't sound your horn or rev the engine.

14.5   You've stopped at a pelican crossing. What should you do if the lights have changed to green but a disabled person is still crossing?

❏ Give way to them   ❏ Drive In front of them

❏ Drive behind them ❏ Sound your horn at them

HC r198

At a pelican crossing, the green light means you may go, but you must give way to anyone still crossing. If someone hasn't finished crossing, be patient. People with mobility difficulties can struggle to cross in the time allowed by the lights.

14.6   Which sign means that there may be people walking along the road?

❏   ❏

❏   ❏

HC p109, KYTS p13

Always check the road signs. They'll inform you of hazards ahead so you know what problems to expect. A number of different signs show pedestrians in different situations. Learn them all so you'll understand the hazards you're likely to meet.

14.7   You're turning left from a main road into a side road. What should you do If people are already crossing the road into which you're turning?

❏ Continue, as you have right of way

❏ Signal to them to continue crossing

❏ Walt and allow them to cross

❏ Sound your horn to warn them of your presence

HC r170, 206

Approaching a junction at the correct speed will allow you enough time to observe and react. Pedestrians crossing here have priority and you must give way to them.

14.8 You're at a road junction, turning into a minor road. What should you do if there are pedestrians crossing the minor road?

❏ Stop and wave the pedestrians across

❏ Sound your horn to let the pedestrians know that you're there

❏ Give way to the pedestrians who are already crossing

❏ Carry on; the pedestrians should give way to you

HC r170, 206
Always look into the road you're entering. If pedestrians are already crossing, be considerate and give way to them. Don't wave or signal them to hurry; they have priority here.

14.9 Why should you check for motorcyclists just before turning right into a side road?

❏ They might be overtaking on your left

❏ They might be following you closely

❏ They might be emerging from the side road

❏ They might be overtaking on your right

DBC s4, DGV s4, HC r180
Never attempt to change direction to the right without checking your right-hand mirror. A motorcyclist might not have seen your signal and could have decided to overtake. This action should be a matter of routine.

14.10 Why is a toucan crossing different from other crossings?

❏ Moped riders can use it

❏ It's controlled by a traffic warden

❏ It's controlled by two flashing lights

❏ Cyclists can use it

HC r125
Pedestrians and cyclists are shown the green light together. The signals are push-button-operated and there's no flashing amber phase.

14.11 What happens at toucan crossings?

❏ You only stop when a pedestrian is waiting

❏ Cyclists aren't permitted

❏ There's a continuously flashing amber beacon

❏ Pedestrians and cyclists may cross

HC r25, KYTS p124
Toucan crossings can be used by cyclists and pedestrians. Some cycle routes lead cyclists to these crossings. Always look out for cyclists, as they're likely to be approaching much faster than pedestrians.

14.12 Where would you see this sign?

❏ In the window of a car taking children to school

❏ At the side of the road

❏ At playground areas

❏ On the rear of a school bus or coach

HC p117
Vehicles that are used to carry children to and from school will be travelling at busy times of the day. Be prepared for a vehicle with this sign to make frequent stops. It might pick up or set down passengers in places other than normal bus stops.

14.13 What does this sign mean?

❏ No route for pedestrians and cyclists

❏ A route for pedestrians only

❏ A route for cyclists only

❏ A route for pedestrians and cyclists

KYTS p36
This shared route is for pedestrians and cyclists only. Be aware that, when it ends, the cyclists will be rejoining the main road.

14.14 What action would you take when elderly people are crossing the road?

❑ Wave them across so they know that you've seen them

❑ Be patient and allow them to cross in their own time

❑ Rev the engine to let them know that you're waiting

❑ Tap the horn in case they're hard of hearing

DBC s4, DGV s4

Don't hurry elderly people across the road by getting too close to them or revving the engine. Be aware that they might take longer to cross. They might also have hearing difficulties and not hear you approaching.

14.15 What should you do if you see two elderly pedestrians about to cross the road ahead?

❑ Expect them to wait for you to pass

❑ Speed up to get past them quickly

❑ Stop and wave them across the road

❑ Be careful; they might misjudge your speed

DBC s4, DGV s4

Elderly pedestrians may have impaired judgement, hearing and/ or vision. Be aware that, if they do start to cross, they could take more time to do so.

14.16 You're approaching a roundabout. What should you do if you see a cyclist signalling to turn right?

❑ Overtake on the right

❑ Give a warning with your horn

❑ Signal the cyclist to move across

❑ Give the cyclist plenty of room

DBC s4, DGV s4, HC r187

Leave plenty of room if you're following a cyclist who's signalling to turn right at a roundabout. Give them space and time to get into the correct lane.

14.17 You're approaching this roundabout and see the cyclist signal right. Why is the cyclist keeping to the left?

❑ It's a quicker route

❑ They're going to turn left instead

❑ The Highway Code doesn't apply to cyclists

❑ They may use the left-hand lane to turn right

DBC s4, DGV s4, HC r187

Cycling in today's heavy traffic can be hazardous. Some cyclists might not feel happy about crossing the path of traffic to take up a position in an outside lane. Be aware of this and understand that, although they're in the left-hand lane, the cyclist might be turning right.

14.18 You're waiting to come out of a side road. Why should you look carefully for motorcycles?

❑ Motorcycles are usually faster than cars

❑ Police patrols often use motorcycles

❑ Motorcycles are small and hard to see

❑ Motorcycles have right of way

DBC s4, DGV s4, HC r211

If you're waiting to emerge from a side road, remember to look for motorcycles. Their small size makes them easy to overlook. Be especially careful if parked vehicles are restricting your view. If you can't see, don't go.

14.19 Why do motorcyclists use dipped headlights in the daytime?

❑ To make themselves more easily seen

❑ To stop the battery overcharging

❑ To improve their vision

❑ To scare wildlife off the road

HC r86

A motorcycle can be lost out of sight behind another vehicle. The use of the headlights helps to make the motorcycle more easily seen.

14.20   Why are motorcyclists advised to wear bright clothing?

❑ They must do so by law

❑ It helps to keep them cool in summer

❑ The colours are popular

❑ To help other road users to see them

HC r86
Although they're advised to wear clothing that's bright or reflective; motorcyclists often wear clothing that's mainly black. This can make them difficult to see, so you must look carefully for them.

14.21   Why do motorcyclists often look over their right shoulder just before turning right?

❑ They need to listen for following traffic

❑ Motorcycles don't have mirrors

❑ Looking around helps them balance as they turn

❑ They need to check for traffic in their blind area

DBC s4, DGV s4, HC r88
Expect a motorcyclist who makes a quick glance over their shoulder to be changing direction. They should do this before turning. By observing this, you'll get an early clue of their intention.

14.22   You're approaching a roundabout. What should you do if there are horses being ridden ahead of you?

❑ Give them plenty of room

❑ Stop and wait for them to get off the road

❑ Sound your horn as a warning

❑ Accelerate past as quickly as possible

HC r214-215
Horse riders often keep to the outside of the roundabout even if they're turning right. Give them room in case they have to cross lanes of traffic.

14.23   What should you do when passing sheep on a road?

❑ Keep close to avoid oncoming traffic

❑ Drive very slowly

❑ Pass quickly but quietly

❑ Briefly sound your horn

HC r214
Slow down and be ready to stop if you see animals in the road ahead. Animals are easily frightened by noise and by vehicles passing too close to them. Stop if signalled to do so by the person in charge of the animals.

14.24   You're driving at night. What does it mean if you see a pedestrian wearing reflective clothing and carrying a red light?

❑ You're approaching roadworks

❑ You're approaching an organised walk

❑ You're approaching a slow-moving vehicle

❑ You're approaching an accident black spot

HC r5
At night, a pedestrian carrying a red light should be at the back of an organised walk. The walkers should keep to the left, but this won't always be the case. Pass them very slowly. Be aware that the pedestrians may have their backs to you and might not know you're approaching.

14.25   What action should you take if there are flashing amber lights under a school warning sign?

❑ Reduce speed until you're clear of the area

❑ Keep up your speed and sound the horn

❑ Increase your speed to clear the area quickly

❑ Wait at the lights until they change to green

HC r208
The flashing amber lights are switched on to warn you that children may be crossing near a school. Drive slowly and be prepared for children running into the road.

14.26   What should you do when you're approaching this zebra crossing?

❑ Prepare to slow down and stop

❑ Stop and wave the pedestrians across

❑ Speed up and pass by quickly

❑ Drive on unless the pedestrians step out

HC r195
Be courteous and prepare to stop. Don't wave people across, as this could be dangerous if another vehicle is approaching the crossing.

14.27 Why must these road markings be kept clear?

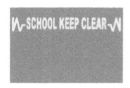

- ☐ To allow schoolchildren to be dropped off
- ☐ To allow teachers to park
- ☐ To allow schoolchildren to be picked up
- ☐ To allow an unobstructed view of the area

HC p116, r243, KYTS p56
Keeping the markings clear ensures that drivers and riders passing and children crossing have a clear, unrestricted view of each other.

14.28 Why mustn't you stop on these road markings?

- ☐ It would obstruct everyone's view of the area
- ☐ It would obstruct teachers' access to the school
- ☐ It would obstruct delivery vehicles' access to the school
- ☐ It would obstruct emergency vehicles' access to the school

HC p116, r243, KYTS p56
These markings are found on the road outside schools. Don't stop or park on them, even to set down or pick up children. The markings are to make sure that drivers, riders and children have a clear view.

14.29 You're following two cyclists as they approach a roundabout in the left-hand lane. In which direction should you expect them to go?

☐ Left ☐ Right ☐ Any direction ☐ Straight ahead

HC r187
If you're following cyclists onto a roundabout, be aware that they might not take the exit you expect. Cyclists approaching in the left hand lane could be turning right but may not have been able to get into the right-hand lane. Give them plenty of room.

14.30 You're travelling behind a moped. What should you do if you want to turn left a short distance ahead?

- ☐ Overtake the moped before the junction
- ☐ Pull alongside the moped and stay level until just before the junction
- ☐ Sound your horn as a warning and turn in front of the moped
- ☐ Stay behind until the moped has passed the junction

HC r182
Passing the moped and then turning into the junction could mean that you cut across in front of the rider. This might cause them to slow down, stop or even lose control.

14.31 You see a horse rider as you approach a roundabout. What should you do if they're signalling right but keeping well to the left?

☐ Proceed as normal ☐ Keep close to them

☐ Cut In front of them ☐ Stay well back

DBC s4, DGV s4, HC r187
Allow horse riders to enter and exit the roundabout in their own time. Don't drive up close behind or alongside them; this could disturb the horse.

14.32 How would you react to drivers who appear to be inexperienced?

- ☐ Sound your horn to warn them of your presence
- ☐ Be patient and prepare for them to react more slowly
- ☐ Flash your headlights to tell them it's safe for them to proceed
- ☐ Overtake them as soon as possible

DBC s4, DGV s4
Many learners aren't confident when they first start to drive. Allow them plenty of room and don't react impatiently when they take their time. Remember that new drivers are inexperienced in dealing with traffic situations, so be patient.

14.33 What should you do if you're following a learner driver who stalls at a junction?

❏ Be patient, as you expect them to make mistakes

❏ Stay very close behind and flash your headlights

❏ Start to rev your engine if they take too long to restart

❏ Immediately steer around them and drive on

DBC s4, DGV s4

Learning is a process of practice and experience. Try to understand this and tolerate others who are at the beginning of this process.

14.34 You're on a country road. What should you expect to see coming towards you on your side of the road?

❏ Motorcycles   ❏ Bicycles

❏ Pedestrians   ❏ Horse riders

HC r154

On a quiet country road, always be aware that there may be a hazard just around the next bend, such as a slow-moving vehicle or pedestrians. There might not be a pavement and people may be walking on your side of the road.

14.35 What should you do when you're following a car driven by an elderly driver?

❏ Expect the driver to drive badly

❏ Flash your lights and overtake

❏ Be aware that the driver's reactions may not be as fast as yours

❏ Stay very close behind but be careful

HC r216

You must show consideration to other road users. Elderly drivers may have slower reactions and they might need more time to deal with a situation. Be tolerant and don't lose patience or show your annoyance.

14.36 You're following a cyclist. What should you do if you wish to turn left a short distance ahead?

❏ Overtake the cyclist before the junction

❏ Pull alongside the cyclist and stay level until after the junction

❏ Hold back until the cyclist has passed the junction

❏ Go around the cyclist on the junction

DBC s4, DGV s4, HC r182

Make allowances for cyclists. Allow them plenty of room, and be aware that they also have to deal with hazards. They might swerve or change direction suddenly to avoid uneven road surfaces.

14.37 A horse rider is in the left-hand lane approaching a roundabout. What should you expect the rider to do?

❏ Go in any direction ❏ Turn right

❏ Turn left   ❏ Go ahead

DBC s4, DGV s4, HC r187

Horses and their riders will move more slowly than other road users. They might not have time to cut across heavy traffic to take up a position in the offside lane when they're turning right; it could also be hazardous for them to do so. Therefore, a horse and rider may approach a roundabout in the left hand lane, even though they're turning right.

14.38 You're at the front of a queue of traffic waiting to turn right into a side road. Why should you check your right-hand mirror just before turning?

❏ To look for pedestrians about to cross

❏ To check for overtaking vehicles

❏ To make sure the side road is clear

❏ To check for emerging traffic

DBC s4, DGV s4

Always check your right-hand mirror and blind spot just before you make a right turn, as another vehicle could be overtaking you. Motorcyclists often filter along the outside of traffic queues. Keep checking all your mirrors while you're waiting to turn, because situations behind you can change quickly.

14.39 You're driving past a line of parked cars. What should you do if you notice a ball bouncing out into the road ahead?

❏ Continue driving at the same speed and sound your horn

❏ Continue driving at the same speed and flash your headlights

❏ Slow down and be prepared to stop for children

❏ Stop and wave the children across to fetch their ball

DBC s4, DGV s4
Beware of children playing in the street and running out into the road. If a ball bounces out from the pavement, slow down and stop if necessary. Don't encourage anyone to fetch the ball from the road. Other road users might not see your signal and you might lead a child into danger.

14.40 What should you do just before turning right from a main road into a side road?

❏ Cancel your right-turn signal

❏ Select first gear

❏ Check for traffic passing on your right

❏ Stop and set the handbrake

DBC s4, DGV s4, HC r180
Motorcyclists can often pass slow or stationary traffic because of the relatively small size of their vehicle. Take a last look in your right-hand mirror to check for motorcyclists and so avoid turning across their path.

14.41 You're driving past a bus that's waiting at a bus stop on the other side of the road. Why should you be careful?

❏ The bus may have broken down

❏ Pedestrians may come from behind the bus

❏ The bus may move off suddenly

❏ The bus may remain stationary

HC r223
Watch out for pedestrians if you see a bus ahead. They may not be able to see you if they're crossing behind the bus.

14.42 How should you overtake horse riders?

❏ Drive up close and overtake as soon as possible

❏ Speed isn't important but allow plenty of room

❏ Use your horn just once to warn them

❏ Drive slowly and leave plenty of room

DBC s4, DGV s4, HC r215
Horses are easily frightened, so pass them slowly and carefully, giving them as much room as possible. On country roads, expect farm animals, horses, pedestrians and farm vehicles. Always be prepared to slow down or stop.

14.43 Where in particular should you look out for motorcyclists?

❏ At a filling station   ❏ At a road junction

❏ Near a service area   ❏ When entering a car park

DBC s4, DGV s4
Motorcyclists and cyclists are smaller and usually more difficult to see than other vehicles. Look out for them at junctions; failing to see them can lead to a collision.

14.44 While driving at night, you see a pedestrian ahead. What does it mean if they're wearing reflective clothing and carrying a red light?

❏ You're approaching men at work

❏ You're approaching an organised walk

❏ You're approaching an incident blackspot

❏ You're approaching slow-moving vehicles

HC r5
Pedestrians who are part of an organised walk using the road at night should wear bright or reflective clothing. The walker in front should display a white light, while the one at the back should display a red light. Be particularly careful, slow down and give the walkers plenty of room.

14.45 Which road users are more vulnerable at night in built-up areas?

❏ Drivers of black taxi cabs

❏ Drivers of double-deck vehicles

❏ Cyclists

❏ Ambulance drivers

DBC s4, DGV s4
Look out for cyclists who don't have lights on. Also be aware that pedestrians – especially those in dark clothing – may be difficult to see.

14.46 You're about to overtake a motorcyclist when they look around over their right shoulder. What's the most likely reason for them doing this?

❑ The rider intends to move to the right

❑ Something has fallen from the machine

❑ The drive chain is slack

❑ The rear tyre is flat

DBC s4, DGV s4, HC r88
Understanding other road users' behaviour can help you anticipate their next action. On this occasion it could prevent a serious incident. This type of assessment is part of the forward planning of a professional driver.

14.47 Why should you allow extra room for motorcyclists when they're riding through roadworks?

❑ There may be a reduced speed limit

❑ There may be temporary traffic lights

❑ They may swerve to avoid potholes

❑ The traffic may be in single file

DBC s4, DGV s4
Motorcyclists can ride through narrow gaps in traffic and generally don't take up as much room as a car. However, other factors, including the road surface, can affect their stability. Give them an extra safety margin whenever possible.

14.48 You're following a motorcyclist along a potholed road. How should you adjust your driving to take account of this situation?

❑ Give them extra room ❑ Drive alongside them

❑ Try to pass them ❑ Stay close behind them

DBC s4, DGV s4
Good forward planning can help you keep other road users out of trouble. Information to help you do this is available if you look for it. Watch for clues: for example, a motorcyclist taking a 'lifesaver' look over their shoulder could be about to change direction.

14.49 Which vehicles are most at risk from spilt diesel fuel?

❑ Motorcycles ❑ Empty tankers

❑ Towed vehicles ❑ Fire engines

DBC s4, DGV s4
Where the road surface has been made slippery (for example, by spilt diesel fuel), motorcyclists are particularly vulnerable to skidding.

14.50 You're driving in a town. What should you do when you see this sign on a stationary bus ahead?

❑ Accelerate quickly

❑ Wait until it moves off

❑ Drive past slowly

❑ Expect the driver will be looking after the children

HC p117, r209
Children getting off the bus will be hidden from your view, and they may not be able to see you. Even if they can see you, they may have poor judgement of danger. You should drive slowly as you pass the bus and be ready to stop.

14.51 What should you do when you're following a scooter on a poor road surface?

❑ Overtake without any delay

❑ Stay close behind until you can pass

❑ Stay well back and allow them room

❑ Sound your horn as you get close

DBC s4, DGV s4
On a poor road surface, the rider may need to move out to avoid potholes. You may not get much warning. A look to the right or a 'lifesaver' check may warn you that they're about to move out. Stay well back and allow the rider plenty of room until you can pass safely.

14.52 At toucan crossings, pedestrians share the crossing with which other road users?

❑ Horse riders ❑ Cyclists ❑ Motorcyclists ❑ Trams

HC r199
A toucan crossing is signal controlled, but unlike a pelican crossing it doesn't have a flashing amber light in the sequence. Cyclists and pedestrians cross together, and cyclists are allowed to ride their bicycles over the crossing.

14.53 You're driving on a dual carriageway. What type of vehicle must use a flashing amber beacon on this road?

❏ An ambulance   ❏ A fire engine

❏ A doctor's car on call   ❏ A mobility scooter

HC r220
Small battery-powered vehicles are often used by disabled people. On unrestricted dual carriageways, these vehicles must show a flashing amber light. Be very careful, as they have a maximum speed of 8 mph. You may see other slow-moving vehicles with amber flashing lights, such as agricultural vehicles.

14.54 You're driving near a school in heavy traffic. What should you do when there are children walking close to the kerb on your side of the road?

❏ Move to the other side of the road

❏ Wave at them to move back from the kerb

❏ Stop for a moment to see what they do

❏ Drive slowly until you're clear of the area

DBC s4, DGV s4
Children can be unpredictable, and when they're in groups they may fool around and push each other into the road. You should drive with extreme caution when you're near them. You need to be ready to stop suddenly.

14.55 You're driving on a road with an uneven surface. What should you do if you're following a motorcyclist along this road?

❏ Allow extra room in case the rider swerves to avoid potholes

❏ Leave less room so the rider can see you in their mirrors

❏ Drive close behind and get ready to overtake

❏ Drive closely to shield the rider

DBC s4, DGV s4
Never follow any road user too closely. This is particularly important when you're following scooter or motorcycle riders, or cyclists. They might brake or swerve suddenly; for example, to avoid a pothole on a road with a poor surface.

14.56 You wish to turn left into a side road. What should you do if there's a cyclist in front as you approach the junction?

❏ Overtake the cyclist before the junction

❏ Wait until the cyclist has passed the junction

❏ Sound your horn to warn the cyclist to wait

❏ Drive alongside and watch the cyclist in your mirrors

HC r182
Stay back and allow the cyclist to proceed. You mustn't cut across in front of them. Also be aware of any cyclists who may try to pass on your left as you slow for the turn.

14.57 You're waiting to turn left at a junction. In your mirror you can see a cyclist moving up between the kerb and the nearside of your vehicle. How should you deal with the cyclist?

❏ Allow them to move in front of you

❏ Move off and make them wait for you

❏ Steer to the left to make them dismount

❏ Tell them to move out of your way

DBC s4, DGV s4
Always be aware of your limited vision around your vehicle, due to its size and shape. Never move off without checking along the nearside of your vehicle. You should be aware of the possibility of cyclists and motorcyclists getting trapped between your vehicle and the kerb.

14.58 You're approaching a roundabout. You see a cyclist signal right. Why do they keep to the left?

❏ It's a quicker route for a cyclist

❏ They're going to turn left

❏ It's a safer route for a cyclist

❏ The Highway Code doesn't apply to cyclists

DBC s4,DGV s4, HC r187
The cyclist may not be able to get into a right-hand lane due to heavy traffic. Give them room, as they may not be taking the exit you expect.

14.59 You're entering a roundabout. What should you do if a cyclist In front of you is signalling to turn right?

❏ Overtake on the right ❏ Sound the horn

❏ Overtake on the left ❏ Allow plenty of room

DBC s4, DGV s4, HC r187

Allow the cyclist plenty of room. Give them space and be prepared for them to change direction. To stay safe, they may travel around the roundabout in the left-hand lane.

14.60 A group of horse riders comes towards you. What should you do if the leading rider's horse becomes nervous of your presence?

❏ Brake gently to a stop until they've passed

❏ Brake quickly to a stop, applying the parking brake

❏ Continue driving, keeping well to the left

❏ Increase speed to pass the riders quickly

DBC s4, DGV s4, HC r215

If any animal you pass on the road becomes unsettled, you should brake gently and come to a stop. A nervous animal is unpredictable, so you should wait until it has settled or passed by. Other road users behind you may have a limited view of the hazard, so use your mirrors and give clear signals if necessary.

14.61 You're emerging from a side road into a queue of traffic. Which of these vehicles is especially hard to see?

❏ Bicycle ❏ Tractor ❏ Milk float ❏ Car

DBC s4, DGV s4

Always check carefully for cyclists when emerging from a junction. Bicycles, being much narrower than any other vehicle, can be quite difficult to see.

14.62 Why are motorcyclists more at risk from other road users?

❏ They're easy to see

❏ They often break down

❏ They can't give arm signals

❏ They're easily overlooked

DBC s4, DGV s4

Always look for the more vulnerable road users, such as motorcyclists, cyclists, pedestrians (especially children), animals and horse riders. All need your consideration. Motorcycles are relatively small, but they can move just as fast as other vehicles, making them easy to overlook.

14.63 Which of these is the main cause of collisions involving motorcycles?

❏ Other drivers ❏ Other motorcyclists

❏ Wet roads ❏ Icy roads

DBC s4, DGV s4

The main reason why there are so many collisions at junctions is that drivers fail to see motorcyclists. A bright jacket or single headlight may help you identify an approaching motorcyclist, but you should be aware that not all motorcyclists wear bright clothing or use their headlights during the day.

14.64 What should you be on the lookout for before changing lanes in slow-moving queuing traffic?

❏ Private-hire taxis ❏ Breakdown vehicles

❏ Filtering motorcyclists ❏ Traffic cones

DRG s4, DGV s4

In slow-moving traffic, particularly on dual carriageways or motorways, always be on the lookout for motorcyclists who approach from behind and filter through narrow gaps between vehicles.

14.65 Which road users are especially at risk at a road junction?

❏ Motorcyclists ❏ Lorry drivers

❏ Car drivers ❏ Bus drivers

DRG s4, DGV s4

Junctions are especially risky for some road users – particularly motorcyclists, cyclists, pedestrians and mobility-scooter users. Their small size means they're easily hidden from view. At busy junctions, scan the near, middle and far distance to identify all hazards before emerging with a long vehicle.

14.66 When are motorcyclists particularly vulnerable?

❏ Near zebra crossings ❏ In gusting winds

❏ When leaving motorways ❏ At traffic lights

DRG s4, DGV s4

Always be concerned for the safety of other road users. Be aware of the various factors and situations where you may have to take action to keep more vulnerable road users safe.

14.67 You're driving towards a zebra crossing. What should you do if you see that a person in a wheelchair is waiting to cross?

❑ Continue on your way

❑ Wave to the person to cross

❑ Wave to the person to wait

❑ Be prepared to stop

HC r195
Prepare to slow down and stop, as you would for a person without a disability. Don't wave them across, as other traffic may not stop.

14.68 How will a school crossing patrol signal you to stop?

❑ By pointing to children on the opposite pavement

❑ By displaying a red light

❑ By displaying a 'stop' sign

❑ By giving you an arm signal

HC p105, r105
If a school crossing patrol steps out into the road with a 'stop' sign, you must stop. Don't wave anyone across the road or get impatient and rev your engine.

14.69 There's a slow-moving motorcyclist ahead of you. What should you do if you're unsure what the rider is going to do?

❑ Pass on the left   ❑ Pass on the right

❑ Stay behind   ❑ Move closer

DRG s4, DGV s4
The motorcyclist might be turning right, changing direction or unsure of their destination. Stay behind until the rider has made a move or you're sure you can pass safely. Don't intimidate them by moving too close.

14.70 Which road users are more vulnerable at road junctions?

❑ Cyclists

❑ Car drivers

❑ Lorry drivers   ❑ Taxi drivers

DBC s4, DGV s4
Road junctions can be especially dangerous for some road users, especially those that are small and more easily overlooked. Effective observation is necessary to ensure you don't overlook anything.

14.71 You're driving on a single carriageway road. What should you do when you see horse riders ahead?

❑ Move into the middle of the road

❑ Check your mirrors and prepare to slow down

❑ Switch on your vehicle's hazard warning lights

❑ Signal right to show you're going to pass them

DBC s4, DSV s4, HC r215
Look well ahead and be ready to deal with any hazards you see coming up, such as animals in the road. Horses are easily scared by the noise of an engine and the size of your vehicle may also be intimidating. Approach them as slowly and quietly as you can.

14.72 As you approach a pelican crossing, the lights change to green. What should you do if an elderly couple are halfway across?

❑ Wave at them to cross as quickly as they can

❑ Rev your engine to make them hurry

❑ Flash your lights in case they haven't heard you

❑ Wait patiently and give them time to finish crossing

DBC s4, DGV s4
When the lights turn to green, you may drive on, but only if the crossing is clear. You should wait for any pedestrians to finish crossing, regardless of their age. Allow them to cross the road at their own pace; don't try to hurry them in any way.

14.73 What should you do when you're following a motorcyclist on an uneven road?

❑ Allow less room, so you can be seen in their mirrors

❑ Overtake them immediately

❑ Allow extra room, in case they swerve to avoid potholes

❑ Allow the same room as you would any other road user

DBC s4, DGV s4
Potholes and raised drain covers in the road can unsteady a motorcyclist. They may suddenly swerve to avoid these uneven surfaces. Watch out at places where the road is in poor condition and this is likely to occur.

14.74   Why do you have to be alert for motorcyclists in queues of traffic?

❑ They may have panniers fitted to their motorcycle

❑ They may ride in single file

❑ They may be filtering between the lanes

❑ They may ride with their headlights on dipped beam

DBC s4, DGV s4

In queuing traffic, motorcyclists may take the opportunity to filter between the lanes. Be aware that they may pass on either side and very close. Stay alert and always check your mirrors and blind spots before moving off, changing lanes or turning.

14.75   You're driving past parked cars. What should you do if you notice a bicycle wheel sticking out between them?

❑ Accelerate past quickly and sound your horn

❑ Slow down and wave the cyclist across

❑ Brake sharply and flash your headlights

❑ Slow down and be prepared to stop for a cyclist

DBC s4, DGV s4

Scan the road as you drive. Try to anticipate hazards by being aware of the places where they're likely to occur; for example, pedestrians and cyclists emerging between parked cars on a busy street. If you're prepared, you'll be able to slow down or stop in good time.

14.76   What do yellow zigzag lines on the road outside a school mean?

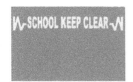

❑ Sound your horn to alert other road users

❑ Stop to allow children to cross

❑ You mustn't wait or park on these lines

❑ You mustn't drive over these lines

HC p116, r234, KYTS p56

Parking on the yellow zigzag lines will block the view of the school entrance. This will endanger the lives of children wanting to cross the road on their way to and from school.

14.77   You're driving on a main road. What should you do just before turning right into a side road?

❑ Adjust your interior mirror

❑ Flash your headlights

❑ Steer over to the left

❑ Check for traffic overtaking on your right

DBC s4, DGV s4, HC r180

Just before turning, a check in the offside mirror will help you to see any cyclist or motorcyclist passing on your offside. This check may help to prevent a serious incident from developing.

14.78   Where should you take particular care to look for motorcyclists and cyclists?

❑ On dual carriageways   ❑ At junctions

❑ At zebra crossings   ❑ In one-way streets

DBC s4, DGV s4, HC r170

Motorcyclists and cyclists may be more difficult to see, especially at junctions. They can be easily hidden by obstructions such as other vehicles, and the small size of an approaching motorcycle may make it difficult to judge its speed and distance. It's vital that you don't emerge until you're sure it's safe.

14.79   What should you do when you're driving through a bus station?

❑ Change your destination boards

❑ Drive through quickly if you're not stopping

❑ Look for people leaving buses

❑ Sound your horn as you enter

DBC s1

Bus stations are busy places. If people are in a rush, they may not always look properly before getting off a bus. Keep your speed down and look for manoeuvring vehicles or pedestrians stepping Into your path.

Section 15 Road and traffic signs

15.1 You're driving a lorry with a maximum authorised mass of 38 tonnes on a single carriageway road in England. What's the speed limit for your vehicle after passing this sign?

- ☐ 40 mph
- ☐ 50 mph
- ☐ 60 mph
- ☐ 70 mph

HC p106, KYTS p20   NI EXEMPT

The national speed limit for a goods vehicle exceeding 7.5 tonnes on a single carriageway road in England and Wales is 50 mph. In Scotland, the limit is 40 mph. The national speed limit varies for different vehicle categories. You must know the limit that applies to the vehicle you're driving.

15.2 You're driving a laden articulated lorry with a maximum authorised mass of 38 tonnes on a dual carriageway in England. What speed limit applies to your vehicle after passing this sign?

- ☐ 40 mph
- ☐ 50 mph
- ☐ 60 mph
- ☐ 70 mph

HC p106, KYTS p20   NI EXEMPT

60 mph may be the legal speed limit for a goods vehicle on a dual carriageway in England and Wales, but it doesn't mean that it's safe to drive at that speed. You should always take into account the road, weather and traffic conditions, and maintain safety margins.

15.3 You're driving an articulated lorry. What should you do when you see this sign?

- ☐ Turn round and find an alternative route
- ☐ Park safely and arrange alternative transport for the goods
- ☐ Inform your vehicle operator and await further instructions
- ☐ Drive past the sign because it doesn't apply to you

KYTS p32

The sign prohibits buses and coaches with more than eight passenger seats and so doesn't apply to you.

15.4 Which of these signs means you can't drive your lorry past this point?

☐   ☐

☐   ☐

KYTS p17

No motor vehicles are allowed past this sign. Although a motorcycle and car are shown, the restriction applies to all motor vehicles.

15.5 You're driving a lorry 30 feet long and towing a trailer 15 feet long. What should you do when you see this sign?

☐ Find an alternative route to your destination

☐ Stop and wait for a police escort

☐ Continue past the sign but reduce your speed

☐ Carry on; the sign applies to the towing vehicle only

KYTS p17
The maximum permitted length of vehicle includes any trailer being towed. Make sure you know the total length of your vehicle.

15.6 You're driving a lorry that's carrying a heavy load. What should you be prepared to do when you see this sign ahead?

☐ Brake to a lower speed

☐ Change to a higher gear

☐ Stop to check your load

☐ Change to a lower gear

KYTS p12
A heavy vehicle will lose speed when climbing a steep hill. Changing to a lower gear will help you to maintain an appropriate speed.

15.7 You're on a motorway. Your lorry has a maximum authorised mass of more than 7.5 tonnes. What does this sign mean to you?

☐ You mustn't use the right-hand lane

☐ You can only use the right-hand lane

☐ You can't leave the motorway at this junction

☐ You can use the middle or right-hand lane

KYTS p129-131
At motorway roadworks, some lanes may be narrower than normal and large vehicles may not be allowed to use those lanes. Look for weight-limit signs to check for any lanes that you can't use. Move to the appropriate lane in good time.

15.8 What's the national speed limit on a motorway for a lorry weighing over 7.5 tonnes?

☐ 50 mph (80 km/h) ☐ 55 mph (88 km/h)

☐ 60 mph (96 km/h) ☐ 70 mph (112 kmlh)

HC p40
Be aware of, and obey, all speed limits. On a motorway, any lorry that's articulated, towing a trailer, or over 7.5 tonnes mustn't exceed 60 mph (96 km/h).

15.9 When must these two signs be used?

☐ When you're carrying a load that overhangs the front or rear of the vehicle by more than 1 metre (3 feet 3 inches)

☐ Whenever your vehicle is being towed

☐ Whenever a police escort is required

☐ When you're carrying a load that overhangs the front or rear of the vehicle by more than 2 metres (6 feet 6 inches)

HC p117
The law requires you to use projection markers for long or wide loads. It's the driver's responsibility to keep the markers clean and securely fixed. They must also be independently lit at night.

15.10 You're driving a lorry weighing more than 7.5 tonnes on a motorway. What does this sign mean?

☐ Maximum speed 40 mph

☐ Maximum speed 50 mph

☐ Maximum speed 60 mph

☐ Maximum speed 70 mph

HC p40, 106
The maximum speed for lorries over 7.5 tonnes maximum authorised mass on a motorway is 60 mph. However, it may not always be appropriate or possible to drive at this speed, because of the weather, volume of traffic and other factors.

15.11 You're driving a lorry weighing more than 7.5 tonnes on a dual carriageway in England. What does this sign mean?

- ❏ Maximum speed 40 mph
- ❏ Maximum speed 50 mph
- ❏ Maximum speed 60 mph
- ❏ Maximum speed 70 mph

HC p40, 106   NI EXEMPT

The maximum speed for lorries over 7.5 tonnes maximum authorised mass on a dual carriageway in England and Wales is 60 mph. In Scotland, the limit is 50 mph. Be aware of the speed limits applying to different types of vehicle on particular roads. This is the maximum speed allowed, but it may not always be safe to drive at this speed, because of the weather, volume of traffic and other factors.

15.12 You're driving a lorry weighing more than 7.5 tonnes on a single carriageway road in England. What does this sign mean?

- ❏ Maximum speed 30 mph
- ❏ Maximum speed 40 mph
- ❏ Maximum speed 50 mph
- ❏ Maximum speed 60 mph

HC p40, 106   NI EXEMPT

In England and Wales, the national speed limit for lorries over 7.5 tonnes maximum authorised mass on a single carriageway road is 50 mph. In Scotland, the limit is 40 mph.

15.13 What's prohibited when a Red Route is in operation?

- ❏ Stopping or parking   ❏ Overtaking
- ❏ Changing lanes   ❏ Straddling the lines

DGV s3, HC p115, KYTS p56-57

The hours of operation of Red Routes vary from one area to another. As a rule, you mustn't stop on a Red Route, but there may be special marked boxes where loading and unloading can be carried out at certain times. Look out for signs giving information about the restrictions in place.

15.14 What does this sign mean?

- ❏ End of restricted speed area
- ❏ End of restricted parking area
- ❏ End of clearway
- ❏ End of cycle route

KYTS p38

Even though there are no restrictions, make sure that you park where you won't cause an obstruction or endanger other road users.

15.15 Which sign means 'No stopping'?

❏   ❏

❏   ❏

KYTS p52-55

Stopping where you see this sign is likely to cause an obstruction, which could lead to traffic delays. Obeying the sign will help keep the traffic flowing.

15.16 What does this sign mean?

- ❏ Give way to traffic from the opposite direction
- ❏ You're entering a one-way street
- ❏ Two-way traffic ahead
- ❏ You have priority over vehicles from the opposite direction

KYTS p73

You have priority over vehicles from the opposite direction. However, if a vehicle approaching from the opposite direction isn't going to stop, you should slow down and give way to avoid confrontation or an incident.

15.17 At a junction, you see this sign partly covered by snow. What does It mean?

- ❑ Crossroads
- ❑ Giveway
- ❑ Stop
- ❑ Turn right

KYTS p9, 16, 29

The 'Stop' sign Is the only sign that's octagonal. This helps you to recognise it even when the wording can't be seen.

15.18 What does this sign mean?

- ❑ Service area 30 miles ahead
- ❑ Maximum speed 30 mph
- ❑ Minimum speed 30 mph
- ❑ Lay-by 30 miles ahead

KYTS p21

This sign is shown where slow-moving vehicles would block the flow of traffic. However, if you need to slow down to avoid an incident, you should do so.

15.19 Which of these signs means turn left ahead?

KYTS p19

This sign gives a clear instruction. You should prepare to negotiate a left-hand tum.

15.20 What does this sign mean?

- ❑ Route for trams
- ❑ Give way to trams
- ❑ Route for buses
- ❑ Give way to buses

KYTS p30

Take extra care when you're driving on roads where trams operate. Look out for road markings and signs that tell you to expect them. Modern trams are very quiet and you might not hear them approaching.

15.21 Which of these signs means that you're entering a one-way street?

KYTS p18-19, 73

If a one-way street has two lanes, you can use either lane and overtake on either side. Use the lane that's more convenient for your destination unless directed by road signs or markings.

15.22 What does this sign mean?

- ❑ Bus station on the right
- ❑ Contraflow bus lane
- ❑ With-flow bus lane
- ❑ Give way to buses

KYTS p33

If you see a contraflow sign, there'll also be markings on the road to indicate the bus lane. Don't use this lane for parking or overtaking.

15.23 Which hazard would be shown in a triangular road sign?

- ❑ Road narrows
- ❑ One-way street
- ❑ Bus lane
- ❑ Minimum speed

KYTS p10-15

A triangular sign is a warning sign. Knowing this, you can prepare for the hazard ahead.

15.24   Which sign means that pedestrians may be walking along the road?

KYTS p13-14
Be cautious, especially if there's a bend in the road and you're unable to see well ahead. If you have to pass pedestrians, leave them plenty of room. You might have to use the right-hand side of the road, so look well ahead and in your mirrors before you pull out.

15.25   What does this sign mean?

- ❏ Side wind
- ❏ Road noise
- ❏ Airport
- ❏ Adverse camber

KYTS p12
Side-wind warning signs are often found on roads that are frequently affected by strong wind. High-sided vehicles, caravans and motorcycles are more susceptible to windy weather, and you should be aware of the difficulties they may be having.

15.26   What does this traffic sign mean?

- ❏ Slippery road ahead
- ❏ Tyres liable to puncture ahead
- ❏ Danger ahead
- ❏ Service area ahead

KYTS p13
A sign showing an exclamation mark (!) tells you that there may be danger ahead. Be ready to slow down for whatever that may be.

15.27   What should you do if you see this sign when you're about to overtake?

- ❏ Overtake the other driver as quickly as possible
- ❏ Move to the right to get a better view
- ❏ Switch your headlights on before overtaking
- ❏ Hold back until you can see clearly ahead

KYTS p13
You won't be able to see any hazards that might be out of sight in the dip. As well as oncoming traffic, there may be cyclists, horse riders, parked vehicles or pedestrians hidden from view. Only start to overtake when you can see the road ahead is clear, giving you enough time to overtake safely.

15.28   What does this sign mean?

- ❏ Uneven road surface
- ❏ Bridge over the road
- ❏ Road ahead ends
- ❏ Water across the road

KYTS p12
This sign is found where a shallow stream crosses the road. Heavy rainfall could increase the flow of water. If the water looks too deep or the stream has swelled over a large distance, stop and find another route.

15.29   You see this traffic light ahead. Which light or lights will come on next?

- ❏ Red alone
- ❏ Red and amber together
- ❏ Green and amber together
- ❏ Green alone

KYTS p102
The amber light means stop. You may only go on if the light changes to amber after you've crossed the stop line or when you're so close to the line that stopping might cause a collision. The amber light is followed by the red light.

You must wait behind the stop line until the green light shows.

15.30 Where would you find these flashing red lights?

☐ At a pelican crossing

☐ At a level crossing

☐ At a zebra crossing

☐ At a school crossing

KYTS p102

These signals can be found at level crossings, some airfields, bridges and emergency access sites. You must stop if the red lights are flashing. At level crossings, if the lights continue to flash after a train has passed, continue to wait because another train Is coming.

15.31 You're driving through roadworks. What information does this sign give you?

☐ Large vehicles must go straight ahead

☐ Traffic is joining from the left

☐ All traffic must leave at the next exit

☐ The distance to the next exit

KYTS p131

This sign gives you advance warning of a junction where the permanent sign is obscured by roadworks.

15.32 What does this sign mean?

☐ Stop only to pick up passengers

☐ No stopping at any time

☐ Stop only to set down passengers

☐ No stopping at peak times

KYTS p52-58

This traffic sign means no stopping on the main carriageway at any time, not even to set down passengers. However, you may stop in a lay-by.

15.33 You're driving on a motorway and there's no traffic ahead. You see this sign. Which lane should you use?

☐ The right-hand lane

☐ The hard shoulder

☐ The left-hand lane

☐ The middle lane

HC r264, KYTS p90

When there's no traffic ahead of you, you should always drive in the left-hand lane.

15.34 Which of these signs shows an uphill gradient?

☐   ☐

☐   ☐

KYTS p12

You'll need to identify the sign in time, so that you can select an appropriate gear.

15.35 Which of these signs means 'uneven road'?

☐   ☐

☐   ☐

KYTS p12

Some signs can look similar to others but each one has a different meaning. For example, this one looks a little like the sign for a hump bridge. Learn the meaning of every sign to prepare yourself for how to react to them.

15.36 What are these advanced stop lines for?

□ To allow room for pedestrians to cross the road

□ To allow space for large vehicles to turn

□ To allow cyclists to position in front of other traffic

□ To allow you to select where to stop

HC r178, KYTS p36
Advanced stop lines allow cyclists to take a position ahead of other traffic. When the green signal shows, they then have the time and space to move off in front of the following traffic.

15.37 What does this arm signal mean?

□ The driver intends to turn left

□ The driver intends to slow down

□ The driver wants you to keep back

□ The driver wants you to go past

HC p103
Sometimes, drivers or riders use arm signals as well as direction indicators and brake lights; for example, in bright sunshine or when approaching a zebra crossing. Using the arm signals shown in The Highway Code can help other road users to understand your intentions.

15.38 What does this motorway sign mean?

□ Use the hard shoulder

□ Contraflow system ahead

□ Overhead bridge repairs

□ All lanes closed ahead

KYTS p91
When the red lights are flashing, don't go beyond this signal. This sign shows that all lanes ahead are closed and you mustn't enter the motorway. Motorway signals are located on the central reservation, to the left of the hard shoulder, on overhead gantries and at the entrance to the motorway.

15.39 What does this sign warn of?

□ Slippery road

□ Double bend

□ Overhead electrified cable

□ Series of bends

DBC s3, DGV s2, KYTS p26
This sign is used to warn of overhead electrified cables and is usually accompanied by a plate indicating the safe height limit.

15.40 Who has priority when you're approaching this sign?

□ Larger vehicles

□ Oncoming traffic

□ Smaller vehicles

□ You have priority

KYTS p73
When you see this sign, you must give way to traffic from the opposite direction, regardless of the size of your vehicle.

15.41 What does this sign mean?

□ Car lane only

□ Single file only

□ Queues likely

□ Keep your distance

KYTS p13
When you see this sign, beware of traffic queues ahead. Check your mirrors and reduce your speed. Research shows that you make poor decisions when you're angry, so you're less likely to spot and respond safely to hazards. Be patient when you're delayed and reduce the possibility of being involved in an incident.

15.42 What does this sign mean?

□ Road flooded

□ Risk of punctures

□ Loose chippings

□ Uneven surface

KYTS p137
This is a warning sign to indicate loose chippings ahead. The sign is usually accompanied by an advisory speed limit. Vehicles travelling too fast for the conditions can throw up chippings or stones. Avoid causing damage to paintwork and windscreens by keeping your speed down.

15.43 What does this sign mean?

☐ You're allowed to carry on, but only with a police escort

☐ You should continue slowly if your weight is above the limit

☐ Don't cross unless the bridge is clear of other vehicles

☐ Don't cross the bridge if your weight exceeds the limit

KYTS p18
Vehicles over the weight shown on the sign may not use the bridge ahead. You must know the weight of your vehicle, including any load. With this knowledge you should plan your route in advance, so that you don't come to a bridge you can't cross. That way, you'll avoid delays and save time and fuel.

15.44 What does this marker count down to?

☐ A motorway slip road

☐ A primary road junction

☐ A concealed level crossing

☐ A roadside rest area

KYTS p27
When you see this sign, reduce your speed. You may well have to stop at the level crossing, or there may already be traffic queuing ahead.

15.45 What does it mean when there are double red lines running along the edge of a road?

☐ Limited loading   ☐ No stopping

☐ Bus route   ☐ Short-term parking

DBC s3, DGV s3, HC p115, KYTS p56-57
Double red lines indicate that you're on a Red Route and in a no-stopping area. Red Routes also have single red lines, with signs showing the times that restrictions are in force. There are also parking and loading boxes, which have signs explaining the restrictions that apply.

15.46 Where would you expect to see these road markings?

☐ At the entrance to a car park

☐ On the approach to an arched bridge

☐ At the start of a cycle lane

☐ On the approach to a lifting barrier

KYTS p24
High vehicles are often directed to the centre of the road to go under an arched bridge. Check that your vehicle doesn't exceed the height restriction indicated. Plan your route in advance to avoid any bridges that your vehicle won't be able to clear.

15.47 You're approaching traffic lights. Only the red light is showing. Which series of lights will show next?

☐ Red and amber, then green

☐ Green, then amber

☐ Amber, then green

☐ Green and amber, then green

KYTS p102
If you know which light is going to show next, you can plan your approach. This will help prevent excessive braking or hesitation at the junction.

15.48 The double white line along the centre of the road is unbroken on your side. When may you cross the line?

❏ To overtake any maintenance vehicle in front

❏ To overtake a pedal cycle travelling at 10 mph or less

❏ To check it's safe to overtake the vehicle in front

❏ To overtake a driver travelling at 20 mph or less

HC r129, KYTS p64

Solid white lines are used where it would be dangerous to overtake. If the solid line is on your side of the road, you may cross it to pass a stationary vehicle, or to overtake a pedal cycle, horse or road-maintenance vehicle that's travelling at 10 mph or less. You may also cross the solid line to enter premises or a side road.

15.49 What should you do when you see this sign ahead?

❏ Accelerate because you have priority

❏ Slow down; the road may be narrow ahead

❏ Stop and give way to oncoming traffic

❏ Maintain your speed; it's just an information sign

HC p113, KYTS p73

When the road narrows, there'll be less room than normal and others may not obey the rules, so slow down and approach with caution. Even when you have priority, you should still be ready to stop.

15.50 Why should you slow down when you see this sign?

❏ Because pedestrians have right of way

❏ There's a 'road race' in progress

❏ There's a pedestrian crossing ahead

❏ Because children may be crossing

HC p109, KYTS p14

see this sign, take extra care with these very vulnerable road users.

15.51 What does this sign mean?

❏ Vehicle carrying dangerous goods in packages

❏ Vehicle broken down ahead

❏ Holiday route

❏ Emergency diversion route for motorway traffic

HC p111, KYTS p107

Major roadworks often cause complicated diversions for large vehicles. Drivers may be advised to follow a special symbol until the original road can be rejoined. Look for the yellow-and-black symbols In these shapes:

• square

• triangle

• diamond

• circle.

They'll often be shown with additional information and will help guide you around the diversion.

15.52 You're driving in fog on a three-lane motorway. Which lane are you in when you can see red reflective studs on your left and white reflective studs on your right?

- ☐ The hard shoulder
- ☐ The middle lane
- ☐ The right-hand lane
- ☐ The left-hand lane

HC r132
White reflective studs separate each of the lanes. Red studs mark the left-hand edge of the carriageway, where the hard shoulder begins.

15.53 Which drivers are given Instructions by diamond-shaped signs?

- ☐ Drivers of lorries
- ☐ Drivers of trams
- ☐ Drivers of buses
- ☐ Drivers of tractors

KYTS p31
You need to show caution when driving in areas where trams operate. You might not hear their approach and they can't change direction to avoid you. There may also be crossing points where you'll need to give way to them, or areas specifically reserved for trams, which you aren't allowed to enter.

15.54 What's a 'Red Route'?

- ☐ An area where special waiting restrictions apply
- ☐ An area where part-time traffic lights operate
- ☐ An area where drivers have to pay a toll
- ☐ An area where night-time and weekend weight limits apply

DBC s3, DGV s3
Red Routes operate in many busy cities and are designed to ensure the route has no obstructions to cause delays during peak periods. Road signs and red road markings identify roads where Red Route waiting and loading restrictions apply.

15.55 You're driving on a motorway. What colour are the reflective studs on the right-hand edge of the carriageway?

- ☐ Amber
- ☐ Green
- ☐ Rcd
- ☐ White

HC r132
Reflective studs on motorways and dual carriageways are provided to help drivers in bad visibility. Reflective studs are coloured

- red on the left-hand edge of the carriageway
- white to indicate lane markings
- green at slip roads and lay-bys
- amber on the right-hand edge of the carriageway, marking the central reservation.

15.56 What's the purpose of green-and-yellow fluorescent studs on a motorway?

- ☐ They mark the lanes in a contraflow system
- ☐ They separate the slip road from the motorway
- ☐ They mark access points for emergency services
- ☐ They separate the edge of the hard shoulder from the grass verge

HC r132
Roadworks can involve complex lane layouts. Reflective green and-yellow fluorescent studs are used to separate the lanes in a contraflow traffic system. As you approach roadworks, look for traffic signs giving you advance information, which may relate to the size or type of vehicle you're driving.

15.57 What does this sign mean?

- ☐ Tramway speed limit
- ☐ Distance to level crossing
- ☐ Maximum passenger capacity
- ☐ Goods-vehicle weight limit

KYTS p31
Trams are becoming increasingly common in large towns and cities, as the move to more environmentally friendly transport continues. They may either cross the road you're driving on or share it with you. Always be aware of their virtually silent approach, and look out for places where you may be required to give way to them.

15.58 Which light won't show to a driver at a puffin crossing?

❑ Flashing amber   ❑ Red

❑ Steady amber   ❑ Green

HC r23
A flashing amber light is shown at pelican crossings, but not at puffin crossings. Puffin crossings have sensors that detect when pedestrians are using the crossing.

15.59 You're approaching a red light at a puffin crossing. Pedestrians are on the crossing. How long will the red light stay on?

❑ Until you start to edge forward onto the crossing

❑ Until the pedestrians have reached a safe position

❑ Until the pedestrians are clear of the front of your vehicle

❑ Until a driver from the opposite direction reaches the crossing

KYTS p123
The traffic light will remain on red to give pedestrians on the crossing time to reach safety. Don't proceed until the green light shows and it's safe to do so.

15.60 A bus-lane sign shows no hours of operation. When is the bus lane in operation?

❑ The bus lane isn't in operation at all

❑ The bus lane is only in operation at peak times

❑ The bus lane is in operation 24 hours a day

❑ The bus lane is only in operation in daylight hours

HC r141
When a bus-lane sign shows no hours of operation, the lane operates all the time.

15.61 What colour follows the green signal at a puffin crossing?

❑ Steady red   ❑ Flashing amber

❑ Steady amber   ❑ Flashing green

KYTS p123
Puffin crossings have sensors that detect when pedestrians are using the crossing. The sensors control the timing of the traffic lights, and this means that there's no flashing amber phase as there is with a pelican crossing.

15.62 What must you do when you're approaching a pelican crossing in its flashing amber phase?

❑ Give way to pedestrians on the crossing

❑ Encourage pedestrians to cross

❑ Wait until the green light appears

❑ Stop even if the crossing Is clear

KYTS p126
When the amber light Is flashing, you must give way to any pedestrians on the crossing. Don't be impatient or encourage pedestrians to cross by waving or flashing your headlights; they or other road users may misunderstand your signal.

15.63 What should the hard shoulder on a motorway be used for?

❑ As a place to stop to answer a mobile phone

❑ As a place to stop when an emergency arises

❑ As a place to stop for a short rest when you're tired

❑ As a place to stop to check a road atlas

HC r264
When an emergency arises, pull onto the hard shoulder and use the emergency telephone to report your problem. You'll be connected to an operator, who will put you through to a breakdown service. Never cross the carriageway or a slip road to use a telephone.

15.64 When must you stop on a motorway?

❑ When you're tired and need to walk in the fresh air

❑ When you're picking up hitchhikers

❑ When you're signalled to do so by flashing red lights

❑ When you need to answer your mobile phone

HC r258
If red lights flash on the overhead signals above your lane, you mustn't go past the signal in that lane. If other lanes aren't displaying flashing red lights, you may go ahead in those lanes if it's clear and you can move into them safely. If red lights flash on a signal in the central reservation or at the side of the road, you mustn't go past the signal in any lane.

15.65   Which sign means 'no overtaking'?

KYTS p18
This sign is placed on sections of road where overtaking would be dangerous. There'll often be a plate underneath the sign, telling you how far the restriction extends. You mustn't overtake until you pass another sign cancelling the restriction.

15.66   What does this motorway sign mean?

☐ Right-hand lane closed ahead

☐ 1 tonne weight limit ahead

☐ Left-hand lane closed ahead

☐ T-junction 1 mile ahead

HC p102, KYTS p90
Four amber lights flash in alternate horizontal pairs to provide a warning and to draw the driver's attention to the message displayed.

15.67   What does this sign mean?

☐ No U-turns   ☐ Two-way traffic

☐ One-way system   ☐ End of one-way system

KYTS p18
You mustn't make a U-turn on roads where this sign is displayed.

15.68   What does this sign mean?

☐ Low bridge   ☐ Tunnel ahead

☐ Accident blackspot ☐ Speed camera

KYTS p12
A tunnel can present a number of dangers to large vehicles. Look out for height or width limits and always be aware of your vehicle's size. Reduce speed and turn on your headlights before entering the tunnel. Remove sunglasses if you're wearing them, and remember, your eyes may take a little time to adjust to the sudden darkness.

15.69   What does this sign mean?

☐ Rumble strips

☐ Road humps

☐ Uneven road

☐ Double hump bridge

KYTS p12
Slow down when you see a warning sign for an uneven road. Be especially careful if you're carrying passengers, livestock or fragile items.

15.70   Why should you slow down when you see this sign?

☐ To reduce the risk of a blow-out

☐ To avoid splashing others with water

☐ To avoid throwing up loose chippings

☐ To prevent grit from blocking your air filter

KYTS p137
This sign is usually accompanied by a reduced speed limit. When chippings fly out from your tyres, they can cause a lot of damage to other vehicles, or injury to pedestrians, cyclists and motorcyclists. Slowing down will reduce the risk.

15.71 You're driving on a smart motorway. What's the speed limit when the hard shoulder is being used as a running lane?

❑ The speed limits displayed are advisory

❑ The national speed limit applies

❑ The set speed limit is displayed

❑ The speed limit is always 30 mph

KYTS p89–91
When you're driving on a smart motorway, speed limits will show above each lane. These limits are shown inside a red circle and must be obeyed. A red cross will usually appear above the hard shoulder. When the hard shoulder is being used as a running lane, an appropriate speed limit will be displayed instead.

15.72 In which part of the United Kingdom do traffic officers operate?

❑ England only

❑ England, Scotland and Wales

❑ England and Wales

❑ England, Wales and Northern Ireland

DBC s4, DGV s4, HC r108
Traffic officers have powers to stop vehicles on safety grounds; for example, if you have an insecure load. They only operate in England. It's an offence not to comply with their directions.

15.73 What's the purpose of an emergency refuge area on a smart motorway?

❑ It's for use in case of emergency or breakdown

❑ It's for use if you think you'll be involved in a road-rage incident

❑ It's for a police patrol to park and watch traffic

❑ It's for construction and road workers to store emergency equipment

DBC s4, DGV s4
Emergency refuge areas may be found next to the hard shoulder on a smart motorway. If possible, you should use one of these areas, rather than the hard shoulder, when you break down. If the hard shoulder is being used as a running lane, take care when you rejoin the motorway.

15.74 What are traffic officers authorised to do?

❑ Carry out enforcement duties

❑ Issue fixed penalty notices

❑ Test drivers suspected of drink-driving

❑ Stop and direct anyone on a motorway

DBC s4, DGV s4, HC r108
Traffic officers don't have enforcement powers, but they're able to stop and direct people on motorways and some 'A' class roads. They only operate in England and work in partnership with the police at incidents. Traffic officers can be recognised by their orange-and-yellow jackets and their vehicles, which have yellow- and-black markings.

15.75 You're on a motorway. What does it mean when a red cross is displayed above the hard shoulder?

❑ Stop in this lane to answer your mobile phone

❑ You may use this lane as a running lane

❑ This lane can be used if you need a rest

❑ You shouldn't use this lane as a running lane

DBC s4, DGV s4, HC p102, KYTS p89
On smart motorways, the hard shoulder can be used as a running lane when a speed limit is shown above it. However, a red cross above the hard shoulder means that this lane shouldn't be used, except for emergencies and breakdowns.

15.76 You're on a smart motorway. What does it mean when a mandatory speed limit is displayed above the hard shoulder?

❑ You shouldn't use the hard shoulder as a running lane

❑ The hard shoulder can be used as a running lane

❑ You can park on the hard shoulder if you feel tired

❑ Large vehicles must use the hard shoulder

DBC s4, DGV s4
If a mandatory speed-limit sign is shown above the hard shoulder, this lane can be used as a running lane. You must stay within the signed speed limit. Look out for any vehicles that have broken down and are blocking the hard shoulder.

15.77 What's the aim of a smart motorway?

❏ To prevent overtaking ❏ To reduce rest stops

❏ To prevent tailgating ❏ To reduce congestion

DBC s4, DGV s4
Smart motorways are intended to reduce congestion and make journey times more reliable. In these areas, the hard shoulder may be used as a running lane to ease congestion at peak times or when an incident occurs. The variable speed limits shown in red circles are mandatory and help to keep traffic flowing at a steady speed.

15.78 You're on a smart motorway. What do the speed-limit signs indicate?

❏ The speed limit on the sign is advisory

❏ The national speed limit will always apply

❏ The speed limit is always 30 mph

❏ The speed limit on the sign must be obeyed

DBC s4, DGV s4
When a smart motorway is in operation, you must follow the instructions shown on the gantries above each lane. There may also be instructions above the hard shoulder. The signals displayed are mandatory and may be enforced with camera technology.

15.79 You're travelling on a motorway. A red cross is displayed on the gantry signals above the hard shoulder and mandatory speed limits are shown above all other lanes. What does the red cross mean?

❏ The hard shoulder can be used as a rest area if you feel tired

❏ The hard shoulder is for emergency or breakdown use only

❏ The hard shoulder can be used as a normal running lane

❏ The hard shoulder has a speed limit of 50 mph

DBC s4, DGV s4
A red cross above the hard shoulder means that it's closed as a running lane and should only be used for emergencies or breakdowns. At busy times, the hard shoulder may be used as a running lane; the red cross will then be replaced by a mandatory speed-limit sign.

15.80 You see this sign on a smart motorway. Which lane can you use?

❏ Any lane except the hard shoulder

❏ The hard shoulder only

❏ The three right-hand lanes only

❏ Permitted lanes, including the hard shoulder

DBC s4, DGV s4
Mandatory speed-limit signs above the hard shoulder and all other lanes show that you're on a smart motorway. In this case, you can use the hard shoulder as a running lane. You must stay within the speed limit shown. Look well ahead for any vehicles that have broken down and are blocking the hard shoulder.

15.81 When can you travel on the hard shoulder of a motorway?

❏ When taking the next exit

❏ When traffic has stopped

❏ When signs show that you can

❏ When traffic is moving slowly

DBC s4, DGV s4
Normally, you should only use the hard shoulder for emergencies and breakdowns. On smart motorways, the hard shoulder may be used as a running lane, but only when speed-limit signs are shown directly above it. This technology has been introduced to ease traffic congestion.

15.82 What does this sign mean?

❏ Soft verges

❏ Only cars may park here

❏ Parking restrictions apply

❏ Fuel and water tanks will leak

KYTS p12
This sign tells you that the verge is soft. If you park here, there's a danger that your vehicle will become stuck. This can be inconvenient and could be costly if you need to be pulled out. In extreme cases, your vehicle may even tip over.

15.83 What does this sign mean?

- ☐ Buses only
- ☐ Bus lane
- ☐ No buses
- ☐ Bus stop

KYTS p32

No buses with more than eight passenger seats are permitted past this sign. Exceptions apply for scheduled services, school and works buses.

15.84 Which road user is sometimes allowed to share a bus lane?

- ☐ Learner driver
- ☐ Lorry driver
- ☐ Disabled driver
- ☐ Taxi driver

HC r141, KYTS p32

The bus-lane signs will indicate which road users are allowed to share the lane with buses and any time restrictions that may apply. Taxis are often allowed to use bus lanes, as these lanes provide a route that has less congestion and can therefore be quicker.

15.85 You're driving a fully loaded coach that's 12 metres long. What should you do when you approach this sign?

- ☐ Don't proceed past the sign but find another route
- ☐ Set down all your passengers at a safe place before the sign
- ☐ Stop and check the legal lettering on the side panel
- ☐ Proceed as normal; the sign doesn't apply to you

KYTS p17

The sign shows the maximum authorised mass for goods vehicles. It's used to restrict heavy lorries (for example, in residential areas), but it doesn't apply to buses and coaches.

Section 16 Answers

1. Vehicle weights and dimensions

1.1 ❏ No goods vehicles over 7.5 tonnes maximum authorised mass
1.2 ❏ Use only the left-hand lane
1.3 ❏ 50 mph
1.4 ❏ When the left-hand lane is closed
1.5 ❏ On traffic-calming humps
1.6 ❏ The ground clearance
1.7 ❏ Stop before the crossing and phone the signal operator
1.8 ❏ Chains
1.9 ❏ 40 mph
1.10 ❏ 35 mph
1.11 ❏ Red/yellow
1.12 ❏ Through a greater arc than the cab
1.13 ❏ Through a greater arc than the cab
1.14 ❏ When turning
1.15 ❏ Unload only within a 'white box' area
1.16 ❏ 60 mph
1.17 ❏ Tri-axles with single wheels
1.18 ❏ The driver has very little warning
1.19 ❏ The pendulum effect
1.20 ❏ To keep the load safe
1.21 ❏ ▰▰▰
1.22 ❏ 2 metres (6 feet 6 inches)
1.23 ❏ When the load's height exceeds 5.25 metres (17 feet 6 inches)
1.24 ❏ 2.9 metres (9 feet 5 inches)
1.25 ❏ Red/white
1.26 ❏ Using twist locks
1.27 ❏ To make room for the trailer cutting in
1.28 ❏ Vehicles over the weight shown are prohibited
1.29 ❏ Overhead electrified cable
1.30 ❏ No vehicles over 14 feet 6 inches (4.4 metres) high
1.31 ❏ Tunnel ahead
1.32 ❏ The distance to a tunnel
1.33 ❏ When driving under overhead cables
1.34 ❏ 5.0 metres (16 feet 6 inches)
1.35 ❏ The police
1.36 ❏ The bridge number
1.37 ❏ Overhead electric cables ahead
1.38 ❏ No vehicles over 6 feet 6 inches (2 metres) wide
1.39 ❏ Lane ahead closed
1.40 ❏ End of restriction
1.41 ❏ In road tunnels
1.42 ❏ Height
1.43 ❏ Its length
1.44 ❏ Icy
1.45 ❏ 10 times
1.46 ❏ 60 mph
1.47 ❏ Your left-hand mirror
1.48 ❏ During gentle acceleration
1.49 ❏ No entry for vehicles over 32 feet 6 inches (9.9 metres) long
1.50 ❏ Avoid going over the roundabout if possible
1.51 ❏ Weight restrictions
1.52 ❏ In the driver's cab
1.53 ❏ Keep to the centre of the arch and give way to oncoming traffic
1.54 ❏ 5.0 metres (16 feet 6 inches)
1.55 ❏ In an off-road parking area
1.56 ❏ When you're overtaking
1.57 ❏ When overtaking
1.58 ❏ Risk of grounding
1.59 ❏ Your vehicle's length
1.60 ❏ Straddle the lanes to make more room for the turn
1.61 ❏ At an authorised speed-limiter centre
1.62 ❏ On the vehicle plate
1.63 ❏ 1 tonne
1.64 ❏ 15
1.65 ❏ By a plate fitted beneath the weight-limit sign
1.66 ❏ At any time of the day
1.67 ❏ 60 mph
1.68 ❏ Buses with a maximum of 16 passenger seats
1.69 ❏ On the side of the vehicle
1.70 ❏ D
1.71 ❏ You might hit something close to the road
1.72 ❏ A plate in the cab showing the limited speed
1.73 ❏ In the driver's cab
1.74 ❏ The weight of your vehicle, with both luggage and passengers
1.75 ❏ By reducing the fuel supplied to the engine
1.76 ❏ The amount of space needed for the vehicle to turn

2. Drivers' hours and rest periods

2.1 ❏ To help road safety
2.2 ❏ Road safety
2.3 ❏ Keep a written record of hours worked
2.4 ❏ Every 24 hours
2.5 ❏ 24 hour
2.6 ❏ Use a spare chart and attach it to the damaged one
2.7 ❏ Remove the chart and make a manual record of the break period
2.8 ❏ 45 minutes
2.9 ❏ Open the window and turn down the heating
2.10 ❏ Stop in a safe place and seek help
2.11 ❏ Make sure all doors and windows are locked
2.12 ❏ Park with the rear doors close to another vehicle

2.13 ❑ Make sure the doors and windows are secure

2.14 ❑ Vary your routes and rest stops

2.15 ❑ On secure premises

2.16 ❑ When it's left unattended

2.17 ❑ The starting point of your day's journey

2.18 ❑ Take the chart with you and use it in the other vehicle

2.19 ❑ Parking in a well-lit lorry park

2.20 ❑ Keep plenty of cool, fresh air moving through the cab

2.21 ❑ Fit an alarm and immobiliser

2.22 ❑ Your local crime-prevention officer

2.23 ❑ 00.00 hours Monday to 24.00 hours the following Sunday

2.24 ❑ Continue your journey but make a manual record

2.25 ❑ They can be heavily fined

2.26 ❑ Carry enough approved charts

2.27 ❑ One week

2.28 ❑ The officer

2.29 ❑ With their name

2.30 ❑ To replace the original chart if it gets dirty

2.31 ❑ 4.5 hours

2.32 ❑ At least 45 minute.

2.33 ❑ 9 hours, extended to 10 hours on two days of the week

2.34 ❑ 9 hours

2.35 ❑ Three days

2.36 ❑ 11 hours

2.37 ❑ 45 hours

2.38 ❑ Use their own tachograph chart

2.39 ❑ As a break in daily driving

2.40 ❑ Driving time

2.41 ❑

2.42 ❑ Driving

2.43 ❑ Other work

2.44 ❑ 34

2.45 ❑ Continue using the same tachograph chart and write an explanation on the back

2.46 ❑ Having insufficient breaks from driving

2.47 ❑ Stop as soon as it's safe to do so

2.48 ❑ Stop as soon as it's safe to do so

2.49 ❑ Leave by the next exit and find a place to stop

2.50 ❑ At a service station

2.51 ❑ Secure the vehicle and lock the doors

2.52 ❑ 30 minutes

2.53 ❑ 10 hours

2.54 ❑ Two days

2.55 ❑ 28

2.56 ❑ One of 15 minutes, plus one of 30

2.57 ❑ Within 7 days

2.58 ❑ Five years

2.59 ❑ The Driver and Vehicle Licensing Agency

2.60 ❑ The Driver and Vehicle Licensing Agency

2.61 ❑ Unlimited

2.62 ❑ At no time

2.63 ❑ Between 00.00 hours on Monday and 24.00 hours the following Sunday

2.64 ❑ Workshop card

2.65 ❑ Control card

2.66 ❑ The Driver and Vehicle Licensing Agency

2.67 ❑ The driver's employer

2.68 ❑ From a plaque on or near the tachograph

2.69 ❑ Every six years

2.70 ❑ Take it with you, and use it in the new vehicle

2.71 ❑ 90 hours

2.72 ❑ Every two years

2.73 ❑ EU only

2.74 ❑ 45 minute

2.75 ❑ If it's fitted with a bunk

2.76 ❑ Ask to see a warrant card

2.77 ❑ Check that the· parking brake is applied

2.78 ❑ When the journey is more than 50 km

3. Braking systems

3.1 ❑ While you're braking on a bend

3.2 ❑ While driving on muddy construction sites

3.3 ❑ Blue

3.4 ❑ Red

3.5 ❑ Auxiliary

3.6 ❑ Drain the air tanks daily

3.7 ❑ Select an appropriate gear before downhill gradients

3.8 ❑ At high engine speed, while in low gears

3.9 ❑ The service brake

3.10 ❑ The vehicle could jack-knife

3.11 ❑ While it's under heavy braking

3.12 ❑ As soon as the vehicle is moving

3.13 ❑ Blue

3.14 ❑ It's the emergency line

3.15 ❑ The trailer auxiliary line should be left unconnected

3.16 ❑ Apply the footbrake firmly and continuously until the vehicle has stopped

3.17 ❑ Brake fade

3.18 ❑ To make the wheels less likely to spin

3.19 ❑ They help you keep steering control while braking heavily

3.20 ❑ Moisture drawn in with the air may freeze and cause a blockage

3.21 ❑ Stop and get help without delay

3.22 ❑ Keep the parking brake on

3.23 ❑ Stop safely in an emergency

3.24 ❑ Before every journey

3.25 ❑ Reduced effectiveness

3.26 ❑ Apply firm, continuous pressure to the brake pedal

3.27 ❑ Reduction of braking effectiveness

3.28 ❑ On a long downhill gradient

3.29 ❑ Use the endurance brake
3.30 ❑ Maintain steering control
3.31 ❑ There's no need to alter the way you brake
3.32 ❑ Down a steep hill
3.33 ❑ When your brakes have failed
3.34 ❑ While driving down long hills
3.35 ❑ An endurance brake (retarder)
3.36 ❑ An endurance brake (retarder)
3.37 ❑ On long downhill slopes
3.38 ❑ When driving in a straight line
3.39 ❑ Be prepared to reduce your speed
3.40 ❑ Drive in a low gear with the footbrake lightly applied
3.41 ❑ The air brakes
3.42 ❑ When the brakes get too hot
3.43 ❑ Use the endurance brake
3.44 ❑ Continuous use of the brakes
3.45 ❑ On slippery roads
3.46 ❑ Because the service brake may not stop you
3.47 ❑ The vacuum pump isn't working
3.48 ❑ The brake pedal feels hard when pressed
3.49 ❑ There isn't enough fluid in the braking system
3.50 ❑ The hydraulic-brake fluid level
3.51 ❑ A buzzer or light
3.52 ❑ Blue
3.53 ❑ Low air pressure
3.54 ❑ The brake system has a loss of vacuum
3.55 ❑ The brake linings
3.56 ❑ Stop and have the fault put right
3.57 ❑ The drive wheels could lock
3.58 ❑ The drive wheels locking
3.59 ❑ Find out whether you need to drain the system manually
3.60 ❑ Frozen moisture in the storage tanks
3.61 ❑ When road speed is 6 mph (10 km/h) or more
3.62 ❑ Service brake
3.63 ❑ Apply the parking brake after stopping
3.64 ❑ Put your foot on the footbrak
3.65 ❑ Improved passenger safety and comfort

4. The driver

4.1 ❑ Go forward if your vehicle will clear the junction
4.2 ❑ It's required by law
4.3 ❑ Check your right-hand mirror and blind spot
4.4 ❑ Headlight dazzle
4.5 ❑ Stay calm and accept the error
4.6 ❑ When you're making deliveries that are less than 50 metres apart
4.7 ❑ You, the driver
4.8 ❑ Traffic further ahead may be stopping
4.9 ❑ Drive on until you find a safe place to stop
4.10 ❑ Shopping areas
4.11 ❑ The noise of your vehicle
4.12 ❑ Drive very slowly
4.13 ❑ When driving close to the kerb
4.14 ❑ Heart disorders

4.15 ❑ Your distance from the controls
4.16 ❑ To protect your neck in a collision
4.17 ❑ When reversing
4.18 ❑ Drop back to leave the correct separation distance
4.19 ❑ Try to avoid splashing the pedestrians
4.20 ❑ Slow down
4.21 ❑ Stop in a safe place
4.22 ❑ To warn others of your presence
4.23 ❑ Be patient and stay well behind
4.24 ❑ Stop on the left as soon as it's safe
4.25 ❑ Signal with the left indicator
4.26 ❑ Find a safe place to stop
4.27 ❑ When you're stopped in a safe place
4.28 ❑ As one continuous crossing
4.29 ❑ Give way to pedestrians already on the crossing
4.30 ❑ Always leave the crossing clear in traffic queues
4.31 ❑ Do nothing and let the driver decide
4.32 ❑ Stop to let it pass as soon as it's safe to do so
4.33 ❑ Yes, because it's a doctor going to an emergency
4.34 ❑ Doctor's car
4.35 ❑ Be patient and wait
4.36 ❑ There may be another vehicle coming
4.37 ❑ The nearside mirror striking the heads of pedestrians
4.38 ❑ Near the brow of a hill
4.39 ❑ Your mirrors are clean
4.40 ❑ Check your nearside mirror
4.41 ❑ Allow the vehicle to overtake
4.42 ❑ Slow down and be ready to stop
4.43 ❑ You'll feel more confident
4.44 ❑ Tiredness
4.45 ❑ It reduces your concentration
4.46 ❑ Insurance premiums
4.47 ❑ Go home by public transport
4.48 ❑ Avoid drinking alcohol completely
4.49 ❑ You may still be over the legal drink-drive limit
4.50 ❑ Some types of medicine can cause your reactions to slow down
4.51 ❑ Only after checking with your doctor
4.52 ❑ Ask your doctor for advice
4.53 ❑ Check the label to see whether the medicine will affect your driving
4.54 ❑ Leave the motorway at the next exit and take a rest
4.55 ❑ Wait until you're fit and well before driving
4.56 ❑ Ensure a supply of fresh air
4.57 ❑ When driving while you're tired
4.58 ❑ Seek medical advice
4.59 ❑ Leave the motorway at the next exit
4.60 ❑ Park in a suitable place and rest
4.61 ❑ Withdrawal of a driving licence
4.62 ❑ Hold the steering wheel firmly
4.63 ❑ It allows easy location by the emergency services

4.64	❏ When you use a mobile phone	5.10	❏ Towards the outside of the bend
4.65	❏ Stop in a safe place before making the call	5.11	❏ Thinking and planning well ahead
4.66	❏ Only when you're suitably parked	5.12	❏ Passengers getting off the bus
4.67	❏ Your attention will be diverted from the road	5.13	❏ At all times
4.68	❏ Check your location from the marker posts on the left	5.14	❏ A fire extinguisher
		5.15	❏ The location of the first-aid equipment
4.69	❏ Stop safely before answering	5.16	❏ They have poor vision and hearing
4.70	❏ Move back to the left when you judge it's safe to do so	5.17	❏ Be courteous and polite
		5.18	❏ To be courteous and polite
4.71	❏ Slow down and give way if it's safe to do so	5.19	❏ Look at them when speaking to them
4.72	❏ Stay where you are and allow them to cross in their own time	5.20	❏ To allow the step height to be raised and lowered
		5.21	❏ The bus may be carrying children
4.73	❏ Pull in when you can	5.22	❏ When children are getting on or off the vehicle
4.74	❏ It will divert your attention		
4.75	❏ Stop in a safe place when you can	5.23	❏ To limit injuries in the event of a rear-end collision
4.76	❏ A false sense of confidence		
4.77	❏ Concentrate on the road ahead	5.24	❏ Keep the interior lit
4.78	❏ It makes it easier for you to steer	5.25	❏ Get all the passengers off the bus
4.79	❏ Keep calm and don't retaliate	5.26	❏ Access for passengers
4.80	❏ Stop and take a break	5.27	❏ So that passengers can see to move around
4.81	❏ Stay calm and don't retaliate	5.28	❏ Those attempting to board the bus
4.82	❏ Switch on your hazard warning lights	5.29	❏ Wait until the passenger has sat down before moving away
4.83	❏ Wait until it's clear in both directions		
4.84	❏ The length of your vehicle	5.30	❏ When children are boarding the bus
4.85	❏ Allow plenty of time for your journey	5.31	❏ Leave a responsible person on the coach
4.86	❏ Have regular meals and rest breaks	5.32	❏ Lampposts
4.87	❏ Bottled water	5.33	❏ 5 tonnes
4.88	❏ Eat a meal at the beginning of your shift	5.34	❏ 15
4.89	❏ Between 2 am and 7 am	5.35	❏ School-bus signs
4.90	❏ 40%	5.36	❏ Stop and have the fault put right
4.91	❏ Heart disease	5.37	❏ Overhanging trees
4.92	❏ Stop and rest	5.38	❏ Helping passengers who need directions
4.93	❏ On motorways	5.39	❏ Fully trained people
4.94	❏ 30 years and under	5.40	❏ Access for disabled people
4.95	❏ Hold the steering wheel firmly and slow down gradually	5.41	❏ The front of the bus
		5.42	❏ Passengers leaving the bus
4.96	❏ When you hold a medical exemption certificate	5.43	❏ Finish issuing tickets to passengers
		5.44	❏ Move passengers to the front of the bus
4.97	❏ You're more likely to fall asleep at the wheel	5.45	❏ The safety and comfort of passengers
4.98	❏ A head restraint	5.46	❏ Make sure you've cancelled any signal
4.99	❏ When you're reversing the vehicle	5.47	❏ By making full use of the internal mirror system
4.100	❏ The emergency-exit location		
4.101	❏ After overtaking, to see whether it's safe to return to the left	5.48	❏ Passengers using the stairs could fall if the bus brakes or swerves
		4.49	❏ Close to the kerb
4.102	❏ Keep junctions clear	5.50	❏ Close to the kerb
		5.51	❏ Check for traffic on the left

5. Carrying passengers

5.1	❏ The safety and comfort of your passengers	5.52	❏ Check it's clear of traffic on the left
5.2	❏ By stopping close to the kerb	5.53	❏ Check mirrors before opening doors
5.3	❏ To improve passenger comfort	5.54	❏ Keep the passenger doors closed until the bus has stopped
5.4	❏ Plan ahead and take early action on all stops		
5.5	❏ To the front of the bus	5.55	❏ When there are no passengers
5.6	❏ Plan ahead and take early action	5.56	❏ No, this isn't allowed
5.7	❏ When the vehicle is cornering	5.57	❏ Passenger comfort will be increased
5.8	❏ Slow down to avoid the need to stop suddenly	5.58	❏ Smile and offer to help them
		5.59	❏ When it can't be seen by the driver
5.9	❏ To keep the passengers safe	5.60	❏ Priority seating

5.61 ❑ Those with disabilities
5.62 ❑ When the boarding device has failed to work
5.63 ❑ When the designated space is occupied
5.64 ❑ In a medical emergency
5.65 ❑ High-visibility vest
5.66 ❑ The boarding device
5.67 ❑ When the lift has stopped working
5.68 ❑ Passengers are standing in a wheelchair space and can't move elsewhere
5.69 ❑ Wait until they're inside the bus

6. The road

6.1 ❑ Leave plenty of room and check your nearside mirror before returning to the left
6.2 ❑ High-level bridges may be closed to certain vehicles in windy weather
6.3 ❑ Build up your speed on the slip road before joining the motorway
6.4 ❑ Plan your route in advance
6.5 ❑ Ease off and drop behind the vehicle you were trying to overtake
6.6 ❑ Tie both curtains open
6.7 ❑ When it's travelling empty
6.8 ❑ To reduce the effect of side wind
6.9 ❑ When travelling empty
6.10 ❑ Lane closures
6.11 ❑ An unladen lorry with box body
6.12 ❑ A motorcycle
6.13 ❑ High-sided lorry
6.14 ❑ When there's a headwind
6.15 ❑ Double your dry-weather separation distance
6.16 ❑ Hose down the wheels
6.17 ❑ It's an offence to deposit mud on a road
6.18 ❑ Solid and level
6.19 ❑ When the motorway has two lanes
6.20 ❑ Stop as soon as it's safe to do so
6.21 ❑ Four seconds
6.22 ❑ When the escort vehicle of an oversized load signals you to pass
6.23 ❑ Use dipped headlights
6.24 ❑ The brakes will be less effective
6.25 ❑ Fallen trees
6.26 ❑ The effect of strong side wind
6.27 ❑ There's ice or frost on the road
6.28 ❑ Check ahead and then your nearside mirror
6.29 ❑ Be prepared to stop in good time
6.30 ❑ On exposed sections
6.31 ❑ Across suspension bridges
6.32 ❑ Ease off the accelerator
6.33 ❑ They can park without lights
6.34 ❑ Wait until the vehicle starts to turn in
6.35 ❑ There's a long uphill gradient ahead
6.36 ❑ The driver's door may suddenly open
6.37 ❑ Use the parking lights
6.38 ❑ When you're cornering
6.39 ❑ More braking effort will be required
6.40 ❑ When turning at tight junctions

6.41 ❑ Anticipate how the weather may affect other road users
6.42 ❑ Open roads
6.43 ❑ On high-level roads
6.44 ❑

6.45 ❑ A safety lane for vehicles blown off course
6.46 ❑ On high-level bridges
6.47 ❑ When it's windy
6.48 ❑ Drive slowly, in a higher gear than normal
6.49 ❑ A motorcycle
6.50 ❑ The buffeting effect
6.51 ❑ They may be blown into your path
6.52 ❑ Car drivers towing caravans
6.53 ❑ Drivers towing caravans
6.54 ❑ To see if the rider is in control of their motorcycle
6.55 ❑ Curtain-sided vehicles
6.56 ❑ Across viaducts
6.57 ❑ The road may still be slippery
6.58 ❑ To reduce the risk of skidding
6.59 ❑ Twice the normal distance
6.60 ❑ Switch on your dipped headlights
6.61 ❑ Your tyres may lose grip
6.62 ❑ Visibility will be reduced by spray from traffic
6.63 ❑ More spray will be thrown up
6.64 ❑ Move out earlier than normal
6.65 ❑ Their vision will be reduced
6.66 ❑ To reduce spray on wet roads
6.67 ❑ Before setting out on every journey
6.68 ❑ Spray reducers
6.69 ❑ Rain
6.70 ❑ Slowly, in a low gear, with engine speed high
6.71 ❑ There may be deep snow ahead
6.72 ❑ To allow for an increased stopping distance
6.73 ❑ To reduce the amount of spray thrown up
6.74 ❑ When visibility is reduced to 100 metres (328 feet) or less
6.75 ❑ Water reducing the tyres' grip on the road
6.76 ❑ It will take longer to stop
6.77 ❑ To avoid splashing them
6.78 ❑ Your view ahead is reduced
6.79 ❑ When you're on a motorway and traffic ahead slows suddenly
6.80 ❑ Children crossing the road
6.81 ❑ Near a school
6.82 ❑ You'll have reduced visibility
6.83 ❑ Speed and distance are harder to judge
6.84 ❑ The left-hand lane
6.85 ❑ Traffic behind in the right-hand lane, returning to the middle lane
6.86 ❑ Check your mirrors carefully
6.87 ❑ The left-hand lane
6.88 ❑ Be ready to adjust your speed
6.89 ❑ Move to the next lane if it's safe
6.90 ❑ Traffic in the centre lane may be travelling much faster than you

6.91 ❑ When the motorway has two lanes
6.92 ❑ Cutting in
6.93 ❑ To enable slow-moving traffic to move further over to the left on uphill gradients
6.94 ❑ You're approaching a long uphill slope
6.95 ❑ When letting faster traffic overtake you
6.96 ❑ Look ahead for road junctions
6.97 ❑ When you would have to break the speed limit
6.98 ❑ By checking your nearside mirror
6.99 ❑ Stay behind the slower vehicle
6.100 ❑ Move back to the left when it's safe to do so
6.101 ❑ Signal right on approach
6.102 ❑ When they need to avoid mounting the kerb
6.103 ❑ Check your mirrors
6.104 ❑ Allow extra room
6.105 ❑ Go in any direction
6.106 ❑ Look well ahead for uphill gradients
6.107 ❑ They may move back to the middle lane as you move out
6.108 ❑ It's facing towards you
6.109 ❑ So that other road users can see the size of your vehicle
6.110 ❑ When visibility falls below 100 metres (328 feet)
6.111 ❑ When visibility is more than 100 metres (328 feet)
6.112 ❑ When the roads are dry
6.113 ❑ Increase your distance from the vehicle in front
6.114 ❑ Slow down
6.115 ❑ At least a two-second gap
6.116 ❑ Drop further back
6.117 ❑ You can see well ahead
6.118 ❑ Ten times as long
6.119 ❑ Brake gently and in good time
6.120 ❑ Gently
6.121 ❑ To keep a safe distance from the vehicle in front when conditions are good
6.122 ❑ Your field of vision will be seriously reduced
6.123 ❑ At least four seconds
6.124 ❑ Brake in good time
6.125 ❑ Make sure that your vehicle is travelling in a straight line
6.126 ❑ You'll take longer to get past
6.127 ❑ A motorcycle
6.128 ❑ At least 53 metres (175 feet)
6.129 ❑ Use dipped headlights
6.130 ❑ Some roads may be closed to certain vehicles in high winds
6.131 ❑ Spray could affect their control
6.132 ❑ Steering will be more difficult
6.133 ❑ Strong wind
6.134 ❑ Pass wide in case they're blown off course
6.135 ❑ Rain
6.136 ❑ To avoid mounting the kerb
6.137 ❑ They must leave their parking lights switched on

6.138 ❑ There may be unseen dips or bends in the road
6.139 ❑ To make them easier to see at junctions
6.140 ❑ On a hump bridge

7. Incidents, accidents and emergencies

7.1 ❑ Cut off the fuel supply
7.2 ❑ How to use fire-fighting equipment
7.3 ❑ 5 metres (16 feet 6 inches)
7.4 ❑ Check that they're breathing
7.5 ❑ Stop at the scene
7.6 ❑ 24 hours
7.7 ❑ It's carrying dangerous good
7.8 ❑ Douse the burns with cool water
7.9 ❑ Apply firm pressure to the wound
7.10 ❑ Warn other traffic
7.11 ❑ Switch on your own hazard warning lights
7.12 ❑ Check the casualties airway
7.13 ❑ Whether their airway is open
7.14 ❑ Check that they're breathing
7.15 ❑ Keep injured people warm and comfortable
7.16 ❑ Deal with the danger from further collisions or fire
7.17 ❑ Reassure them confidently
7.18 ❑ Warn other traffic to prevent further collisions
7.19 ❑ Reassure them confidently
7.20 ❑ Warn other traffic
7.21 ❑ Until medical help arrives and takes over
7.22 ❑ When they can breathe without help
7.23 ❑ Try to stem the flow of blood
7.24 ❑ Apply firm pressure to the wound
7.25 ❑ Because there's further danger
7.26 ❑ Leave them where they are
7.27 ❑ Keep them in the vehicle
7.28 ❑ Your driving licence
7.29 ❑ By talking to them quietly and firmly
7.30 ❑ You could cause more injury
7.31 ❑ A length of wood
7.32 ❑ Facing the oncoming traffic
7.33 ❑ Water (red)
7.34 ❑ Call for help using the nearest emergency telephone
7.35 ❑ Shut off the fuel supply
7.36 ❑ Remove your sunglasses
7.37 ❑ Use dipped headlights
7.38 ❑ Tune your radio to a local channel
7.39 ❑ Keep a safe distance from the vehicle in front
7.40 ❑ Switch on hazard warning lights
7.41 ❑ Drive it out of the tunnel if you can do so
7.42 ❑ Follow the instructions given by variable message signs
7.43 ❑ Douse the burns with cool water
7.44 ❑ By opening their airway
7.45 ❑ Stop, then report the incident to the police within 24 hours
7.46 ❑ Switch off the engine and switch on hazard warning lights

7.47	☐ Stop at the side of the road and switch off the engine
7.48	☐ Rapid shallow breathing
7.49	☐ Drive out of the tunnel
7.50	☐ Talk to them quietly and firmly
7.51	☐ Rapid pulse and sweating
7.52	☐ Make sure the emergency services have been called
7.53	☐ Tell your passengers what's happening without upsetting them
7.54	☐ Switch off the fuel supply
7.55	☐ Report the incident to the police within 24 hours
7.56	☐ Keep them warm
7.57	☐ When they can breathe on their own
7.58	☐ Get medical help
7.59	☐ To reduce the risk of injury from a rear-end collision
7.60	☐ Immediately, to the railway authority
7.61	☐ Get the passengers off and keep them together
7.62	☐ Get everyone off the bus quickly and safely
7.63	☐ Move your passengers to the nearest tunnel exit

8. Vehicle condition

8.1	☐ To stop mud dropping onto the road
8.2	☐ To make sure bricks or debris aren't wedged between the wheels
8.3	☐ The diff-lock is disengaged
8.4	☐ Stop on the hard shoulder and phone for assistance
8.5	☐ 1 mm
8.6	☐ Release the trailer parking brake
8.7	☐ Regularly
8.8	☐ The power steering is faulty
8.9	☐ Soon after initial tightening
8.10	☐ The kingpin release handle
8.11	☐ Monthly
8.12	☐ Eyelet coupling
8.13	☐ To connect the tractor unit to the trailer
8.14	☐ Every 6000 miles (10 000 km)
8.15	☐ It expands
8.16	☐ Air pressure
8.17	☐ Park and phone for assistance
8.18	☐ Using a tyre with exposed ply or cord
8.19	☐ Drain the tanks daily
8.20	☐ Braking-system fault
8.21	☐ Stop on the hard shoulder as soon as possible
8.22	☐ On the left of the road
8.23	☐ Park and get help
8.24	☐ A fault with the power-assisted steering
8.25	☐ Park and phone for help
8.26	☐ To remove moisture drawn in from the atmosphere
8.27	☐ Leave the vehicle parked and report the fault immediately

8.28	☐ Low oil pressure
8.29	☐ Three-quarters
8.30	☐ Immediately
8.31	☐ Anti-waxing additives
8.32	☐ Don't drive until they're repaired
8.33	☐ Look for a check switch on the dashboard
8.34	☐ They'll be more likely to overheat and disintegrate
8.35	☐ You'll break the law and risk prosecution
8.36	☐ To heat the combustion chambers
8.37	☐ Into the combustion chamber
8.38	☐ It could increase pressure in the engine and cause damage
8.39	☐ To protect the coolant from freezing
8.40	☐ Replace the valve
8.41	☐ When the engine is cold
8.42	☐ All year round
8.43	☐ Low oil pressure
8.44	☐ There's an electrical fault
8.45	☐ Maximum load
8.46	☐ It will reduce breakdowns
8.47	☐ Use wheel chocks if available
8.48	☐ Shortly afterwards
8.49	☐ By regular servicing
8.50	☐ To reduce friction and wear
8.51	☐ On flat ground
8.52	☐ Some gaskets might be damaged
8.53	☐ Apply the parking brake
8.54	☐ Apply the trailer parking brake
8.55	☐ Before any journey
8.56	☐ Stop in a safe place and get help
8.57	☐ Tyres
8.58	☐ Running tyres under-inflated
8.59	☐ To change either up or down in gear
8.60	☐ To give quicker acceleration
8.61	☐ Faulty power steering
8.62	☐ Scattered debris
8.63	☐ It will be prohibited from further use until the defects are rectified
8.64	☐ The Traffic Commissioner
8.65	☐ It may break down
8.66	☐ The engine may be damaged
8.67	☐ Speed capability
8.68	☐ Reduced rolling resistance
8.69	☐ Tighten the nuts evenly with a torque wrench
8.70	☐ They have a reduced rolling resistance
8.71	☐ The vehicle handbook
8.72	☐ Workshop manuals
8.73	☐ Loss of power
8.74	☐ To collect metal particles from the oil
8.75	☐ Torque wrench
8.76	☐ The fuel partly solidifying
8.77	☐ The diesel from solidifying
8.78	☐ To check for any defects
8.79	☐ It expands
8.80	☐ A system for reporting vehicle defects
8.81	☐ You may scrub the rear tyres
8.82	☐ Drive at a very low speed

8.83 ❏ 1 mm
8.84 ❏ Get it repaired before continuing
8.85 ❏ Have the fault checked before setting off
8.86 ❏ Punctures can be more difficult to detect
8.87 ❏ The tyres on the smaller wheels are more likely to overheat
8.88 ❏ Daily
8.89 ❏ Allow the engine to idle
8.90 ❏ Every day before starting out
8.91 ❏ Allow the engine to idle, then switch it off
8.92 ❏ Wait for the breakdown services
8.93 ❏ At least once a week when they're cold
8.94 ❏ When needing brisk acceleration
8.95 ❏ Faulty power steering
8.96 ❏ Punctures can be difficult to detect
8.97 ❏ To top up the oil or water levels
8.98 ❏ They're more difficult to detect
8.99 ❏ The tyre pressures are all correct
8.100 ❏ The tyres will wear more quickly
8.101 ❏ Park on a firm, level surface

9. Leaving the vehicle

9.1 ❏ Your nearside mirror doesn't strike the head of a pedestrian
9.2 ❏ Check the rear-view mirrors
9.3 ❏ At a service area
9.4 ❏ In a lorry park
9.5 ❏ Using the mirrors
9.6 ❏ Slippery walkways
9.7 ❏ Use a suitable set of steps
9.8 ❏ There'll be a risk of theft or hijack
9.9 ❏ Roof markings
9.10 ❏ Before opening your door
9.11 ❏ Apply the parking brake
9.12 ❏ Switch off the engine
9.13 ❏ Vehicles passing near the door
9.14 ❏ When approaching queuing traffic on a motorway
9.15 ❏ Whenever you leave the vehicle
9.16 ❏ Stop the engine
9.17 ❏ When on motorways or dual carriageways, to warn drivers behind of a hazard ahead
9.18 ❏ Look ahead when the load is secure
9.19 ❏ Have a stable position
9.20 ❏ In a stable position
9.21 ❏ When children are getting off a school bus
9.22 ❏ When you're parked close to another vehicle
9.23 ❏ Take everything with them
9.24 ❏ Apply the parking brake
9.25 ❏ Apply the parking brake
9.26 ❏ High-visibility vest

10. Vehicle loading

10.1 ❏ Spread the load evenly
10.2 ❏ The container must be secured using the locking levers
10.3 ❏
10.4 ❏ To stop wind and rain from getting under the sheets
10.5 ❏ A dolly knot
10.6 ❏ Ropes can wear and snap
10.7 ❏ To stop the load from blowing away
10.8 ❏ Park and resecure the load before continuing
10.9 ❏ Baffle plates
10.10 ❏ It will try to push the vehicle forward
10.11 ❏ Keep pressure on the brake pedal until you've stopped
10.12 ❏ Glass
10.13 ❏ 3.5 metres (11 feet 5 inches)
10.14 ❏ When it's unloaded
10.15 ❏ Try to move forward with the trailer parking brake on
10.16 ❏ The trailer brake is applied
10.17 ❏ Stow it away safely
10.18 ❏ The surface is firm and level
10.19 ❏ To give a view down each side of the trailer
10.20 ❏ A short-wheelbase empty vehicle
10.21 ❏ Steel plates
10.22 ❏ Tubular metal
10.23 ❏ Over the rear axles
10.24 ❏ Tied down securely
10.25 ❏ An unladen trailer
10.26 ❏ When empty
10.27 ❏ Driving too fast
10.28 ❏ The lorry may overturn when cornering
10.29 ❏ In high winds
10.30 ❏ Restraining straps
10.31 ❏ The load will push the lorry straight on
10.32 ❏ Your could lose control of your vehicle
10.33 ❏ Use chains and tensioners
10.34 ❏ Place chocks under the wheels
10.35 ❏ When only the top deck is loaded
10.36 ❏ Demount the body without a crane or lift
10.37 ❏ Diamond
10.38 ❏ To reduce the wave effect
10.39 ❏
10.40 ❏ Make sure the vehicle is on a firm, level surface
10.41 ❏ The railway authority
10.42 ❏ The maximum load the vehicle can carry
10.43 ❏ Hygiene procedures
10.44 ❏ Lower the stabilising legs
10.45 ❏ Heavy items near the centre line, light items towards the sides
10.46 ❏ Walk forward near the edges
10.47 ❏ Frozen foods

10.48 ☐ Practical experience In the care of animals
10.49 ☐ Create compartments using moveable panels
10.50 ☐ 25 tonnes
10.51 ☐ You might overload an axle
10.52 ☐ Reduced braking efficiency
10.53 ☐ Damage to the road surface
10.54 ☐ Covered
10.55 ☐ Rope hook
10.56 ☐ Split-link
10.57 ☐ 10 mm
10.58 ☐ Rear
10.59 ☐ To prevent any spillage
10.60 ☐ Perishable foods
10.61 ☐ Chemicals

10.62 ☐

10.63 ☐ Oxidising agents

10.64 ☐

10.65 ☐

10.66 ☐ Check the load by carefully entering through the rear door or opposite curtain
10.67 ☐ Protection from the weather
10.68 ☐ Vehicle stabilisers
10.69 ☐ Between the shoulder and the waist
10.70 ☐ 30 tonnes

11. Restricted view

11.1 ☐ Parking
11.2 ☐ The site should be level
11.3 ☐ Check the blind spots before you start moving
11.4 ☐ There's a motorcycle on the left
11.5 ☐ Brake smoothly and allow it to emerge
11.6 ☐ Get someone to guide you into the bay
11.7 ☐ The motorcyclist from the right passing the parked van
11.8 ☐ On the road
11.9 ☐ When traffic is merging from the right or left
11.10 ☐ It increases your blind spots
11.11 ☐ The motorcyclist
11.12 ☐ The nearside mirror
11.13 ☐ The offside mirror
11.14 ☐ Use your mirrors and look behind
11.15 ☐ After passing cars parked on the left
11.16 ☐ Mirrors, signal, manoeuvre
11.17 ☐ With-flow bus and cycle lane

11.18 ☐ Adjust your seat properly
11.19 ☐ Between 7.00 am and 11.30 pm
11.20 ☐ Your view ahead will be reduced
11.21 ☐ They can be hidden in blind spots
11.22 ☐ Someone may be overtaking you
11.23 ☐ The left-hand mirror
11.24 ☐ Cyclists on your left
11.25 ☐ Use the left-hand of the two lanes
11.26 ☐ You'll need to take all-round observation
11.27 ☐ An area of road that can't be seen, even with mirrors
11.28 ☐ It will have more blind spots than smaller vehicles
11.29 ☐ Ease forward until you can see clearly in all directions
11.30 ☐ Look all around
11.31 ☐ Be cautious and keep looking all around
11.32 ☐ When you're pulling into park at the kerb
11.33 ☐ The blind area close in front
11.34 ☐ Open the window and look down and round to the right
11.35 ☐ Cyclists and pedestrians
11.36 ☐ The front wheel in relation to the kerb

12. Essential documents

12.1 ☐ A valid ADR driver training certificate
12.2 ☐ The driver
12.3 ☐ Four
12.4 ☐ A trailer up to 750 kg
12.5 ☐ Hygiene procedures
12.6 ☐ Your national driving licence
12.7 ☐ Partial blindness
12.8 ☐ Your entitlement to drive all motor vehicles
12.9 ☐ The Driver and Vehicle Licensing Agency
12.10 ☐ Until the vehicle is taxed, sold or scrapped
12.11 ☐ A notification to tell DVLA that a vehicle isn't being used on the road
12.12 ☐ Unlimited
12.13 ☐ Up to £2000
12.14 ☐ The vehicle hirer
12.15 ☐ By using an effective vehicle security system
12.16 ☐ Your operator documentation
12.17 ☐ For each person they bring in
12.18 ☐ 35 hours
12.19 ☐ Five years
12.20 ☐ 35 hours
12.21 ☐ An eyesight test
12.22 ☐ D
12.23 ☐ For national security
12.24 ☐ To prevent the carriage of illegal immigrants
12.25 ☐ A list of passengers
12.26 ☐ D
12.27 ☐ 750 kg
12.28 ☐ You can tow a trailer not exceeding 750 kg
12.29 ☐ D
12.30 ☐ D
12.31 ☐ The Traffic Commissioner

13. Environmental issues

13.1 ☐ They'll reduce the wind resistance
13.2 ☐ Fuel consumption
13.3 ☐ Fit wind deflectors
13.4 ☐ Five years
13.5 ☐ Braking in good time
13.6 ☐ Drag effect
13.7 ☐ Fit a cab-mounted wind deflector
13.8 ☐ For authorised purposes only
13.9 ☐ To prevent rubbish from falling out of it
13.10 ☐ Make sure the lorry is always attended
13.11 ☐ Police permission
13.12 ☐ Changing filters regularly
13.13 ☐ Save fuel
13.14 ☐ Red diesel
13.15 ☐ To reduce aerodynamic drag
13.16 ☐ Road surfaces
13.17 ☐ It uses electricity
13.18 ☐ Lorries
13.19 ☐ Underground services
13.20 ☐ By braking in good time
13.21 ☐ By using bypasses and avoiding town centres
13.22 ☐ Plan routes to avoid busy times and congestion
13.23 ☐ That the filler cap is properly closed and secure
13.24 ☐ Close and secure the filler cap
13.25 ☐ The road may be very slippery
13.26 ☐ Vehicles with faulty suspension
13.27 ☐ By planning routes to avoid congestion
13.28 ☐ Low-sulphur diesel
13.29 ☐ Low-sulphur diesel
13.30 ☐ Securely close the filler caps
13.31 ☐ Before reversing on a road that has a 30 mph speed limit
13.32 ☐ Continuous use of the air conditioning
13.33 ☐ To reduce wear to roads
13.34 ☐ Between 11.30 pm and 7.00 am
13.35 ☐ You'll be breaking the law
13.36 ☐ Damage to the road surface
13.37 ☐ Plan journeys to avoid busy times
13.38 ☐ Switch off the engine
13.39 ☐ Poorly maintained vehicles
13.40 ☐ Motorcyclists
13.41 ☐ To warn another road user who poses a danger
13.42 ☐ Motorcycles
13.43 ☐ Get a replacement before driving
13.44 ☐ Look at a map
13.45 ☐ A motoring organisation
13.46 ☐ Use a route planner on the internet
13.47 ☐ Print or write down the route
13.48 ☐ It will help to ease congestion
13.49 ☐ You're less likely to be delayed
13.50 ☐ Your original route may be blocked
13.51 ☐ You'll reduce fuel consumption by about 15%
13.52 ☐ Missing out some gears
13.53 ☐ Green
13.54 ☐ You would damage the engine

13.55 ☐ Reduced engine emissions
13.56 ☐ They have a reduced rolling resistance
13.57 ☐ An excessive amount of fuel will be used
13.58 ☐ A reduction in fuel consumption
13.59 ☐ Exhaust emissions
13.60 ☐ Being aware of hazards
13.61 ☐ Cruise control
13.62 ☐ You'll use less fuel
13.63 ☐ Using air conditioning
13.64 ☐ Air conditioning
13.65 ☐ By switching off your engine
13.66 ☐ To reduce exhaust emissions
13.67 ☐ Switch off your engine
13.68 ☐ Increase it by about 15%
13.69 ☐ With the engine ticking over
13.70 ☐ Your filler caps are securely closed

14. Other road users

14.1 ☐ Motorcyclists
14.2 ☐ Motorcycles
14.3 ☐ Keep calm and be patient
14.4 ☐ Sounding your horn
14.5 ☐ Give way to them
14.6 ☐

14.7 ☐ Walt and allow them to cros
14.8 ☐ Give way to the pedestrians who are already crossing
14.9 ☐ They might be overtaking on your right
14.10 ☐ Cyclists can use it
14.11 ☐ Pedestrians and cyclists may cross
14.12 ☐ On the rear of a school bus or coach
14.13 ☐ A route for pedestrians and cyclists
14.14 ☐ Be patient and allow them to cross in their own time
14.15 ☐ Be careful; they might misjudge your speed
14.16 ☐ Give the cyclist plenty of room
14.17 ☐ They may use the left-hand lane to turn right
14.18 ☐ Motorcycles are small and hard to see
14.19 ☐ To make themselves more easily seen
14.20 ☐ To help other road users to see them
14.21 ☐ They need to check for traffic in their blind area
14.22 ☐ Give them plenty of room
14.23 ☐ Drive very slowly
14.24 ☐ You're approaching an organised walk
14.25 ☐ Reduce speed until you're clear of the area
14.26 ☐ Prepare to slow down and stop
14.27 ☐ To allow an unobstructed view of the area
14.28 ☐ It would obstruct everyone's view of the area
14.29 ☐ Any direction
14.30 ☐ Stay behind until the moped has passed the junction
14.31 ☐ Stay well back

14.32 ☐ Be patient and prepare for them to react more slowly

14.33 ☐ Be patient, as you expect them to make mistakes

14.34 ☐ Pedestrians

14.35 ☐ Be aware that the driver's reactions may not be as fast as yours

14.36 ☐ Hold back until the cyclist has passed the junction

14.37 ☐ Go in any direction

14.38 ☐ To check for overtaking vehicles

14.39 ☐ Slow down and be prepared to stop for children

14.40 ☐ Check for traffic passing on your right

14.41 ☐ Pedestrians may come from behind the bus

14.42 ☐ Drive slowly and leave plenty of room

14.43 ☐ At a road junction

14.44 ☐ You're approaching an organised walk

14.45 ☐ Cyclists

14.46 ☐ The rider intends to move to the right

14.47 ☐ They may swerve to avoid potholes

14.48 ☐ Give them extra room

14.49 ☐ Motorcycles

14.50 ☐ Drive past slowly

14.51 ☐ Stay well back and allow them room

14.52 ☐ Cyclists

14.53 ☐ A mobility scooter

14.54 ☐ Drive slowly until you're clear of the area

14.55 ☐ Allow extra room in case the rider swerves to avoid potholes

14.56 ☐ Wait until the cyclist has passed the junction

14.57 ☐ Allow them to move in front of you

14.58 ☐ It's a quicker route for a cyclist

14.59 ☐ Allow plenty of room

14.60 ☐ Brake gently to a stop until they've passed

14.61 ☐ Bicycle

14.62 ☐ They're easily overlooked

14.63 ☐ Other drivers

14.64 ☐ Filtering motorcyclists

14.65 ☐ Motorcyclists

14.66 ☐ In gusting winds

14.67 ☐ Be prepared to stop

14.68 ☐ By displaying a 'stop' sign

14.69 ☐ Stay behind

14.70 ☐ Cyclists

14.71 ☐ Check your mirrors and prepare to slow down

14.72 ☐ Wait patiently and give them time to finish crossing

14.73 ☐ Allow extra room, in case they swerve to avoid potholes

14.74 ☐ They may be filtering between the lanes

14.75 ☐ Slow down and be prepared to stop for a cyclist

14.76 ☐ You mustn't wait or park on these lines

14.77 ☐ Check for traffic overtaking on your right

14.78 ☐ At junctions

14.79 ☐ Look for people leaving buses

15. Road traffic signs

15.1 ☐ 50 mph

15.2 ☐ 60 mph

15.3 ☐ Drive past the sign because it doesn't apply to you

15.4 ☐

15.5 ☐ Find an alternative route to your destination

15.6 ☐ Change to a lower gear

15.7 ☐ You mustn't use the right-hand lane

15.8 ☐ 60 mph (96 km/h)

15.9 ☐ When you're carrying a load that overhangs the front or rear of the vehicle by more than 2 metres (6 feet 6 inches)

15.10 ☐ Maximum speed 60 mph

15.11 ☐ Maximum speed 60 mph

15.12 ☐ Maximum speed 50 mph

15.13 ☐ Stopping or parking

15.14 ☐ End of restricted parking area

15.15 ☐

15.16 ☐ You have priority over vehicles from the opposite direction

15.17 ☐ Stop

15.18 ☐ Maximum speed 30 mph

15.19 ☐

15.20 ☐ Route for trams

15.21 ☐

15.22 ☐ Contraflow bus lane

15.23 ☐ Road narrows

15.24 ☐

15.25 ☐ Side wind

15.26 ☐ Danger ahead

15.27 ☐ Hold back until you can see clearly ahead

15.28 ☐ Water across the road

15.29 ☐ Red alone

15.30 ☐ At a level crossing

15.31 ☐ The distance to the next exit

15.32 ☐ No stopping at any time

15.33 ☐ The left-hand lane

15.34

15.35

15.36 ❏ To allow cyclists to position in front of other traffic
15.37 ❏ The driver intends to turn left
15.38 ❏ All lanes closed ahead
15.39 ❏ Overhead electrified cable
15.40 ❏ Oncoming traffic
15.41 ❏ Queues likely
15.42 ❏ Loose chippings
15.43 ❏ Don't cross the bridge if your weight exceeds the limit
15.44 ❏ A concealed level crossing
15.45 ❏ No stopping
15.46 ❏ On the approach to an arched bridge
15.47 ❏ Red and amber, then green
15.48 ❏ To overtake a pedal cycle travelling at 10 mph or less
15.49 ❏ Slow down; the road may be narrow ahead
15.50 ❏ Because children may be crossing
15.51 ❏ Emergency diversion route for motorway traffic
15.52 ❏ The left-hand lane
15.53 ❏ Drivers of trams
15.54 ❏ An area where special waiting restrictions apply
15.55 ❏ Amber
15.56 ❏ They mark the lanes in a contraflow system
15.57 ❏ Tramway speed limit

15.58 ❏ Flashing amber
15.59 ❏ Until the pedestrians have reached a safe position
15.60 ❏ The bus lane is in operation 24 hours a day
15.61 ❏ Steady amber
15.62 ❏ Give way to pedestrians on the crossing
15.63 ❏ As a place to stop when an emergency arises
15.64 ❏ When you're signalled to do so by flashing red lights
15.65 ❏

15.66 ❏ Right-hand lane closed ahead
15.67 ❏ No U-turns
15.68 ❏ Tunnel ahead
15.69 ❏ Uneven road
15.70 ❏ To avoid throwing up loose chippings
15.71 ❏ The set speed limit is displayed
15.72 ❏ England only
15.73 ❏ It's for use in case of emergency or breakdown
15.74 ❏ Stop and direct anyone on a motorway
15.75 ❏ You may use this lane as a running lane
15.76 ❏ The hard shoulder can be used as a running lane
15.77 ❏ To reduce congestion
15.78 ❏ The speed limit on the sign must be obeyed
15.79 ❏ The hard shoulder is for emergency or breakdown use only
15.80 ❏ Permitted lanes, including the hard shoulder
15.81 ❏ When signs show that you can
15.82 ❏ Soft verges
15.83 ❏ No buses
15.84 ❏ Taxi driver
15.85 ❏ Proceed as normal; the sign doesn't apply to you

Part 2

Advice for passing LGV driving test

Advice for Passing LGV Driving Test

Choosing a Training School: Considerations

Avoid brokers at all costs-they will take your money and deliver as little as possible. They often say that they have 30 plus training centres around the country. No genuine trainer has and so they are easy to spot.

It's also important to bear in mind that there are some poor training schools out there.

Questions to keep in mind:

- Training schools reputation? Check them out thoroughly, do your research and try to find some genuine reviews before making any payment. Gaining an LGV licence is an expensive undertaking – choosing the wrong school could be a costly mistake.

- Do they offer one-on-one training or is it two learner drivers being taught in one truck at the same time? There is twice the hands-on driving experience if it's one-on-one!

- Can you take an assessment drive?

- Are they reasonably priced? Or does it seem too cheap? Be careful paying peanuts, because this can sometimes result in attracting monkeys.

- What is their average pass rate?

- Can you visit the school?

- Are the vehicles in good condition?

- Lesson duration?

- Do the instructors have the DVSA (Driving Standards Agency) qualification? Note: this is a voluntary qualification, not mandatory.

- Which LGV test centre do they use?

Five day intensive courses.

Intensive courses allow trainees to distance themselves from other life distractions and to become fully immersed in the training. On an intensive course, it is possible to lose concentration and to start making mistakes during one of the five consecutive days. This may or may not happen. If it does, do not lose confidence, it is perfectly natural, the mind will only focus intensely for a certain period of time before wandering. Concentration will and always does return.

About Your Practical Test

What to Expect ...

You must bring your photocard driving licence. If you don't have your photocard driving licence then your paper licence and a valid passport will suffice.

Your test will be cancelled and you'll lose your fee if you don't bring these on the day.

Ideally take a 40 minute pre-test lesson, then arrive at the test centre about 15 minutes prior to your test, so that you're not hurried or waiting for too long.

Remember to switch off your mobile phone and any other personal distractions.

Your practical test will last about 1 hour 30 minutes and includes:

- Practical road driving

- Off-road exercises

- Vehicle safety questions

- 10 minutes of independent driving during which your examiner will ask you to follow signs or follow directions to reach a destination.

Practical road driving – during this, your examiner will assess your ability to operate, control the vehicle and carry out various tasks.

- Moving off from a stationary position, checking mirrors and blind spot.

- Use of the vehicle controls

- Move away at an angle, uphill and downhill

- Do a controlled stop

- Use the mirrors

- Give appropriate signals

- Show awareness and anticipation of other road users' intentions.

- Manage your progress and control your vehicle speed.

- Deal with hazards

- Select a safe space to stop.

The off road exercises will include:

- An 'S' shaped reverse into a bay.

- Follow your instructor's advice and fix a reversing marker to the rear mud guard of the truck. This will help get the truck aligned into the designated box.

- Taking your seat belt off just prior to carrying out the reversing exercise may make the manoeuver easier. Remember to fasten your seat belt immediately after the exercise is complete.

- You can take up to 2 shunts for the reversing exercise if required.

- You are permitted to get out of the vehicle once, so make good use of the first shunt to ensure the rear of the truck is close to or in place.

- Also showing the uncoupling and re-coupling procedure if you're taking a test with a trailer.

You can still pass your practical test with up to 15 minor faults. In the event of a mistake, simply move on and do not dwell on it.

Lorry and bus 'show me, tell me' vehicle safety questions

1. About the questions

You'll be asked some vehicle safety questions during your test for one of these categories of licence:

- C1 – Medium sized lorry
- C – Large goods lorry
- D1 – Minibus
- D – Bus and coach

- C1+E – Medium sized lorry with trailer
- C+E – Large goods lorry with trailer
- D1+E – Minibus with trailer
- D+E – Bus and coach with trailer

The questions ...

2.1 Show me how you would check that all doors including cargo doors are secure.

All doors must be closed and locking levers for cargo doors are set in the recommended secured position.

2.2 Show me how you would check for air leaks on this vehicle.

Charge the air tanks, consult gauges for drops in air pressure. Walk round vehicle listening for any obvious leaks.

2.3 Tell me the main safety factors involved in loading this vehicle.

The load should be evenly distributed throughout the length of the vehicle so as not to affect control while the vehicle is being driven. Any load must be carried so that it does not endanger other road users. It must be securely stowed within the size and weight limits for the vehicle. The load needs to be secure so that it cannot move or fall from the vehicle when cornering or braking.

2.4 Tell me how you would check the condition of the reflectors on this vehicle.

Ensure that all reflectors are fitted, clean, and functional (not cracked or broken).

2.5 Tell me how you would check the condition of the windscreen and windows on this vehicle.

The windscreen and windows must be clean, clear and free from defects. No mascots or sticker that restrict view.

2.6 Show me how you would check the condition of the mudguards on this vehicle.

As part of daily walk-round check ensure mudguards and spray suppression equipment are secure.

2.7 Tell me how you would check your tyres to ensure that they are correctly inflated, have sufficient tread depth and that their general condition is safe to use on the road.

Follow manufacturer's guide, using appropriate equipment, check and adjust pressures when tyres are cold. Must have a tread depth of at least 1mm across ¾ of the breadth of the tread and in a continuous band around the entire circumference. There should be no cuts, damage or signs of cord visible at the sidewalls.

2.8 Tell me how you would check the condition of the windscreen wipers on this vehicle.

Windscreen wipers must operate. Blades should be in good condition.

2.9 Tell me how you would check the condition of the body is safe on this vehicle.

As part of a daily walk-round check, ensure the body is fully roadworthy and there are no significant defects. No loose panels or items, which could endanger other road users. All inspection panels must be secure.

2.10 Show me how you would check for the correct air pressure on this vehicle.

Ensure gauges are reading the correct pressures for the vehicle and that all warning lights are extinguished and audible warning devices are not sounding.

2.11 Identify where you would check the engine oil level and tell me how you would check that the engine has sufficient oil.

Identify dipstick/oil level indicator, describe check of oil level against the minimum/maximum markers.

2.12 Show me how you would check the wheel nuts are secure on this vehicle.

A visual check to identify any nuts that are obviously loose, and check that the wheel nut indicators (if fitted) are in alignment.

2.13 Show me how you would check the operation (specify horn, warning device for reversing) of the audible warning devices on this vehicle.

Demonstrate use of control.

2.14 Tell me how you would check the condition of the suspension on this vehicle.

As part of a daily walk-round check, suspension should be checked for any obvious signs of deterioration or damage.

2.15 Show me how you would check that the brake lights are working on this vehicle (I can assist you, if you need to switch the ignition on, please don't start the engine).

Operate brake pedal, make use of reflections in windows, garage doors, etc, or ask someone to help.

2.16 Identify where you would check the engine coolant level and tell me how you would check that the engine has the correct level.

Identify high/low level markings on header tank where fitted or radiator filler cap, and describe how to top up to correct level.

2.17 Tell me how you would check that the headlamps, sidelights and tail lights are working.

Explain: Operate switch (turn on ignition if necessary), walk round vehicle.

2.18 Show me how you would replace the tachograph disc on this vehicle.

Candidate to demonstrate how to insert tachograph disc. Digital tachographs may require an explanation if the candidate does not have a digital card.

2.19 Tell me how you would operate the loading mechanism on this vehicle (vehicle specific i.e. tail lift).

Candidates should be able to explain briefly the correct operation and safe working practice of specific machinery fitted to the vehicle, eg tail lift, kneeling bus.

2.20 Show me / explain how you would check that the power assisted steering is working.

If the steering becomes heavy the system may not be working properly. Before starting a journey two simple checks can be made. Gentle pressure on the steering wheel, maintained while the engine is started, should result in a slight but noticeable movement as the system begins to operate. Alternatively turning the steering wheel just after moving off will give an immediate indication that the power assistance is functioning.

2.21 Show me how you would check that the direction indicators are working.

Applying the indicators or hazard warning switch and check functioning of all indicators.

2.22 Identify where the windscreen washer reservoir is and tell me how you would check the windscreen washer level.

Identify reservoir and explain how to check level.

2.23 Show me what instrument checks you would make before and after starting the engine on this vehicle.

Check to make sure all gauges and warning systems are working. Ensure that all gauges are reading correctly and that warning lights / audible warning devices are extinguished before moving away.

2.24 Show me where the first aid equipment is kept on this vehicle.

Candidate to indicate equipment if carried. Where equipment is not present, candidates should be able to explain under what circumstances (ie vehicle types, loads carried) it must be provided.

2.25 Show me how you would clean the windscreen using the windscreen washer and wipers.

Operate control to wash and wipe windscreen (turn ignition on if necessary).

2.26 Show me how you would set the windscreen demister to clear the windows effectively.

Set all relevant controls including; fan, temperature, air direction / source and heated screen to clear windscreen and windows. Engine does not have to be started for this demonstration.

2.27 Show me how you would switch on the rear fog light(s) and explain when you would use it/them (no need to exit vehicle).

Operate switch (turn on ignition and dipped headlights if necessary). Check warning light is on. Explain use.

2.28 Show me how you switch your headlight from dipped to main beam.

Operate switch (with ignition or engine on if necessary), check with main beam warning light.

After you've taken the practical test your examiner will tell you if you've passed and explain how you did.

You'll pass your test if you make:

- 15 or less minor faults.

- No serious or dangerous faults.

If you fail, you can book another driving test straight away, but you can't take it for another 3 clear working days.

Useful contacts for learners:

- Booking your theory test (https://www.gov.uk/book-theory-test)

- Book your driving test (https://www.gov.uk/book-driving-test)

- In the case of your test being cancelled by the DVSA at short notice you can apply for a refund of expenses here (https://www.gov.uk/government/publications/application-for-refunding-out-of-pocket-expenses)

Psychology – The examiner and you

The examiner is likely to be from an ex-police or military background. These people take dangerous vehicles and their personal role in public safety very seriously. To gain their confidence, a demonstration of the following is necessary:

- Competence, ability to keep the vehicle fully under control at all times.

- Anticipation, forward thinking, awareness of all road users and of possible hazards ahead of time.

- Road positioning, choosing the correct lane at the right time/taking up two lanes where necessary.

Driver's Attitude

A good attitude, responsible and confident.

Note

Ex-forces people often mix socially with people of similar experience and not more alternative types. Due to negative media stereotyping, an unconscious misunderstanding of more alternative people can sometimes occur.

With this in mind: If you are alternative looking, to gain respect and not to be misunderstood, it may be worth considering being a bit conformist for a few hours. Achieved simply by doing what is necessary not to stand out. One thing is for sure they will not change for you.

Note

I do not believe in discrimination of any kind.

My Test

I included this section on my test experience for information purposes only - it's not an exercise in tutoring or self indulgence. My hope was simply that including this might help someone in what I know is a very tough, expensive and vital challenge when trying to get into this industry.

I took an intensive five day LGV 1 training course in Bristol. The trainer was Ex Military and used a stick to jab me in the ribs if I made a mistake. The idea being if I repeated the same mistake I would connect it with those jabs and remember. I would say this technique worked.

I took 1 to 1 training which provided more hands on driving time. I knuckled down and focussed hard. The first three days really went well and my confidence grew. That was until the mock test on the 4th day. On that day, I couldn't do anything right. I bounced off curbs, pulled out on cars at junctions and messed up on the reversing. My confidence started to crash. The instructor was a good man and he told me that during his career he'd seen this happen many times before. It was just the mind letting go for a day after intensively focussing for long periods and that my concentration would return. He was right, it did.

The Day of the Test

I had a very poor night's sleep. Knowing that I would need to be fully awake and alert on the test I had a very strong coffee. It didn't help my nerves but totally woke me up. Fortunately on the pre-drive lesson to the test centre I found that my focus had fully returned.

During the day I incurred five main problems on the drive:

- **Focus.** My trainer had taught me a seven second rule of checking the mirrors including actually turning my head slightly to demonstrate to the examiner that I was doing so. This necessary distraction made concentrating on all other aspects of the test very difficult indeed.

- **Hesitancy.** On approaching a busy roundabout with oncoming traffic, I couldn't assess whether the gaps between vehicles were quite big enough for me to be able to pull out.

- **Random.** I encountered a group of schoolchildren who, on seeing me coming, decided it would be a good idea to wind me up by wandering in and out of the road in front of the truck. They continued to do this for at least a minute or two, by this time my blood pressure was going through the roof (I thought to myself, bless them because the children are our future. Not really, if the examiner hadn't been there and I had a shotgun, things would have been a very different :-)

- **Knowing the route.** At a short distance ahead I could see a few people waiting to cross a pedestrian crossing. I didn't know if they had pushed the button, all I knew was that the lights were showing no sign of changing. The road ahead of me was clear but I had to make a decision to accelerate or just go on very steadily. My decision was to just crawl up to the lights. Just as I arrived the lights suddenly changed to red, even at this low speed, I had to stop sharply, at that moment the examiner slammed his clipboard down hard onto the dashboard, as if to make out I'd almost sent him through the windscreen (didn't do my nerves much good).

- I was driving down a busy but narrow road. It had parked cars down both sides and I had to make a decision to commit to going through–I knew if I met another large vehicle it would be impossible to pass. Just as I committed I saw a bin lorry oncoming in the distance. Luckily the driver may have guessed there was a test going on and kindly stopped to let me through.

Summary

Focus. I pushed myself to get into the zone, told myself only to think about the test itself and dismiss all thoughts of the past or future. "Pass or fail, money, I'll worry about that when I've finished". Some thoughts did arise and I just ignored them.

Hesitancy. I displayed hesitancy at the busy roundabout and pedestrian crossing. At the time I had no doubt that if I obstructed and caused another vehicle to slow down and alter their course that this would be an instant fail. If I'd gone through the red light I'd also have failed. Whereas to err on the side of caution and try to keep the truck wheels rolling and use up some possible hesitancy points, would be at least a possible pass if the rest of the drive went well.

Knowing the route was a big key. Because I knew the roads the constant mirror checking wasn't as big an issue. Other advantages were: pre-knowing speed limits, tight turns, awkward obstacles, traffic light systems, steep hills, narrow roads etc.

Random. Kids and bin lorry experience. These events were completely out of my control. I was very fortunate that on the day things went my way. I understand the test pass rate is 33%, as one in three people pass first time. This shows the level of difficulty and things that can happen on the day to affect the outcome. Whatever you do, try not to go through the whole test and then fail on the Highway Code questions!! Examiners see this part of the test as equally important.

Note

In my experience coffee did help with alertness but I wouldn't recommend it to a non coffee drinker.

Examiners Assessment Criteria

Examiner Fault System Explained.

There are three main types of fault recorded. Minor, serious and dangerous.

Minor Faults. Examples: undue hesitancy, gear crunching, insufficient use of mirrors, insufficient road progress etc.

When a driver makes a mistake a fault is noted down on the examiners test report in the relevant section.

If the driver commits the same mistake again it will be noted again in the same section. Same mistake a third time the examiner can and probably will change the fault from minor to serious.

To Summarise. If a driver has 15 points to play with and they make a few small errors which are noted in various sections of the test sheet, they will probably pass. If they make three of the same errors they could well fail.

Serious Faults. Examples. Pulling out in front of another vehicle causing it to alter course. Truck or trailer mounting the curb, going through a red light at a crossing ,etc. The likelihood of a driver failing their test after committing one or more serious faults is extremely high.

Dangerous Faults. Examples include: going the wrong way down a one-way road, almost hitting a pedestrian, colliding with another vehicle etc. A dangerous fault is an immediate fail.

Researched Most Common Test Mistakes,Faults/Fails

Response to signs and road markings

- Driving unnecessarily over central dividing line.

- Not correctly following lane directional arrows

- Stopping inside a yellow box junction when the exit is not clear.

- Not coming to a dead stop at a stop sign (stop means stop!)

Not moving off under control

- Rolling back on an uphill start

- Moving off with handbrake on

- Trying to move off in neutral

- Moving off in wrong gear

- Repeated stalling

Mistakes at junctions or when turning

- Improper mirror signal manoeuvre

- Unnecessarily cutting corners

- Mounting the kerb

Road positioning/normal driving

- Driving too far from / too close to kerb

- Not driving in a bus lane when allowed and safe to do so

- On a roundabout creeping forward beyond the white line, whilst waiting for an opportunity to enter.. (deemed as being in a position likely to cause another vehicle to alter course. Serious Fault)

- Straying across lanes on a roundabout.

- Not increasing or decreasing speed according to road signs.

Not maintaining control/steering

- Erratic / jerky

- Crossing hands

- Striking a kerb

- Not having both hands on the wheel where possible(two hands)

Not responding to signals

- Not moving off on a green filter arrow when safe to do so

- Not going on a green light when safe to do so.

- Driving through a red light

- Not reducing speed on approach to traffic lights(failure to show caution)

Use of mirrors

- Not checking prior to signal, manoeuvring

- Not being fully aware of cyclists and overtaking motorcyclists

- Not checking mirrors often enough

- Not being seen to check!!!(move head)

Moving off /safety

- Not checking mirrors, blind spot and road ahead.

- Incorrect indicating

Reversing excercise

- On approach. Positioning the vehicle too far forward

- During. Hitting cones

- Finishing.Failing to position rear of vehicle inside the required zone (remember to fasten seatbelt)

Correcting Bad Habits

To pass the test you will have to drive in a certain way adhering to all the rules. Demonstrate a high ability to concentrate, attention to detail, a high level of control over the vehicle and good road sense and road manners.

Bad habits built up over time can easily be your undoing on the test day. They don't just disappear overnight. Either get rid of them or be aware of which ones prevail and could effectively be your Achilles heel on the day.

Usual culprits that scupper people are incorrect mirror signal manoeuvre:

Using crossed hands instead of shuffling the wheel,

Poor choice of gears,

Tailgating other vehicles,

Poor road positioning,

Erratic steering and braking,

Incorrect road speed,

Forgetting to signal on entering and exiting a roundabout,

Pulling out in front of other vehicles leaving them insufficient room,

Pulling away from the curb without checking the blindspot/looking over their shoulder,

Lack of anticipation,

Improper handbrake use,

Poor reversing skills

The Solution

Make a concerted effort to practice away the old habits. During the few weeks leading up to the test, drive your car or van as if it's examination day. Make driving to the rules become second nature. Not having to worry about making mistakes due to bad habits will free up more headspace and concentration for all of the other necessary details of the exercise. Note if you have a car- fold up the interior mirror and use side mirrors.

To Summarise

Stack the odds in your favour by:

choosing the best driving school

Assessing test centre entrance and exit

learning most of the route

driving the route

knowing the difficult junctions

knowing the speed limits

keeping the same vehicle

overcoming bad habits

anticipation, forward thinking of the road

anticipating other motorists intentions

avoid lack of road progress

avoid hesitancy, where appropriate keep the wheels rolling

knowing the highway code

focus focus focus

confident calm and concentrated

Conclusion

I fully understand how time-consuming and expensive it is to gain an lgv licence. I also understand that everyone is different. What works for one person may not work for another. I recommend you cherry pick from the information provided, whatever works best for you. I hope this chapter helps with the challenge of passing your test.

Part 3

The Essential New Truckers' Handbook

Chapter 1
Tachograph and Digicard

Introduction

This chapter focuses on the tachograph unit that truck drivers must use as an everyday part of their job. It includes a step-by-step guide of how to enter a manual entry, plus various information on the driver's digicard, which must be inserted into the tachograph unit.

One important reason why the manual entry procedure was introduced was in order to give DVSA (the Driver and Vehicle Standards Agency) proof that mandatory checks have been undertaken.

The fifteen minutes at the start of the shift during which the tachograph must be set to 'other work' (the cross hammers symbol) covers you in the event of an inspection. DVSA takes this as proof that vehicle inspection checks have been carried out.

I have provided a detailed easy to follow guide, which I hope will make things easier.

It is a bit complex at first, but, after completing it a few times, it will become second nature. Before you get the hang of it, if you are really struggling, you might want to try this alternative (plan B) strategy:

- Press OK on the tachograph vehicle unit (VU) to all questions asked.

- Once this is completed, change the tachograph symbol to 'other work' (crossed hammers).

- **Now do not move the truck for 15 minutes, whilst you carry out vehicle checks.**

Users Guide to Manual Entry
- Siemens Tachograph Unit

Symbols ^{h} = Rest Period. X = Other Work. $\blacksquare$ = POA $\odot$ = Driving

 The pictures on either side of this text show an example of a driver's card. The picture on the left shows the driver's details and photo ID. The one on the right shows the chip and the direction that the card needs to be inserted into the tachograph.

Step 1)   Turn on ignition and one of these screens will appear.

A}
17:07	$\odot$	0km/h
X	123456.7km	^{h}

B}
!$\odot\blacksquare$ driving	
without card	28

If box "B" 'driving without a card' appears', press OK.

Step 2)   Insert your driver's card in card slot 1, making sure that the chip is facing forward and upward, and then wait for

The above sequence will happen automatically. When the last screen appears, the 'yes' symbol will be flashing. Press OK to proceed.

Step 3) The next screen (**A**) shows the date and time that the card was last withdrawn on the top line. It also shows the date and time that the card has been inserted today on the bottom line. The 'rest' symbol will be flashing.

Now follow these steps in order using the up, down forward and back buttons.

Change the symbol to 'other work' X, and press OK.
Change the date to the last shift date and press OK.
Change the time to the last shift finish time and press OK.
After completion of these steps you will arrive at screen (**B**).

A)
```
M 02.02.15     12:08
h 07.02.15     17:07
```

B)
```
→  M 02.02.15     12:30  ←
→  X 07.02.15     17:07
```

Now (**C**) change the time to the start time of today's shift and press OK. Then (**D**) Change the symbol to 'other work' X and press OK.

C)
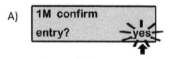
```
M 02.02.15     12:30
h 07.02.15     17:00  ←
```

D)

```
M 07.02.15     17:00
X 07.02.15     17:07
```

Step 4) A) Confirm manual entry and press OK.

B) Begin country, press OK.

C) The final screen, you are now ready to go.

A)
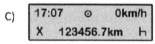
```
1M confirm
entry?          yes
```

B)
```
•   begin country
:UK:
```

C)

```
17:07   ⊙   0km/h
X   123456.7km   h
```

D)
```
!⊙ driving
without card     28
```

Note: If box "D" 'driving without a card' appears', press OK.
If you make a mistake at any time, press the back button.
Warning, once you confirm manual entry, there is no going back.

Driver's Digicard Information

A driver digicard stores information on dates and times worked, vehicles driven, duty periods, rest etc.

It expires after 5 years. To apply for a new card, you must complete the form D777B/DL that is available from the DVLA.

The card will retain information for 28 working days. This information needs to be downloaded before the 28th day to avoid the information being overwritten.

If the card appears to be malfunctioning it is worth trying it in another vehicle to establish if the card is at fault.

Always remember your digicard, as, unless it is lost or stolen, it is illegal to drive the vehicle without it.

Do a printout at the end of each day.

Lost/stolen digicard:

If the card is lost or stolen you must apply for a new one within 7 days. Following an application for a new card, you are able to drive without it for a maximum of 15 consecutive days (not working days).

If the card is stolen, this must be reported to the police and a crime reference number obtained.

Whilst waiting for your new digicard you must keep manual records. At the start of a shift, press print on the tachograph. On the printout, you must write down the vehicle's licence plate registration number. You must also write down enough information to identify you as the driver of the vehicle. For example, driver's licence number, driver card number and signature. Also, include your shift start time and the actual time you started driving.

At the end of a shift, press print on the tachograph. On the printout, write down the vehicle's licence plate registration number along with all periods of other work (whether you were in the vehicle or away from it), periods of availability and rest. Then ensure again that you include enough information to identify you as the driver.

Remember that these printouts count as official work records. As the driver, it is your responsibility to make sure that all work records are able to be understood easily and kept clean and presentable.

By law, it is required that you keep this printout with you for 28 days before handing it in to the company. If the company asks to retain it at the end of your shift, then you should photocopy it. If you are stopped by DVSA, they will want to see it.

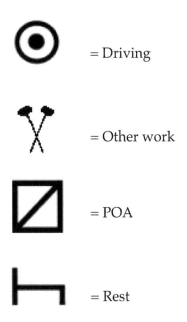

= Driving

= Other work

= POA

= Rest

Chapter 2

Official Working Time Regulations (WTR)

Introduction

The aim of this chapter is to give you all the important information regarding WTRs. Subjects are subtitled and bullet pointed for ease of reference.

These EU regulations were introduced in April 2005. They are a bit of a double-edged sword. On the one hand, they add restrictions and put pressure on drivers by adding a second set of times and breaks to adhere to. On the other hand, these regulations safeguard drivers against being exploited – forced to work too many hours. They also ensure that drivers are entitled to definite breaks every 6 hours.

To newcomers, the information in this chapter may seem a little daunting at first. Don't let this faze you. I have made sure to explain the essential parts of these overcomplicated regulations in as simple and comprehensive a manner as possible. In Chapter 3, under 'Drivers' Hours Rules simplified', point 7, 10 and 11 will be helpful until you get a good grasp of these complicated rules.

Working Time Regulations (WTR)

Hours of work:

- Drivers are required, on average, to work no more than 48 hours per week.

- This average is calculated over a period of time, known as a 'reference period'.

- One working year (52 weeks) is made up of three reference periods: two reference periods which last 17 weeks and one reference period which lasts 18 weeks.

- In this way, the three reference periods add up to a full working year: $17 + 17 + 18 = 52$.

- Please be aware that these stipulations may be slightly altered if you are part of either a 'collective agreement' or a 'workforce agreement'.

  - A collective agreement is an amendment to standard working time regulations which is reached via negotiation between an employer and a trade union.

  - A workforce agreement is an amendment to standard working time regulations which is reached via negotiation between an employer and workforce representatives.

- There are two possible amendments to standard working time regulations concerning reference periods. Having a 'fixed reference period by agreement' means that:

  - Start and end dates of reference periods can differ from the standard industry dates.

  - The average weekly working hours can be calculated over two 26–week reference periods, rather than three reference periods.

- These two reference periods will still add up to a full working year: $26 + 26 = 52$.

- Having a 'rolling reference period' means that:

  - A continuous, weekly updating average is taken over the previous 17 weeks. The first 17-week period of work is calculated in the standard way; however, after this the average is updated weekly. For example, in the 18th week, the average is calculated over the 17-week period spanning working weeks 2–18.

- Despite being required to work no more than 48 hours per week on average, you may work anywhere up to 60 hours in any single week starting at 00.00 on a Monday morning.

- You may not exceed more than 10 hours in any single 24-hour period if you are working at night. The night work limits can only be exceeded where there is a work force or collective agreement in place.

  - If driving a goods vehicle, you are legally considered to have worked a night shift if you have worked between 00.00 and 04.00.

  - If driving a passenger-carrying vehicle, you are legally considered to have worked a night shift if you have worked between 01.00 and 05.00.

Daily rest:

- As a driver, you are required to take 11 consecutive hours in each 24-hour period with the ability to reduce this to 9 consecutive hours up to 3 times per week.

  - Doing this makes no difference to the rest of your weekly working hours.

- Alternatively, daily rest can be split into 2 periods. Where this is done the first period must be at least 3 hours and the second period must be a minimum of 9 hours, so that total daily rest is at least 12 hours in these circumstances.

- Mobile workers should not exceed 6 consecutive hours without taking a break.

- If working hours total up to 6 hours per day a 15 minute break must be taken, up to 9 hours, 30 minute break must be taken.

- If working times total more than 9 hours per day, breaks should increase to a minimum of 45 minutes.

- Any breaks can be divided into 15-minute periods.

Weekly rest:

- WTR requires the driver to take 45 consecutive hours' weekly rest. This can be reduced to 24 hours providing that any reduction is made up for within 3 weeks.

Periods of availability (POA):

- POA is waiting time, the periods of which should be known in advance.

- POA criteria:

  o The mobile worker should not be required to remain at work-station (typically the vehicle).

  o The mobile worker must remain available to answer calls and resume work on request.

  o The duration of POA must be known in advance. Either before departure or just prior to the start of period in question.

Useful tips:

- If you do enter into either a collective or workforce agreement:

  o Make sure you find out exactly how this will affect you and alter your weekly duties.

- o Ensure that you keep in contact with other employees to ensure that your understanding of this agreement matches theirs.

- If it is your contractual duty to calculate your own working time:

  - o Make sure to subtract rests, breaks and POAs from your total time worked.

  - o Make sure to subtract any sick days, holidays etc. from your total time worked.

  - o Remember, keeping accurate daily written records will help you in this task.

  - o Ensure that all records are kept (filed or backed up on a computer for at least two years).

Chapter 3
Drivers' Hours Rules

Introduction

This chapter is split into three parts. The first section is the official drivers' hours rules. Don't worry if you find this a little confusing as, in the second section, I give a simplified, concise version of this information. This will hopefully make the first section a little easier to understand. The second section will also allow you to revise the relevant information whenever you need to. The third section contains some tips and advice regarding drivers' hours rules.

Note: the information contained in this chapter is the most important with regards to keeping your license safe and needs to be adhered to at all times.

Drivers' Hours Rules (official version)

Driving period

A driving period is the accumulation of actual driving
time between two break periods or following a rest period.

Daily driving time

You may not exceed 9 hours' actual driving time per day. However, this can
legally be extended to 10 hours twice a week. Doing this makes no difference
to the rest of your weekly actual driving hours.

Weekly driving time

You should not exceed 56 hours in total.

Fortnightly driving time

You should not exceed 90 hours' total driving time in any two consecutive
weeks.

Break periods

After 4½ hours of continuous driving have elapsed, an uninterrupted break
of 45 minutes must be taken.

A break of 45 minutes can be replaced by a 15-minute break followed by a
30-minute break. You could, for example, drive for 2 hours, take a 15-minute
break, drive for a further 2½ hours and then take a 30-minute break. During
this break period, you may not legally do any form of work (even written
work).

Please note, however, that you may not take a 30-minute break followed by a 15-minute break. This is to ensure that you are properly rested for your next period of driving.

Daily rest

Daily rest can be reduced from 11 hours to 9 hours three times a week. Doing this makes no difference to the total number of your rest hours.

A daily rest period is usually 11 uninterrupted hours but can be split into two: first minimum 3 hours, second minimum 9 hours. This means altogether 12 hours' rest. This would not count as a reduction in a daily rest period.

Weekly rest

A week is a period of time between 00.00 Monday and 24.00 Sunday. Weekly rest is generally an uninterrupted period of 45 hours. This can be reduced to 24 hours; however, you are legally required to make up this rest time within three weeks of taking the reduced rest. If, for example, you take a reduced weekly rest period of 24 uninterrupted hours, within three weeks you must take a weekly rest period of 66 uninterrupted hours.

A new weekly rest period commences after six 24-hour periods have elapsed since the last weekly rest period.

Rest taken as compensation for a reduced weekly rest period shall be attached to another rest period of at least 9 hours. The reduction must be compensated for 'en bloc' – it may not be split.

Where a driver chooses to take daily rest and reduced weekly rest periods away from base, these may be taken in the vehicle as long as it has suitable sleeping facilities and the vehicle is stationary.

A weekly rest period which begins in one week and continues into the following week may be attached to either of these weeks.

Drivers' Hours Rules simplified

1   Maximum driving time 9 hours per day. This can be extended to 10 hours twice a week.

2   Take 45-minute break after 4½ hours of driving.

3   The break can be split into 15 minutes, then 30 minutes: not 30 followed by 15. (Over-complicated, much easier to take full 45 minutes.)

4   Park up and take break on or ideally before 4½ hours (1 minute over is illegal).

5   If driving for 10 hours, you will need two 45-minute breaks.

6   If using Digicard VU tachograph machine, be sure to take 46 or 47-minute break (sometimes VU is not accurate enough and will show 45 minutes as 44½ – this now becomes an illegal break and will generate an infringement!).

7   Maximum 6 consecutive shifts in 1 week.

8   Ensure you take 11 hours' rest between end of one shift and start of next. This can be reduced to 9 hours twice a week.

9   Weekly rest period is 45 hours.

10 Maximum driving time in 1 week is 56 hours. If driving 2 consecutive weeks, maximum hours must be 90. (Example: 56 hours 1st week, then 34 hours 2nd week.)

11   If your total driving and working time equals 45 hours or less in 1 week and you then take a rest period of 45 hours or more, you will be totally compliant with drivers' hours rules and working time rules.

12   Maximum total shift duration is 15 hours during the day, 10 hours during the night.

Drivers' Hours Rules tips and advice

1   Make a note of the time you actually start driving.

2   Set alarm on phone for 4 hours on (acts as a reminder and also allows 30 minutes to find a place to park up).

3   When on break remember to alter symbol on VU to rest (bed symbol) then either press down button on VU to see break time or set alarm for 46 minutes, then again make a note of the time you resume driving.

4   Reset alarm for 4 hours on.

5   At any time, if you press down arrow, VU should show exact driving time. (Only records time when the truck wheels are actually turning, not stuck in traffic etc.)

6   New types of VU will flash on 4 hours and 15 minutes as warning to take a break.

7   Remember to take minimum of 15-minute break within 6 hours of starting working, regardless of whether or not you have driven 4½ hours (working time regulation).

Chapter 4
Mock-up of New Driver's Shift

Introduction

These mock shift pages are intended to be of help during the first shift or three. Revision of these pages before starting a new job may be useful – to give reminders and some advice.

The first shift I ever did was on an articulated truck. At the very first drop, I managed to smash the passenger side mirror off whilst manoeuvring past a large skip. I ended up with a three-inch mirror gaffer-taped on and a long drive to Plymouth ahead. When I reported the incident, I said that I had parked up at a service station in order to buy a sandwich and had returned to the truck to find that the mirror had been smashed off, clearly by another truck. It was certainly not the most relaxing day I've ever had, but still, you gotta laugh!

Hopefully your first shift will go a lot better than mine did! However, remember that everyone makes mistakes when first starting out. Don't let this knock your confidence. This chapter should help you be confident that you are as prepared as possible for what awaits you in your first shift. Having a good idea of the structure of a driver's shift before you start will allow for an easier, less stressful transition into this line of work.

Mock-up of new driver's shift

1   Report to transport office. Fill in the paperwork provided
     (Q&A self-explanatory). Typical questions are: last shift date,
     start/finish times, POA, rest (calculated from end time of
     previous shift and new shift start time), driving licence
     number etc.

2   Office staff will take a photocopy of your licence, CPC card
     and digicard.

3   Handover of keys, driver's sheets, delivery addresses and
     hopefully maps and location of truck and trailer.

4   Find truck, switch on ignition, insert digicard into VU.
     Answer questions by continuously pressing 'OK' or by doing
     a manual entry. Then change symbol to cross hammers ('other
     work'). *Now do not move truck for 15 minutes!!*
     (See Chapter 1 for advice on VU.)

5   Start vehicle checks and paperwork. (See Chapter 5.)

6   Locate and couple up to trailer, do all checks to vehicle and
     also check load correct and secure. (See Chapters 5 and 7.)

7   Complete paperwork and plan route.

8   Now make a note of the time you actually start driving, then
     set alarm on phone for 4 hours' time. This acts as a reminder
     and allows 30 minutes to find a park-up. At any time, if you
     need to check how much actual driving time has elapsed, just
     press down arrow on VU. (See Chapter 3.)

9   If you are unable to find truck or trailer, ask the shunter or another driver.

10 Make sure that within 6 hours of putting digicard into VU (starting actual work) or within 4½ hours' continuous driving, a break is taken – a 45-minute break is required when driving, a 30-minute break is required when doing other work. I recommend taking a 45-minute break on whichever one of these occurs first. (See Chapters 2 and 3.)

11 When on break, remember to alter VU to bed symbol (rest).

Note: If required press 'down' button on VU to see up-to-the-minute break time taken. I recommend taking a full 46 or 47-minute break.

12 For POA (basically time kept waiting), remember to alter symbol on VU.

13 Do all feasible deliveries and keep to all breaks.

14 Return to depot, drop off trailer, do checks and fuel up.

15 Park up truck. Do printout from VU and keep it. Eject card.

16 Hand in all completed paperwork, keys etc. (See Chapter 6.)

17 Office will download digicard.

18 Finish.

19 Make a note in diary of date and start/finish shift times/POA and any problems incurred.

20   Be sure to have 11 hours' rest from end of shift to start of next shift. Can reduce to 9 hours three times a week. (See Chapter 3.)

Note: maximum shift duration is 15 hours for a day shift and 10 hours for a night shift.

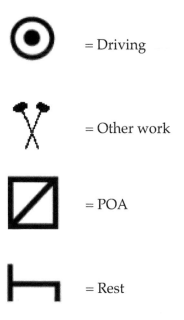

= Driving

= Other work

= POA

= Rest

Shift Check List

The shift check list included in this section is one which I have created and use to help make life a bit easier. I make sure that I have one, attached to a clip board, whilst I am on the job; to act as a task-reminder at the start of my day. It also helps me to keep an eye on my hours during a shift. As the shift progresses, I continue to fill in the sheet with break times, P.O.A. times etc. This helps me to keep track of everything I've done, and everything that I still need to do. In order to make filling it out as clear as possible, I have included a filled in example and a blank example. It's not necessary to use this list, but you my find it helpful to do so.

SHIFT CHECK LIST

- Insert Digi Card, Card Time in = ___0=800___

- Manuel Entry, Stationary For 15 min (Vehicle Checks).

- Fuel Level = ___¾___

- Trailer Height = ___13'6___

- Trailer Brake On? ___✓___

- BayLight Green? ___✓___

- Bridge Tag? ___✓___

- Alter Sat Nav? ___✗___

- Start Drive (Set Alarm On Phone).

- Start Drive Time = ___08:50___

- Drive Break (47mins)

    - After 4½ hrs driving

        - Alter Tacho Symbol – on break

        - Break time = ___13.20___ to ___14.07___

    - Working Time Directive – Break Must Be Taken After 6 hrs.

- Lock On Dock, Fuel Up.

- Vehicle Checks.

- Print Out, Take Card Out.

- POA = ___45 min___

- Time Sheet.

- End Shift Time = ___19.30___

SHIFT CHECK LIST

- Insert Digi Card, Card Time in = _____
- Manuel Entry, Stationary For 15 min (Vehicle Checks).
- Fuel Level = _____
- Trailer Height = _____
- Trailer Brake On? ____
- BayLight Green? ____
- Bridge Tag? ____
- Alter Sat Nav? ____
- Start Drive (Set Alarm On Phone).
- Start Drive Time = _____
- Drive Break (47mins)
  - After 4½ hrs driving
    - Alter Tacho Symbol – on break
    - Break time = _____ to _____
  - Working Time Directive – Break Must Be Taken After 6 hrs.
- Lock On Dock, Fuel Up.
- Vehicle Checks.
- Print Out, Take Card Out.
- POA = _____
- Time Sheet.
- End Shift Time = _____

Chapter 5
Mandatory Vehicle Inspection Checks

Introduction

This chapter outlines the mandatory vehicle checks which you, as the driver, must carry out. I have also included examples of paperwork and checklists likely to be given to you to fill in. These are quite self-explanatory, but you do need to be quite thorough as you could find yourself blamed for any damage or defects which are overlooked. It can also threaten your licence if any defects are discovered after you have signed the paperwork. This paperwork is legally binding, so be sure not to rush. Only sign it if you're confident that you have been thorough in your checks.

Note: if you are disturbed or distracted whilst completing these checks, or the paperwork, it's advisable to **retrace** previous steps taken before continuing. Remember, it is completely the driver's responsibility once the vehicle hits the road!

Cab Front

Mirrors

O License

Screen damage

Horn

Wipers and washers

Lights/Indicators

Leaks

Cab Back

Lights

GS08
PHA

Left

Trailer brake

Oil and water

Fuel tank top

Legs up

Tyres

Height adjuster correct

Right

Airleaks

In-cab height indicator

MOT date

Load secure and door closed

Wheel nuts

Mudguard secure

Dog clip-in

Service line correct

Back

Lights

Number plate

Vehicle Check Sheet 1

Fill each box with a '☑' if the condition is satisfactory
or a '☒' if there is a defect.

TRUCK CHECK	JOURNEY	
	BEFORE	AFTER
Brake lines and coupling – present in good working order		
Fuel cap and seal – present free from leaks		
Levels & leaks – engine oil, water, fuel, AdBlue		
Lights – operational, in good working order		
MOT disc – valid, clearly displayed		
Road fund & O licence discs – valid, clearly displayed		
Tyres – inflation, tread depth, in good working order		
Wings, mudguards and spray suppression equipment – satisfactory condition and secure		
Excessive engine exhaust smoke – visual check		
Indicators – in good working order		
Mirrors – presentable, in good working order		
Service week sticker – valid, displayed – number to be written		
Wheels – satisfactory condition, fixings secure		
Wipers & washers – satisfactory condition, in good working order		
Digital tachograph fitted – spare print roll present		
Horn – in good working order		
Seating – satisfactory condition & secure		
Air leaks – listen for leaks		
Glass & windscreen – presentable, good condition, free from obstruction		
In-cab height indicator – present and correctly set		
Seat belt – in good working order		

Vehicle Check Sheet 2

Fill each box with a '☑' if the condition is satisfactory
or a '☒' if there is a defect.

TRUCK CHECK	JOURNEY	
	BEFORE	AFTER
Rear door shutter – in good working order		
Reflectors – free from damage		
Service week sticker – valid, clearly displayed – number to be written		
Tyres – inflation, tread depth, damage		
Wheels – satisfactory and secure		
Wings, mudguards and spray suppression equipment – satisfactory condition and secure		
Indicators – in good working order		
Landing legs warning device – in good working order		
Marker boards – satisfactory condition, free from damage		
Lights – in good working order, free from damage		
Mavis rail – operational		
Load security restraint in place – 2 bars/straps at rear		
MOT disc – valid, displayed – MOT month to be written		
Number plate satisfactory condition, and secure		
Park brake operational/air leaks – aural check		

Chapter 6

Example of A Driver's Transport Sheet

Introduction

This chapter provides an example of a typical driver's sheet. It's important to fill in each driver's sheet correctly. At the end of the shift, all paperwork is handed in to the transport office and all information is entered into their system. If there are a lot of inaccuracies, it creates extra work and hassle for the office workers. Remember, it is your responsibility to fill out all paperwork accurately. Not taking the time to do this can be interpreted as a lack of courtesy to the office staff whom you rely on. (A stitch in time saves nine.) The best way to stay as hassle-free as possible is to study this sheet before you start a new job and then ensure that you take the time to familiarise yourself with your new company's driver sheet. Please bear in mind that the sheet provided is an over-simplified example.

This example sheet is based on supermarket delivery work. Other work, such as general haulages, Royal Mail etc., utilises a very similar format.

Transport Sheet

DATE	DRIVER ID	NAME	SHIFT START	SHIFT END	ACT HOURS	CONTRACT HOURS
15-8-15	731	RICHARD GOVADS	10 00	2200	12	/

EMPLOYER (AGENCY)

ACME

TYPE OF TACHOGRAPH USED			
DIGITAL	ANALOGUE	SPARE ROLL	
✓		✓	

WORKING HOURS	PERIODS OF AVAILABLITY		TOTAL HOURS	BREAKS AND RESTS
12	30 MIN		11¼	3¾

TRACTOR

JOURNEY NO.	FULL REGISTRATION	ODO START	ODO FINISH	TOTAL	FUEL(LTR)	GAS	AD BLUE	GAS/OIL/RIGID	MPG
101	KLM115	102000	102280	280	128	/	2	½	

DELIVERIES   STORE= S   BACKHAUL= B   CAGE COLLECTION= C

JOURNEY NO. CODE	JOURNEY CODE	STORE NAME	DU'S DEL R/PALLETS	BOARDS	START/FINISH TEMP/TEMP	TRAILER NO.	START FRIDGE GAS	OIL	RIGID	DEPART DEPOT	ARRIVE DESTINATION	TIME ON BAY	DEPART DESTINATION	RETURN DC	GAS/OIL (LITRES)
101	—	Plymouth	18	12		042				1100	1410	1420	1545		
101	—	Torquay Central	9	3		042					1740	1750	1845	21-15	18

Driver's Signature...R...G.Govads...   Manager's Signature........................

Chapter 7
Coupling Procedures

Introduction

This chapter shows the various scenarios to do with coupling and uncoupling. The diagrams show some of the problems that can be encountered if you are not on your game. It's quite a straightforward procedure; however, make sure that you do not let time constraints pressure you into feeling rushed or distracted. This is where mistakes happen. Take enough time to carry out this task properly. If you do get distracted, by someone or something, make sure you **retrace** previous steps before proceeding.

Artic Coupling Procedure (split)

a. Reverse up to the trailer, handbrake on, check trailer brake is on (pulled out), fifth wheel bar (handle) pulled out. **Is the trailer height correct?**

b. Reverse halfway under the trailer – handbrake on, connect service lines – airline.

c. Reverse under until pin locks in.

d. Select first gear and tug trailer twice.

e. Handbrake on, fit fifth wheel clip (dog clip).

f. Trailer brake off.

g. Wind up legs.

h. Fit number plate.

Artic Coupling Procedure (close)

a. Reverse up to trailer, handbrake on, check trailer brake is on, fifth wheel bar pulled out. **Is the trailer height correct?** (If Mavis rail fitted slide it all the way across.)

b. Reverse under the trailer until the pin locks in.

c. Select first gear, tug trailer twice.

d. Handbrake on, fit dog clip.

e. Fit service/airlines.

f. Trailer brake off.

g. Wind up legs.

h. Fit number plate.

Artic Uncoupling Procedure

a. Handbrake on.

b. Trailer brake on.

c. Wind legs down.

d. Service/airlines disconnected.

e. Remove number plate.

f. Pull fifth wheel locking lever out (unlocked position).

g. Double-check all procedures.

h. Drive out.

Considerations during coupling

If the trailer is at an incorrect height, use the handheld suspension unit to raise or lower the truck to match the trailer height.

If you are still unsure if the trailer is too high, you can reverse under most of the way, raise the truck up until you feel the weight of the trailer and then reverse the last few inches until the pin locks in.

Note: Some companies do not allow split coupling. Always check with each company transport office.

Always, always check trailer brake is on! Once you fit the airline the brakes will automatically release. During split coupling, there is an extreme danger of the trailer rolling forward, if the yard is on a downwards incline, and of you therefore being crushed between it and the cab.

The object of the tug test is to ensure that the pin is locked in. Give the trailer two strong tugs but do not drag it forward as this will risk damage to the legs etc.

Mavis rail (Montracon articulated vehicle interconnection system): This modern technology is fitted on newer trailers. It is located on the bulkhead (front of trailer). It allows the service lines and airlines to be connected from the ground without having to climb onto the back of the truck. Pull one or two levers (pins) and the whole rail slides out.

a.   Make sure to lock it back into its original position when you are finished.

b.   Be very careful of other traffic whilst using it, because **you will have your back to any possible danger!!!**

Bad coupling example A shows a trailer which is too high, therefore missing the pin. This will result in damage to the rear of the cab and to the trailer bulkhead.

Bad coupling example B shows a trailer which is too low. This will cause damage to rear lights and mudguards.

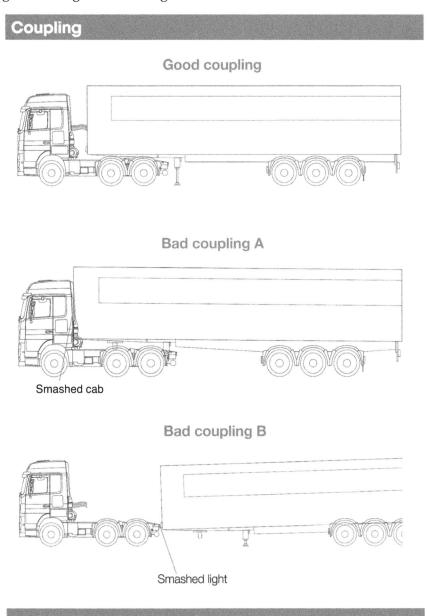

Coupling

Good coupling

Bad coupling A

Smashed cab

Bad coupling B

Smashed light

Chapter 8
Loading and Unloading

Introduction

The aim of this chapter is to help you gain an understanding of safe loading and unloading. With regard to loading/unloading equipment, I have outlined the safe use and carriage of roller cages and pallets, and essential tips for the use of pump trucks. I have also included pictures and a description of how to use height adjusters and tail lifts, and a list of considerations to keep in mind whilst you are loading/unloading.

Roller cages

In the event of a full load of roller cages, you need to have at least a minimum of 2 load restraining bars spaced out evenly every 5 rows. If rollers are very heavy, i.e. containing drinks, tins, etc. you will need 2 bars every 3 rows – pallets require 2 bars or straps every 4 or 5 rows.

When unloading on an incline, always level the vehicle by raising or lowering the suspension on the truck or trailer or both. **Never** remove straps or bars if the vehicle is not level. Each roller could easily weigh up to 500kg each. This system applies to both arctic and rigid trucks.

↖ Load-restraining bar

Ratchet Strap →

← Cup

Note: Extreme danger to you and others! If one or more rows start to move, you **will not** stop them! You could be crushed in the corner of the trailer or the roller cage could fall off the back and potentially hit someone else.

When manually handling cages, always push or pull. Don't walk alongside them; if a wheel brakes there is high risk of injury.

Roller cage

Pump trucks

A pump truck acts as a manual version of a forklift. Its main purpose is for loading and unloading pallets of goods. Pump the handle backwards and forwards to lift up the pallets. Press the handle/lever to lower.

If using one inside a trailer, you must ensure the vehicle is level! A pallet can easily weigh up to 10 times a person's body weight. It can run away as you give chase down the trailer. Pump trucks don't have brakes; the only way to stop them is by lowering the pallet. Just remember to take it slow until you get used to using one.

Trailer height adjuster

Located near passenger-side rear corner. Usually push it inwards and rotate lever left or right to lower or raise; pull it back out until it clicks and it should self-level the trailer to correct height.

Truck height adjuster

Located either behind driver's seat or on the side of the seat. When adjusting suspension height, either leave control pad on seat or write a note to self and put on dashboard as a reminder (this prevents forgetting, which can cause damage to tyres or suspension airbags).

Tail lift operation

Some trucks have an isolator switch in the cab. This needs to be in the 'on' position to operate the tail lift. Switches and buttons are usually found on the near side of the trailer; there are usually more buttons inside the trailer (near side just inside the trailer). A little lever clip will need to be pushed or pulled to unfold the lift.

Warning: whilst raising the lift, there is a serious risk of crushing your toes if you get them trapped between the lift and the trailer floor. Also, **never ever try to free an underslung tail lift if it jams!** If it suddenly moves it will turn your hands into marmalade. Instead, get help or walk away.

Release clip

Upright

Operating buttons and switches

Operating buttons and switches

Underslung

1. Leave sidelights switched on in truck in order to be able to work interior trailer lights.

2. When unloading or loading or carrying out checks etc. change VU symbol to 'other work' (cross hammers).

3. If you are kept waiting to be loaded or unloaded, change the symbol to 'POA' (supposed to be waiting time known in advance, not always the case). When you drive away, usually the VU symbol will automatically change itself to the driving symbol.

4. Load safety tips – always check the load yourself and always make sure it is fully secure. **Never** trust that someone else has chained, strapped or barred up the load properly. The loaders could have changed shift halfway, been distracted, been short of equipment or not cared!

5. **Important:** try not to be hurried when completing the task of loading/unloading. Your safety comes first, the load second. Also, if for any reason you have to move the truck halfway through, keep calm and collected. Remember, you are in the middle of a process, so **retrace** previous steps if you need to. Always, always **re-secure** the load before moving!

Chapter 9
Manoeuvring

Introduction

The aim of this chapter is to show you the recommended positioning techniques to aid the manoeuvring of vehicles onto bays in busy yards. 2 types of scenario will be focused on:

- Manoeuvring in a spacious yard.

- Manoeuvring in a tight yard.

You should find this information useful, as you never know how much space you will be given. With practise, manoeuvring becomes much easier.

Manoeuvring

Spacious yard

If yard protocol allows, approach the bays offside on. Drive along the rank until you reach the required bay. Swing the truck up towards the opposite row of bays. The idea here is to leave the rear of the trailer positioned towards the intended bay, as it makes it easier for reversing in.

Tight (small) yard

You need a different approach for a tight yard. Ideally, you should aim to be offside on and centrally positioned. Line up the back of the trailer with the intended bay, then jack-knife the trailer 180 degrees onto the bay.

Note) In tight yards, this manoeuvre is very difficult until you get the hang of it, to avoid causing damage. If you need help, **ask!** If you find the yard folk are not very friendly, you could offer a cash incentive in exchange for assistance, such as a fiver. (Shame on any man who takes it rather than helping for free!!).

Chapter **10**
Key Safe (Lock on Dock)

Introduction

This chapter focuses on the key safe procedure. This system was designed to prevent accidents and injuries. In the past, there were a lot of incidents of trucks pulling off bays whilst loading or unloading was still taking place. This resulted in many injuries to loaders, some serious. For example forklifts and pump trucks came crashing down off the docks.

Here are a few scenarios of why, in the past, drivers have prematurely driven off:

1. The driver fell asleep and woke up after some time to find that all was quiet. He/she checked the time. Half asleep, he/she believed that loading/unloading must have finished and so drove off.

2. The driver could hear that loading was underway. He/she was under pressure to get to the next destination and therefore a bit distracted. After a while, all went quiet. Not thinking clearly, he/she believed that loading/unloading had finished. Perhaps, due to past experience, he/she thought that there had been a change of shift in the warehouse and that the previous loader must have forgotten to change the bay light to green. He/she therefore drove off.

Please be aware that not all yards use the key safe procedure. In these situations, it is good to keep these scenarios in mind whilst loading/unloading is taking place.

Key safe (lock on dock) procedure

<u>Arctic (class 1), rigid (class 2)</u>

The usual procedure is to put the ignition keys onto a chain. The warehouse staff will pull them up and keep hold of them until the truck is loaded. Keep an eye on the mirror; on completion the bay light will change to green and the keys will be dropped.

On the rare occasion that the keys are either hanging on the chain or in the truck, but the bay light is still on red:

- Go and speak to warehouse staff.

- Check all is fine.

- Get bay light changed to green.

- Drive off.

- **Never** ever drive off on a red bay light!

Artic (Class 1)

Picking up trailers

- Check bay light on green.

- Reverse up to trailer.

- Fetch key from hook/chain next to building.

- Undo lock on airline (trailer).

- Put key and lock back on hook/chain. Commence coupling up to trailer.

Dropping trailers

- Reverse trailer safely into empty bay.

- Uncouple truck from trailer.

- Fetch key and lock from hook/chain next to building.

- Secure lock to airline on trailer.

- Return key.

- Press button to change bay light to red.

Safety tips

a. Always check bay light on green before attempting to couple up.

b. Never reverse under trailer on red bay light.

Note: don't forget to remove trailer number plate.

Chapter **11**

Refrigerated Trailers and Tautliners

Introduction

Please find, in this chapter, a thorough guide to using two of the most commonly used trailers – refrigerated and tautliner trailers. The same, or very similar, steps also apply to Class 2 rigid trucks. Technology on trucks is ever-changing; however, all are basically similar to operate.

User's Guide to Refrigerated Trailers

Typically, the transporting temperature for ambient and chilled loads is +3°C, and, for frozen loads, the transporting temperature is -20°C.

Usually there are movable drop-down curtains inside the trailer to create two separate compartments; this makes it possible to have both an ambient and a frozen load in one trailer.

Operation

1. Flick the switch marked 'start/run' from 'off' to 'start/run'. Wait a few seconds; an alarm will sound, then the fridge will start up.

2. Use the switch/button marked '1/2' to select compartment 1/2, then press up/down arrows to alter the temperature and press '=' button to confirm.

The red diesel (gas oil) fuel tank is underslung beneath the trailer. The fuel gauge is located on the side of the tank. Always check that the cap is tight and that the rubber seal is intact. One third to half a tank of fuel should usually see out a 10-hour shift.

Tri-axle fridge trailer:

Adjustable curtains:

User's Guide to Tautliners

Front End Pole	Front Curtain Tensioning Ratchet	Lower Chassis Rail	Curtain Tensioning Strap	Rear Curtain Tensioning Ratchet	Rear End Pole

Curtain tensioning strap. In this example, the strap is in the closed tense position. To release strap, lift lever [a], pull the rear strap down and unhook hook [b] from lower chassis rail.

To secure the strap, pull the hook [b] under the lower chassis rail and secure to rail. Then pull down on the upper strap until taut and then pull down lever [a] until it clips into place.

Typical corner tensioning ratchet. To release push handle firmly inwards. To tension, pull handle forwards and backward until the curtain is tight.

How to open the curtains:

Release the curtain tensioning straps, as described above, to the extent you need to open the curtain. Next release the corner tensioning ratchet and pull out the curtain attached to the corner pole. Push the pole upwards until the bottom of the pole is free of the ratchet and pull outward. Lower the pole until it is free of the top securing pin. Pull the curtain back in the required direction.

Curtain	Central
Slide	Slide Rail
Rail	Support Bar

Warning:

Never take out both corner poles at the same time; you risk pulling the curtain off the curtain rail and it is very difficult to re-attach.

How to close the curtains:

Pull the curtain closed and lift the top of the corner pole up until it is located in the top securing pin, hold it up and locate the bottom of the pole onto ratchet. Use the ratchet to tension the curtain and then do up the curtain straps as described on the preceding page.

Safety:

When it is windy the curtains, strap hooks and in particular the corner pole can flap about uncontrollably. This can result in serious injury or damage. To prevent this it is advisable to only open the curtains to the minimum required. Also it is advisable to pull the hooks up to release lever and use the curtain strap nearest the curtain pole to clip it into place on either the lower chassis rail or one of the tensioned straps.

Chapter **12**
Gearboxes

Introduction

Shown in this chapter are various types of gearboxes. I have chosen to focus on the most commonly found gearboxes in the industry today. Diagrams and descriptions of how to use each model are included.

A – Range Change

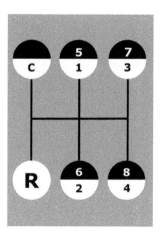

This is essentially a 16-speed gearbox – 4 gears in a low range, 4 gears in a high range and a splitter (overdrive) which allows for half-gears. 'C' stands for 'crawler gear', which is useful for very steep inclines.

Go through gears 1 to 4, pull up the switch on the front of the stick. To access gears 5-8, use the other switch for splitter gears.

B – Range Change (SCANIA)

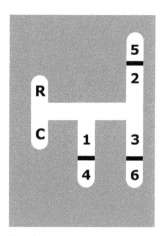

This box is fitted to SCANIA trucks. It is basically the same as example A; the only difference is that it only contains 3 gears in a low range and 3 gears in a high range.

C – Splitter

A splitter box is a 16-speed gearbox. Go through gears 1-4, then pull the stick sideways towards the driver's seat to change the range and access gears 5–8. It should be obvious when you are changing range – feel the resistance through the stick. The switch on the side is for half-gears (overdrive).

D – Automatic

In this example of an automatic gearbox, select 'A' for full-automatic mode. Select 'M' to drive in manual mode. When in manual mode, use the switches on the side of the stick to change gear.

Chapter 13
Roping and Sheeting

Introduction

Explained below are the basics for the roping and sheeting of an open load.

Note) it is <u>necessary</u> that, prior to attempting this task, you undergo full training in the exact placing of sheets, straps and ropes, and in the tying of the various knots used. Rest assured, you won't be expected to attempt any of these procedures until you have been shown by a professional.

Example A - Ropes not tight enough, tensioned unevenly:

Example B - Sheets placed in wrong order:

Roping and Sheeting

The basic principles of roping and sheeting are as follows:

Ideally, you should find a quiet, sheltered part of the yard where you won't be disturbed or distracted.

To secure down a load using one sheet –
Start at either end of the trailer. Roll the sheet out towards the opposite end of the trailer. When rolling the sheet out, be sure to keep it taught and to expel any trapped air as you go. Once the load is covered, secure all ropes and/or straps tightly, making sure they're all evenly tensioned.

To secure down a load using two sheets –
Start at the rear end of the trailer. Attach the first sheet over the rear end of the trailer, then attach the second sheet over the front end of the trailer. Make sure that the front sheet overlaps with the rear sheet (this stops the wind from getting underneath the rear sheet, which could loosten it and cause it to start to lift it whilst in transit).

Note) In windy conditions, you should only roll your sheeting out a little bit at a time and secure as you go.

Please take the time to note the following **dangers:**

- Walking on top of a load that's unstable and could move.

- Walking on top of a load which has an unsecured sheet, as there is a possibility of you falling down into a space in between the load.

- Being blown off the top of the load when the wind lifts the unsecured sheet.

- The load coming loose, shifting, falling off the trailer.

Chapter **14**
Maximum Vehicle Laden Weights

Introduction

Included below is a useful but not uncomplicated table regarding the legal maximum vehicle laden (gross) weights of various goods vehicles. It was produced by the Department of Transport in 2003, for the use of Magistrates when presiding over cases of overloading. Since this is the information magistrates use when deciding whether or not a particular goods vehicle was overloaded, you can't go too far wrong if you abide by the weights on this table.

A Simplified Guide To Lorry Types And Weights

Recommended Description			Identifier	UK Maximum Gross Weight (tonnes)	Shape
LIGHT GOODS VEHICLES			2 axles	3.5	no rear side windows
L O R R I E S		SMALLER 2-AXLE LORRIES	2 axles	Over 3.5 7.5	
		BIGGER 2-AXLE LORRIES	2 axles	Over 7.5 18	
	HEAVY	MULTI- AXLE LORRIES	3 axles rigid	25 26*	
			3 axles artic.	26	
	GOODS		4 axles rigid	30 32*	
	VEHICLES		4 axles artic.	36 38*	
	(Vehicles over 7.5 tonnes gross require a Heavy Goods Vehicle Driver's Licence)		Vehicle and draw-bar trailer 4 axles	30 36**	
			5 axles or more artic. See note (a)	40	
			Vehicle and draw-bar trailer 5 axles See note (a)	40**	
			6 axles artic. See note (b)	41*	
			6 axles draw-bar See note (b)	41* and **	
			5 or 6 axles artic. See notes (b) and (c)	44* and ***	
			6 axles draw-bar	44*,** and ***	
			6 axles artic. See note (b) and (d)	44*	
			6 axles draw-bar See note (b) and (d)	44* and **	

* If the driving axle is not a steering axle, has twin tyres and road friendly suspension, or if each driving axle is fitted with twin tyres and the maximum weight for each axle does not exceed 8.55 tonnes.

** Distance between the rear axle of the motor vehicle and the front axle of the trailer is not less than 3 metres.

*** If the vehicle is being used for combined transport.

(a) 5 axles or more artic and the 5 axles or more drawbar could alternatively have a 3 axle motor vehicle and a 2 axle trailer.

(b) Conditions:

- each vehicle must have at least 3 axles.

- drive axle has twin tyre and road friendly suspension and maximum of 10.5 tonnes, or each driving axle is fitted with twin tyres and has a maximum of 8.5 tonnes.

- trailer has road friendly suspension.

(c) Conditions for operation on 5 axles:

- must have 3 axles on tractor unit.

- single container 40ft in length (conforming to standards laid down by the International Standards Organisation) being carried only.

- vehicle being used for international journey.

(d) Powered by a low pollution engine

Maximum Vehicle Laden Weights

For the purposes of full disclosure, please note that under UK law, there are two sets of regulations concerning maximum vehicle laden (gross) weights, which a company can choose to abide by:

1. The Authorised Weight Regulations 1998.

2. The Road Vehicles (Construction and Use) Regulations 1986.

Companies can abide by either set of regulations, but not a combination of the two. For this reason, I <u>strongly</u> suggest that you check with the company that you are working for, as to what the laden (gross) weights of their vehicles are, before you take any of them out on the road.

Source – Department of Transport – 'A Simplified Guide to Lorry Types and Weights' – 2003.

Used in accordance with the Open Government Licence for public sector information:

http://www.nationalarchives.gov.uk/doc/open-government-licence/version/3/

Chapter 15

Environmentally Friendly - Fuel Saving - Driving

Introduction

Featured here are tips and techniques to drive a truck economically.

Nowadays, companies are very keen on this topic. This is hardly surprising, considering the price of fuel and the fact that an average fully loaded 44 ton truck burns through a gallon of diesel every 6–9 miles. Companies are, therefore, looking to all options to increase miles per gallon.

Note) In a successful attempt to cut costs, some larger companies (such as supermarkets) are now removing one of the two fitted fuel tanks and replacing it with a gas tank. Their trucks would then run on duel fuel, which lowers fuel costs.

Eco-driving

The following set of tips will help you to save as much fuel as possible:

- Avoid unnecessary idling in cold weather if waiting to be loaded/unloaded. Switch off the engine and use night (cab) heater.

- Adjust your driving style to one of forward thinking and anticipation. By reading the road ahead, it can be possible to see obstacles and hazards before reaching them; thus avoiding a lot of heavy braking and accelerating (keeping up momentum).

- Approach traffic lights gradually, avoiding (where possible) coming to a complete stop.

- Set your air deflector to correct height and angle.

- Change gear in the middle of the rev range.

- Check and correct all tyre pressures.

- Avoid speeding.

- Pull sheets/curtains on the trailer tight.

Chapter **16**

ADR – Accord Dangereux Routier

(European agreement concerning the international carriage of dangerous goods by road, relating to e.g. petrol tankers, chemical tankers and explosive transporters.)

Introduction

This chapter refers to hazardous loads. It contains a short explanation of the qualifications needed, course durations and costs. The courses are individually tailored to each category of dangerous goods. All details are to be found online. These details are far too extensive and ever-changing to go into in depth here.

Courses vary from 3–7 days and they cover transporting the following.

- Explosives.

- Gasses.

- Flammable liquids.

- Flammable solids.

- Oxidising substances.

- Organic peroxides.

- Toxic & infectious substances.

- Radioactives.

- Corrosive substances.

- Miscellaneous substances.

Costs vary between £350 & £700.

Chapter **17**
Mineral Products Qualification Council – MPQC

Introduction

For a driver to go to work hauling aggregates, earth or liquids, he or she must first gain a MPQC qualification. It is a very simple and straightforward course.

It covers: quarry work, tippers, truck mixers and tankers.

Drivers require an MPQC Driver Skills Card to undertake this kind of work. The aim of the course is an increased awareness of health & safety and environmental issues.

This is a 1-day course, which includes:

- Personal protective equipment (PPE).

- Preventing workplace accidents.

- Reporting incidents.

- Vehicle pre-start checks.

- Safe driving behaviour.

- Vehicle access and egress.

- Site hazards.

- Entering and leaving customer sites.

- Environmental issues.

- Vehicle-specific hazards.

Costs for this course vary between £150 and £250, and it may count as 7 hours (1 day) towards CPC course.

Chapter 18
Umbrella Companies

Introduction

If you are new to umbrella companies, you are probably wondering:

- What is an umbrella company?

- How does it work?

- What should I do?

An umbrella company is a company which takes the role of an employer for a worker contracted through an agency.

The majority of agencies, and some companies, will only employ a driver if they are registered with one of these organisations.

- You join an umbrella company by registering online or over the phone.

- You sign an employment contract between yourself and the umbrella company.

When you join an umbrella company, study the information that they send you, as procedures differ slightly from company to company. However, they all basically work in the following way:

- At the end of the week you submit your hours and expenses to the umbrella company using their online facility.

- The umbrella company invoices the agency/company you are working for.

- The umbrella company pays you through a PAYE (pay as you earn) system after the deduction of allowable business expenses.

- At the end of the tax year, you will receive a P60 (government statement issued to taxpayers at the end of a tax year).

- Also, if relevant, you will receive a P11D (expenses and benefits form) for any beneficial expenses claimed.

The umbrella company will take an administration fee directly from your wages before paying them into your bank. Always establish what their fee is as this can vary. Try to sign up to a well-established company if possible. The company or agency you are interested in working with should recommend one to you.

Ensure that you keep a record of dates, hours and companies that you've driven for, in order to ensure that you are receiving the correct salary. Always get your time sheet signed at the end of each shift. These sheets are supplied by either the company or the agency.

It is also a good idea to keep your tachograph printouts, as, if there is any dispute with regards to pay, this provides evidence of the hours you've worked etc.

Chapter **19**
Pre-Employment Examination Questions

Introduction

This chapter is comprehensive and covers most, if not all, of the questions and answers that a driver will need to know in order to pass an agency or company pre-job exam. If you study the information corresponding to these answers, you can't go wrong.

The first section covers questions and answers. The second section covers the analogue tachograph. The third section covers the Highway Code. Each subject is relevant and likely to be included, in part or in full, in a pre-job exam.

Note: it is advisable to study these pages every time you're about to change agency or company. You will need to answer 75–85% of these questions correctly in order to pass.

PRE-EMPLOYMENT QUESTIONS AND ANSWERS

Q1: A driver is required to take a statutory break after an accumulated period of driving not exceeding?

A) 3.5 hours   B) 5 hours   C) 4.5 hours   D) 4 hours

Q2: The requirement of a normal weekly rest period is?

A) 47 hours   B) 45 hours   C) 44 hours   D) 40 hours

Q3: A fortnightly driving period must not exceed?

A) 107 hours   B) 100 hours   C) 94 hours   D) 90 hours

Q4: The maximum number of hours that can be worked in a single week starting 00.00hrs on Monday is?

A) 44 hours   B) 50 hours   C) 56 hours   D) 60 hours

Q5: If splitting a 45-minute break over two periods, rules dictate the first break taken must be?

A) 30 minutes   B) 10 minutes   C) 15 minutes   D) 20 minutes

Q6: What is a period of availability?

A) Waiting time known in advance

B) Extra vehicle loading time

C) Waiting time not known in advance

D) Extra vehicle unloading time

Q7: What is classed as night-time for a heavy goods vehicle driver?

A) 01.00 – 04.00   B) 02.00 – 06.00   C) 00.00 – 04.00   D) 23.00 – 03.00

Q8: Under work time directive rules, after how many hours worked must a driver take a break?

A) 4 hours   B) 5 hours   C) 4.5 hours   D) 6 hours

Q9: If working between 6 and 9 hours, what should be the minimum break duration?

A) 60 minutes   B) 45 minutes   C) 30 minutes   D) 50 minutes

Q10: What is the maximum day shift duration for a heavy goods vehicle driver?

A) 10 hours   B) 15 hours   C) 12 hours   D) 14 hours

Q11: Generally, EU drivers' hours rules dictate that the average number of hours' driving in a day is?

A) 10 hours   B) 11 hours   C) 9 hours   D) 12 hours

Q12: Drivers can do up to how many extended driving shifts in a six-day period?

A) 1   B) 3   C) 2   D) 4

Q13: Weekly rest can be reduced to a minimum of?

A) 25 hours   B) 16 hours   C)   24 hours   D)   34 hours

Q14: Under normal circumstances, a driver is allowed to extend driving time twice a week to?

A) 11 hours   B) 9.5 hours   C)   10 hours   D)   12 hours

Q15: A reduction of weekly rest must be compensated for by when?

A)   End of 3rd week following the week of reduction

B)   End of 1st week following the week of reduction

C)   End of 2nd week following the week of reduction

D)   End of 4th week following the week of reduction

Q16: Pick two answers below to this question: Who is responsible for a vehicle found to be overloaded?

A)   The company B)   The loader   C)   The driver   D)   The shunter

Q17: How long is a driver's digicard valid for?

A) 4 years   B) 10 years   C)   5 years   D)   15 years

Q18: How long do you have to report a lost or stolen digicard?

A) 10 days   B) 7 days   C)   15 days   D)   14 days

Q19: How many days of information, on average, does a driver's digicard hold?

A) 28 days   B)   60 days   C)   30 days   D)   90 days

Q20: When inserting a driver's digicard into a VU, which position and direction should the chip and arrow be in?

A) Chip facing up and arrow pointing backwards

B) Chip facing up and arrow pointing forwards

C) Chip facing down and arrow pointing backwards

D) Chip facing down and arrow pointing forwards

Q21: If you are driving a vehicle with a tachograph fitted, you must download the information on the digicard within?

A) 24 days   B)   7 days   C)   28 days   D)   14 days

Q22: If the tachograph unit breaks during a shift, what should the driver do?

A) Call the depot B)   Park up   C)   Keep a written record D)   Try to fix it

Q23: Name 4 checks a driver should do on a vehicle.

A)   B)   C)   D)

Note: refer to chapter 5, vehicle checks.

Q24: What is the usual height of an unmarked bridge?

A)   15ft/4.5m   B)   16ft 6in/5.0m

C)   15ft 6in/4.7m   D)   16ft/4.8m

Q25: What is the legal speed limit for a heavy goods vehicle on:

- A-roads?

A)   40mph   B)   45mph   C)   50mph   D)   55mph

- Dual carriageways?

A)   40mph   B)   55mph   C)   50mph   D)   60mph

- Motorways?

A)   60mph   B)   65mph   C)   56mph   D)   55mph

Q26: What is the speed limiter on a heavy goods vehicle set to?

A)   50mph   B)   56mph   C)   55mph   D)   60mph

Q27: Do periods of availability (POAs) count towards a mobile worker's working time?

A)   Yes B)   No

Q28: Do breaks count towards a mobile worker's working time?

A)   Yes B)   No

Q29: Which two of the following factors are the most effective in making a vehicle more fuel-efficient?

A)   The driver   B)   Tyres

C)   Lubricants   D)   Aerodynamics

Q30: What is PPE?

A)   Protective personal equipment

B)   Personal protective equipment

C)   Professional protective equipment

Q31: In any 24-hour period, what is the standard minimum required rest period?

A)   9 hours   B)   10 hours   C)   11 hours   D)   12 hours

Q32: The daily rest period can be reduced 3 times a week; what is the minimum reduced daily rest period allowed?

A)   7 hours   B)   8 hours   C)   9 hours   D)   10 hours

Q33: What is the maximum number of hours that a person can work in 1 week, according to the EU work time directive?

A)   55 hours   B)   65 hours   C)   60 hours   D)   70 hours

Example of analogue tachograph chart

Tachograph Disc

Date recordings started

Driver's surname and Christian name

Date recordings ended

Registration number

Closing odometer reading

Opening odometer reading

Clock time

⊙= Driving
𝟀 = Other work
☑= POA
⊢= Rest

Speed trace

Place where the chart started

Place where the chart ended

Distance trace – each completed upwards and downwards movement equals 10 km

Road markings

No waiting during
times shown

Loading bay

No waiting at
any time

No loading or unloading
at the time shown

No loading or unloading
at any time

Steep hill upwards

Steep hill downwards

Fallen or falling rocks

Hump bridge

Side winds

Uneven ground

Risk of grounding

Opening or swing bridge ahead

No vehicle over width shown

No vehicle over height shown

No vehicle or combination of vehicles over length shown

Available width of head room indicated

Weak bridge

Distance over which series of road humps extends

No goods vehicles over maximum gross weight shown (in tonnes) except for loading

Vehicle markings

Left   Central   Right

The panel illustrated is for flammable liquids.

The above panel will be displayed by vehicles carrying certain dangerous goods in packages

Oxidizing substance

Non-flammable compressed gas

Side marker

End marker

Chapter 20
Jobs at a Glance

Introduction

Below is a list of commonly found jobs, including brief descriptions, hours involved etc. This should give a window into what's out there. Everybody's different. One person might enjoy long distance and the open road. Another might enjoy multi-drop, which is more challenging and includes more physical exercise. Still another might prefer the steady, less pressurised environment provided by supermarkets, the Post Office etc.

This chapter is designed to show the types of work that are out there. It includes a brief look at what each type of job is like, so as to help with the decision of which to go for. It is always more fulfilling to have the type of job which best suits you.

Skips (Class 2)

Short hours, usually 7am–5pm weekdays and 7am–1pm Saturdays. This is usually local work. You should expect this type of work to be very dirty. It's a busy job; drivers are expected to get on and do as many skips as possible on top of collecting cash from customers. It will risk your licence if anything drops off onto the road, so be careful not to rush.

Tippers (Class 1 and 2)

On muck shifting and aggregate deliveries, it's usually 7am–5pm weekdays and 7am–1pm Saturdays. This job is all about getting as many loads in as possible in a day. Again, you should expect this to be fairly dirty work. It may risk your licence if you are over-weight on earth-shifting work. Quarry work is OK because truck is weighed.

Multi-drop (Class 1 and 2)

Reasonably high-pressured job; it can be time-sensitive regarding deliveries. There's also the risk of personal injury due to hurrying whilst loading and unloading. The job becomes easier if you are allocated a regular route and get to know where the drops are. A good knowledge of the local area always helps. Average 10–15 hour shifts.

Brewery deliveries (Class 1 and 2)

Usually 7am–5pm. This is local work, similar to multi-drop, but with less pressure. You will get plenty of exercise on the job. Plus the chance of getting a regular route is reasonably high.

General haulage (Class 1 and 2)

General haulage could involve transporting anything from palletised goods to car parts. The companies in this field are very competitive. Employers usually expect you to work lots of hours, so there is no guarantee of getting home every night, especially if you are doing long distance. Start and finish times vary. Can be unsociable hours and fairly flat-out work; however, it is relatively easy to get work in this area. It might be a good way to earn some much needed experience, though it may very well be a baptism by fire. Expect 10–15 hour shifts.

Supermarkets (Class 1 and 2)

Class 1 – usually 2 drops a day or 2 trailer swaps. Rarely more than 6. Class 2 – between 2 and 5 drops. Employers usually expect you to have a couple of years' experience. Expect good equipment and working conditions – goods are usually palletised and caged, making the process quite simple. You will not be pressured to speed out on the road, but expect employers to be quite pedantic about paperwork and driver behaviour. Varying start times, 10 hours is an average shift.

Shipping containers (Class 1)

This is mainly long distance work. Many companies do not expect the driver to load and unload due to insurance. Various start times. Average 10–12 hour shifts.

Car transporters (Class 1)

Experience in this line of work is crucial. Good pay due to added pressure because of high insurance costs to companies regarding damage to cars etc. Obvious considerations for driver include hazards such as low-hanging branches, theft etc. You will be expected to load and unload – drive cars up and down the ramps without damaging them. Various start times. Average 10–12 hour shifts.

ADR (Class 1 and 2)

Good pay, driver required to do lots of training. There are extensive rules and regulations. Can be dangerous, involves hauling potentially explosive loads. Various start times. Average 10–12 hour shifts.

Music theatre and film work (Class 1 and 2)

Much of this is seasonal work, but it is well paid and interesting. Nice people. Hours vary wildly. Potentially a lot of down time on location.

Chapter **21**

Jobs Abroad

Introduction

This chapter is a brief look at the job opportunities abroad. There are many countries which a UK driver could consider going to work in. I have chosen to focus on the examples given due to the probability of work and the standard of living.

Job Opportunities Abroad

The country most interested in hiring UK LGV1 drivers is Canada. You have to go through an agency; they do all the necessary paperwork, e.g. temporary visa, plus arrange a job. It costs around £3,000 in stage payments. You need to take a short LGV test for left-hand drive trucks in Canada. The government criterion is to fill long haul vacancies. If all goes well, it equates to only 3 years' long distance interstate driving before you are entitled to full residency. On average, 3 weeks out of 4 will be spent living in the truck. You can apply for full residency after working for 18 months. This may take a further 12 to 18 months

to be processed. Once residency is granted, you can change to whatever job suits you. You will need to be very careful and check out the agency before using them. Some have been known to be bogus scam artists.

If you are considering emigrating to Canada, a humorous and informative web resource is Trucker Josh VLOGS on YouTube: www.youtube.com/user/truckerjosh456 .

Australia and New Zealand are also possibilities, but are much harder to get into. And you will need to work for 5 years before any company can sponsor you for residency; this still may or may not be granted. It's a gamble, but sometimes nothing ventured, nothing gained. On a plus point, being right-hand drive, there is no LGV test to take. UK licences are valid.

Good luck if you decide to emigrate!

Chapter **22**
Optional Electrical Equipment

Introduction

This chapter outlines some of the very helpful, optional electrical equipment that is available. I have chosen to focus on two types of equipment: sat navs and the Pure Highway DAB radio adaptor. One will ensure that you don't get lost and lose time on deliveries, the other will ensure that you don't die of boredom on the way there.

As far as my experience with sat navs goes, this information is very accurate.

Sat navs

Sat navs are an absolutely tremendous bit of kit. They take a serious amount of pressure out of the job. When you key in the dimensions and weight etc. the sat nav will help to guide you away from any potential hazards such as low bridges, weak bridges and weight restricted roads.

The **best** sat navs by far are the big name brands. The most expensive models cost around £350 to £400. I found others priced at £50 to £300 pretty much useless.

Note: I recommend fitting it lower down on the windscreen and putting a small pillow or something similarly soft underneath it. I have had the unit come loose and drop off a few times: a very valuable piece of equipment to break!

Pure Highway DAB radio adaptor

When out on the road, good entertainment is good company. If your truck doesn't have a digital radio, it is possible to transfer a DAB signal into your truck radio through a Pure Highway device.

This device plugs into the cigarette lighter/electrical power-point. It has its own aerial. Simply set the frequency on the device, then set the radio to the same frequency. It enables access to all DAB channels, including 6 Music (real quality entertainment!). It costs around £70. The signal is very good in most places, but it can be lost in rural areas. It's a great bit of kit!

Note: the aerial it's supplied with is not designed to be installed numerous times. In order to avoid numerous aerial purchases, you should consider buying a magmount aerial which is compatible with a Pure Highway. A magmount aerial has a thicker cable and, as it is magnetic, will easily stick to anything metal in the cab. It should cost around £10 and can be found online.

Chapter 23
Road Safety/Useful Information

Introduction

This chapter contains useful tips and advice for various situations which drivers may find themselves in. My main piece of advice is – never forget how much time and money went into gaining your LGV or PCV licence and how easy it is to lose it. If you are unsure of something, ask for help. If you ever find yourself being pressured into doing something illegal, just walk away. There's always another day, another job. The laws are so strong now; it's just not worth the risk!

Road safety

Please take note of the following, potentially dangerous scenarios that you could run into:

Temporary road works

Be aware that some temporary road work sites do not have signs placed far enough back to give you enough, or even any, warning. During busy times, such as rush hour, cars may be queuing way back beyond sight of the signs. Therefore, always ensure that you slow down when approaching a blind bend, because a fully-laden truck will not be able to stop at a moment's notice. This is not an uncommon situation; you will come across it in the course of your career.

Cresting a hill

When cresting a hill you should also ensure that you reduce your speed. As with the previous scenario, you never know what awaits you on the other side. There could potentially be a queue of traffic, a broken-down vehicle or somebody waiting to turn.

Turning off the motorway

If, when you are planning to turn onto a slip road, your vision is obscured whilst following another truck or coach, ensure you slow down in order to create space to see. There could potentially be a queue of traffic that you are not aware of.

Blind spots

Beware of blind spots in your viewing mirrors. If you are changing lanes in heavy traffic, do the manoeuvre very slowly in order to give anybody in that lane a chance to let you know they are there.

Tyres

Check the tread depth, and for splits in the side walls of the tyre. Tyres that are just on, or around, the legal limit of 1mm at the start of a shift can wear down and become illegal during the same day if you are travelling long distance, especially in hot weather. It's 3 points on your licence plus a fine for each defective tyre. Four illegal tyres and it could be game over! Check and double-check. Ask someone if in doubt; don't take it out! Defective tyres can and do burst.

Manoeuvring

If you are unsure whether you are able to manoeuvre around a tight bend in a built-up area, then, when it's safe, take up two lanes. At times this is the only way possible to get around.

Tyre scrub build up/Spring summer

During the hotter period of the year scrub builds up on the road surface. In itself not a real problem until the first heavy rain shower which turns it back into oil. Be ready for this hazard, it affects heavy vehicles in a much more severe way. The road can very suddenly turn into a skating ring.

Autumn

Same scenario, but add a covering of wet leaves and the road becomes even slippier. Hit the brakes and truck just slides.

Wasps, bees and spiders

These can be an instantaneous hazard. There are numerous accidents every year due to driver's attention being diverted away from the road for a second or two.

I've personally heard of at least one fatality. A passing car driver saw an oncoming truck driver doing battle with a bee. The truck veered off the road and hit a farm wall head on.

Slamming into reverse

Avoid stopping quickly and then instantly beginning to reverse. Give time for a possible cyclist or motorcyclist to take evasive action (they do not have a reverse gear and you will not hear them). I have seen a motorcyclist backpedalling a heavy bike for all he was worth, trying to get out the way of a quickly reversing truck.

Blind spots/cyclists listening to music

Cyclists and motorcyclists have a nasty habit of creeping up the nearside of trucks undetected or stopping directly in front, below windscreen level at a set of traffic lights/junction. Be mindful of them getting part of their clothing or bag caught up on the side of the truck and being dragged underneath. In the past there have been several very serious incidents of cyclists/motorcyclists sitting in the blind spots of truck mirrors. In a rush the truck driver suddenly changed his/her mind about which route to take. Without indicating they turned suddenly, thus leaving no time for the person to react (you can guess the rest).

Black ice

This is an unseen danger, especially found on untreated roads and shady areas after the temperature drops below freezing. I spoke to an artic driver who hit a stretch of black ice whilst driving at speed in the middle lane of a motorway. The trailer started sliding sideward pulling the tractor unit out of line (pre-jack knife) He managed to gently ease off the accelerator and slowly, as the speed decreased, it all came back under control and into line. He was fortunate.

Blinding low winter sun

A real hazard, especially when travelling towards the sun whilst cresting a hill. I know of a driver who crested a hill and was sun blinded and completely unable to see anything for a few seconds. At the last moment, still partially blinded, he saw a queue of traffic. He swerved to the left to avoid it and by doing so accidentally hit a lady walking her dog. The driver, subsequently traumatised, then faced manslaughter charges for over two years until the case was finally dropped.

Where safe to do so, if you can't see- slow down. Drive defensively to anticipate the sun's level.

Different truck/trailer heights

Identical looking trucks and trailers can be deceivingly lower or higher than you might expect. Always look for the height written on them. A matter of a few inches may be the difference between clearing a low bridge on the same route that you came in on.

Note: a brand-new truck or trailer can have a shiny, slippery floor making for a much higher possibility of load moving in transit. Load needs to be secured tightly to prevent it moving, causing a risk of truck rollover on tight bends.

Mobile phone

This is obviously a major distraction to concentration and a big risk to license. A much bigger problem occurs in the event of an accident involving a fatality. The driver can then possibly be charged with manslaughter. I have heard tell of a driver being involved in an accident. The police seized his phone and inserted a code. By doing this they were able to see all phone use prior to the accident.

Horses

Horses are very easily spooked when they come into close proximity with a moving truck-ideally pull over to the side of the road, switch off your engine then let them pass. If it's a tight space then very slowly crawl past them whilst looking for any possible signals from the rider to advance, or stop and switch off.

Navigation

A trucker's atlas is always a very useful item to have in the cab. It will indicate all bridge heights and weight restrictions etc. Usually around £10 to purchase.

Useful Information

Included here is a short list of work-wear and useful gear.

Work-wear:

- Steel toecap boots

- High-visibility jacket or vest

- Gloves

- Waterproofs

Useful gear:

- Map

- Notepad and pens

- Torch

- Screwdrivers

- Mole grips

- Adjustable spanner

- Bungee straps

- Duct tape

- Ice scraper

- Disinfectant wet wipes

- Plasters and bandages

Tips and advice

1. Keep diary of dates, hours worked, rest, POA and of any problems etc. Also, ensure you keep the tacho printouts.

2. Away from yard, photocopy company driver sheet etc. (can be difficult to use). This gives you time to study and get used to it on your own terms (be secretive about it).

3. Set the height to current trailer to avoid bridge strikes. If you are stopped by DVSA and it is incorrect, there is a high probability of a fine.

4. During blindsided reversing, if the trailer becomes impossible to see because of the articulation angle, pull out the passenger mirror a click or two.

5. Try, if possible, not to rely too heavily on the person giving guidance in a manoeuvre through a tight space. If safe, keep getting out to check yourself. If there is an accident, 9 times out of 10 the driver will get the blame.

6. Adjusting the lift axle into the up position can be useful in wet conditions whilst tug testing after coupling to trailer (puts more weight onto drive axle). This also aids traction on slippery ramps, inclines and during tight manoeuvres.

7. Check wheel nuts by eye and by hand, try at least 3 on each wheel.

8. Hijackers usually target expensive loads such as cigarettes and alcohol, but not always. Anything that can be sold on a market stall is fair game. It has also been known for them to target new trucks and trailers for re-sale abroad. If you are stopped by DVSA, it is apparently within a driver's rights to lock the cab doors and shout through the window or write on paper a message to state that you will not open up, but will follow a DVSA vehicle to one of their designated yards. Criminals have been known to impersonate DVSA and police officers.

An article published recently said that there is a concern over stolen DVSA security uniforms in the northwest being used in bogus stops on goods vehicles. The advice given is that all DVSA vehicles have a roof bar matrix sign. DVSA do not use vehicles with rear window matrix signs. Magic, that's all right then!??

9. Every transport company must have an O licence (operator's licence), which should be displayed in the windscreen of the vehicle.

10. A lot of new trucks have automatic gearboxes. Select 'drive' ('D') or automatic ('A'), depending on the box. Some gear levers are counter-intuitive i.e. push the lever forward to reverse, pull it back to go forward.

11. Coupling heights – if you are unsure if a trailer is too high to couple to, reverse halfway under until the fifth wheel is only half visible. Lift the truck suspension until you feel the weight of the trailer and then reverse under.

12. Take extreme care to ensure that the handbrake is always applied correctly during coupling and uncoupling procedures. **A runaway is definitely no fun!**

13. A good system after coupling up is to follow this sequence:

    - Fit the fifth wheel dog clip.
    - Take the trailer brake off.
    - Wind up the legs.
    - Fit the number plate, then carry out all necessary checks.

14. If the airline is difficult to fit, jiggling it can help. Alternatively, repeatedly press the foot brake in order to lower the air pressure.

15. Many a driver's undoing is being distracted by someone or something, during the coupling/uncoupling process. If this happens, retrace all previous steps taken in the sequence **before** carrying on.

16. Top-heavy loads are dangerous. Go steadily and carefully around bends. There is a possible risk of rollover, injuries to you (the driver), and of completely crushing a car if it's alongside. (Double-decker trailers and containers are the most risky.)

17. AdBlue is a type of chemical solution designed to reduce a vehicle's nitrogen oxide emissions. All modern goods vehicles are fitted with an AdBlue tank. Roughly, 1 litre should last 100 miles.

18. All drivers must complete 35 hours of periodic training every five years on an ongoing basis to be able to drive a truck or bus. Periodic training is delivered through courses that consist in length of a total of 35 hours, split into five 7-hour days. The easiest, least intense way of doing this is a day a month for five months before the expiry date. Prices usually start at £250 and run right up to £600. Shop around for the best deal.

19. Depending on which company you work for, your vehicle may be fitted with an Isotrak system. Isotrak systems are used by some transport companies in order to track trucks, trailers and loads. An Isotrak system can also be used as a contact link between a driver and their company office. If your company does use Isotrak systems, they should provide you with full instruction and training. Although it looks complicated, it is fairly simple to use.

20. Audiobooks can be a great way of keeping yourself entertained on the road. You could potentially learn something whilst you work or just listen to interesting stories.

21. Tail lift. Isolator switches can also sometimes be located inside and outside the back corner of truck or trailer

Chapter 24
Driver Fatigue

Driver fatigue and falling asleep at the wheel

How to know when you are suffering from serious driver fatigue – **example scenario:**

Your eyelids become heavy and constantly try to close, your head starts to nod. You can't stop yawning and you find it hard to focus.

Suddenly you become aware of the rumble strips; you blink hard and realise that you have veered onto the hard shoulder for a moment and quickly straighten the wheel. You were asleep; this time you were lucky ...

Serious fatigue symptoms:

- Frequent blinking, difficulty focusing and droopy eyelids.

- Daydreaming/scrambled thoughts.

- Missing exits and street signs, an inability to remember last few miles driven.

- Constant yawning/sore eyes.

- Head feels heavy.

- Drifting across lanes, hitting the rumble strip of hard shoulder and tailgating.

- Suddenly being aware of getting too close to another vehicle.

- Feeling restless, irritable and confused.

Temporary cures:

- Open both windows and turn up the radio loud.

- Sugary foods and caffeine-containing drinks.

- Pinch yourself to feel slight pain, and keep pinching.

- Say something aloud or sing.

If absolutely exhausted, you will have no prior warning or control over falling asleep, it will just happen. **Pull over and stop!** Take a 20-minute sleep break, get up, take a brisk walk. If you are still exhausted, sleep for another hour or two. Sometimes you have to just give in to the situation; it is better to accept any potential repercussions for being late etc. rather than endanger yourself or an innocent person/family. **There are other people's lives in your hands, not just your own!**

Note: (motorway driving): If you need to stop immediately you can park up at the top end of the motorway slip road just after the 'motorway start/end' sign and sleep there.

Summary

I hope that you have found this book a useful guide to the world of trucking. Remember to revise the example examination questions if you decide to switch to a different company.

I want to leave you with a final piece of advice. Remember not to rush. It is easier said than done. You may be employed by people who try to pressure you into completing more deliveries than are legally possible in the time allocated. However, rushing leads to mistakes. Excessive risk-taking carries potentially dangerous consequences. Whether you have 1 delivery or 50, if they don't get done due to circumstances beyond your control, they don't get done. Your licence and personal safety are far more important.

On the road you will encounter many potentially stressful situations. You cannot control these situations, but you can control your reaction to them. If you stay calm and focussed, you are far more likely to come home safe and happy at the end of the day.

Acknowledgements

With very special thank-yous for all your help!

Danny Omz
Cody
Donna Hamilton
Michael Kingston
Uri Freixa
Nick Cosstick
Chris Bradley

Photo contributors:

Bob Spears
Marko Kudjerski
Triston
Arham Javed
Babish
Daniel Rosenberg
Hafez Thaikulathil

If you would like to contribute to the next edition and for general enquiries please contact jellymantrucking@yahoo.co.uk.

Lightning Source UK Ltd.
Milton Keynes UK
UKHW020938050921
389903UK00002B/3

9 781911 589556